Twice the Work

THE HAYMARKET SERIES

Editors: Mike Davis and Michael Sprinker

The Haymarket Series offers original studies in politics, history and culture, with a focus on North America. Representing views across the American left on a wide range of subjects, the series will be of interest to socialists both in the USA and throughout the world. A century after the first May Day, the American left remains in the shadow of those martyrs whom the Haymarket Series honors and commemorates. These studies testify to the living legacy of political activism and commitment for which they gave their lives.

Twice the Work of Free Labor

The Political Economy of Convict Labor
in the New South

———————◆———————

ALEX LICHTENSTEIN

VERSO

London · New York

First published by Verso 1996
© Alex Lichtenstein 1996
All rights reserved

Verso
UK: 6 Meard Street, London W1V 3HR
USA: 180 Varick Street, New York NY 10014-4606
Verso is the imprint of New Left Books

British Library Cataloguing in Publication Data
A catalogue record for this book is available from the British Library

Library of Congress Cataloging-in-Publication Data
Lichtenstein, Alex
    Twice the work of free labor : the political economy of convict
labor in the New South / Alex Lichtenstein.
        p.   cm. — (The Haymarket Series)
    Includes bibliographical references (p.   ) and index.
    ISBN 1-85984-991-1. — ISBN 1-85984-086-8 (pbk.)
    1. Convict labor—Economic aspects—Southern States. 2. Prison
industries—Economic aspects—Southern States. 3. Afro-American
prisoners—Southern States—Social Conditions. 4. Prisons and race
relations—Southern States. 5. Southern States—Economic policy.
6. Southern States—Economic conditions. 7. Southern States—
Politics and government.   I. Title.   II. Series.
HV8929.A132L53   1995   95-9404
331.5'1'0975—dc20   CIP

ISBN 1-85984-991-1
ISBN 1-85984-086-8 (pbk)

Typeset in Monotype Baskerville
by Lucy Morton, London SE12

Printed and bound in Great Britain by Biddles Ltd,
Guildford and King's Lynn

For Sybil

Contents

List of Tables and Figures

Acknowledgements

Many individuals deserve thanks for helping me bring this project to fruition. Those colleagues and comrades who have smoothed the path to completion by generously contributing their ideas, encouragement, or just plain good company, include: Ed Ayers, Amy Bentley, Nancy Bercaw, Vernon Burton, Dan Carter, Dan Cohen, Saul Cornell, Mary Ellen Curtin, Pete Daniel, Drew Faust, Andy Feffer, Brett Gary, John Gennari, Rob Gregg, Gary Fink, John French, Jim Grossman, Rick Halpern, Karl Ittmann, Antoine Joseph, Michael Katz, Cliff Kuhn, Walter Licht, Sybil Lipschultz, Matt Mancini, Harry McKown, Doug Munro, Jim Oakes, Joyce Peterson, Jan Radway, John Rodrigue, Leslie Rowland, Karin Shapiro, Gerald Shenk, Michael Sprinker, Ken Strauss, Shirley Wajda, Bill Westerman, Jon Wiener, Harold Woodman, Rich Yeselson, and Bob Zieger. I also appreciate comments I received when portions of this work were presented to Florida International University's history department in 1989, the Southern Labor Studies Conference in 1991, the Commonwealth Fund Conference, University College London in 1992, and the Newberry Library Lunchtime Colloquium in 1994.

In different form, portions of Chapters 4, 6, and 7 have previously appeared in Melvyn Stokes and Rick Halpern, eds., *Race and Class in the American South since 1990* (Oxford: Berg Publishers, 1994); Gary M. Fink and Merl Reed, eds., *Race, Class, and Community in Southern Labor History* (Tuscaloosa: University of Alabama Press, 1994); and the *Journal of Southern History* 59 (February 1993), respectively. I thank the readers for these publications for their helpful comments, and the publishers for permission to rework some of that material here.

Though they may not all agree with the point of view expressed in these pages, without exception special thanks are due to every member of Florida International University's history department. Knowing these colleagues has reconfirmed my belief that a democratic and non-hierarchical work environment promotes a free interchange of ideas and an atmosphere conducive to scholarship. I know how this must look; but my colleagues know I wouldn't say it if I didn't mean it. All junior scholars should be so fortunate.

Librarians and archivists everywhere I went greeted this project with enthusiasm, and provided me with invaluable aid. I would especially like to thank Dale Couch, Andy Phrydas, and Virginia Shadron at the Georgia Department of Archives and History; Nelson Morgan at University of Georgia Special Collections; and Jim Murray at the Birmingham Public Library.

Institutional and research support came from the University of Pennsylvania, the Mellon Foundation, a North Caroliniana Archie K. Davis Fellowship (twice), a National Endowment for the Humanities Travel to Collections Grant, a Florida International University Foundation Summer Research Grant, a pair of research mini-grants from FIU, and some much-needed carrel space at the Newberry Library in Chicago.

Special mention goes to Tom and Peggy Buergenthal, whose hospitality and generosity made an extended research trip to Atlanta possible.

At bottom, this book is written out of a now half-forgotten sense of political commitment. Three people whose devotion to prisoners' rights nourished that commitment deserve acknowledgement: Jane Motz of the American Friends Service Committee, and Carol Bergman and Jill Raymond of the National Moratorium on Prison Construction.

Family members have nourished different commitments. Cynthia, Gene, Andrew, Miranda, and Mary Lichtenstein have all contributed to my sense that writing this was a worthy endeavor. My other extended family, Harold, Gloria, Amy, and Nicole Lipschultz have also been consistently supportive and understanding. Most of all, however, the task of writing this book has coincided with the expansion of my immediate family. Sybil Lipschultz has seen this project through as a partner from its genesis until the last grueling weeks of its completion. Her intellectual and emotional support has made all the difference each step of the way. Our good fortune in sharing the joys of parenthood has only sweetened bringing the work to a conclusion. Hannah, next time you knock on my study door and ask "Daddy, are you all done working?", I think I'll say "Yes."

As soon as peoples whose production still moves within the lower forms of slave labour ... are drawn into a world market dominated by a capitalist mode of production ... the civilized horrors of over-work are grafted onto the barbaric horrors of slavery.

Karl Marx, *Capital* Volume 1

What hold can another manufacturer have upon his workmen, equal to what my manufacturer would have upon his? What other master is there that can reduce his workmen, if idle, to a situation next to starving, without suffering them to go elsewhere?... And who, so far from being able to raise their wages by combination, are obliged to take whatever pittance he thinks it most to his interest to allow?

Jeremy Bentham, *Panopticon*

The way prisons are run and their inmates treated gives a faithful picture of a society, especially of the ideas and methods of those who dominate that society.

Milovan Djilas, *Of Prisons and Ideas*

Preface

More than a decade ago I worked briefly for a small and quixotic organization, the National Moratorium on Prison Construction. The Moratorium, as it was called, advanced the decidedly unpopular idea that American prisons and American crime had nothing to do with one another. Instead, they – we – contended that America's ballooning incarceration rate stemmed from a politicized definition of criminal behavior, a racist criminal justice system, cynical "law-and-order" politicians, and a host of special interests that profited from prison expansion. This last included prison contractors and architects, counties desperate for new jobs and revenue-generating "industry," and businesses that directly exploited prison labor. Except as a function of political opportunism, prison expansion was not a response to the crime rate, the Moratorium insisted. Quite the contrary: if the states paid (or borrowed) to build new prison cells, the machinery of justice would fill them before the concrete dried.

I must admit, at the time I found this radical analysis disquieting and even a bit improbable. Unfortunately, the intervening years of criminal justice policy in this country have proved it true in almost all of its particulars. Incredibly, between 1984 and 1994 the already large state and federal prison population more than doubled, surpassing the one million mark for the first time (this figure does not even include jail inmates). Back in 1980 there were 330,000 prisoners in the United States. A recent study found the incarceration rate at over 500 for every 100,000 Americans, an astounding number far beyond virtually every other nation in the world. (The garrison city-state of Singapore, for example, has an incarceration rate of 229 for every 100,000 people.) If these numbers are broken down by race, they tell an even more disturbing story. African-Americans suffer incarceration at a rate at least six times that of whites; at the end of 1992, 2,678 out of every 100,000 black males in the USA were in prison; a widely reported study of punishment in Washington, DC found 15 per cent of all black male residents aged 18–35 in prison or jail. And so on.[1]

Most observers agree that the single most important factor in the increase in incarceration has been the so-called "war on drugs," a war prosecuted primarily against racial minorities. In 1980 drug offenses sent fewer than 10,000 people to state prisons; between 1990 and 1992, the Bureau of Justice Statistics recorded an annual average of more than 100,000 drug convictions. This new frontier of punishment is only one aspect of the increasing criminalization of behavior that the carceral state associates with the poor; as a National Center on Institutions and Alternatives (NCIA) study suggests, "most of the hundreds of thousands of black youths and young men being dragged into the criminal justice system ... are being arrested for misdemeanors, minor property crimes, and non-violent drug offenses." The increasing racial disparity which has come to define a penal system that appears to know no bounds is a "predictable consequence of having replaced the social safety net with a dragnet," the NCIA concludes.[2]

The oft-cited fact that more African-American men are in prison than attending college indicates the distance reaction has carried us from the promises of the civil-rights era and the Great Society programs of thirty years ago. For African-Americans living a century ago on the cusp of freedom much the same pattern of raised hopes and dashed expectations defined the era of Radical Reconstruction and its aftermath. Within a generation the post-emancipation dreams of land ownership, the right to vote, civic equality, and economic independence, had been deferred. They were replaced by a lengthy struggle against landlessness, disfranchisement, segregation, lynching, and a host of legal and extralegal means of keeping the black person dependent upon the white. An important component of this tightly woven net of oppression, exploitation, and terror was the South's notorious penal system. Most tellingly, prior to the 1920s African-Americans convicted of breaking the laws – petty and grand – in the New South found themselves "farmed out" to the highest bidder, and destined to labor for this "lessee" for the duration of their sentence or their life, whichever came first. Actually, "farmed out" is a misnomer: southern convicts built railroads, mined coal, made brick, labored in the forest industries, and paved roads far more often than they picked cotton.

This book is a study of that labor system, known then as the convict-lease, and of the public chain gang which replaced it during the South's version of the Progressive Era. With the exception of brief excursions to the convict coal mines of Alabama and Tennessee, and the roads of North Carolina, my narrative follows the development of convict labor in a single state, Georgia, from Reconstruction until the Great Depression. Of course, Georgia need not be singled out as unique in its willingness to use the penal system to exploit black labor. Throughout the South convict-leasing remained the predominant form of punishment until the closing years of the nineteenth century, and contributed to the region's industrial and commercial expansion. Convicts built rail lines across the peaks of western North Carolina; they worked in the mines opened by the New South's most powerful corporation, the Tennessee Coal and Iron Company, and dug the coal and iron that made Birmingham the "Pittsburgh of the South"; they drained swampland and built levees in the Mississippi Delta; they produced fertilizer in the phosphate pits of Florida. Moreover, in its willingness to abandon the profits generated by leasing and shift to chain-gang labor on the county roads in 1908, Georgia was neither a pioneer nor a laggard. Mississippi and Tennessee abolished leasing in the 1890s, for example, replacing the system with the infamous state-run Parchman penal farm and a state-owned coal mine respectively. Florida and Alabama, on the other hand, remained committed to leasing well into the 1920s when they finally removed convicts from the turpentine and coal industries and placed them on the roads, as Georgia had two decades earlier.[3]

But I have chosen to focus on Georgia for several reasons. Not only did this large state, with a black population of half a million at emancipation, have forty years experience with convict-leasing, but over that time its prisoners labored in a diverse array of industries, all of them important to the state's postbellum economic transformation. This allows me to examine the workings of the convict-lease in railroad construction, coal mining, brickmaking, and the forest industries (turpentine and lumber), while retaining a coherent political narrative. Georgia also provides an exceptional example of the Progressive Era transition from the privatized convict-lease to the public chain gang. The instant economic impact of this transformation, its ideological importance as a "reform" measure parroted by other states, and the obvious unwillingness to ameliorate conditions for the convicts, 90 per cent of whom were black when the state abolished leasing in 1908, all merit attention. Finally, the postbellum history of Georgia's penal system offers a clear illustration of how convict labor helped forge the peculiar New South "Bourbon" political alliance, by accommodating the labor needs of an emerging class of industrialists without eroding the racial domination essential to planters.

Despite the focus on Georgia, I believe my argument is equally applicable to the rest of the New South. Even in states such as Mississippi or Louisiana with little or no pretense to industrial or infrastructural development, convicts worked in the most "modern" sector of the plantation economy, large-scale cotton or sugar plantations. Of course, I invite other scholars to corroborate, disprove, or modify my conclusions for other states, as the case may be. But I seek to make these larger claims because, ultimately, this book is meant to be a study in race and political economy. In regarding forced labor as a decidedly modern feature of the New South, *Twice the Work of Free Labor* joins a growing number of studies that reject the dichotomy between a modern and antimodern South, and instead seek to link the region's most appalling features to the process of modernization itself. As John Cell suggests in his 1982 book, *The Highest Stage of White Supremacy*, segregation was an invention of modern race and class relations, not a holdover from a more "backward" social order. In much the same vein this book posits southern convict labor as a relation of production suited to modernization while maintaining a commitment to a restrictive racial order.[4]

To this end I mostly tell the story of the political, social, and economic forces that encouraged powerful whites to turn to forced black labor in an effort to exploit their region's resources and bring its economy into the modern world. As a result, the convicts themselves generally remain in the background, victims of historical forces greater than their individual destinies. This book is not a social history of crime, and in what follows I try to avoid succumbing to the temptation to romanticize the actions and lives of southern convicts as rebels or outlaws. No doubt some African-American convicts were like Henry Nisbet, who had murdered nine men, all "of his own race, which he always declared he abhorred," and hardly deserve romanticization. Others, like Seaborn Smith, sent to the penitentiary for burglary and then pardoned when he was found "entirely innocent of the crime," were victims of the southern brand of criminal justice, so deeply compromised by racism.[5] Most lay somewhere in between, many of them given harsh sentences for petty transgressions of laws specifically designed to control impoverished African-Americans. The convict labor system of the South, however, effectively erased these distinctions, reducing all prisoners, vicious, petty, and innocent alike, to a commodity. Indeed, one of the few complaints whites registered about the system was its failure to separate adults from children, women from men, hardened criminals from those who landed in the penitentiary by what whites saw as misfortune or poor judgement.[6]

Convicts, of course, were also human beings with familial ties to free kin and social ties to their fellow prisoners. Convict life – the work songs, crap games, knife fights, religious worship, practical jokes, comradeship, and sexual or romantic encounters with convict "gal-boys" – went on. And like slaves everywhere, southern convicts resisted their condition, by attempting to escape, penning desperate half-literate pleas for mercy to the governor, or petitioning for pardons. They also frequently refused to work at the pace dictated by their tormentors, something I do address in detail in Chapter 6. The sad truth, however, is that more often than not to tell the story from "below" is to recount horrific tales of racial brutality and torture. The social and cultural history of southern convicts remains to be written, but any account will have to scrupulously avoid what, in another context, Lawrence Langer calls the "persisting myth about the triumph of the spirit that colors the disaster with a rosy tinge and helps us to manage the unimaginable without having to look at its naked and ugly face."[7]

For my part, I only provide a glimpse of that "naked and ugly face." I have deliberately eschewed writing an exposé of the horrors of the convict-lease and chain gang (as if such was needed). To be sure, convict labor in the South was steeped in brutality; the rawhide whip, iron shackle, sweat box, convict cage, and bloodhound were its most potent instruments for eighty years. This book is not an account of that brutality per se, however. An entire volume could be filled with the atrocities committed in southern convict camps; but this approach ultimately serves to distance the subject, to banish it to the realm of the benighted South and set it off as some terrible aberration in an other-wise slow but healthy march toward progress. Such an account of convict labor lends itself to a faulty interpretation. For the use of the penal system to recruit and control black labor stood at the cutting edge of southern politics and economic development, not in its dark corners. Far from representing a lag in southern modernity, convict labor was a central component in the region's modernization.

Many "leading men" of the New South leased convicts to expand their enterprises, and suffered very little opprobrium for doing so. After I discovered in her papers that Rebecca Lattimer Felton, one of Georgia's staunchest critics of convict-leasing, was quite intimate with Joseph E. Brown, the state's pre-eminent lessee of convicts, and even purchased convict-mined coal from his mines at a cut-rate price, I abandoned any effort to distinguish between the benighted New South and the progressive one.[8] In fact, the two cannot be separated. The horrors of the southern penal system were not some anomaly in an otherwise decent society, just as today's expanding prison state cannot be divorced from the political and economic forces reshaping American society, especially its urban race relations. The point is that punishment in the postbellum South lay at the heart of the changes sweeping that society, and played a central role in the evolution of the region's race relations, forms of labor exploitation, and burgeoning capitalist development. Any attempt to relegate convict labor to the realm of extreme racial brutality and set it apart from the main currents of the New South risks misconstruing its fundamental significance to the social order.

While doing research for this book I spent part of a summer in Atlanta. During my stay I had the privilege of witnessing the showcase city of the newest New South host the 1988 Democratic Convention. One scorching hot afternoon in Piedmont Park I heard Jesse Jackson refer (erroneously) to the city as "the cradle of the Old South," and (correctly) as "the crucible of the New." In the latter respect, Atlanta did not disappoint. While the upscale delegates enjoyed glistening downtown Atlanta's hotels, restaurants (including a nauseating recreation of "Old" southern hospitality, Miss Pittypat's Porch, complete with black "mammies" as hostesses), bars and convention centers, a group called Justice for Janitors made it known that the men and women who would clean Atlanta when the crowds were gone had complaints about the new regime. And indeed, as the *Washington Post* remarked a year later, "a mile from the glitzy skyscrapers of prosperous, rich, expanding 'Hotlanta' stand the squat, unairconditioned apartments of the nation's oldest public housing project ...; booming Atlanta is dogged by the second-highest poverty rate in the country."[9] The architectural magnificence of John Portman's postmodern lobbies and atrium could not successfully obscure the harsh underlying class realities that continue to plague the city. This, I thought, was an irony that Jesse could appreciate.

Of course this striking contrast should not have surprised me. There is no reason why the most recent incarnation of the New South should be exempt from the racial and class injustices that have characterized much of the region's history. While exploring the cityscape and its past I was struck by this sense of continuity, even while Atlanta and the rest of the South have undergone massive changes. In and among Portman's testaments to the new Atlanta remain landmarks of earlier proclamations of a New South: the First National Bank building; the Cyclorama, dramatizing the burning of the antebellum town and demonstrating the phoenix-like vigor of the postbellum city; the marvelous old Victorian neighborhood of Inman Park; antiquated factories and mills; the Federal

Penitentiary, erected in 1905. In the course of my research I discovered that all of these traces of an older Atlanta were intimately connected to convict labor.

Immediately after the Civil War, Atlanta grew as a rail center; many of the state's Reconstruction railroads were built by convicts. The factories and mills of the 1880s and 1890s were fueled by coal dug by convicts. The personal fortunes that built the downtown banks and office buildings and monuments like the Cyclorama at the turn of the century were gained by men who leased convicts, men who were the city's business and civic elite. The bricks that fortified the Federal Penitentiary, where Eugene Debs was imprisoned in the 1920s, were manufactured by convicts at the Chattahoochee Brick Company. In fact, this company, owned by one of the city's leading citizens and one-time mayor, provided the bricks for many of Atlanta's buildings. The development of Inman Park, the city's first "streetcar suburb" was encouraged and financed by Joel Hurt, a lessee of convicts. And, in the twentieth century, the renowned Peachtree Street and the rest of Atlanta's well-paved roads and modern transportation infrastructure, which helped cement its place as the commercial hub of the modern South, were originally laid by convicts. All this coincided with my emerging argument that from Reconstruction through the Progressive Era southern convict labor lay at the heart of transformations in the region's political economy.

On all those research trips I never did get to eat at Miss Pittypat's Porch. What I did take away from my forays into one of the "darker phases of the South," however, was the conviction that progress and modernization are not necessarily salves of injustice. To the contrary, I found that far from being a barbarous relic of the Old South, convict labor was in many ways in the vanguard of the region's first tentative, ambivalent, steps towards modernity. In what follows I hope to make this view plausible.

New South Slavery

The old is dying and the new cannot be born. In the interregnum, a
great variety of morbid symptoms appear.

Antonio Gramsci[1]

It is one of the rarer ironies of the period that the Redeemers of ...
Georgia should have come to be known as "Bourbons." No group of
Southern rulers less deserved that much abused epithet, with its implications of obstinate adherence to the old loyalties and abhorrence of the
new.

C. Vann Woodward[2]

In *Gone With the Wind*, when Scarlett O'Hara leased a handful of convicts
from the state of Georgia to work in her sawmills she quickly discovered
that her foreman "accomplished more with five convicts than ... with
his crew of ten free negroes." Her friends and family, still wedded to
Margaret Mitchell's version of the more gentile values of the Old South,
felt nothing but shame at this transaction. True, confronted with the
necessary brutality of working convicts for profit, Scarlett's "conscience
battled with her desire for money." But as with so many of the entrepreneurs of the New South, this proved an uneven contest. "'Oh, I'll
think of them later,' she decided, and pushed the thought into the
lumber room of her mind and shut the door upon it."[3]

At around the same time that Mitchell published her historical novel,
an ex-slave recounted a piece of what he dubbed "folklore" to an in-
terviewer from the Works Progress Administration. When freed, this
former slave recalled, "I figguered [*sic*], like de balance of 'em, dat ole
massa wus jes' tryin' to get outen feedin' us." As a result, he continued
to help himself, as he thought was his right, to his master's corn crib
and potato kiln, "collectin'," as he put it. His ex-master asked him to

do some plow work, offering to pay him in corn and potatoes – which he of course refused, continuing his "collectin'." One night, however, the freedman put his hand in the corn crib and was caught in a racoon trap his former master had placed there. In the morning the planter arrived, and said, "I is free too," and told his former slave that he was no longer obligated to feed him, so "start plowing, or I'll land you in de chain gang fur stealin'."[4]

Forty years prior to the publication of *Gone With the Wind*, in 1896, a black convict named Henry Hatcher applied to the governor of Georgia for a pardon. In 1893 Hatcher had traveled from Alabama to Gordon County, Georgia, "under the promise of high wages" from his employer, the Southern Cross-Tie Company. While Hatcher was cutting ties in Georgia the company failed, and could not meet its payroll. "After they had refused to pay him anything for his labor" Hatcher entered the company store and took clothing and shoes "in part payment for the work he had done." The county court sentenced him to eight years hard labor in Georgia's penitentiary for the crime of burglary. The record does not indicate whether as a convict Hatcher continued to cut cross-ties for one of his erstwhile employers' competitors, worked in the nearby coal mines, or was sent to the Chattahoochee brick yard outside of Atlanta. In this instance, the governor showed mercy. Hatcher served only three years of his sentence.[5]

These three anecdotes, drawn from fiction, "folklore," and fact, together illustrate the main features of criminal justice in the New South. For the lessees of convicts, like Scarlett O'Hara bearers of a novel set of moral and economic calculations, black prisoners represented a labor force that would help them produce commodities for the market. For planters denied recourse to the slave whip, the chain gang served as an important element of rural labor discipline with which to control "their" sharecroppers. And for African-Americans like Henry Hatcher, who exercised their new found mobility and defended their hard-won right to compensation for their labor, the penitentiary was often their fate.

Henry Hatcher served his time in a penal system remarkably akin to slavery. Ironically, this system emerged immediately on the heels of the passage of the Thirteenth Amendment to the Constitution, which was intended to abolish bondage but permitted involuntary servitude solely as a punishment for crime. This form of punishment persisted in the southern states for nearly a century after emancipation. The vast majority of southern convicts were black; punishment and rehabilitation were distinctly subordinated to labor exploitation; and prisoners were leased as laborers to the region's capitalists, or worked as state slaves on the chain gang.

The postbellum South saw the growth of a unique penal system, the convict lease. Rather than house convicts in a penitentiary, after 1865 southern states leased them to the highest bidder, who was then responsible for feeding, clothing, and restraining the convicts. In return, the lessee received the right to use the convicts' labor as he desired. This in itself was not unusual; nineteenth-century northern prisons had several systems of penal labor which often included contracting the prisoners' labor out to private entrepreneurs. Yet only in the South did the state entirely give up its control of the convict population to the contractor; and only in the South did the physical "penitentiary" become virtually synonymous with the various private enterprises in which convicts labored.[6]

The development of the convict lease is commonly attributed to the legacy of slavery, the destruction of southern penitentiary buildings during the Civil War, postwar fiscal retrenchment, political corruption, and a general lack of concern for convicts, most of whom were black. Not surprisingly, the system was subject to many abuses, most notably the corruption engendered by collusion between lessees and politicians (often the same people), and the cruelties inflicted on convicts by lessees interested only in extracting labor. By the early twentieth century these scandals stimulated enough Progressive Era reform impulse and humanitarian outrage to abolish the convict lease in most southern states. In Georgia this occurred in 1908. After the abolition of leasing, in Georgia and many other southern states, convicts became the inalienable property of the state, and labored to construct and repair county and municipal roads. In this way the penal system was made to benefit all of a state's citizens, rather than a few entrepreneurs who had used convict labor for their personal gain.

This is the traditional narrative, which, while historically accurate, remains inadequate. By focusing on the workings of the convict lease in Georgia, and drawing corroborative examples from surrounding states, I examine how it operated not merely as a corrupt and unjust penal system, but as a system of labor recruitment, control, and exploitation particularly suited to the political economy of a post-emancipation society. From a purely penological point of view, the convict lease was a fiscally conservative means of coping with a new burden: the ex-slaves who were emancipated from the dominion of the slaveholder only to be subject to the authority of the state. But from a broader perspective, the lease was much more than a convenient fiscal and penal stopgap; it stood as a system of forced labor in an age of emancipation.[7]

During this age of emancipation the American South underwent not one but two wrenching and potentially incongruous economic transformations. Like plantation societies throughout the nineteenth-century world, the abolition of slavery and challenge of free labor relations encouraged landed classes to seek new forms of control over agricultural labor. In all post-emancipation societies the balance between the possibility of land ownership and self-sufficiency for ex-slaves and their dependence on wage labor determined the tightness of this labor control. In the US South planters effectively transformed ex-slaves into an agricultural proletariat with a gamut of labor relations ranging from tenancy to sharecropping to debt-peonage. The necessary political corollary of this labor system was the preservation of white supremacy.[8]

Southern planters resorted to coercion in the face of the freedpeoples' insistence that emancipation gave them the right to define their own conditions of work, to provide or withhold their labor at will. Simultaneously, however, and in contrast to other post-emancipation societies, the South also began to industrialize at a rapid rate.[9] And as in any industrializing society, the owners of capital sought mechanisms to "free" laborers from the means of production and subsistence so they would have to bring their labor to the marketplace, regardless of their race. Black labor recruitment to industry was hindered, however, by the resistance of landowners, who wanted to maintain a hold on the laborers they had fought so hard to constrain. But, like their counterparts in the agricultural sector, southern capitalists also found their designs thwarted by a nascent working class willing to work for wages only on their own terms: on a tentative basis, with little commitment to full-time wage labor in a single firm. In harmony with the planters, the single most common complaint voiced by southern industrialists was their inability to command a reliable, predictable labor force. Leasing convicts was one of the most successful solutions to this problem.

Postbellum planters and industrialists both found ways to benefit from the spread of market relations and yet blunt the free labor market that often accompanies this social transformation. The extension of sharecropping, tenancy, and merchants' liens to the Upcountry, the "southern enclosure" that undermined self-sufficient economies, the close links between railroad expansion and commercial monocrop agriculture, and the growth of textile mills which drew on the newly created pool of landless whites in the Piedmont and Upcountry, were all prominent features of the emerging political economy of the New South.[10] But these developments did not herald the dissolution of "traditional" patterns of labor exploitation and racial domination, for they did not require a loosening of the grip that black-belt planters had on their laborers. To the contrary, the total control that planters sought over the black agricultural workforce was extended and re-created in other economic sectors with various degrees of success. In the cotton-mill villages the paternalism of company town, company store and company housing severely limited the options of the landless whites who entered the mills. And in the South's coal and iron mines, railroad camps, brickyards, sawmills and turpentine camps, capitalists often relied on the forced labor of convicts as a spur towards industrial development.

The common experience of post-emancipation societies with coercive agrarian labor relations undermines the antinomy of slave and free labor, and instead suggests the spectrum of labor relations that lies in between. Despite its overwhelmingly industrial character, southern convict labor can be glimpsed in this twilight between permanent ownership of the laborer's person and the ostensibly free contractual relationship of capitalist labor markets. In the tentative and uneven transition to free labor in the postbellum South, the forced labor embodied in the penal system was the most obvious "continuity" with the slavery that had defined the old regime. Yet it also proved highly adaptable to – and even instrumental in – the most dramatic social and economic transformations of the era. The southern postbellum penal system cannot be understood without reference to the end of slavery and the transition to free labor; the extent to which labor relations in the New South duplicated or diverged from those of the Old South; the attempts to industrialize the South, and the relationship of the state to industrial development in a predominantly agrarian society; and the identity and ideology of the elite that directed – or limited – the pace and scope of that development. In short, convict labor rests at the nexus of the key elements in the ongoing debate over the distinctiveness of the New South and the evolution of its race and class relations. Above all, convict labor made modern economic development of the South's resources compatible with the maintenance of racial domination.

The convict lease appeared in an era in which the abolition of slavery and the spread of capitalist wage-labor relations were held up as dramatic worldwide examples of moral and economic progress.[11] In the United States this new era was ushered in by a Civil War which symbolically marked the triumph of industrial capitalism over an agrarian feudalism, of free labor over slavery. Yet, despite the completeness of the northern victory, and the undeniably massive transformation entailed by the destruction of slavery, there is little agreement about the degree to which the outcome effected a genuine revolution in the direction of the southern economy or the identity and ideology of its dominant class.

Robert S. Cotterill, in his 1948 presidential address to the Southern Historical Association, dismissed any distinction between an "Old

South" and a "New South," claiming that "in no essential way did the war [between the states] alter or deflect the course of southern development.... There is, in very fact, no Old South and no New. There is only The South. Fundamentally, as it was in the beginning it is now, and, if God please, it shall be evermore." Indeed, the supposed cultural hallmarks of southern exceptionalism and continuity – agrarianism, organic conservatism, hierarchy, religiosity – have been persistently noted by writers as diverse as Alexis de Tocqueville, Allen Tate, and Eugene Genovese, suggesting that fundamentally antimodern values have always characterized the region, perhaps right up to the present. Others, most recently Shearer Davis Bowman, have argued for continuity on the basis that the antebellum and postbellum South were both essentially capitalist societies, despite the existence of slavery in the former.[12]

More plausible – and influential – than either of these models is the view associated with C. Vann Woodward, who perhaps heard Cotterill's 1948 address. Three years later his *Origins of the New South* laid out the still persuasive case for discontinuity. In Woodward's account, which remains the bench-mark for studies of the New South, the Civil War and Reconstruction utterly destroyed the power, property, and pretensions of the antebellum planter elite, and replaced them with a class of ruthless capitalist entrepreneurs wedded to economic development, industrialization and growth, and thoroughly bourgeois values.[13] Ever since *Origins of the New South* historians have continued to argue about the identity, ideology, and economic interests of the New South's ruling class. Following Woodward, some have portrayed a New South dominated by bourgeois modernizers – merchants and capitalists who shaped social relations in a way that completely transformed the South. Others, most notoriously Jonathan Wiener, have suggested that "antibourgeois agrarians" remained hegemonic; in the not-so-New South they built a social order dependent on unfree agricultural labor and hostility to industrial development – what Wiener calls, following Barrington Moore, the "Prussian Road" to modernization.[14]

As originally formulated, however, the "Prussian Road" consists of both "the preservation of the traditional agrarian social structure" *and* the economic empowerment of a nascent bourgeois-industrial class.[15] Since the agrarian elite retains social and political supremacy ("hegemony") in this coalition, the path to "modern society" is undemocratic at best, fully fascist at worst.[16] Actually, Eugene Genovese, not Barrington Moore, appears to be the first person to apply the Prussian analogy to the southern United States – but, ironically, with reference to the antebellum South. In the *Political Economy of Slavery*

Genovese argued that "the commitment of [southern industrialists] to slavery forced them to adjust their vision of an industrialized South to one dominated by a broadened slaveholders' regime" and that this "necessarily meant a Prussian road to industrialism, paved with authoritarianism, benevolent despotism, and aristocratic pretension." However, the war liquidated this possibility along with the slaveholders as a class.[17] Moore himself advances a similar thesis with the counter-factual proposition that a southern victory would certainly have led to "a latifundia economy, a dominant antidemocratic aristocracy, and a weak and dependent commercial and industrial class, unable and un-willing to push forward to political democracy." The outcome of the Civil War left a far more ambiguous legacy, in Moore's view, since "when Southern 'Junkers' were no longer slaveholders and had acquired a larger tincture of urban business and when Northern capitalists faced radical rumblings, the classic conservative coalition was possible."[18]

On the one hand, this view seems in accord with Woodward's version of the bourgeoisification of the southern elite and their role as *compradors* in a "colonial" southern economy; on the other hand, where Woodward saw the leaders of the New South as cloaked in the time-honored disguise of the "Lost Cause," Moore seemed to imply that the new southern elite in fact consisted of old "Junkers" clothed in new garb. It is this latter implication that Woodward's radical critics – the "New Continuarians" in his words – seized upon more than twenty-five years after the publication of *Origins of the New South*. In Wiener's view, for instance, "planter persistence" led to a labor-repressive agrarian society, dominated by a planter class which used its political power to ham-string industrial development in Alabama. Sharecropping was the determining "relation of production" in Alabama's political economy. In this model of the Prussian Road, "Junker" hegemony in Alabama meant political authoritarianism, unfree black labor (at least in the agricultural sector) bound to the land by lien laws, vagrancy and anti-enticement statutes, debt-peonage, racial custom, and the threat of extralegal violence. The result was chronic underdevelopment of the state's resources. Above all, this is taken as an argument for the con-tinuity of the "antibourgeois" South, unshaken by the destruction of slavery.[19]

The attack from the "New Continuarians" of the left on the entire notion of a "New" South raises the right questions. What vision of economic development did the New South elite champion? Were they interested in reconstituting the plantation system, and subordinating manufacturing to the continued reliance on monocrop agriculture produced by a bound labor force? Or were they more "capitalist" in orientation, redirecting capital into railroads, coal mines, cotton mills, and real estate, in order to build a new South based on manufacturing, economic development, speculation, and free labor? Finally, how were race and labor relations shaped by whichever of these visions dominated the New South? Did the political economy of the postbellum South rest on virtual slavery, particularly in the agricultural sector, or was it dependent upon the triumph of free labor relations, particularly wage labor, over the legacy of slavery?[20] Yet the focus on the *personnel* of the respective ruling classes of the Old and New Souths can be misleading. While the persistence of particular wealthy individuals or families from the ante- to the postbellum elite "may be interesting sociologically," as Gavin Wright says, it was the way the class that owned the means of production extracted labor from the class that did not that constituted them as a class. "If after the Revolution, the members of a class vigorously pursue goals they staunchly opposed before, in what economic sense has that class survived?," Wright asks. Whatever the ties by blood, money, or even ideology the New South elite had to the Old, their provenance was far less significant than the means they used to exercise class power, make a profit by exploiting labor, or shape the economic future of their region.[21]

While the Prussian Road analogy has had holes punched in it on a number of counts, many of its critics seemed to have missed this crucial point. Its applicability at a local or state, or even regional, level has been questioned, since Barrington Moore's view of power, politics and the economy was developed at the national level.[22] Michael O'Brien has noted that Prussia itself was characterized by state intervention in the economy, while Alabama "inherited an essentially laissez-faire political economy," and debunked the analogy on almost every other point as well.[23] Of course the fact that the primary victims of antidemocratic development were of a different race than the ersatz Junkers also strains the analogy. But Wiener himself has always insisted that for him the "Prussian Road" was never more than a metaphor for the distinctive path to modern American capitalism taken by the South. In contrast to the North, southern development prior to the 1930s depended on "labor repressive" mechanisms far more than on an untrammeled market in "free labor."[24]

Despite Wiener's emphasis on the plantation South, however, this qualitative difference from northern development was not confined to the agricultural sector. In fact, the Prussian Road thesis forces us to examine whether or not the interests of planters and industrialists in the New South actually clashed. Much of the literature assumes this to be the case. If planters emerged hegemonic, then the ways of the Old

South would be perpetuated; if the industrialists were the victors, then a New South – of rapacious or benevolent capitalism, depending on one's point of view – arose from the ashes. But the incompatibility of labor-repressive agriculture and industrial development departs from historical reality as well as the theoretical Prussian Road, which, after all, includes the development of modern industry. Indeed, as we shall see, much of Wiener's otherwise persuasive case rests on a major fallacy: the supposed stunted economic growth of Birmingham, Alabama.

Dwight Billings, a sociologist whose work is often lumped together with Wiener's, presents a similar case for continuity based on the Prussian Road thesis, but with an argument closer in spirit to Moore's original formulation. Like Wiener, Billings emphatically rejects the notion that a "new" middle class took over the reins of economic development in the New South. However, where Wiener defines the new order by its reliance on labor-repressive agriculture at the *expense* of industrial development, Billings argues that postbellum modernization and industrialization depended on the *extension* of labor-repressive social relations to nonagricultural development. In North Carolina his example of this process is the paternalistic structure of the textile industry. In this version of the Prussian Road the postwar planter class allied itself with "nascent industry," providing not only the capital for manufacturing, but the ideology and mechanisms of labor control and extraction as well. "The hallmark of conservative modernization is the preservation of the traditional agrarian social structure ... simultaneously with the sponsoring of industrial development," concludes Billings.[25]

The history of the convict lease system, in Georgia and elsewhere, clearly demonstrates that the class interests and ideologies of planters and industrialists were not necessarily incompatible. On the one hand, convict lessees seemed to be advocates of a "Prussian" path to development; that is, they were reluctant to accept the use of free contractual labor in their enterprises, and preferred the bound labor of convicts. Yet they were hardly anticapitalists or agrarians. Some of the most prominent industrialists and financiers of Georgia, Alabama, and Tennessee leased convicts from the state. In fact, they were the quintessential New South capitalist entrepreneurs, directors of industrial firms, railroads, banks and real estate companies. But they were also "laborlords" as slaveholders had been before them, buying, selling, and exploiting the labor of convicts. This combination of "bourgeois" and "antibourgeois" characteristics points to a potentially new way of looking at an important sector of the ruling class of the New South.

One of the issues raised by identifying this class of industrialists linked to coercive labor relations is the relationship between forced labor and economic development. The effort to distinguish continuity and change, to demonstrate the hegemony of agrarian or bourgeois, planter or industrialist in the New South, frequently relies on the faulty notion that unfree labor will be swept away by "modernization," and that, conversely, the perpetuation of "bound" labor will entail underdevelopment. For Woodward's followers, the fall of the planter class entailed the liquidation of a political economy based on unfree plantation labor; alternatively, the persistence of "archaic" social structures – the plantation, forced labor, racial barriers to political or economic advancement – is linked to underdevelopment and the failure to industrialize.[26] In particular, the absence or presence of the defining feature of the Old South's economy, unfree labor, determines whether the New South was "capitalist" in a modern sense or not. But most analyses of the post-Civil War southern political economy have only considered the degree to which *agricultural* labor was free or unfree.[27]

As a result, the degree of freedom in New South labor relations generally has been measured by the status of the former slaves who became laborers on plantations and farms. From one point of view, if agricultural labor relations were particularly coercive, the social order necessary to maintain this state of affairs hindered economic development. Hence the South remained "backward." Alternatively, if plantation labor was relatively "free," then the social legacy of slavery was effectively abolished, and reasons for the region's persistent poverty would have to be sought elsewhere. On the latter side are the believers in the almighty market, who argue that sharecropping and tenancy developed naturally, and were noncoercive "risk-sharing" mechanisms. On the former are historians who emphasize racism, lien laws, debt-peonage, the Klan, and a host of other "nonmarket" factors that "bound" croppers and tenants to the land, the landowner and the merchant.[28] The focus of this debate serves to perpetuate the view that industrialization would threaten agrarian interests, since its reliance on free wage labor would undermine plantation labor control by creating an alternative labor market for blacks. Conversely, those who argue that free labor relations triumphed in the South after the Civil War point to the fact that "industries developed [and] railroads spread over the land," which they believe could only have occurred if labor relations were noncoercive in all sectors of the economy.[29]

Both of these views slight the possibility that industrial capitalism can benefit from "a conservative, often undemocratic, social and political climate," in the words of James Cobb, and that in the post-bellum South "certain elements of the social and political organization of a fading plantation society [were] not just compatible with but almost integral to the establishment of a new industrial one."[30] Indeed, many recent studies of the New South suggest that segregation, disfranchisement, lynching, peonage, poverty, and racism were as often indices of southern "progress" as they were of backwardness.[31] Convict labor might well be added to this list. In fact, economic "modernization" did occur in the New South; a new class of southern entrepreneurs and industrialists helped promote this "modernization;" and they did not hesitate to rely on forced labor – penal slavery – to make it possible.

This apparent anomaly can be best understood if the political economy of the postbellum South is considered a "transition period between one dominant mode of production [slavery] and another [capitalism]," as Barbara Fields puts it, in which all southerners "found themselves drawn into the orbit of the capitalist market: but on the basis neither of the old social relations nor of mature capitalist ones." This particular model of underdevelopment reframes the question of continuity and discontinuity, and casts new light on the issue of whether the social relations of the New South were "capitalist" or not. From this vantage point industrialization and unfree labor do not preclude each other, and a theory of modernization that equates the development of a society's productive forces with the notion of "progress" can be challenged. For in this "transitional" period, "hybrid forms [of capitalist social relations] made up of relics of slavery grafted onto developing new labor relations" defined the organization of production.[32]

In the agricultural sector of the postbellum South the most notorious "hybrid form" of course was sharecropping, and its lever was the crop-lien. Outside of agriculture, convict labor exemplified a "hybrid form" linked to several classic symptoms of underdevelopment. The growth of capitalism in the postbellum South was hindered by a lack of infrastructure, high transport charges, and a weak home market. There was a shortage of local capital, and a consequent dependence on outside investment. An emphasis on the extractive sector failed to stimulate much value-added manufacturing, and left southern enterprises particularly vulnerable to economic fluctuations.[33] Finally, the available labor force appeared reluctant to enter the wage-labor market on a steady basis. Indeed, it was this very existence of "free" labor, willing and able to exercise mobility, that New South industrialists found unreliable. All of these factors inevitably led southern capitalists to "tighten the screws" on the labor they were able to obtain, much as landowners and merchants did in the agricultural sector.[34]

Indeed, agriculture and industry in the New South were equally structured by – and dependent on – an isolated, low-wage labor market.[35] In a region poor in capital and rich in natural resources, and in which wealth was based on the sudden transformation of "laborlords" into "landlords," a low-wage labor market accounts for both southern "backwardness" and the economic development that occurred.[36] Gavin Wright has shown that by any measure – railroad construction, increased number of manufacturing establishments, agricultural productivity, value-added growth in manufacturing, increase in per-capita income – the South did achieve economic and industrial growth in the latter part of the nineteenth century. In fact, "rates of industrialization and industrial growth in the South were quite respectable by historical standards" in this period.[37] The fact that this growth relied on a heavy dose of continuity acceptable to both planters and industrialists – an isolated labor market, cheap labor, and repressive social and race relations – is far more significant than the relative strength of either class.[38] Material interests provided the basis for planter–industrialist cooperation: "at the center of the common core of planter–industrialist interests was the need for an adequate supply of low-cost labor," as Cobb puts it.[39]

This, however, is only one side of the coin, for it does us no good to explain southern economic isolation by referring to its low-wage labor market, and to then attribute this labor market to southern isolation. This is especially true in light of the fact that the most common complaint of planters and industrialists alike was the difficulty of recruiting and retaining adequate labor. How do we reconcile the presence of a low-wage labor market with fears of chronic labor scarcity? Despite the best efforts of whites to reinvent slavery, African-Americans insisted on their status as free laborers, and attempted to exercise their right to mobility. As they gained leverage, however, the spread of modern forms of labor negotiation merely fostered renewed coercive intervention in the labor market. In an ongoing struggle, landowners and merchants devised methods to keep blacks landless, impoverished and dependent. But this did not necessitate hostility to industrial development: the emerging class of capitalist entrepreneurs had no particular commitment to free labor relations. They sought solutions to the "labor problem" as vigorously as did their counterparts in the agricultural sector.

In his comparative study of Alabama and South Africa, Stanley Greenberg has argued that

> the labor market in an emerging capitalist order almost never responds spontaneously and generously to the needs of the new employers of labor.... Free wage labor as a principle and the labor market as an institution do not provide a sufficient supply of wage laborers at a wage rate acceptable to the

emerging bourgeoisie.... The primary industries in early capitalist development, particularly mining and the railroads, repeatedly turned away from the market in labor and toward the state.[40]

This counter-tendency to "modernization" is particularly true, Greenberg shows, in societies that seek to reconcile the interests of commercial agriculture and emerging industry, while simultaneously maintaining racial domination. From this comparative perspective, early capitalist development tends to intensify the "racial order" rather than dissolve it. Hand in hand with economic development comes a "state racial apparatus" which promotes labor control and the maintenance of racial lines. The tight control of labor in the agricultural sector is not undermined by economic development; instead repressive labor relations are used to foster that development. More often than not, the justification invoked for this is the problem of a "labor shortage."

But this "labor shortage" is an ideological fiction for the persistent attempts by an "undisciplined" working class to seek alternatives to steady wage labor wherever possible, or to seek improvement in their conditions of labor through mobility. For ex-slaves and their children the right to leave one employer for another was second only to the desire to work for one's self as freedom's most precious gift. For employers of labor – in agriculture and industry alike – this aspiration represented emancipation's greatest challenge to their assumptions and power. Rather than dependence on such an unreliable free labor market, capitalists in the New South "used the norms controlling race and labor issues to help organize and control their own labor force."[41]

In the New South, other than Jim Crow laws, the single most dramatic and direct expression of this "state racial apparatus" was the convict lease system.[42] New South capitalists in Georgia and elsewhere were able to use the state to recruit and discipline a convict labor force, and thus were able to develop their states' resources without creating a wage labor force, and without undermining planters' control of black labor. In fact, quite the opposite: the penal system could be used as a powerful sanction against rural blacks who challenged the racial order upon which agricultural labor control relied. From this vantage point the convict lease was not the persistence of a "precapitalist" form of labor coercion, but the extension and elaboration of a new forced-labor system wholly compatible with regional industrial development and the continuation of racial domination. Since it reinforced, rather than disrupted, the forms of social control necessary for extreme labor exploitation in the South's plantation districts, this was a form of "modernization" acceptable to planter and industrialist alike.

* * *

"Much nonsense has been written about the New South," proclaimed historian Holland Thompson in a 1910 paper published in an issue of the *Annals of the American Academy of Political and Social Science* devoted to "The New South." "Every change in form has been hailed as a change in substance," he continued, "and we have been told many times that the Old South is dead, and that an entirely new and different South has risen from the ruins. These expressions have been generally the product of imagination and hope rather than reality and fact." But Thompson did observe that there was a reason to hope for change, as the full impact of industrialization would at last begin to reshape southern social relations. "What no amount of coercion could accomplish is being done by the silent working of economic forces," he concluded. By the end of the decade, Thompson could confidently assert that "today a New South may be said to be everywhere apparent."[43]

Thompson's optimistic faith that industrial development and progress would dissolve "traditional" or "premodern" ways was a staple of New South boosterism and propaganda whose modern-day equivalent is "modernization theory." But his initial skepticism was warranted. The convict lease cannot simply be understood as an unusually resilient "premodern" social relation whose presence in the New South was an aberration, an unfortunate reminder of a less enlightened or "progressive" era; nor should its replacement by the state and county "chain gang" in Thompson's era be taken solely as the victory of Progressive Era humanitarianism.

Its harshest contemporary critics – and there were many – insisted the convict lease was a barbaric relic out of step with the genuine desire for progress and national acceptance that the most enlightened members of the New South sought for their region. Historians have tended to agree with this view, while obscuring the economic significance of the lease. The lease system is commonly portrayed as a stain on the "honor" of the New South, which undermined the legitimacy of the ruling class and their "real" interest in progress or nostalgic attachment to paternalism. But in Whiggish fashion, this historiography presents the abolition of the convict lease as the inevitable triumph of humanitarianism over barbarism, paternalism over naked self-interest, the "reconciliation of progress and tradition."[44] Once crusading reformers exposed its cruelties, "liberal and progressive leaders, business men, ministers and teachers,"[45] the press, and public opinion united to abolish the convict lease in the early decades of the twentieth century.[46] But the defenders and beneficiaries of the New South's peculiar penal system had hardly been enemies of progress. Nor were the advocates of a new penal system – the chain gang – unqualified opponents of using forced black labor to foster economic development. They simply disagreed about the uses to which that labor would be put.

O. Nigel Bolland has pointed out that, when examining forced labor systems, "the interests of those who control the labor should ... be considered, in order to distinguish, for example, between labor for the public good and labor for private profit."[47] This is a crucial distinction when considering the class interests behind the lease and those behind its abolition, and their contrasting views of economic development. Convicts leased to the brick, coal and turpentine industries worked in the extractive sector. While profitable for individual entrepreneurs, and important for construction, industrial expansion, or export, this form of forced labor did not necessarily promote commercial development of the state the way public works might. It also competed with free labor. The tensions between these contrasting models of economic growth, and the interests behind them, were embodied in the private-sector exploitation of convicts in the convict lease and the alternative of the publicly controlled chain gang. In Georgia this conflict culminated in the 1908 law which outlawed the private leasing of convicts and mandated their use by counties on the roads.

The abolition of the convict lease in Georgia pitted Progressive reformers, the labor movement, the good roads movement, and agrarian and commercial interests against the lessees. But this did not mean that the real "New South" had at last shaken off the remnants of the Old. The practice of leasing out convicts to private contractors for use in extractive industries passed away, but the state itself took over the task of exploiting convict labor for economic development by building a transportation infrastructure, ironically with help from the federal government. In the years immediately following the abolition of leasing, Georgia used its chain gangs to make immense strides in macadamizing, repairing, and surfacing its mostly dirt roads.[48] This road work appeared most significant in Fulton County, surrounding Atlanta – one of the commercial hubs of the New South. But this measurable "progress" still relied on a significant continuity, one which lasted into the mid twentieth century: forced black labor.

Georgia's black convicts, who still outnumbered white prisoners nearly ten to one in 1908, were as much the victims as the beneficiaries of this "reform." Indeed, only four years after the advent of the chain gang, up went a new cry for reform. "Georgia ... daily degrades and drives men deeper into hell" by working them in chain gangs on the roads, proclaimed Georgia's Men and Religion Forward Movement in 1913. "Boast not of roads today," chastened these Methodist reformers. "Each foot of them has been built at frightful cost." But it was not until two decades later that Georgia's chain gang achieved national infamy, with the publication of Robert Elliot Burns's *I am a Fugitive from the Georgia Chain Gang!*, and the release of the subsequent Hollywood film based on this book.[49]

The purpose of *I am a Fugitive*, like most muckraking accounts of southern prisons, was to suggest how out of step with modern life Dixie remained, even in the 1930s. In this regard, Burns's account was a typical "Yankee" description of a benighted South, isolated, backward, corrupt, and dominated by ill-educated crackers and hillbillies lording it over simple "darkies." The penal system stood as the most atrocious feature of a politically and culturally undeveloped section of the country, "the Sahara of the Bozart," in H.L. Mencken's language. "The chain gang is simply a vicious, medieval custom ... and is so archaic and barbarous as to be a national disgrace," was the most damning indictment hurled by Burns at his tormentors. But of course in 1922, when Burns had first been arrested in Atlanta, Georgia's chain gang was a recent innovation. Ironically, Burns effected his escape from an isolated county convict camp by riding in an automobile. The modern means of transport which rescued the fugitive from medieval tortures was made possible by the very "archaic" penal system he decried. In all likelihood the paved road on which Burns rode from the backcountry to the outskirts of Atlanta had been improved by convict labor.[50]

Perhaps southern Progressivism "reformed" the convict lease system, but the nature of this reform raises important questions about the role of the state in coercing black labor for economic development. While humanitarian motives should not be dismissed altogether, the class interests that backed this new use of convicts had their own notions about the relationship between penal systems and economic development. The chain gangs which built the roads of the twentieth-century South became an enduring symbol of southern backwardness, brutality, and racism; in fact, they were the embodiment of the Progressive ideals of southern modernization, penal reform, and racial moderation. In this duality the southern chain gang replicated the most significant feature of the convict lease system it had superseded.

"Except as a Punishment for Crime"

Neither slavery nor involuntary servitude, except as a punishment for crime whereof the party shall have been duly convicted, shall exist within the United States, or any place subject to their jurisdiction.

Thirteenth Amendment to the US Constitution

Describing the brutal beating and salting she received for stealing one of her master's pigs, ex-slave Marrinda Singleton recalled that "when dey get through with you, you wouldn't want to steal no' more.... If you see a pig a mile off you'd feel like running from 'im." Deprived of this harsh means of deterrence, postbellum whites had recourse to the law, which while perhaps less direct might prove equally severe. Thus when Jim Watkins stole fifteen pounds of meat from a rural Georgia smokehouse in 1876 he received a fifteen-year sentence for burglary. True, Watkins did obtain a pardon when the governor reviewed his case – after he had served his sentence. The 1889 case of Colonel G.G. Flynt, a white landowner in Monroe County, offers a revealing contrast. Convicted of carrying a concealed weapon, Flynt faced the choice of a $50 fine or a sentence to the county chain gang. He explained that he had carried the weapon because of a dispute with one of his black tenants, who had quit while still owing him money. "I carried a pistol ... only because I apprehended an assault from the negroes," Flynt informed Governor John Brown Gordon. "To have to pay the fine would be a humiliation I certainly don't deserve," he complained. Governor Gordon pardoned him immediately. The possibility that he might have had to work as a convict with black men he might normally employ was not even a consideration.[1]

For whites no longer able to mete out arbitrary punishment to their former black chattel, the criminal justice system served as a prime means

of racial control and labor exploitation in the New South. But for African-Americans, this same system became a powerful symbol of injustice, linking the punishment of crime and their former status as slaves as
forms of white oppression. This view derived from both the harsh treatment blacks experienced in the convict system, and the obvious racial
double standard with which Georgia's white solicitors (prosecutors),
judges, and juries enforced the law. "The black man will be discrimi-
nated against in most instances where the case is squarely between him
and a white man," claimed Bishop Henry Turner, one of the African-
Americans who had served in Georgia's Reconstruction legislature. As
Georgia's leading black newspaper, the *Savannah Tribune*, frequently remarked, "upon the least pretext colored persons accused are convicted
and given heavy sentences" while whites accused of similar offenses were
acquitted.[2] Penitentiaries in the antebellum South had been used to
mete out justice to whites; but the brutality of convict leasing, and its
association with slavery, bred a reluctance to prosecute or punish whites
in the New South. This dramatic transformation in the form, function,
and racial implications of southern punishment accompanied the political, social, and economic upheavals of Reconstruction.

"It is universally conceded that convicts should be employed at some
useful labor," began the 1886 US Bureau of Labor report devoted to
convict labor.[3] The report went on to describe four different systems of
prison labor found in the United States. The most prevalent method of
convict labor was the contract system in which the physical plant – the
penitentiary – remained under state control, but an outside contractor
supervised production and marketed the convict-made goods. These
prison-factories, predominantly located in the industrial states of the
Northeast and Midwest, manufactured boots and shoes, barrels,
clothing, furniture, stoves, cigars, and other value-added products. The
"piece-price system," while less widespread, was a variation on the
contract system. The contractor simply furnished the materials, while
the state supervised production, returning the finished goods to the
contractor for marketing.[4]

   However, due to the objection of both organized labor and capital
to the competition engendered by prison contracting, by the 1880s some
states returned to the public account system. Under public account the
penitentiary became a state-run factory; the prison authorities purchased
materials, supervised production, and marketed the final product, ideally
to other state institutions. Finally, there was the notorious lease system,
concentrated in the southern states, "the most remunerative of any in
vogue," returning in profits to the states that used it nearly four times

their operating expenses. "Under the lease system," the Bureau of Labor report noted, "the total receipts of the state leasing its prisoners are profits, there being no running expenses beyond the payment of a few salaries."[5]

In 1886, of the 64,349 prisoners in the country, 9,699 were worked under the lease system. In Georgia, 1,560 felony convicts were leased as a labor force to entrepreneurs who worked them in their private enterprises. In all, thirteen states "farmed out" their convicts in this manner, rather than work them within the walls of a state penitentiary. In ten of those states slavery as a system of labor, and the state-run penitentiary as a system of punishment, had both held sway in the antebellum period.[6]

The prevalence of the lease system in former slave states lends credence to the common view that the postbellum southern penal system could be traced to the "legacy" of slavery, a tradition of black forced labor that could not be dislodged by emancipation and Reconstruction.[7] Yet, without denying the significance of this continuity, it is important to recognize that the convict lease was far more than just a functional replacement for slavery. As one account of the lease has emphasized, it "must be viewed in relation to the new demands of the postbellum South and not merely as the inertia of the antebellum South.... Convict labor depended upon both the heritage of slavery and the allure of industrial capitalism."[8] Convict labor in the postbellum South continued a tradition of forced labor; yet it hastened the concentration of coerced labor in industry, rather than agriculture. But the true paradox of the convict lease was that while it embodied some continuity in labor and race relations, the adjustments in the political economy of labor coercion coincided with a rapid departure from southern penal traditions, which until then had paralleled those in the industrializing northern states.

In fact the application of forced labor to the process of industrialization in an agrarian economy had important roots in the Old South, and, especially, the Confederacy. Slavery was an overwhelmingly agricultural institution, but not because slave labor was unadaptable to industry. Robert Starobin has estimated that thousands of slaves labored in industrial enterprises in the Old South, from coal mines, to iron foundries, to railroad construction, and other basic industries, many of which leased convicts after the Civil War. During the war itself, when manpower was short and industrial production was a dire necessity, many slaves entered the industrial labor force, again setting an important precedent for forced industrial labor in the postbellum period.[9] In northwest Georgia, for instance, war production gave the nascent iron industry a powerful boost, and "wartime manpower shortages and production demands accelerated a shift from free to slave labor that had begun in some branches of Georgia's iron industry during the 1850's."[10] One author has argued that the entire southern iron industry depended on slave labor, and that up to 10,000 slaves labored in antebellum iron works.[11]

Similarly, during the last decades of the antebellum period many railroad contractors replaced free labor with slaves.[12] One of these, Lemuel P. Grant, bequeathed the tradition to his brother and nephew, John T. and William D. Grant, whose firm was one of the first lessees of Georgia convicts.[13] And while urban slavery was negligible in antebellum Atlanta, two of the largest slaveholders in the city were industrialists, a foundry owner and a brick manufacturer. As with antebellum iron and railroad work, the Civil War intensified the importance of slave labor in urban industry.[14] In general, "Southern businessmen were convinced that slaves were the most stable industrial work force available" in the antebellum period.[15]

Yet it was not a workforce that was always readily available, especially before the war made industrialization imperative; one study has noted that southern coal operators sought slave labor in the antebellum period but had difficulty obtaining it, since "masters were reluctant to hire their Negroes for such employment."[16] After emancipation the lack of available industrial slaves ceased to be a problem; the state was more than willing to hire out black convicts, especially as reconstruction (in the economic sense) and industrialization became priorities. Of the 9,699 convicts leased out by southern states in 1886, only 1,978, or 20 per cent, were engaged in farm labor. In Georgia only 100–150 of the over 1,500 convicts worked in agriculture, and many of these were "invalids" at the state farm, supposedly too weak to be acceptable to lessees.[17] The rest were employed in brickyards, lumber camps, coal and iron mining, the turpentine industry, and railroad construction – the very industries which had relied on industrial slaves before emancipation. In this respect the "continuity" between slavery and convict labor is as much a sign of the compatibility of forced labor and modernization as it is of the enduring legacy of southern economic "backwardness."

The ideology of the convict lease also entailed both continuity and adaptation to a new set of social relations. The use of black convicts in southern industry reflected the refusal by many whites to accept the ideological tenets of emancipation and free labor relations, even in an economy undergoing transformations brought about in part by the destruction of slavery. The lessees regarded black labor as a commodity inseparable from the convicts themselves, much as slaveholders had regarded slaves. But in the New South the "social death" entailed by the enslavement of the laborers was ostensibly rooted in their criminality, not just their race. This marked a shift from what Orlando Patterson has called "intrusive" slavery to "extrusive" slavery. The "intrusive" slave stood as an outsider, the alien – in the antebellum South, the black African, whose enslavement whites justified by a belief in black racial inferiority. But "in the extrusive mode the slave became an outsider because he did not (or no longer) belonged ... he was an internal exile, one who had been deprived of all claims of community.... [He] became the enemy because he had fallen."[18] In the eyes of postbellum whites, convicts became outcasts from a community defined by white supremacy, and thus subject to enslavement; felony prisoners were even denied citizenship upon their return.

Yet continuities in southern racial ideology made this shift to extrusive slavery possible. The well-worn notion that blacks would only work under the threat of compulsion bolstered the forced labor central to the postwar southern penal system, a system socially legitimized by the supposed need to respond to the threat of so-called "negro criminality." Both its labor regime and its penological rationale virtually dismissed the possibility of "reforming" or rehabilitating the black lawbreaker. Reformation only entered the discourse of convict labor when the abysmal conditions found in southern convict camps were defended on the grounds that they represented an improvement over the health and welfare of the "average negro laborer," or when the hard labor required by convicts coincided with the "unskilled" heavy labor held suitable for blacks.[19] These of course were the postbellum South's "special" conditions which southern whites repeatedly used to justify the divergence of their penal system from the penitentiary model prevalent in the rest of the nation.

But this divergence was not just geographic; the convict lease also marked a radical break with the penal policy of the Old South. As the most thorough scholar of nineteenth-century southern crime and punishment has noted, "in virtually every facet of their antebellum history the penitentiaries of North and South were far more similar than different."[20] Thus the postbellum South departed from its own penal traditions, as well as from the developments in the northern states.

Criminologist E.T. Hiller, in his 1914 survey of the previous century of penal labor in the United States, noted this remarkable divergence. Hiller wrote at a time when all except a handful of southern states had abolished private exploitation of convict labor, both in the forms of contract labor and the convict lease, and replaced them with road gangs or state penal farms.[21] He saw the return of convict labor to public control as the last in a series of stages in the development of compulsory penal labor in the United States, which had alternated between private and public control.[22] According to Hiller, the tension between the "utilitarian" desire to make prison labor remunerative and the "humanitarian" desire to reform the criminal determined the ultimate motive – rehabilitation or profit – of prison labor. During the nineteenth century the form this labor took became increasingly dependent on the forces of the market and the conditions of production. Thus the state-run congregate factory system of convict labor "was suited to the new and changing industrial conditions of the [early nineteenth century]." But the private contract system won favor by mid century because it profited the state, had few administrative burdens, and removed the state from the marketplace. By the Civil War era the industrial penitentiary – both state-run and contracted – was commonplace in both sections.[23] And the defining feature of nineteenth-century incarceration, North and South, was in fact "hard labor."[24]

But just as we can find important precedents for forced labor in key sectors of Georgia's antebellum economy, we can also detect a southern ambivalence about penitentiary labor that emerged in the 1850s, and undoubtedly contributed to the reluctance to return to the old penal system in the postwar period. Northern states had contracted out penitentiary labor because the state was unable to assume mounting administrative burdens, to overcome the inelasticity of local markets, or to provide the capital to mechanize penitentiary workshops properly. The resulting stagnation of prison industry led to the privatization of prison labor until the contract system predominated in northern prisons.[25] Similar problems plagued Georgia's antebellum penitentiary, and the legislature grumbled continually about its drain on the state's resources.

Production at Georgia's antebellum prison was unprofitable for several reasons. First, due to its isolated location in the heart of the plantation belt, the Milledgeville penitentiary was unable to tap any markets for its goods "beyond the immediate vicinity." Moreover, this geographic disadvantage increased the cost of production, since raw materials had to be brought from long distances. The quality of prison-manufactured goods was poor, and thus these goods were unable to "compete with similar articles in the markets of the country." Finally, "mechanics, manufacturers, and dealers" objected to prison competition.[26] As a result of these problems, during the 1850s the legislature several times considered moving the penitentiary to the granite quarries at Stone Mountain near Atlanta, putting the convicts to work in mines and iron furnaces near the Western and Atlantic rail line in northwest Georgia, or, alternatively, leasing the entire prison to a private contractor.[27] All three of these suggestions were taken up again after the war, but in Georgia, unlike northern states with similar problems, contractors never gained control over prison labor in the antebellum period.

Perhaps this was because southern prison labor was carried out on a much smaller scale – due both to industrial conditions and the racially restricted pool of available felons – and thus less quickly outgrew the state's administrative and fiscal capabilities even while prison production mirrored the predominant system in the northern states. Furthermore, the opportunities for the "merchant capitalist" so eager to reap a profit from northern prisons seemed less promising in the South. As a result the contract system penetrated the southern penitentiary much more tentatively.[28] Despite the legislature's complaints about its burdensome nature, Georgia's antebellum penitentiary received only 1,343 prisoners between 1817 and 1853, and at the end of the antebellum period held only 245 convicts – the most ever. Over this 36-year period nearly all of these convicts were white.[29]

The most striking difference between the antebellum penitentiaries of the North and South was their magnitude, and Georgia was no exception. In 1850, Georgia with a total population of 900,000 had only 43 prisoners, and convicted only 80. Massachusetts, with comparable population, convicted 7,250, and held 1,236 people in its penitentiary that year. This was because in the South a large proportion of the class most likely to be imprisoned was subject to the direct penal authority of slaveowners more often than the state. And when slaves were prosecuted by the law, punishment was corporal or capital, rather than incarcerative. One comparative study argues that in the South the slave plantation served the same function as the northern penitentiary: social control of the working class. Indeed, in both societies, forms of punishment and forms of production were closely related: "while the plantation represented commercial agriculture in a slave society in its most highly developed form, the Massachusetts State Prison took its cue (and its system of labor and discipline) from the new industrial order [of the nineteenth century]," this study argues.[30] As a result, in the antebellum South there were never enough prisoners to carry on prison production on the scale of the northern penitentiaries. In Georgia, the prison was not self-supporting, and in fact the legislature appropriated an average of $11,000 a year in the antebellum period for the penitentiary. But while this led to the occasional campaigns to lease – or even abolish – the penitentiary, it did not appear to be an emergency; despite the frequent outcry that the penitentiary did not pay, Georgia's antebellum penal system remained relatively stable.[31]

The Georgia penitentiary did manage to find one area of profitable production before the Civil War: manufacturing rolling stock for the state-owned Western and Atlantic Railroad, which guaranteed a market. The principal keeper's (state warden's) report for 1852–53 noted that the "car-shop" was "a most profitable enterprise" – and he consequently offered to lease the penitentiary himself. Between January and October 1853 the penitentiary manufactured thirty-five box cars, five "break" cars, twenty platform cars, and fifteen stock cars, with only thirty convicts working in this shop (the prison held 138 in 1853). This enterprise alone cleared $9,625, and the principal keeper asked the governor for the funds to enlarge the operation to employ up to ninety convicts, and to do away with the tanning shop, which proved unprofitable. Still, even while some convicts labored in the "car shop," others worked outside the prison, constructing a rail line to the penitentiary. This branch line would "prove a great facility in carrying out the business which now chiefly occupies the time of the inmates," since it could ease the transport of work material, and the finished product could be rolled directly from the prison onto the track.[32] This outdoor labor on a railroad set a significant precedent.

The principal keeper's optimism proved brief and unwarranted; four years later his successor complained about the "dilapidated condition of the penitentiary," and the fact that he did not have the facilities to put enough convicts to work. Rather than move or lease the penitentiary, Georgia's legislators had simply chosen to ignore it, and failed to appropriate any funds for the prison in 1854 and 1855.[33] Since the legislature disregarded the earlier plea for expansion, by 1857 the principal keeper informed the governor that "for the want of room to work the convicts inside the walls we are compelled to look outside for employment," and by 1858 he recommended removal of the convicts from the penitentiary altogether. "It is impossible to make the institution pay expenses while engaged in the manufacture of articles where costly materials are used," he complained, "as a large majority of the convicts are loafers and vagabonds who have never been accustomed to labor, and consequently are not mechanics or tradesmen of any kind." He urged that the penitentiary be moved to a point on the Western and Atlantic where convicts could be put to work rolling iron for the railroad; "material will cost but a trifle," and this would "afford constant labor for the convicts and be a source of revenue to the State."[34] Thus by the end of the antebellum period the system of factory prison labor in Georgia had reached its limits, and even white convicts were deemed suitable only for the heavy labor normally done by slaves.

The demands of the Civil War economy briefly resuscitated prison production in Georgia. As in the North, production needs for basic goods and labor shortages augmented the role of prison industry in the wartime economy, especially in the weakly industrialized Confederacy. In 1862 Georgia's convicts manufactured shoes, wagons, furniture, and salt sacks, and also worked in the state arsenal. No prison appropriations were needed during Civil War years, and the penitentiary even managed to turn a profit.[35]

But military exigencies soon overcame the prison's usefulness as a factory. Only twenty-eight felons were sent to the penitentiary in 1862, and in 1864 as General Sherman approached central Georgia, Governor Brown offered a full pardon to any prisoner willing to bear arms for the Confederacy, and the convicts obliged. Apparently the convicts were mustered as a guerrilla force to harass Sherman's troops; but the effectiveness and commitment of these unusual recruits is disputed.[36] The penitentiary building itself lay directly in Sherman's path, at Milledgeville, the state capital. Since it was a war-production factory, Union troops razed the prison workshops. By one historian's account, at the end of the conflict "the penitentiary and its shops were nearly all destroyed, and those convicts who had not been discharged had escaped." Only four convicts remained in the custody of the state in 1865.[37] Deprived of a slave labor force that had been crucial to heavy industrial labor, already uncertain about the practicality of penitentiary labor, and fearful of the social impact of nearly half a million freedpeople, white Georgians began to reconstruct a penal system suitable to their greatly changed conditions.

The Civil War and its aftereffects at once shattered the penitentiary system of the South and reinforced the North's prison-factories. In the North "social and industrial disturbances of the War period augmented the magnitude of prison industry under the contract system."[38] The market for the type of goods manufactured by prison industry grew rapidly, and in the postwar period the available population of felons – the unemployed, the vagrant, immigrants, demobilized soldiers, and criminals – also swelled.[39] In the South, however, despite an initial surge in prison production, the eventual result of the war was the virtual collapse of the penitentiary. The penal system was so weakened in Georgia, that the 1866 legislature made death the punishment for convict insurrection.[40] Most significant, however, was the state's sudden domain over the freedpeople, whose behavior had previously been the concern of their owners more often than the criminal justice system. The antebellum South's penitentiaries had always been intended for whites, which shaped both their labor systems and their relatively small scale. Emancipation effectively erased this determining factor in southern punishment. The state's capacity to punish now focused on ex-slaves who fell afoul of the law. This sharpened the distinction between the type of penal labor deemed appropriate for African-Americans and that which continued to be associated with white convicts.[41]

The postbellum decision to lease convicts was not merely an abandonment of the "humanitarian" goals of penology and penal labor, an abdication made possible by a racism no longer mitigated by paternalism. Nor was it simply a temporary fiscal expedient made necessary by the trials of war, emancipation, and Reconstruction. These factors were important, but the lease also entailed an explicit rejection of the factory-based penitentiary system in favor of penal labor that appeared more appropriate to Reconstruction Georgia's economic needs as well as the sudden preponderance of black convicts.

In his impassioned exposé of the convict lease in the 1880s, southern crusader George Washington Cable noted a peculiar southern justification for the lease. In northern prisons, he was told, convicts were capable of the "skilled" work demanded of them in prison workshops, and in fact derived useful training in carrying on prison labor. But southern convicts – that is, blacks – could not engage in this sort of work, and were incapable of being trained to do so. Cable, of course, took pains to debunk this racist view, and contended that blacks could learn skilled labor while in prison. Yet he failed to observe the fact that one reason the lease initially developed might have been the desire to *avoid* giving blacks training that could undermine their restricted place in the southern labor market, lest "the penitentiary become a school for the promotion of bad men over good."[42]

Ironically, Cable did point out that even under the labor system prevailing in northern prisons skilled labor was not the norm. He complained that northern convicts were "set to some simple task, some minute fraction of the work of manufacturing some article, a task that he learns to do at most in a few days" and bemoaned the fact that this left the convict "without a trade."[43] Again, he seemed oblivious to the fact that this served to socialize an unskilled labor force to its location in an industrializing economy and proletarianized labor market.[44] Yet Cable did hit upon one of the important factors that militated against the re-establishment of factory-penitentiaries in the South: the prevalent belief that "the Negro is not well adapted for such employment as is furnished in factories."[45] The southern penal system was not unique in its compatibility with specific developments in a regional economy and labor market, but merely in the specific forms that relationship took – forms dictated by the unique political economy of race and class relations in the postbellum South.

On 1 January 1869 the principal keeper of the Georgia penitentiary reported that it was difficult for him to keep the refurbished prison workshops open, and that he found his stock of material practically exhausted. Although he operated a tan yard, a smithy, a woodworking shop, a shoe manufactory, and a brickyard within the walls of the penitentiary, these enterprises could not be made profitable.[46] Only twenty-four convicts were at work inside the prison – and only eight worked in a shoe shop capable of employing fifty prisoners. In all, one hundred convicts – twenty-nine white, seventy-one black – remained inside the penitentiary, but most of them were too sick to work. On the other hand, the principal keeper had "farmed out" 243 "able-bodied" convicts to railroad contractors; these prisoners, most of them black, were "confined" within the penitentiary only on paper. The sick convicts inside the penitentiary had been rejected or returned by the labor contractors who "make the penitentiary their hospital." The principal keeper had hoped to return the prison to car manufacturing – the only prison industry which had been profitable in the 1850s – but "the substraction [sic] of so much of the able-bodied and efficient labor has so crippled my [work]force that I deem it imprudent to begin the business," he complained.[47] By the beginning of the next year, 1870, the convict force grading the railroads had swelled to nearly 400, with 329 black convicts and only 65 whites; the penitentiary itself was virtually abandoned, with only 7 prisoners remaining. Even the weak and sick convicts had been leased.[48]

But it would be a mistake to think that this state of affairs followed inevitably from the pressures of war, emancipation, and Reconstruction. During the initial years of Reconstruction the development of a penal policy, like much else in Georgia, was tentative, and, because of the politically fluid situation, fraught with uncertainty. Charles Jenkins, Georgia's presidential Reconstruction governor – a prewar Whig elected by the first Democrat-dominated Reconstruction convention in November 1865 – appointed a three-man committee to report on the status of the Milledgeville penitentiary and recommend alternative locations. The committee's report, conveyed to Jenkins on 2 November 1866, demonstrated the uncertainty surrounding the question of postbellum convict labor, and the far from fixed "solution" to the new penal problem posed by the freedpeople.

Their first concern was that by September 1866 they found 177 convicts in the penitentiary, and that "from the proportion of Negro Convicts it is very manifest that the new order of things will result in a far greater number of convicts being sent to the penitentiary" than ever before. Foremost in the committee's mind was the need to create more room than existed at the Milledgeville penitentiary, in order to accommodate what was feared to be an inevitable influx of a vast vagrant and criminal population generated by emancipation. In a self-fulfilling prophecy the penitentiary "was soon filled to overflowing with negro convicts, as all men of common sense saw would be the case as soon as freedom was conferred upon the slave population." Many – perhaps 40 per cent – of convictions in 1866 and 1867 resulted from the stringent prosecution of the petty crime of "simple larceny," which netted sentences of three to seven years.[49]

No doubt some convicts were guilty of just that – simple larceny. But there is reason to believe that for many newly emancipated rural blacks petty theft proved an excellent means of defending their tenuous hold on independence and freedom from debt, a potent "weapon of the weak." Even as the state broadened definitions of criminal trespass in the rural South during the early years of Reconstruction, agricultural laborers contested redefinitions of property rights and exchange relations with a well-developed moral economy, as they persisted in "stealing what had previously been theirs by customary right."[50] At "the dawn of freedom" a Georgia planter seemed to recognize that theft was not the expression of a racial trait, but a rational economic calculation. "Of at least 3000 hands in Burke Cty," he complained to the Freedmen's Bureau in the fall of 1865, "there are not 50 who will even talk of making arrangements for the next year.... They are stealing every thing eatable, evidently with the view of having something to eat, so as not to be driven by necessity to labour" – starvation presumably being the only thing that could drive landless free workers to sell their labor for a wage.[51]

Similarly, as the system of sharecropping spread across the black belt, the rights of sharecroppers to control and dispose of the crop were correspondingly narrowed. The sharecropper "only has a right to go on the land to plant, work, and gather the crop.... The case of the cropper is rather a mode of paying wages than a tenancy," declared Georgia's Supreme Court in 1872. Not only did this imply that the customary "right" of provision grounds, developed under slavery, remained at the planter's discretion; it also meant that "the cropper's share of the crop is not his until he has complied with his bargain,"[52] effectively tying all his exchange relations to the landlord and relinquishing any ownership in the crop. This was in marked contrast to the control over shared crops that freedpeople had sought immediately following emancipation, control that increasingly could only be reclaimed by the "criminal" action of simple larceny or "larceny after trust."[53]

Unlike most southern states, Georgia apparently did not immediately enact a battery of new criminal laws designed to entrap the freedpeople. In fact, the 1866 legislature reduced a whole series of crimes to misdemeanors. It is conceivable, however, that the reduction of many felonies to misdemeanors had a dual purpose. On the one hand, whites could pay a fine – or have it paid for them – and go free. On the other, blacks, unable to pay a fine, would be sent to the "chain gang" in their county, or might even be leased with the felony convicts. Alternatively, a white landowner might pay the fine for a black misdemeanant, and he or she could "work it off" as a debt peon.[54]

Still, existing felony laws were sufficiently severe and arbitrary that blacks found themselves with long penitentiary sentences for petty crimes, and whites seemed to avoid prison sentences altogether. Of the 205 convicts sent to the Georgia penitentiary in 1868, 177 were black, and only 28 were white. Thus black convictions alone were nearly twice the number of total convictions in any single year during the 1850s; at the same time, the number of whites being sent to prison by Georgia's courts was substantially *reduced*. By 1 January 1870, 145 of these black convicts remained in Georgia's penal system, now leased to Grant, Alexander & Company, railroad contractors, but only 11 of 28 whites sent to prison in 1868 were still imprisoned. Eighty-six of the 145 black convicts had been sentenced for burglary, a crime whose definition was "clarified" by the 1866 legislature, and 17 of these 86 had received life sentences. Georgia's cities and the counties in the plantation belt – the two areas most affected by the social tensions and black labor mobility unleashed by emancipation – sent 136 of these 145 black convicts to the penitentiary in 1868.[55]

Whether this was due to the state's attention to crimes previously punished by slaveowners, draconian legal codes aimed at driving the freedpeople to labor for their former masters, racially biased application of the laws, the "ignorance" of the freedpeople or merely their poverty, several questions were raised by the penitentiary's new function of racial control. The costs of an expanded penal system, the possibility – or lack thereof – of reforming these new "criminals," and the suitability of the freedpeople to penitentiary labor were all concerns raised by the committee appointed by Governor Jenkins. Ostensibly providing a report on the "location" of the penitentiary, the committee extended their own mandate to discuss a broad range of penological questions that touched on labor and race, fiscal responsibility, and economic development.

While their report claimed that "it [was] impracticable to have a proper Penitentiary System when the main object ... is the expense to be avoided and the profits to be realized from it," they nevertheless urged in their recommendations that penal labor be made compatible with the development of Georgia's economic resources. The committee characterized the history of *all* penal institution – in Georgia and elsewhere – as a failed effort to reform criminals, and contended that the best hope was that convicts would be "turned out no worse men than when they were received." Having thus dismissed two centuries of reformative penology, they noted that punishment was a crucial component of any penal regime, and that in this area "there [was] great room for improvement" in the Georgia penitentiary.[56]

Oddly, they argued that by itself penal labor did not constitute punishment, and in fact "labor in the Penitentiary is a relief and not a punishment" – particularly the "mechanical labor" that had been carried on at the penitentiary throughout its history. This unusual rejection of the rehabilitative and punitive aspects of prison labor was compatible with the committee's most pressing concern about the current state of the Georgia penitentiary: its "utter unsuitableness [*sic*] for any other kind of labor except the mechanical trades."[57]

The critique of factory prison labor embodied in the committee's report derived from two mutually reinforcing sources, both closely bound up with the penal system's new role in punishing ex-slaves. First, the committee developed a republican attack on the tendency of prison labor to degrade the status of the free mechanic, an attack which gained strength in northern states in the decades following the Civil War. "The almost universal practice of instructing convicts in the various mechanical trades, has aroused a deep feeling with that portion of the people in every section of the Country," began the committee's report to Governor Jenkins. Furthermore, prison labor was "offensive to the just pride of that worthy and estimable portion of our community [the white working men]. They feel that the natural effect is to degrade their vocation, by turning out from the walls of the Penitentiary the worst characters as rivals and associates in their business."[58]

In Georgia, a state with a small class of "mechanics," such appeals to the interests of the working man were infrequent, and surprising coming from a committee headed by Howell Cobb, hardly a Radical Republican.[59] Indeed, Cobb was one of Georgia's most partisan defenders of the agrarian old order, a firm opponent of Reconstruction, and a disbeliever in the capacity of free black labor. He was joined on the committee, however, by Mark Cooper. While an ardent "states' rights Democrat of the strictest school," Cooper had also been a prominent antebellum industrialist in Georgia. Born in 1800, at the age of thirty-three he had built one of the state's first cotton mills, backed railroad construction in northwest Georgia, and invested in an iron furnace and rolling mill in the region in the 1840s.[60] Together with the third member of the committee, John Fitten, Cobb and Cooper suggested to the governor that he heed the "mechanics' appeal," and that the state abandon altogether a penitentiary based on craft labor inside prison workshops. Men like Cobb, who still owned a plantation in central Georgia, sought to control recalcitrant black workers; Cooper hoped to develop the state's resources. Perhaps the politics of Reconstruction dictated their unusual shared approach. Both Democrats and Radical Republicans, agriculturalists and industrialists, sought the crucial support of the large class of whites susceptible to this appeal: unionists, yeomen, men who had never owned slaves, and the state's nascent white working class.

Second, the committee thought this course of action especially appropriate in a state such as Georgia because "our Penitentiary has the prospect of being filled to overflowing with the very worst portion of the Negro population," and Georgians could not "expect ... respectable citizens to put their sons at a trade, when the State is educating the most infamous characters in the same trade, to compete and associate with them in the pursuit of their daily occupation."[61] It was this potential training of blacks to compete with white artisans and craftsmen, or even to work side-by-side with them upon release, that appeared so offensive both to the committee, and, supposedly, to the mechanics for whom they claimed to speak.

But Cobb, Cooper and Fitten nonetheless foresaw productive uses for the large numbers of black convicts who were rapidly outstripping the capacity of the refurbished Milledgeville penitentiary to incarcerate them. They recommended a comprehensive system of convict labor that would make the most of the state's natural resources, help foster economic development, and concentrate convicts in "more manual or rough work," which would presumably emphasize punishment, rather than training. First, they suggested, the convicts should be removed to the granite quarries of Stone Mountain. There they would find the stone for building a new penitentiary, and the quarries would subsequently "furnish work for the convicts for all time to come." Convict labor could produce cheap stone, which Georgia's growing cities and towns – particularly nearby Atlanta – would use for new buildings and roads. An added advantage of this kind of work was that "they will thus be withdrawn from all other mechanical trades."[62] The committee also envisioned a new penitentiary at Stone Mountain as a base for a far more grandiose scheme. The quarries were accessible to the state-owned Western and Atlantic railroad, which ran through Atlanta and on into an area of Appalachian northwest Georgia "known to be abundant in minerals and natural resources." The convicts at Stone Mountain could be put on a "convict train" and worked at different points up and down the line "in the Iron, Copper, Marble and Slate mines which abound there."[63]

Thus, while quarrying granite seemed like a worthwhile task for the convicts, in fact the committee found the proximity of the state railroad the most attractive aspect of the proposed new location. The Western and Atlantic would provide the opportunity to "use convict labor for the development of the mineral and other resources" which supposedly were crucial to Georgia's economic recovery and progress. One previous difficulty with the penitentiary had been the reluctance of Georgia's taxpayers to support it; but if the penitentiary could "be made useful in developing [the state's] great resources" it would prove popular with the people. In addition to the granite quarries and the numerous mines, the committee also suggested the importance of lime quarries, and the Etowah iron works, antebellum Georgia's premier iron furnace, which they felt the state might want to buy in order to work convicts there. Free labor seemed incapable of exploiting these resources, they claimed. Moreover, the convicts could even "be employed in doing the work on the [Western and Atlantic rail-] road for which large sums are paid out annually to hired labor" – a notable exception to the concern for the rights of "mechanics." In fact, a few months earlier, the legislature had made provision for the working of misdemeanor convicts on the Western and Atlantic, but Governor Jenkins had so far refrained from placing them there.[64] Overall, locating the new penitentiary on the state railroad simplified matters of transport and would take into account "all the varied interests involved in the development of [Georgia's] resources."[65]

As it turned out one of these "varied interests" appeared to be a member of the governor's committee. The owner of the Etowah iron works was none other than Mark Cooper himself, who had long had extensive interests in the iron ore industry of northwest Georgia. Only a month after making the recommendations that sought to use Georgia's convicts to develop this region, Cooper incorporated the Iron and Mining Company of Dade County, which lay directly on the line of the Western and Atlantic. Such conflicts of interest went unnoticed – or unquestioned – at the time, and merely set the tone for future discussions of the convict question, in which self-interested entrepreneurs often took a hand. In fact, Cooper's new company opened the mines that would later pass into the hands of Georgia's Civil War governor, Joseph E. Brown. Brown, an unshakeable defender of the slaveholder's republic, readily adapted himself to the contingencies of the postbellum era. He retained the political influence secured by his defense of the Confederacy even while he embraced the program of economic modernization associated with the New South. Under Brown's stewardship in the 1880s and 1890s the Dade Coal Mines would lease hundreds of convicts, and exploit the rich resources of northwest Georgia much as the 1866 committee had envisioned.[66]

For whatever reason, the committee's report did not entirely convince Governor Jenkins, and he transmitted it to the legislature ten days later, on 12 November, with his doubts appended. Contravening his appointed committee's recommendations, but responding to their racial arguments, he urged the General Assembly to retain the extant Milledgeville penitentiary for white convicts, and to adopt the proposed alternatives for blacks. "The quarrying of granite, limestone, and other minerals ... might be advantageously done by Colored Convicts in a new locality, whilst in the present one, other employments might be prosecuted by [whites]," suggested Jenkins.[67]

The governor pointed to what he saw as the speciousness of the committee's hostility to "mechanical" prison labor, claiming that he personally did "not perceive that [mechanics] will be degraded by having their handicraft taught to or practiced by convicts." "Similarity of occupation does not by any means necessitate social intercourse or imply social equality," he concluded. And would not the problem of competition or association equally apply to *any* kind of penal labor in any case, asked Jenkins? Mining, too, could be degraded by convict workers from this perspective, he argued. Since the "Mechanic Arts" were "eminently fitted to be prosecuted within a small area, which may be easily and securely walled in," such work was appropriate to the penitentiary, as it always had been, North and South.

Still, he agreed that the penal system's new charges – ex-slaves – could be set to work on the quarries, mines and railroads of the state. The report submitted to the governor had suggested the races be kept separate when sent to the penitentiary, but did not "propose to discriminate in punishment between the two races, [since] our only purpose is to repudiate the idea of social equality" – though it was evident that the committee expected the vast majority of the convicts to be black. Jenkins carried the implicit racial views of the report to their logical conclusion: craft labor and industrial training for white prisoners; heavy, dangerous, punitive manual labor for blacks.[68] Unfortunately for the few whites unlucky enough to be caught up in Georgia's postbellum penal system, Jenkins's recommendations were never followed. The forced labor deemed suitable for African-Americans was driven by economic forces that, once set in motion, made little distinction according to race. That privilege was reserved for the court system, whose noted reluctance to punish white offenders was one of the ironic results of convict leasing.[69]

Despite the emphasis on making convict labor a cost-free way to maintain a penal system compatible with the development of Georgia's resources, the committee ultimately recommended the appropriation of $150,000 to establish the new penitentiary system. This represented a considerable sum, which made antebellum expenditures appear frugal by comparison. Pursuing his own agenda, in 1866 Governor Jenkins requested and got from the General Assembly enough funds to rebuild the workshops in the Milledgeville Penitentiary.[70] The legislature, however, continued to express interest in using convicts on the Western and Atlantic railroad. The day after Jenkins conveyed the report and his own recommendations to them, legislators passed a resolution requesting him to "provide information on the following points": first, was it "practicable to use the inmates of the Penitentiary in building bridges, water tanks and freight cars for the State road [the Western and Atlantic]"; and second, could the convicts also be used to roll iron for the railroad and "[do] other heavy manual labor connected therewith."[71]

They must have found the results of this inquiry discouraging, however, for by the end of the legislative session the General Assembly passed an Act which would set Georgia's penal system on a wholly different course. Up until this point even the notion that private capital might benefit from using cheap convict labor had generally been tempered by the assumption that the labor would remain "under the control of the State."[72] But on 28 December 1866 the General Assembly passed legislation to "farm out the penitentiary ... to such persons as shall take it on the best terms," for up to five years.[73]

One of the greatest ironies of Reconstruction politics in Georgia – and there were many – is that of the several penal options available to them, the military and the Congressional Reconstruction governors who succeeded Jenkins's conservative regime seized upon the convict lease. General Thomas Ruger, Jenkins's appointed military replacement, and Rufus Bullock, the Republican governor elected in Georgia's most "radical" phase of Reconstruction, appeared more willing than their predecessor to use penal labor in the service of the sort of state–capital cooperative economic development envisaged by Cobb and Cooper's

1866 report. During Presidential Reconstruction Georgia's legislature made provisions for several dispositions of the state's convicts. On the one hand, on Governor Jenkins's recommendation, they appropriated funds to rebuild the penitentiary buildings and workshops in Milledgeville. At the same time, taking their cue from the committee, they promised a workforce of convicts to the Cartersville and Van Wert Railroad to help build a feeder line to the state railroad in the northwestern corner of the state. Yet it seemed that both of these actions were superseded by the leasing of the penitentiary in the closing days of 1866.[74] However, these legislative initiatives only enabled, but did not necessarily require, the governor to take action. And Governor Jenkins, until his removal by the US Army in early 1868, appeared content with keeping the ever-growing number of convicts confined within the remnants of the Milledgeville penitentiary.[75]

A confluence of factors, not the least of which was the legislature's hope simply to dispose of the responsibility and expense of maintaining a penal system now almost entirely concerned with the black population, made the convict lease possible in Georgia. Still, this decision depended on the willingness to abandon the traditional humanitarian rationale that had helped shape North American penology during the nineteenth century, an abandonment greatly aided by prevailing assumptions about race. Similarly, the belief that blacks were suited only for heavy, unskilled labor, coupled with artisan antipathy to the competition of emancipated slaves, drew Georgians away from faith in the usefulness of factory prison labor. The antebellum experience had weakened confidence in the productivity and profitability of this form of prison labor in any case; the new race relations created by emancipation made it appear to whites as wholly inappropriate.

These conditions, which developed in the immediate aftermath of the Civil War, helped tilt Georgia's penal policy towards leasing. But it was the US military and subsequent Radical Republican regime that found convict labor, railroad construction, and the privatization of the penal system compatible with their plans for the economic reconstruction of Georgia. Decades later, apologists for Georgia's atrocious penal system liked to claim it was a "system [of punishment] we inherited and got thrust upon us by people who were not as much interested in our welfare as we are ourselves."[76] While manipulated as part of the ongoing assault on the legacy of Reconstruction, these sentiments were not entirely inaccurate. Political affairs in Georgia were tumultuous during the late 1860s as Reconstruction reached its high point. When they acceded to power with the aid of the US Army in 1868–69 the Republicans attempted to redraw the map of Georgia politics. Yet in penal matters they readily followed the course charted in the waning days of the 1866 legislature they had supplanted.

In the wake of the destruction wrought by the war, the party that had brought about the demise of slavery swept southward with a vision of progress and economic expansion for the defeated states. Railroads would have to be built; mines would have to be dug; cities would have to grow; factories, furnaces and mills would have to be established. Historians have rightly noted that a free labor ideology was an important component of the political and economic changes the Republicans hoped to carry to the South.[77] Yet the early history of the convict lease stands as a stark reminder of the limits of this ideology. Even while they were committed to the destruction of the last remnants of human bondage, the Republicans found in industrial slavery a telling precedent for certain aspects of their economic program, particularly railroad construction. If, as one Confederate general pointed out to recalcitrant Georgians, the language of the Thirteenth Amendment still allowed the southern states to use the criminal law to sell blacks back into bondage,[78] it took the Republicans' faith in state-aided industrial development to make the convict lease a reality. The political economy of Radical Reconstruction forged the chains that would bind Georgia's convicts for the rest of the century.

===================================== 3 =====================================

"Out of Their Long Shirts and Into Georgia Stripes": Reconstruction, Redemption, and the Convict Lease

Who built the seven gates of Thebes?
The books are filled with names of kings.
Was it kings who hauled the craggy blocks of stone?
Bertolt Brecht, "A Worker Reads History"[1]

Quamly Walker of Wilkinson County worked as a convict for the Dade Coal Company for fifteen years. In 1876 he and nine other men had been convicted under Georgia's anti-Klan statute of conspiring to assault a black man, Rack Beall. Only one other detail of this all too rare enforcement of a law designed to protect black rights stands out: Walker and his co-conspirators were also black.[2] Such a cynical application of a Reconstruction-era legal form to the very people it was designed to protect exemplifies the opportunism of Georgia's defenders of white supremacy. Similarly, the state's "Redeemers" embraced and benefited from a penal system whose corruption, brutality, and economic program they insisted on associating with their erstwhile enemies, the Radical Republicans.

Within the twists and turns of Reconstruction and Redemption politics in Georgia appeared an ongoing debate about the disposition of the state's convicts, a debate which took into account race, punishment, and the needs of a devastated economy, but which did not readily cleave to otherwise sharply defined partisan objectives. In the six years following the Civil War political turmoil engulfed the state, as four short-lived administrations came and went in rapid succession. As we have seen, convict leasing was first proposed in Georgia during Presidential Reconstruction as a means to bring order to the state's penal

37

system, to stabilize race and labor relations, and to encourage economic development. But the first lease contract was signed after Georgia submitted to martial law, once the Radicals in Washington had terminated President Andrew Johnson's half-hearted attempt to remake the South. The Republicans who governed Georgia from 1868 to 1871 then expanded the convict lease as part of their attempt to use the state to foster economic growth, particularly by liberally granting state aid – in the form of bond endorsements and the provision of forced labor – to railroads. Finally, even while the 1871 and 1872 Democratic "redeemer" legislatures began the process of disentangling the Republicans' railroad projects, they also explicitly recognized the convict lease contracts made by the Republican governor, Rufus Bullock, and provided for the continued lease of the penitentiary – at a better return for the state. In an era notable for its lack of consensus, the policy of "farming out" convicts to industrialists and railroad entrepreneurs, with the goal of stimulating economic development, proved amenable to the advocates of Presidential Reconstruction in 1866, the US Military, the Radical Republicans, and the "Redeemers" alike. Above all, forced industrial labor was quite compatible with the political economy promulgated by the conservative regime that seized the reins of power in Georgia after the failure of Reconstruction.

In many ways public aid for the railroads embodied the contradictions of the Republicans' failed "revolution" in the South. The generous state support for economic development knit together a diverse political coalition and built an extensive patronage network; simultaneously, this engendered terrible corruption. Newly laid rail lines helped restore the South's shattered economy; yet overextended and weakly capitalized projects led to collapse, receivership, and the dominance of southern development by northern capital during the 1870s. Finally, railroads lay at the heart of the Republicans' attempt to remake the South in the North's image, and to transform a slaveholders' regime into a democratic capitalist society; but much of the railroad labor in the Reconstruction South was done by African-American penal slaves.[3]

If Reconstruction thus entailed an effort to counter the hegemony of the planter class while maintaining a form of slavery, Redemption marked the apparent triumph of the old regime, and yet permitted a certain degree of industrial expansion – especially if it relied on forced labor. Although the "Redeemers" of Georgia in good part justified their *coup d'état* by the defalcations and liberal state aid of the Republicans, they readily continued to provide the railroads with penal labor. Whatever else differentiated the phases of Reconstruction and its overthrow, the convict lease marked a continuity. The political roots of Radical

Reconstruction in Georgia proved shallow, but in fact the political economy of Redemption "meant the open acceptance on a bipartisan, statewide level of the 'new era' which Joseph E. Brown had long since proclaimed the true result of the Civil War." Promoters of industry quickly accommodated themselves to the new regime.[4]

The creation of a political economy that could simultaneously reject the Republican agenda and yet not entirely close off the opportunities for economic and industrial development entailed several requirements. In order to forge a political coalition that would include Georgia's planters as well as its "progressive" business class, the black agricultural labor force would have to be tightly controlled. Second, securing of capital and the recruitment of an industrial labor force would have to occur, but without weakening the authoritarian social order of the black belt. This meant that southern industry would have to attract northern capital, and perhaps draw on a labor pool consisting of immigrants or dispossessed upcountry whites, particularly in rural areas. In order to attract outside capital, wages would have to be low; but to recruit an immigrant labor force, pay and work conditions would have to be competitive with what was offered in the urban industrial North.

The southern textile industry overcame these contradictions by capitalizing on the rapid growth of a landless class of rural whites in the Piedmont, as well as by recruiting underpaid women and children. The availability of this labor was generated in part by the transformations in southern agriculture, landholding, and credit patterns that followed from the strict patterns of labor control, sharecropping, and debt that spread like a cancer from the black belt.[5] Indeed, the textile sector's traditionally "white" character made it the only significant New South industry that never sought a convict labor force. Textile operators' reluctance to hire black convicts stemmed from the racist belief that African-Americans were inherently unsuited to indoor factory labor; the general rule that convicts could be employed "at any labor consistent with reasonable punishment and their physical ability, except in factories where women are employed"; and the refusal of white textile workers to work or compete with black workers, free or convict. In the rare instance that convicts entered a cotton mill, as they did in Alabama, they tended to be "white boys who have had experience with cotton mill work."[6] But other New South industries, particularly those that traditionally relied on black workers and were located in rural or isolated regions, had a more difficult time recruiting a stable free labor force, and often looked elsewhere.

Convict labor reconciled the contradiction of capitalist development and racial repression that faced the "Redeemer" political coalition.

Convicts provided industrialists with a cheap and consistent labor force attractive to outside capital. But the recruitment of this form of labor in no way loosened the planters' grip on labor in the agricultural sector. In fact, the legal mechanisms of labor control used to subordinate blacks in the plantation belt actually helped create the pool of convict laborers made available to Georgia's mines, iron furnaces, railroads, turpentine camps, and brickyards. Planters could turn to the law as a crucial weapon in their daily struggles with black sharecroppers over appropriation, labor, and mobility. "Nearly half of the Negro prisoners [in Georgia] are confined for crimes against property," noted the 1904 Atlanta University study of negro crime. The same study printed a report from Crawford County, in the heart of the state's black belt, which noted that African-Americans were often punished for "breaking contracts." Correspondents, black and white, writing to the university's conference on crime suggested that it was "transient" workers and the "gang-laborer Negro" not tied to a particular planter that composed the state's "criminal class."[7]

This trend had begun decades before, in the first five years of restored Democratic rule in Georgia (1873–78), during which the number of leased prisoners convicted of larceny increased threefold; by 1878, 270 convicts, the vast majority of them African-American, suffered the severity of the penal system for the crime of simple larceny.[8] Thus the convict lease was a method of labor "recruitment" and control ideally suited to the "Bourbon" political coalition forged by planters and New South industrialists in post-Reconstruction Georgia.

I

In 1866, Mark Cooper and Howell Cobb had both brought their wartime experience with industrial slavery to their ambitious plans for the use of forced black labor to aid postwar development. Cooper had worked slaves rolling iron for the Confederacy in the foundry he now hoped to sell to the state. Howell Cobb, as a Confederate general, was experienced in the impressment of slaves for non-agricultural heavy labor, such as fortification building, during the war.[9] What they both foresaw was essentially the continuation of state impressment of black labor for the task of rebuilding Georgia's shattered economy and infrastructure.

For example, in their report to the governor, Cooper and Cobb noted that the state owned some lime quarries in Polk County, near the town of Van Wert. During the war a company had been organized to work these lime deposits to provide limestone for Confederate iron furnaces; now this same company "desire[d] to arrange for the employment of convict labor in the working of the quarry." To rely on free labor might make this venture unprofitable, they contended, for "the great difficulty [the Company] has encountered since the close of the War grows out of the expense of labor." But "in their judgment [this] could be remedied by the employment of the cheap convict labor under the control of the State."[10]

Governor Jenkins and the legislature did not respond directly to this particular appeal, but they did grant a railroad charter in December 1866 that served as a model for state-sponsored economic development that relied on the labor of convicts. On 13 December – two weeks before passing the first convict lease legislation – the legislature granted incorporation to the Cartersville and Van Wert Railroad Company, which planned to construct a rail link from the Western and Atlantic Railroad in Cartersville to Van Wert, in Polk County – the exact location of the state-owned lime quarries. This in itself was not unusual; all phases of Reconstruction in Georgia saw a frenzy of incorporations of railroad and mining companies. Many roads were also issued aid in the form of state-endorsed bonds, particularly at the high tide of Radical Reconstruction. What the Cartersville and Van Wert received from the state, however, was a labor force.

"Whereas said Cartersville and Van Wert Railroad is a feeder to the Western and Atlantic Railroad, thereby developing vast mineral resources of the State, and leading to extensive forests of pine," the General Assembly authorized the principal keeper of the penitentiary "to detail from the convicts and chain gangs such a number of laborers to work on the grading" of the railroad. The railroad company would relieve the state of the expense of clothing, food and custody, and in exchange would receive a slave labor force to build its railway.[11] This state aid in the form of labor, first devised during Presidential Reconstruction, set an important precedent for the Radical regime to follow, linking convicts, railroads, and economic reconstruction.

The Cartersville and Van Wert did not receive its labor force during Presidential Reconstruction; nor were any convicts leased in 1866 or 1867, as Governor Jenkins continued to insist that the Milledgeville penitentiary could be rehabilitated. But in January 1868 Jenkins was deposed and by military decree General Thomas Ruger was appointed in his stead to impose Congressional Reconstruction on the state. In late April 1868 General Ruger requested a report from the principal keeper on the condition and finances of the penitentiary, and the "value of all salable items on hand." A week earlier Ruger and the principal keeper had already agreed to furnish William Fort with "one hundred able bodied and healthy Negro convicts, now confined in the said Penitentiary" for one year, to work on the Georgia and Alabama Railroad in north Georgia. Ruger expected Fort to pay all the expenses of keeping the convicts, and in addition pay the state $2,500 for their use.[12]

Shortly thereafter Ruger received a communication from S.F. Stephens, president of the Cartersville and Van Wert Railroad, which had yet to take advantage of the convicts allotted to the company in 1866. Perhaps spurred by Fort's success in acquiring a labor force, Stephens reminded General Ruger that "the legislature [in 1866] regarded the immense state interest and lumber business that would be developed of ... much importance to the State road [the Western and Atlantic] and general interests of the state." Indeed, the legislature had "made the express provision in the charter for the free use of the convict labor without charge" for work on the Cartersville and Van Wert line. Referring to the sixteen-month delay since the company's initial charter, Stephens explained that "by General Pope's order and our poverty we have heretofore regarded it unwise to start the work. But this summer a little bread stuff will be to spare and we think by your permission to take one Hundred hands." Just so the general would not miss his meaning, Stephens reiterated that the construction of his railroad would contribute to "our efforts to build up again." Despite the fact that this arrangement had been made under the now discredited 1866 legislature, Ruger readily responded, informing Stephens that all the state needed was his bond, and the convicts would be sent to north Georgia.[13]

Apparently the use of convicts in railroad construction satisfied all parties concerned, for in early July Ruger made a second lease with Fort and his partner Joseph Printup, who planned to work one hundred more convicts on the Selma, Rome and Dalton Railroad, also in north Georgia. This time the lessees paid the state $1,000 for their labor force.[14] Ruger's reasons for leasing the convicts to railway entrepreneurs were not recorded at the time. Ten years later the principal keeper noted that while leasing was initially authorized under a Democratic governor, a US military commander actually carried out the act. Governor Jenkins "did not execute the law [to lease the convicts], being removed from office by the General Government." But "the military commander, his successor, soon found the negro convicts accumulating and filling up the Penitentiary to such an extent, that, by the stress of circumstances ... [he] was forced to lease them out."[15] This analysis was consistent with the Redemption critique of military Reconstruction. The Democrats who had "redeemed" white supremacy in 1872 naturally sought to imply that the US Army and its Republican lackeys feared the supposedly vagrant class of ex-slaves as much as did white Georgians, but were unwilling to admit it.

Whether Ruger was responding to the need to dispose of an ever-growing number of convicts, the pressing task of rebuilding Georgia's railroads, or some other undisclosed inducement, is not made clear by the record. In any event, the general's willingness to bind out the state's convicts did not run counter to the Army's and the Freedmen's Bureau's basic goals of returning the freedpeople to work and restoring the southern economy. If the labor contract stood as the *sine qua non* of Reconstruction agricultural production, the convict lease provided a ready means of recruitment for the heavy labor of grading railroads. Similarly, the lease was also legitimized by the contractual ideology so central to the political economy of Reconstruction. In this instance, however, the lease contract bound the state to capital, rather than employers to free labor. And despite its resemblance to slavery, convict labor was perfectly in accord with the Thirteenth Amendment. In fact, Georgia's 1867 Constitution, which Ruger was bound to enforce, included a dramatic penal reform, indicative of the destruction of slave codes: whipping as a punishment for crime was abolished; hard labor, however – labor enforced by the threat of corporal punishment – was not.[16]

Ruger's elected replacement, the Republican governor Rufus B. Bullock, was an avid booster of Georgia's railway network, and willingly continued the precedent set under Ruger's short reign. Bullock was inaugurated in July 1868 (shortly after Ruger's second lease), and early on he made it clear that in his view "the foundation of all prosperity is the successful development of our internal resources."[17] As the "party of progress" the Republicans set as their main task the "building of railroads" and the resulting encouragement of "manufacturing and economic diversification." As one historian has put it, the southern Republican party was "expected to play the role of midwife to the region's transportation revolution." Under Bullock's stewardship Georgia was no exception to this trend.[18]

In Georgia the state had occasionally fostered economic development and internal improvements in the past, particularly in antebellum support for the Western and Atlantic Railroad.[19] And the legislature of Presidential Reconstruction did begin to endorse state aid to railroads. But the Republican regime and the Reconstruction constitution of 1867 provided unprecedented "vigorous public support for economic development."[20] Much of this support came in the form of state endorsements of bonds which would help secure capital for the Republican program of railroad construction and expansion. Immediate increases in taxable property were "directly stimulated by the lines of railroads," Bullock claimed. Indeed, the importance of this aid to railroads has been obscured by its enduring association with the corruption of the Bullock regime and its retainers, many of whom profited from stock-watering and junk-bond deals tied to chimerical financing schemes and mythical rail lines. Yet, as Bullock hastened to point out in his defense, in the era of Radical Reconstruction in Georgia, from 1867 to 1871, 600 miles of new track were laid. Much of it, however, was graded by the labor of convicts. Between the end of the war and 1875, the 844 miles of track constructed in Georgia was second in the South only to Alabama.[21] State aid in the form of financial security went hand in glove with state provision of forced labor.

II

Railroad construction in Reconstruction Georgia had several competing goals. The development of Atlanta as a major commercial and urban industrial enclave, which could shift Georgia's economic focus away from the cotton belt and the seaboard to the Piedmont, was pitted against the ambitions of antebellum black-belt commercial centers, which sought to forge new links between interior cities and the coast. Remote areas hoped to attract railroads to exploit timber and mineral resources, or else gain increased access to exterior markets, either northward or at the seaboard. Much of the financial jockeying of the period revolved around these rival economic goals. Yet all parties agreed that the first task of economic reconstruction was the repair of a basic transportation infrastructure that had been destroyed by the war.[22]

Key links in Georgia's railway system had lain in the path of Sherman's troops, who tore up hundreds of miles of track and virtually destroyed the Macon and Western and the Central of Georgia. Eighty-four miles of the Western and Atlantic were damaged, 80 miles of the Georgia Railroad from Atlanta to the Oconee River, and 139 miles of the Central from Gordon to Savannah stood in dire need of repair in 1865.[23] But railroad contractors soon discovered that "more hands had to be employed on the road as less work seemed to be done than under the slave system."[24] Because of competition for labor, the Central of Georgia had a difficult time recruiting "a stable force of 400 to 450 laborers at low wages to repair the tracks." And contractors on the Atlantic and Gulf Railroad expressed dissatisfaction with free black labor, since the freedmen had a habit of leaving the company's employ before even a month was up, even foregoing their pay. Of course the fact that their compensation was mostly in the form of "rations" may have contributed to their capriciousness.[25] As in the agricultural sector, the freedpeople were willing to work only on their own terms, and might even choose to withdraw their labor altogether.[26]

In addition to labor problems, the shortage of capital for the expansion of new rail links, let alone the repair of the existing ones, posed the gravest problem.[27] The "financial embarrassment" brought about by the war and defeat made private investors overly cautious, and this induced the General Assembly to endorse the bonds of railroad companies from 1866 onward.[28] The economic program of Georgia's Radical Republicans included relief for debtors, homestead exemptions, free schools, laws governing hours and wages, and aid to railroads. But whatever sharp differences divided the Radicals from Democrats and even the more moderate forces in their own party on most of these issues, both parties and all factions found common cause for the time being in the expansion of the state's transportation system.[29] In the postwar era railroads became an economic panacea for Republicans and Democrats alike. As one historian of nineteenth-century Georgia has argued, "prewar aspirations combined with post-war devastation to make railroads appear the only route to salvation [during Reconstruction]."[30]

Admittedly, the Republicans made the most dramatic thrusts in this direction, and sought railroad development far beyond restoration of the antebellum network. "Georgia wants more railroads, more rolling-mills and foundries, more machine-shops, more mining operations, more cotton-mills, industrial energy.... It is to this kind of reconstruction that the attention of the people should be directed," proclaimed the *Daily New Era*, Atlanta's staunch Republican voice, in 1866.[31] Yet the un-reconstructed 1866 legislature which made the first provisions to lease the state's convicts also attempted to guarantee the endorsement of bonds to help finance four new rail lines – including the Atlanta and Charlotte Air-Line, the Griffin and North Alabama, and the Macon and Brunswick, all of which would shortly rely upon convicts to grade their roadbeds.[32] However, just as he refused to act on the lease law, the parsimonious Governor Jenkins vetoed all but one bond endorsement, the Macon and Brunswick. The others had to wait for a fully reconstructed legislature and a Radical executive; but it was a short wait. The 1868 legislature endorsed the bonds of three railroad companies; the 1869 legislature supported four more; and in 1870, twenty-nine railroad companies received Georgia's endorsement of their bonds. By 1870 potential aid of $30 million had been granted to the railroads.[33]

Not surprisingly, many of these projects never got off the ground. And of those that did, the vast majority landed in receivership, or had their bonds repudiated in the wake of Redemption after 1871. Nevertheless, between 1865 and 1880 five new major rail lines crisscrossed Georgia's countryside, opening up new markets, stimulating the growth of Atlanta, commercializing the Upcountry, and encouraging extractive industry. By 1880 Georgia had increased its track from 1,404 miles in 1860 to 2,432 miles, more than any southern state save Texas.[34] In nearly every case of a successfully completed railroad the essential but extremely arduous labor of grading the hundreds of miles of roadbed prior to laying the track was done by a force of convicts leased from the state.

Convict labor played a particularly important role in the earliest stages of Reconstruction railway construction because of the contingent nature of state aid. Despite the financial free-for-all that railroad projects seemed to initiate, the usual bond endorsement was predicated upon demonstration of progress towards construction of the rail line. Bullock always claimed that "state aid" was a misnomer for his program. The state took on no real burdens, he insisted, because "no indorsements are given until the extent of the [rail]road indorsed for is in actual operation." By guaranteeing payment on the bonds, Georgia merely helped railroads attract enough capital to "pay for half the cost of the continuation of construction" once a few miles were built. The typical act endorsing railroad bonds required that five or ten miles of track be laid *first*, and then bonds would be endorsed at $10–$15,000 per mile completed, and for each five or ten miles subsequently laid.[35]

Thus, even with state backing of their bonds, in the late 1860s and early 1870s in the capital-scarce South railroad firms and their labor contractors faced the dilemma of laying track before they could secure a reliable source of investment capital. They needed a stable, cheap, and readily available labor force at a fixed cost, which would not hinder rapid initial construction by quitting, going on strike, demanding higher wages, or having to be reconstituted at each new section of the line to be graded. Railroads relying on free labor for this work were plagued with problems. During harvest of the cotton crop labor was all but unavailable; contract immigrant labor frequently deserted on the slightest pretext; and labor shortages forced wages as high as $1.75 a day on some lines. Railroad promoters were notorious for their underestimates of costs, and this was partly due to these labor difficulties. The payroll for the Marietta and North Georgia railroad, which used both free and convict workers to pierce the Blue Ridge, shows that nearly 60 per cent of the free laborers worked less than fifteen days a month. They commonly worked for $1.00 a day.[36] Convict labor, which might cost the company only the prisoners' subsistence, or perhaps an additional $10–$50 per laborer per *year* as a leasing fee, was an ideal solution to these problems.

Between 1869 and 1871 alone, Georgia's convicts graded the roadbeds of at least 469 miles of new rail lines. The lease system worked in tandem with the state's bond endorsements to make this construction possible.[37] In some cases the labor came first, providing the assurance for a future endorsement of bonds; in other cases, the state endorsed the bonds pending the first few miles of construction, and the track graded by convicts triggered the endorsement. Clearly Georgia's railroad boom did not just depend on state aid in the financial sector alone; the penal system's ability to provide labor, under the auspices of private railroad contractors who leased the convicts, was equally significant.

The first leases made by General Ruger in the spring of 1868, for example, gave the labor contractors Fort and Printup a labor force of two hundred convicts, which they worked on the Georgia and Alabama and then the Selma, Rome and Dalton railroads.[38] By 1869 the Selma, Rome and Dalton line had completed nearly thirty-seven miles of track in northwest Georgia. The other early branch line designed to link the Western and Atlantic to mining regions in north Georgia was the Cartersville and Van Wert, which as we have seen was the first railroad to be given legislative authorization to use convicts, and requested them under Ruger's regime in 1868. In 1869 the state endorsed Cartersville and Van Wert's bonds; twenty-three miles of track were laid the following year.[39]

But these smaller projects were rapidly superseded in scale and importance by Governor Bullock's lease of the entire penitentiary to the railroad contractors Grant, Alexander and Company in 1869, and the accompanying flood of railroad bond endorsements the following year. The Grant family had long been involved in railroad contracting and construction. Lemuel P. Grant was an antebellum railroad entrepreneur both in Atlanta and the cotton belt. He helped build the Central of Georgia, the Macon and Western, and the Western and Atlantic Railroads before the war in partnership with his brother John T. Grant.[40] During the war Captain Lemuel P. Grant directed the wartime use of slaves in railroad work as late as 1864.[41] In the post-bellum era, John T. Grant and his son William joined with Thomas Alexander – another antebellum railroad contractor – to form Grant, Alexander & Company, the firm that oversaw the majority of Georgia's Reconstruction railroad expansion.[42]

In November 1868 Governor Bullock contracted with Grant,

Alexander & Company to furnish them with between one hundred and five hundred convicts at $10 per head per annum – about 3 cents a day. At the end of the year Grant, Alexander & Company held 109 convicts, while Fort and Printup still worked 134 convicts under the lease made with General Ruger, and 100 convicts remained inside the penitentiary, many of them deemed by the contractors too sickly to work.[43] Uncomfortable with the gradual loss of state control over the prisoners, and finding it increasingly difficult to work convicts at trades within the penitentiary, the principal keeper suggested that the state itself contract to grade a railroad. Noting that the General Assembly had just endorsed the bonds of the Macon and Augusta Railroad, "which runs in a stone's throw of the Penitentiary," he thought the railroad could pay the state $50 per convict per annum to work on the railway. This would avoid interposing the lessee and labor contractor between the state and the railroad companies.[44]

His request went unheeded, and a year later, on 1 January 1870, the entire penitentiary, including the remaining buildings in Milledgeville, was in the hands of Grant, Alexander & Company. The state convicts were employed "almost exclusively outside the walls of the penitentiary" in grading railroads.[45] In June 1869, Bullock had leased the penitentiary and all of its unfortunate occupants for two years to Grant, Alexander & Company, who were to work the convicts "on any Public Works in the State of Georgia."[46] The conditions of this new lease provided labor to the railroad contractors free of charge. As William Grant explained it, the contractors did not pay for the convicts, but they did "relieve the State of all expense except the salary of the Principal Keeper."[47] Blacks sentenced for misdemeanors in county courts also joined the railroad force, serving short sentences for such offenses as simple larceny or "sleeping with a white woman," as one convict put it.[48]

By providing a slave labor force for railroad construction, Bullock with one stroke divested the state of fiscal responsibility for the penal system and fostered the "Public Works" regarded by Republicans as paramount to the state's economic interest and their own political program. Despite the pleas of the principal keeper, Grant, Alexander & Company had already begun working some of their convicts on the Macon and Augusta from mid 1869 onward, and worked up to two hundred convicts on this line.[49] Running past the Milledgeville penitentiary, through the heart of the cotton belt from Macon to Augusta, this was a road whose "completion to Macon [was] of great importance to the agricultural, commercial and manufacturing interests of Georgia."[50] Under the 1868 Act providing the Macon and Augusta with state aid, bonds would be endorsed at $10,000 for each ten miles of track that was completed; convicts helped make this possible. By the end of 1870, all seventy-seven miles of this railroad were completed, which must have pleased its acting president, Governor Rufus Bullock.[51]

On this project the existing penitentiary still could operate as a barracks, now controlled by Grant, Alexander & Company, where the convicts returned each night after working on the nearby railroad. But convicts were also worked farther afield, undermining the only remaining function of the antebellum penitentiary. On the Macon and Brunswick Railroad convicts were confined in temporary stockades spread out over eighty miles of the line to be graded, from Macon southward.[52] Under Grant, Alexander & Company's control the Georgia "penitentiary" soon became nothing more than mobile squads of forced laborers, to be detailed to whatever project the contractors were engaged in. The convict lease was "the destruction of the *penitentiary* system of imprisonment so called, which the world has been struggling to attain for a century and more," lamented penal reformer E.C. Wines in 1880, though he still evidently was willing to regard the US South as part of the "civilized world."[53]

The city of Macon, in addition to linking with Augusta, sought a new outlet to the seaboard with the Macon and Brunswick Railroad, the only rail line to receive a bond endorsement in 1866, and consequently Grant, Alexander & Company's first project with their convict labor force. The legislature endorsed bonds as ten-mile sections were extended through the timber and wiregrass of southeast Georgia, opening the land to the timber and naval-stores industries.[54] Grant, Alexander & Company worked 113 convicts on this line under their November 1868 contract with Bullock, and continued the work at least through 1869, during which they laid 150 miles of track. "The road was completed in December 1869," Poor's *Manual of Railroads* reported.[55]

The same year that the Macon and Brunswick was completed, the port of Brunswick promoted aid for the Brunswick and Albany Railroad, which could "tap the rich black-belt region of Southwest Georgia."[56] Sixty-five miles of this rail link had been built in the antebellum period, with the help of European and northern investors. But the General Assembly of 1869 noted that the track had been torn up by *Confederate* forces during the war, and much of its hardware had been diverted to the Western and Atlantic. Thus the owners of the Brunswick and Albany felt they were entitled to damages from the state, but would forego this if their bonds were endorsed. The legislature capitulated, and endorsed the bonds contingent upon the railroad putting twenty miles in working order. In addition, the act endorsing the bonds required the Brunswick and Albany to build fifty miles a year to continue to receive aid from the state.[57] Once again Grant, Alexander & Company's convict force played a key role in the early stages of construction. By summer 1870, convicts had begun grading the Brunswick and Albany, and on 1 January 1871, 196 of the state's 385 convicts were still working on this line. "The Road is being pushed very rapidly ... and will be open for the cotton business of this season," boasted the Brunswick and Albany's president, as he tried to peddle the railroad's bonds to European investors. In 1871 alone the Brunswick and Albany laid 171 miles of new track, and another 70 miles were "graded and [ready] to be completed by November."[58]

The southern half of the state was not the only beneficiary of the combination of endorsed bonds and the provision of convict labor. One of the major rail projects of this era was the Atlanta and Charlotte Air-Line, also known as the Georgia Air-Line, which ran from Atlanta northeast to the Carolinas and, eventually, Richmond, Virginia. Advocates projected this line as a major artery linking Atlanta to the entire Eastern Piedmont in Georgia and beyond. In 1866 Governor Jenkins had vetoed state aid to the Air-Line, but the 1868 legislature successfully endorsed bonds at $12,000 per mile, provided that the Air-Line demonstrated that it could lay twenty miles of track.[59] The General Assembly felt that the Air-Line was "a work of great general as well as local value and importance to a large portion of the good people of this state," and would be instrumental in "developing the resources of a large and valuable portion of the state hitherto unprovided with railroad advantages."[60] By June 1870 Grant, Alexander & Company had 172 convicts (including 58 misdemeanor convicts) grading the Air-Line, and as many as 200 had worked on the line.[61] The requisite twenty miles of track were laid in 1870, and in the years 1871 and 1872 convicts helped grade the roadbed for eighty more miles, up to the South Carolina line.[62] Throughout this period the railroad's president emphasized to stockholders the need to finish construction as quickly as possible because of chronic shortages of capital.[63]

One other line on which Grant, Alexander & Company worked convicts provides an interesting example of the close relationship between state endorsement of bonds and the advantages of using forced labor to grade railroad beds quickly. The Griffin and North Alabama railroad – projected to run from Griffin, in Spalding County, through Coweta, and on to Carroll County near the Alabama line, thus linking Piedmont to Upcountry – had its endorsements vetoed by the governor in 1866.[64] Nevertheless, the railroad contractors were commissioned to work convicts on this line in late 1869 and early 1870. By the time the 1870 General Assembly met, thirty-six miles of track had been laid, and many more miles had been graded and were ready for track. With this demonstrated progress and security, the legislature endorsed the Griffin and Alabama's bonds in October 1870; twenty-five more miles were laid by 1872.[65]

III

A species of historical explanation posits that after the Civil War new commercial centers "sprung up," Atlanta "rose from the ashes," railroads "penetrated" the Upcountry or "spread across" south Georgia. But such anthropomorphism mystifies the hard labor that made it possible for railroad contractors to lay so much track so rapidly during Reconstruction. The rigors of grading railroad beds at breakneck speed shaped the initial conditions of labor for Georgia's postwar convicts. From the beginning occasional critics expressed concern about the inhumanity of the forced labor on the railroads, culminating in a legislative investigation of the lease in the spring of 1870. As early as 1868 the keeper of the penitentiary himself – perhaps resentful of his slipping control of the institution – complained that "a humane treatment of [the convicts employed on the Selma, Rome and Dalton Railroad] is entirely ignored. Their mortuary record is pointed to as full vindication of this charge," he concluded. Sixteen of the 211 convicts working on this railroad died between May and December 1868. He also noted that the contractors had a habit of overworking the convicts to the point of exhaustion or disease, returning the sick convicts to the penitentiary, and then demanding fresh, healthy replacements to fill their quota of leased laborers.[66]

In fact, by the end of 1868 the Milledgeville penitentiary had devolved to a sick farm, transfer point and barracks for the railroad contractors, and, once work on the Macon and Augusta was completed in 1870, was practically abandoned altogether. Inside the state-run workshops made obsolete by the lease, convicts had been set to a variety of tasks, manufacturing completed goods at a relatively reasonable pace (although punishments inside the penitentiary had been equally as brutal as those inflicted outside).[67] By contrast, grading a railroad bed for a private contractor pushing to meet a strict timetable was difficult, dangerous and relentless work from sun-up to sundown, frequently in harsh conditions. On top of this, the prisoners often had to walk to and from the particular "cut" in which they were working, sometimes located several miles from the stockade.[68] One convict claimed that on the Air-Line he had worked sixteen hours a day, though state rules called for ten hours in the winter and twelve during summer.[69] Another testified that his work gang started out from the stockade before daylight, ate breakfast while on the way to work, ate lunch while in the "cut," and returned after dark.[70] Several convicts also complained that they worked in rain and mud, and the contractors refused to delay work due to bad weather. When asked by the committee investigating the convict lease in 1870 if the "convicts [could] be worked profitably to the lessees" while limiting hours to ten in the summer and eight in the winter, Thomas Alexander declined to answer the question.[71]

But keeping the convicts out working on the line the maximum number of hours was not the contractors' only concern. They needed to devise a system to encourage their recalcitrant labor force to work at a steady and effective pace during these long hours. Grading a railroad bed was mechanically simple but backbreaking and highly dangerous work. A "squad" of several convicts, often working in chains, shoveled, picked and blasted at earth and rock, while others loaded wheelbarrows with the debris and rolled it up the dirt and rock embankments of the "cut," which could reach heights of one hundred feet.[72] Overseers enforced the pace of labor with the lash, and convicts were "whipped when they gave out and could not do as much work as [the contractor] wanted them to do."[73]

Generally the weaker "hands" and the female convicts did the wheelbarrow work, but contractors determined this division of labor with a brutal method. Initially, the same amount of work was required of all convicts working in a "cut," and "the overseer would stand on the bank and count the shovelfuls of dirt. If he saw [a convict] throw two shovelfuls to another man's one, he would whip that man."[74] One convict, who claimed that he could handle the pace of work because he had "a better constitution than any man on the work," testified that he saw many men whipped for not keeping up with him.[75] After several beatings for not keeping pace, the weaker members of a squad would be detailed to removing the dirt with wheelbarrows.[76] Several convicts claimed to witness beatings that resulted in death for "laziness," or "playing off," or feigning sickness.[77] These victims of the lease system paid the ultimate penalty for their attempts to resist forced labor by one of the few methods available to convicts, malingering. Yet by doing so convicts reinforced the racist assumption that governed the exploitation of black prison labor in the first place: the idea that compulsion was a necessary form of labor discipline.

Whipping itself was not unique to the lease system or to the South of course. As William Grant correctly pointed out in his testimony to the 1870 investigative committee, "corporeal [sic] punishment has been a custom in the [Georgia] Penitentiary from the date of its inception," and in 1868 Massachusetts alone prohibited whipping as a "means of enforcing discipline" in its penal system. In their own report following the investigation, the committee also noted that in several northern states "the lash is used, with other punishment, to enforce good order and discipline."[78] Several members of the committee did express concern because Georgia's Reconstruction Constitution of 1867 prohibited whipping as a punishment for crime. But Grant, invoking time-honored white paternalism, cleverly insisted that this did not "apply to a parent whipping his child, a teacher his pupil, or to the internal discipline of the Penitentiary."[79] In the initial lease made under Georgia's brief military regime, General Ruger had outlawed whipping on the Selma, Rome and Dalton Railroad, perhaps aware of its resemblance to slave-labor discipline. But according to the testimony of several convicts this was to no avail.[80] By 1870 even Captain Christopher of the US Military, who dutifully investigated charges that convicts had been whipped to death, accepted the contractors' view that "order and discipline could [not] be maintained without the lash."[81]

While the investigating committee ultimately found little to criticize in the convict lease, even they noted that "in some instances prisoners have been required to do more labor than they could physically endure." However, they blamed this on inexperienced overseers who could not "properly estimate a man's physical ability," rather than a penal system whose economic logic meant pushing every convict to the limit of endurance. With time, they felt, these limits could be tested and set; the more egregious instances of cruelty (resulting in death) occurred "when the present system was new and the proper management yet to be learned."[82]

Yet on the railroads "discipline" referred to the pace of labor more than to penological security and stability. In fact, railroad gangs were as porous as a sieve: between 1866 and 1878, 555 convicts made their escape, one-sixth of the entire number sent to the penitentiary during those years.[83] One of Grant, Alexander & Company's overseers claimed that he whipped convicts for "disobeying orders, for not working, for impudence, for running away or plotting to run away, for fighting, for stealing from each other, and for abusing stock."[84] But from the testimony of the convicts the whip appeared to have but one overwhelming purpose: the enforcement of continual, fast-paced labor. "If you were not a good hand, and had been accused of being lazy, they would tell you they would give you some medicine," one convict told the investigators – "the strap." In fact, "the treatment is rougher on the railroads [than in the Penitentiary], by their having more work to do," admitted a guard; it was the contractors' determination to exact the maximum amount of labor from convicts they had already paid for that dictated this goal of "order and discipline."[85] Together the fundamental concern of private contractors with methods of extracting a maximum amount of labor, and their pecuniary interest in barely maintaining the prisoners' subsistence, shaped the uniquely brutal nature of the South's penal system. If punishment resulted in death, more convicts were always available, and terror might speed the pace of labor in the rest of the gang. For the next four decades the state would continue to acquiesce in these consistent features of Georgia's penal system.

Many deaths by whipping did in fact occur when convicts claimed to be unable to continue work, often due to sickness and fatigue, and the overseer would administer some "medicine" with the lash.[86] This was not always a response to deliberate malingering. Sickly, aged and weak convicts cost the company money, since they still had to be fed and cared for, yet provided less labor. One overseer had "wanted to kill [a sick convict]," since he was "no account and Grant, Alexander & Co. could not afford to feed him for nothing." Another contractor complained that the convicts had been "worked down by Printup & Co. on the Rome Railroad," and now "Grant, Alexander & Co. could not afford to be feeding a set of damned sick negros [sic]."[87]

The desire to drive convicts to the limit, and yet care for them under less than sanitary conditions which might undermine their capacity for hard labor, was a tension that ran through this labor system throughout its existence. The number of deaths inflicted by cruel punishment in 1869 and 1870 was contestable, but all agreed that on the Air-Line alone sixteen convicts perished between January and June 1870, fifteen of them from disease. Grant, Alexander & Company contended that this was because the sick convicts from all the railroad projects had been concentrated on this one line, but deaths under the lease system were far more frequent than they had been in the state-controlled penitentiary in any case. Over four hundred convicts perished during the first twelve years of leasing in Georgia, four times the number of deaths recorded in the entire history of the state's antebellum penitentiary.[88]

The mortality of convict railroad workers contrasted sharply with that of free labor employed at similar work. Joseph Sears, a railroad contractor who relied on a free workforce, stated that he had worked nearly twice as many laborers as Grant, Alexander & Company had on the Air-Line and had seen only two deaths over a six-month period. While admitting that grading a railroad was difficult work, he claimed that his laborers preferred it to farming, and that he was so enamored of free black workers that he had sent to South Carolina to hire some more. When asked what rules he had for "requiring men to work," he replied that he had "no rules, except to discharge them when they do not work to suit me."[89] Free railroad workers in Georgia recognized that Grant, Alexander & Company rejected this apparently novel form of labor discipline; they told Captain Christopher during his enquiries that "they would not work for Grant, Alexander & Co. for any amount of money."[90] Nevertheless, there are several examples of convicts serving out their time on the railroad and then staying on as "free" workers in order to accumulate some cash. Frequently, though, they complained of not receiving their pay, still being treated (and disciplined) as if they were convicts, or finding their wages deducted by charges to the prison commissary.[91]

There is scant direct evidence for Grant, Alexander & Company's reasons for relying on convicts, who, as another contractor observed, "don't appear to work harder," were frequently sick (or pretended to be), attempted to escape, had to be worked in chains, and required expensive oversight. Perhaps these disadvantages were offset by the cheapness of the labor – which under the Bullock lease of 1869 was practically free – but flexibility, mobility, and regularity were of greater concern. Construction delays would not be tolerated by capital-scarce railroad companies anxious to begin collecting revenue. Grant, Alexander & Company were grading several railroads simultaneously; assembling and maintaining a labor force on short notice, sometimes in remote locations, was not easy to do. Free workers on the Marietta and North Georgia, for example, would sign on county by county as the line extended through their localities, and then quit when it passed on; but this form of labor recruitment was fraught with uncertainties and seasonal in nature.[92] Convict labor could be shifted from project to project with relative ease, at a fixed cost, regardless of the time of year.

Many convicts testified to having worked for short periods on several different rail lines. One man began on the Macon and Augusta near the Milledgeville penitentiary in October 1869. After seventeen days he was sent to the Griffin and Alabama – in northwest Georgia – for three months. After that he found himself working on the Air-Line for four months until he received a pardon.[93] A misdemeanor convict from Augusta served a twelve-month sentence working on four different railroads in all corners of the state.[94] And each rail line in itself might have squads stretched out over many miles of countryside, housed in several crude stockades. The uncertain conditions which rendered consistent recruitment of free workers difficult made a stable convict labor force particularly appealing. Finally, as noted, the railroad contractors who received the convict lease had antebellum experience managing an industrial slave labor force.

Strangely, although the 1870 legislative committee included three of Reconstruction Georgia's black legislators, and elicited a harrowing portrait of the convicts' working conditions, it produced few complaints about the lease system itself. While remarking that punishment did occasionally descend to the level of sadism, their report to the full General Assembly also allowed that "while inhumanity should be prohibited on the one hand, any discipline in the other direction would give importance to criminals and dignity to crime [and] should be avoided." As for the tales of brutality recounted by the convicts themselves, the committee concluded that "the one whipped, burning under the sting of the lash, and provoked to feelings of revenge, is hardly competent to fully judge and describe the punishment." However, the investigators did recommend that Sunday labor be prohibited, the number of lashes should be limited to twenty-five, the regulated hours of labor should be counted from the morning departure until the evening return to the stockade, and more attention should be given to the moral and religious life of the convicts. When this version of the report reached the floor, one of the black committee members, Bishop Henry M. Turner, sought to amend it and denied having signed it in the first place. Another black legislator introduced a resolution demanding termination of the lease, and a third called Governor Bullock a "murderer." Conflict over the lease revealed a deep fissure between black Republicans and their white allies.[95]

The leasing of convicts itself went unquestioned, even though the principal keeper, John Darnell, had expressed in his most recent report to the governor his belief that "farming out" the convicts was "demoralizing." In fact, Darnell had revived the idea of moving the prison to Stone Mountain so the convicts could quarry granite for the state or work on the Western and Atlantic Railroad – especially if Atlanta were to replace Milledgeville as the state capital, as the Republicans proposed. At the very least if the lease was to continue, he argued, it should be kept within the walls of the penitentiary. "The system of 'farming out' convicts to *private* contractors, and thereby paralyzing competition, is contrary to the best interests of the state," he claimed.[96]

Apparently the investigation and its results mollified Darnell, for in his 1870 report a year later he said the lessees had greatly improved their management, and the treatment of the convicts was humane.[97] Not everyone was as convinced of this as the principal keeper, however. One response to the 1870 investigation was a mass meeting held in Richmond County which produced a petition signed by two hundred citizens demanding the termination of Grant, Alexander & Company's contract with the state. The petition protested the "horrible cruelties that are being practiced upon the convicts hired to Grant, Alexander & Co.... [For example,] whipping of men to death by heartless and merciless overseers when too sick to perform an equal amount of work with those in health." Still, they made no mention of the fear of competition from convict labor – a common objection in northern states, and a concern voiced by the principal keeper in his critical report – nor did they object to the leasing of convicts per se, merely the conduct of the particular lessees.[98]

Despite the cruelties it exposed, the 1870 investigation was followed by a consensus among politically powerful whites that the lease was an effective penal system appropriate to the fiscal constraints and racial tensions of the era, particularly as Reconstruction met its untimely demise. Redemption came hard on the heels of the "orgy" of bond endorsements and grandiose railroad schemes that discredited the Radicals, and it resulted in the undoing of much of the liberal state aid granted by Bullock and his cronies. But as Bullock pointed out in the 1880s, the same political forces that excoriated him for his "bogus" bond endorsements benefited from the economic prosperity generated by the new rail lines. Similarly, Bullock was held responsible for a convict lease system which his detractors readily endorsed. Indeed, the "Redeemers" showed no interest in repudiating Georgia's emerging penal policy, which regarded convicts as both a potential source of badly needed revenue and a labor force which could be detailed for development of the state's resources. One month after Georgia's Democrats swept back into power in the 1871 elections, the legislature re-authorized the convict lease. In this respect, the state's abdication of penal responsibility, the Democrat's apparent antipathy to positive government and obsession with racial control, and the unabated desire for economic development neatly coincided.[99]

IV

In one of his first messages to the General Assembly in 1872, the new Democratic governor, James Milton Smith, noted the increasing number of convicts who had fallen into the hands of the railroad contractors: 475 by July 1872. "This marked increase in the number of convicts is not due to the augmentation of crime in the state," he reassured the legislators who trusted Redemption's promise of stability, "but is believed to be the result entirely of a more rigid enforcement of the laws" now that the lax Republicans had been swept aside. In fact, an increased number of convicts might even benefit the state. Smith pointed out that previously the penitentiary was "a source of expense to the state," but the need to appropriate money for a penal system had now ceased. "On the contrary," the governor concluded, "it will probably be productive of considerable revenue," since he had recently renewed Grant, Alexander & Company's lease at $50 per convict.[100]

The realization that the convict lease might benefit the state as well as the private contractors who took advantage of the cheap labor it provided had been developing for several years. The year 1869 was the last in which the legislature appropriated any money to maintain Georgia's penal system.[101] A consistent goal of leasing the convicts was to end the necessity for state support for the penitentiary in a period of fiscal limitations. But even in the first years of the lease the principal keeper had expressed concern that "unless the State shall receive a greater annual hire, the farming out of the Penitentiary convicts must prove an expense instead of a source of income to the State," since it cost nearly $60 to receive, process and then discharge each convict on their way to and from the railroad camps.[102] As we have seen, Governor Bullock had addressed this problem by leasing the entire operation, free of charge, to Grant, Alexander & Company. But with the increasing number of prisoners, and no let-up in the demand for railroad laborers, it soon became clear that the state might profit by a lease on a per-capita basis, so that revenue would rise with the number of prisoners. The Redemption legislature of 1871 adopted this approach, and by 1873 the principal keeper could report a revenue of over $35,000 for a single twelve-month period. He enthusiastically contrasted this to the $570,545 the penitentiary had cost the state from its inception until 1869.[103]

The lessees, of course, happily endorsed the view that the convict lease was the only way the penal system could be made to pay its own way. Thomas Alexander had told the investigating committee in 1870 that he did not "think it possible for the large number of convicts now being punished to be profitably employed within the walls of the Penitentiary."[104] Numbers alone did not dictate the choice of a penal system, however; the race of the majority of new prisoners played an important part in the perpetuation of the lease. Much as Howell Cobb and Mark Cooper had six years earlier, the principal keeper in 1872, John T. Brown, emphasized the alleged incompatibility of blacks with traditional forms of penal labor. Even when there were only two hundred *white* convicts, in antebellum days, and they were "kept at such mechanical and industrial employments as were and are profitable," the penitentiary still could not pay for itself, Brown pointed out. After emancipation, however, the convicts were predominantly black, and thus supposedly had "less natural capacity to make their labor profitable at mechanical or other pursuits besides the simplest and roughest."[105]

By January 1874 the convict population had swelled to 616, and 524 of the prisoners were black; even if the state wanted to return to the antebellum system a new prison would have to be built, since the number of convicts had surpassed the old building's capacity. Yet Brown recognized that "the [white] people of the state would oppose the old system of mechanical indoor labor," since with five hundred black "ignorant, idle, dissolute [convicts] what could we reasonably expect" other than an increasing drain on the state's finances. Under these new conditions only the lease system could possibly make Georgia's penal system self-supporting (or profitable), he asserted. "Now [the freedman] has all the privilege of a white man, among which is that of being punished like a white man in the Penitentiary," remarked the principal keeper, with some irony. Even this "privilege," like so many others promised by emancipation, was not forthcoming.[106] Quite the reverse: as with the common fate of postwar black and white agricultural laborers, the system of penal oppression constructed for African-Americans also fell heavily on those whites unlucky enough and socially isolated enough to run afoul of the law.

It is clear that the criminal justice system in the postbellum South was directed at blacks. One historian of crime in postbellum Georgia has concluded that "property crime was nothing less than the price paid by the dominant culture and its elites for structuring Black-Belt society the way they did."[107] Thus during the 1870s while the number of whites in the penal system doubled, this represented only an overall increase of fifty-four convicts. The rapid increase to over one thousand prisoners by 1880 was due almost solely to the long-term convictions meted out to blacks, a trend which would continue for decades (see Table 3.1). Ten-year sentences for burglary, for example, were not uncommon for African-Americans.[108]

The racial ideology of Redemption and the increasing number of black convicts reinforced one another. John Brown, the principal keeper, made the connections clear in his annual reports. "We seldom get an old 'cuffee' from the rural districts, who was trained, in ante-bellum days, to gain his bread by the sweat of his brow," he reported in 1875. Instead he claimed, the penitentiary was filled with preachers, teachers, politicians, and "negro boys" ten to fifteen years old, pathetic victims of the "teachings of carpetbaggers and scalawags." From the brief impact of Reconstruction, "the poor creatures have been so stirred up, and confused on the subjects of politics and religion, that they have

Table 3.1 Number of Convicts in Georgia Penitentiary, by Race, Selected Years

	White		Black	
	no.	%	*no.*	%
1871	61	16	324	84
1874	90	15	524	85
1875	95	13	630	87
1876	91	10	835	90
1877	114	10	994	90
1880	115	10	1,071	90
1886	149	10	1,378	90
1890	168	10	1,520	90
1896	193	8	2,164	92
1900	258	12	1,900	88
1904	256	11	2,059	89
1909	262	10	2,296	90
1871–80 increase	54		747	
% of this increase	7		93	

Source: Georgia Principal Keeper's *Reports*.

forgotten common respect for themselves." Unless Georgia's young blacks found better advisers to replace those recently overthrown by Redemption, who could teach them "to work for their living," Brown warned, "these young vagrants will get out of their long shirts and into 'Georgia Stripes'." Brown continued to stress that the problem was one of youth, the so-called "new negro," uninhibited by antebellum deference. By 1876 there were three hundred African-Americans between the ages of twelve and twenty in the penitentiary. Older blacks would have to teach their progeny the "duties of good citizens" or "they will continue to retrograde." Otherwise, "those who were trained as slaves shall have died, [leaving] only a race of depraved vagabonds."[109]

In fact, Brown implied that this transition had already occurred, and expanded his view of the criminality of blacks while insisting that a reformative approach to penology in Georgia had become obsolete. "No plan which might be adopted is likely to accomplish the reform of the class constituting the great majority of the convicts," he claimed. Instead, reform should focus on the "colored masses" who remained outside of the penitentiary. This was so because in his view "the only difference existing between the colored convicts and the colored population at large" was that "the former have been caught in the commission of crimes, while the latter have not." Other defenders of the lease went even further. The Reverend H.H. Tucker, one-time chancellor of the University of Georgia, complained that while "the convicts are of two races, what is paradise to one is purgatory to the other." For Georgia's blacks, he averred, a stint in the penitentiary "contributes to social distinction" since they could "pose as heroes or martyrs." Incredibly, Tucker's only complaint about the convict lease was "the great leniency of the system." The greatest hardship black convicts faced, he claimed, was "the deprivation of liberty, liquor, and lust." "They wear a chain, but to them it is no great hardship," Tucker concluded.[110]

The hypocrisy of these views is revealed by the case of Nathan Bailey, a black man "induced to swear falsely by some white men, to one of whom his father belonged in days of slavery." Bailey received a four-year sentence for perjury, while one of his equally guilty white confederates went free "for the fact of influential family relations." His perjury "amounted almost to durress [sic]," an advocate claimed, since Bailey was the tenant of the person who urged him to lie on the stand in exchange for a mule. "Being an old family negro [he] was under the dominion of the white man," the solicitor noted. Brown lamented the fact that convicts were "lionized" by the black community, but it is no wonder blacks were "unwilling to discover the clear distinction between unwarranted prosecution and the just enforcement of the law's penalties."[111]

In point of fact, Georgia's black press tended to urge "a moral sentiment that will cause [Negroes] to do right and keep out of the clutches of the law," even while it condemned penal conditions and the state's double standard of justice. "There is no doubt there are many colored persons convicted who are innocent," noted the Savannah *Tribune*, and "many white men who are guilty of crimes have been allowed to go free." Ultimately, the black community's reluctance to recognize the "justice" of Georgia's penal system might be explained by the fact that the principal keeper's half-hearted paternalism was unknown in the convict camps. Observing that deaths on the railroads had steadily mounted from 1870 until 1875, Brown himself admitted that "casualties would have been fewer if the colored convicts were property, having a value to preserve."[112]

V

Begun under the Republicans, the new transportation network that convicts helped build in the 1870s and on into the 1880s had a significant impact on Georgia's postbellum economy. The integration of the previously self-sufficient Upcountry into the "vortex" of the commercial cotton economy, the phenomenal growth of Atlanta as the commercial, financial and ideological center of the New South, and the city's manufacturing sector's access to raw materials all can be traced to railroad development. Further, Georgia's industrial progress was based on its rich endowment of natural resources – timber, coal, iron – and the railroads made access to these resources and transportation to market possible. These developments did not cease with the fall of the Republicans; Georgia's railroad mileage increased by 59 per cent in the decade after 1865, but it doubled again between 1875 and 1890.[113]

State *financial* aid to railroads abruptly halted when the Democrats acceded to power in 1871 and 1872, it is true. But the "Redeemers" did not abandon the "gospel of prosperity" linked to railroads. To the contrary, "the Henry Gradys and Joseph Browns adapted the Gospel of Prosperity to fit their own ends.... The spokesmen of the New South were the progeny of Republican doctrines," and accordingly they enthusiastically continued to use the state to make a convict labor force available to contractors throughout the 1870s. The same legislature that in 1874 proposed a state constitutional amendment repudiating all railroad bonds, the following day extended the convict lease until the end of the decade.[114] By itself, Redemption did not radically alter Georgia's penal system. The military and the Republicans established the main elements of the convict lease – the type of labor it required, its economic rationale, and even its racial justification. But these were all elaborated upon by the succeeding regime.

Perhaps the most striking continuity in Georgia's penal policy appears in the realm of political economy, for this is where Reconstruction and Redemption are held to have clashed. If the plantation oligarchy resumed power in the 1870s we would expect to find the most thoroughly coerced labor – convicts – diverted to agriculture. Such was not the case. Early in his term, Governor James M. Smith discovered that even while railroad bonds were being repudiated, railway promoters still sought a convict labor force as a means to attract private capital. James S. Boynton, the president of the Griffin, Monticello and Madison Railroad wrote Smith in early February 1872 in order to secure between 100 and 150 convicts "to work on this Road, Which is in its infancy yet somewhat healthy and vigorous." Boynton, a Confederate war hero who then served as a county-court judge, assured the governor that "if we can procure a number of convicts it will give capitalist[s] and subscribers a confidence amounting to the certainty of success."[115]

The state might not be able to back a railroad project with its credit, but labor seemed to serve the same purpose as an inducement for further investment and development. Boynton, who had just finished serving a term as mayor of the town of Griffin and would later become president of the State Senate, told Governor Smith that, if "you can put my friend [Joseph] Johnson in a way to secure this number of convicts you will place us in a position to complete this Road and then work up another favorite project of ours to wit the building of a Railroad from [Griffin] to Columbus.... If we can get this labor it will enable us to put the road in running order ... for the trade of the ensuing season," he concluded. Boynton declared his firm ready to pay an annual fee of $36 per convict, and he enlisted the support of the Spalding County Ordinary (Judge), who sent the governor an additional letter of introduction for Boynton's agent, Joseph Johnson.[116]

Competition for the convicts was brisk, however. In January and February 1872, Governor Smith received at least six other bids for convicts, some of which stretched the definition of "public works," to which the lease act of December 1871 ostensibly limited convict labor. Another railroad firm applied for fifty convicts at $30 each "to construct the Memphis Branch Rail Road running ... through what is believed to be a very rich coal region" near the Alabama line. This group of investors emphasized that their purpose was "to build the Road and share whatever benefit may flow therefrom with the Community at large." In fact, the Memphis Branch had received state aid in 1870 because the Reconstruction legislature agreed that the railroad would "be of incalculable benefit to the state and people, by developing resources of a large and valuable region of the country, encouraging the manufacture of iron ... as well as opening up a vast undeveloped coal region."[117]

The entrepreneurs bidding for convict labor had calculated the benefit quite carefully. Alfred Shorter and Hugh Coltman, two of the directors of the Memphis Branch, also owned the Etna Iron Company, which had applied to lease convicts of its own to work the iron mines of Polk County. Shorter had been an antebellum slaveholder and an investor in railroads and iron in northwest Georgia, as well as a Whig politician. After the war he was "recognized ... as the area's leading financier and businessman." In this capacity he now provided the first hint that enterprising capitalists could use forced labor to expand upon the "public" economic benefits of railway work, and to begin to rely on convict labor to integrate the extractive economy of northwest Georgia.[118] Another company bidding for the convicts included as one of its partners John T. Brown, appointed principal keeper of the penitentiary the following year by Governor Smith.[119]

In the end the governor took the easiest course and renewed the lease of Grant, Alexander and Company for two more years, until

1 April 1874. The state would now receive $50 for each convict provided, as the principal keeper had suggested. The convicts continued to extend the Air-Line, and began work on the Georgia Western and the Northeastern railroads. Throughout the decade railroad builders continued to expect – and received – special aid linked to the convict lease, despite the Redeemer's alleged antipathy to public support of private corporations. After two years, for instance, the Northeastern Railroad had graded thirty-eight miles of road, from Athens to the main trunk of the Air-Line. At that point they proposed to "iron, equip and put in running order" twenty miles of the line, after which they expected the Democratic governor's endorsement of the railroad's bonds approved by the Reconstruction administration! The railroad's attorneys informed Governor Smith that they believed the company exempt from the recent law repealing all state aid to railroads. The governor granted the company's request, and the bonds were issued in 1878.[120]

The Northeastern was no exception, for Georgia's Democratic legislators and governors did not hesitate to provide other rail projects with convicts, free of charge, during the 1870s. The leasing act of 1876, for example, furnished the Marietta and North Georgia Railroad with 250 convicts for three years, "before any disposition is made of the convicts," and also required the governor to give preference in accepting bids to railroad companies attempting to renew their lease in order to complete their work.[121]

Railroad work done by convicts continued throughout the 1880s, when over four hundred prisoners still labored on the Georgia Midland, the Atlanta and Hawkinsville, and the Chattahoochee, Rome and Carrolton lines.[122] But by the mid 1880s this represented only slightly more than one-fourth of Georgia's total convict labor force. Even as the Democrats continued a penal policy that bound together conservative state fiscal policies, forced labor, and a "gospel of prosperity" dependent on rail line expansion, New South entrepreneurs began to recognize that convicts might be used profitably in other sectors of the economy. As early as 1873 the principal keeper began to anticipate both the necessity and the difficulty of shifting the convict labor force from railroad work to other branches of developing industry. In his report of that year he noted the remarkable adaptability of forced labor to railroads. The railroads were unique in requiring little initial outlay of capital in order to utilize convict labor. The convicts worked on purely labor-intensive projects – grading the roadbed for rail lines – which was easily completed at low cost. This then stimulated investment which would provide the capital to iron the road and purchase rolling stock. But in most other industries "so heavy a force" of labor usually needed a "heavy outlay of capital" in order to make their labor worthwhile to investors.[123]

The principal keeper, John T. Brown, expressed concern because the lease was due to expire in one year, on 1 April 1874, and since "the lessees have completed nearly all the railroad work in the state" (this turned out to be a considerable exaggeration), some other form of labor for the convicts would have to be discovered. Not only that, "already the lessees experience difficulty in finding work for the convicts to do," most likely as a result of the Panic of 1873, which threw many railroads into receivership. It was imperative to prevent idleness, which could cost a labor contractor with no work and convicts on hand up to $700 a day, Brown claimed.

By now there were too many prisoners to be returned to the old penitentiary buildings, so the principal keeper recommended a ten-year lease, beginning in 1874, to "a company of sharp businessmen." The right entrepreneurs with enough capital "could afford to invest in the lease ... for a term of ten years, with a view to working the minerals of North Georgia, or any other enterprise requiring a strong and reliable [labor] force," Brown argued. This was preferable to the one- or two-year leases previously made, because in an era of shaky investments "under a short term, with a chance of competition for the labor, or a change of the plan before they could mature or realize upon their investment, [capitalists] would be deterred from venturing upon such an undertaking." Unlike the work of railroad contractors, other large-scale enterprises would not have the flexible and temporary nature that made forced labor desirable, except as a long-term capital investment.[124]

The 1874 legislature did not heed the principal keeper's recommendation, and authorized the governor to make new leases from one to five years in length. Yet a subtle change in the wording of the lease Act did open up new possibilities. Under the terms of the 1871 law, convicts were to be worked on "any public works in the State of Georgia"; but the 1874 act read "on any public *or private* works in the State of Georgia." This made it possible to lease convicts to mine owners, brickyard operators, manufacturers of pig iron, or planters.[125]

Indeed, in the scramble for convicts that ensued in 1874 and 1875, all of these interests competed with the railroad contractors for their share of the labor of over six hundred convicts. Despite the principal keeper's dire predictions, many potential lessees sought a small number of convicts for a short term, perhaps unsure whether this form of labor recruitment would be a success or not. J.T. Meador bid for a one-year lease of fifty convicts to work his granite quarries on Stone Mountain and to mine gold in Carroll County. Henry Stevens, who had worked slaves in his Baldwin County brick plant until it was destroyed by General Sherman, hoped to go back into business with "as few as 20 or 25" convicts for work "about the mill and pottery." And J.P. Bondurant, who had worked some convicts on the Air-Line, wanted thirty "men and boys" for his brick works in Atlanta. In fact, in Augusta, brickyards had already begun to rely on convict laborers, obtaining them from Richmond County's misdemeanor chain gang, which otherwise worked on Augusta's roads. Yet "the number received from [the county court] alone will not be sufficient to carry on my business," complained D. Hallahan, a brickyard operator, in a letter to the governor. Consequently, he repeatedly asked if the state would supplement his labor force with fifty felony convicts. Another prospective lessee wanted fifty convicts for railroad and mining work near Cartersville, but, aware of the high mortality rate on similar projects, assured the governor that this would consist of *"no dangerous work."*[126]

The handful of planters who hoped to take advantage of convict labor thought they were in a better position to preserve the health and safety of prisoners than manufacturers, mine owners, and railroad contractors. "We understand the objections to the chaingang [sic] system to be that the convicts are too often overworked, worked in places dangerous to their health and life – neglect in sickness – allowing trusties [convict guards] – carelessness as to food, lodging and clothing, and carelessness in permitting escapes," wrote Robert Hester, a state senator. As an alternative, he urged the governor to lease convicts to A.C. Mathews, an Elbert County landowner, who would treat his charges with the paternalistic care only a planter could supposedly bestow.[127]

Another advocate of plantation labor for convicts was the Thomasville *Times*, a south Georgia paper whose editors wrote the governor seeking to advertise the lease. "We see you are advertising to let the Penitentiary convicts to farmers etc.," they wrote, claiming their paper represented an excellent agricultural region "whose planters are on a[n] easier footing [than elsewhere]" and could provide well for the convicts. Other planters, eager to acquire a cheap and totally dependent labor force, still expressed concerns voiced by industrialists seeking convicts. R. Montfort, J.T. Gray and W.S. Bateman wanted forty convicts to work their land and stated that they "would like to get them for as long as we could so we could fix up to keep them right." And Robert J. Jones of Hancock County appended this request to his bid for fifty prisoners: "colored convicts preferred."[128]

Of course the Grants sought to continue their lease past 1874. They now wanted three hundred convicts for a period of five years, and they hoped to keep the same convicts that had already been working on the

Georgia Western and Northeastern rail lines. However, they still faced the prospect of sporadic railroad work, because of the Panic of 1873 and the repudiation and default of state bonds. To cover themselves they made it clear in their bid that they planned "to work them in different portions of the state where work can be found." As labor contractors, they needed a large and flexible labor force; but they were now competing with their erstwhile partner, Thomas Alexander, who attempted to monopolize the lease with his own bid. "I know it is in the interest of the state, desirable to yourself, the principal keeper, and all the convicts ... that one Co. should controll [sic] the whole," he wrote to the governor. Generously, he proclaimed his readiness to match any other bid the state might receive.[129]

The Grants did obtain over two hundred convicts from the 1874 lease, but as they had foreseen they were soon unable "to procure large jobs at remunerative prices," and they divided the convict force among brickyards, mining operations, and small railroad projects such as the Elberton Air-Line. Contrary to the principal keeper's prediction that "the experiment of turning the labor of convicts in a new channel [other than railroads] is attended with its difficulties," lessees found it easy to diversify the labor of their prisoners, and the state happily obliged them. The 1874 lease divided Georgia's 616 felony prisoners among seven different companies engaged in four different kinds of work. In addition to the 200 convicts leased to the Grants, 185 other prisoners went to railroad contractors, brickmakers, and the like. And a pair of Washington County planters, T.J. Smith and William C. Riddle, received 115 convicts for five years, at the low price of $11 per capita per annum, "for general agricultural farm and saw and grist mill work." As the principal keeper pointed out, Smith and Riddle were "the first in this state to try the experiment of working convicts on farms."[130]

But other lessees put convicts to work for the first time in quite a different enterprise: mining. George D. Harris of Bartow County paid $20 per capita to set forty-seven convicts to work digging ore at his Bartow Iron Works. Harris's lease was later revoked, due to ill treatment of the convicts. The principal keeper reported that Harris served food to the convicts on their work shovels; that over eleven months, eight of Harris's convicts died; and that Harris illegally subleased his convicts for $1 a day (twenty times what he paid for them).[131] But this malfeasance failed to discredit mining as an appropriate industry for convicts. If working convicts at the Bartow Iron Works turned out to be a disaster, a similar lease to the recently opened Dade Coal Mines in the extreme northwest corner of the state proved quite the opposite.

When the lease was made in April 1874 the Dade Coal Company, owned by Joseph E. Brown, acquired 88 of the 616 convicts available. As convictions mounted throughout the year – there were 283 from 1 April until the end of 1874 – the state sent 93 more convicts to the coal mines. By the end of 1874, 152 of the state's 725 convicts worked in the Dade mines, and the company had paid not even $800 for nine months of labor. Despite the fact that thirteen convicts died in the mines in this same period, the principal keeper insisted "the locality and character of this work renders it the safest and most reliable prison in the state." Perhaps this was because the convicts worked underground, and as a result only one escaped (in these same nine months, sixty-three convicts escaped from the rest of the convict camps). And while the convicts did complain about the conditions of labor in the mines at first, by the end of October the principal keeper noted a "marked change" in their attitude. Thanks to the task system, and payments for overwork, he claimed, convict miners "seemed to take an interest in their labors, and were working with spirit" by the end of the year.[132]

VI

As Redemption tightened its grip on Georgia, the 1876 legislature sought to dispose of the convicts for a lengthy period, and relieve the state of any fiscal responsibility for the penal system. The lease law passed that year required the governor to "farm out" the convicts for a period of twenty years, as soon as the 1874 leases expired. In addition, the Act mandated that all convicts with sentences of five years or more – including the nearly fifty lifetime prisoners – were to be employed in the mines. The principal keeper enthusiastically supported the new lease law, claiming that "the long term of the new lease will warrant the investment of capital," and yield the state an annual revenue of $25,000. Moreover, the lessees would obtain their labor at a *fixed* cost, paying to the state their proportion of this fee, rather than for convicts per capita. To facilitate this arrangement, three "penitentiary companies" were organized by "men of great wealth and business experience." Between them these companies put up a bond of $100,000, and included such noteworthy investors as Joseph E. Brown, his brother Julius, the Grants, Thomas Alexander, General John B. Gordon (later elected governor), and a Boston capitalist, Jacob W. Seaver. The contract the state made with these companies stipulated that the lessees would not "inflict corporal punishment upon [the convicts], unless the same shall be necessary to secure discipline."[133]

Although the boards of these paper "companies" overlapped, Penitentiary Company Number One was essentially the Dade Coal Company, owned by Joseph E. Brown. In many ways Brown stands as the ideal representative of the peculiar alliance that lay at the heart of the "Bourbon system" that followed Redemption in Georgia. Brown was an upcountry planter, without strong ties to the antebellum black-belt slavocracy. Nevertheless, he had been governor of Confederate Georgia; but he joined the Republicans during the early stages of Reconstruction, seeing submission to the "new era" as inevitable – and profitable for sharp investors like himself (for example, he leased the Western and Atlantic Railroad from the state). After Redemption he switched back to the Democrats, opened his coal mines, and emerged as a leading New South industrialist. Brown was a spokesman for economic development and a prominent member of the "Bourbon Triumvirate," serving as one of Georgia's US senators; he was probably the most powerful man in the state until his death in 1894. The history of convict leasing in Georgia is closely tied to the development of "Joe Brown's Mines" in Dade County. By the terms of the 1876 lease, his company was guaranteed three hundred "able-bodied long term men" for labor in the mines.[134]

Brown is a significant figure, for he embodied the Janus-faced nature of Redemption and its beneficiaries. Other than hostility to Reconstruction and black political power, the various political and economic factions lumped under the rubric "Redeemers" had little in common. Georgia's 1877 State Constitution has been characterized as "the most profoundly conservative Constitution in Georgia history…. [It] prohibited virtually anything that might encourage the emergence of a New South in Georgia," and heralded the triumph of the planter regime.[135] Yet, in practice, Bourbonism in Georgia was a compromise between the bearers of the "traditional" values of an agrarian society and advocates of New South modernization. By preserving rigid labor control while stimulating industrial development, convict labor helped make this uneasy coalition possible. Men like Joseph Brown sought a labor force every bit as coerced as slaves had been, but hoped to use this labor to build their version of the New South. Convict leasing made the habit of compelling black labor compatible with industrial development. As a result of the political economy of Redemption, the South began to enter the national capitalist economy – albeit as an impoverished junior partner – but retained its own "distinctive system of repressive labor relations."[136]

As long as it did not disrupt the forms of social and racial control necessary to maintain the planters' New South, the Redeemers did not discourage the development of an industrial sector, even one aided by northern capital. The textile industry, for example, met with little planter opposition because it drew on a *white* labor pool, and did not undermine control of black labor. Mining and other extractive industries which recruited blacks were more controversial – unless they relied on convict labor. Indeed, strict laws against breaking contracts and harsh sentences for petty theft served the dual purpose of disciplining rural labor and increasing the pool of convicts for Georgia's coal mines, brickyards, lumber mills, and railroad camps. By 1886, penal farms in Georgia contributed only 4 per cent of the total value of commodities produced by the state's convict labor force. Instead the convict lease was used to provide forced labor to Georgia's nascent extractive industries. Thus the legal mechanisms of social and racial control devoted to the perpetuation of plantation society could also channel forced black labor into a developing industrial sector.[137]

By the end of the 1870s, Georgia's convict camps swelled with prisoners convicted of property crimes: 346 for burglary, 351 for larceny, including 27 for "larceny after trust" (breaking contracts), 36 for stealing stock, and 30 for misdemeanors. A growing number of convicts were characterized by two traits: most of them were African-American, and they were convicted in plantation belt or urban counties. White Georgians marshaled the law to control black workers who threatened the "traditional" order of agrarian society, either by challenging it directly or by migrating to the city.[138]

These new convicts included black men like Lee Chapman, who "came to Atlanta friendless and penniless, not having enough money to procure a meal" in 1888. Chapman went into a stable and picked up a pair of gloves he found there; when approached, he panicked and ran. With no money for counsel to defend him, he received a ten-year sentence for burglary, which he served in Joseph Brown's Dade coal mines. Another recruit for Brown's mines was Charley Hill, a black boy of fourteen, sentenced to four years for horse stealing even though "he only rode the horse off from the place where he had been at work not intending to the steal the horse." Rural Johnson County sentenced Bony Waters to four years for "larceny of a bale of cotton." Waters had only procured the mule team which another man used to haul off the cotton. Alfred Flynn served twelve years in the Amoskeag lumber camp for robbery. He had held the stake in a trick card game used to bilk another man of the proceeds from his just-sold cotton crop. A fourteen year old, Ed Porter from rural Marion County, also black, got twenty years for burglary after an older man sent him inside to rob a storehouse he had broken open. Because Porter's family were "hard working, quiet and peaceable colored citizens," he was pardoned after serving nine years![139]

To be sure, those convicted of violent crimes made up a good proportion of Georgia's convicts – 32 per cent in 1878, for example. Still, those found guilty of heinous crimes in New South Georgia included men like Bill Slaughter, convicted of murder in 1882. He and twenty-four other black railroad workers received long sentences for their participation in a "race riot" in which a white man was killed. "If the conditions of parties, as to race, had been reversed," admitted the presiding judge, "I very much doubt whether there would have been a conviction." Similarly, in 1883 Doc Wilson of Bibb County "killed a white man [in a quarrel] and there was considerable excitement and prejudice against him," making a plea of self-defense or voluntary manslaughter impossible. Wilson was sent to the coal mines with a life sentence for murder. All too frequently, however, blacks in Georgia went to the penitentiary for killing other blacks, like Henry Armstrong who served thirteen years for killing Gabe Ferguson, who accused Armstrong of turning hogs into his corn patch.[140]

Yet it should be noted that the number of violent offenders represents those *incarcerated*, not convicted. Over time there naturally was a growing concentration of prisoners convicted for life or very long terms for murder, arson, rape, and other violent crimes, while those sent to the penitentiary for burglary, larceny and misdemeanors came and went. Despite this fact, by 1888, 60 per cent of the prisoners in Georgia's convict camps were there for property offenses; the percentage of those *convicted* of property crimes was thus even higher. Even at the Dade coal mines, where long sentences were the norm, by 1882 half the black prisoners were there for burglary, larceny, and other non-violent property crimes.[141] Many African-Americans who rejected their "place" in the agrarian social order found themselves bound instead to labor in the new infrastructural, extractive, and industrial areas of Georgia's postbellum economy.

The sweeping vision of change offered by Radical Republicanism included state expenditure to stimulate growth, regional economic development that provided alternatives to plantation work for black laborers, and the development of a Republican working class that could make political demands and create political competition. These remained the implacable enemies of the Bourbon system. But rather than draining fiscal resources, Georgia's penal system was both a source of revenue and an aid to economic development acceptable to planters. Mines, iron furnaces, brickyards, and turpentine camps that relied on convict labor did not undermine the mechanisms of rural labor control so central to Georgia's postbellum agrarian political economy. To the contrary, the "more rigid enforcement of the laws" that supported and justified the lease also helped limit the autonomy of black agricultural workers.

Thus it is no coincidence that Georgia's conservative counter-revolution wrote its constitution only one year after the convict lease was extended for two more decades, guaranteeing the state's industrialists a large pool of forced labor. This readily available cheap labor force was attractive to northern capital, and obviated the need to seek outside immigration or "entice" black workers from the plantations in order to develop the South's resources. Convict labor accommodated the labor needs of industrial and extractive enterprises while keeping in check the threatening social transformations associated with modernization. What anti-enticement laws, crop-liens, and vagrancy statutes were to the planters, the convict lease was to an emerging class of industrial entrepreneurs, in Georgia and elsewhere.

4

"Under the Taint of Prison Labor": The Convict Lease and the Industrialization of the New South

> In your devotion to your peculiar system of labor you have forgotten that iron and coal are the most potent agents of civilization.
>
> Republican Senator William "Pig-iron" Kelley, to a southern audience, 1867[1]

Unlike penal systems, geological formations fail to respect the arbitrary lines of state borders. In a regional context Georgia's coal deposits, worked almost entirely by between three hundred and eight hundred convicts, consisted of a mere two hundred square miles of the vast Appalachian coalfield. By contrast, Tennessee had 5,100 square miles of exploitable coal lands, and Alabama had anywhere between 5,000 and 8,000 square miles (see Figure 4.1). Since coal rested at the base of an industrial pyramid encompassing coke and pig-iron production, the output of coke ovens and blast furnaces of these adjacent states dwarfed that of Georgia.[2] While never approaching the proportion of mine labor in Georgia, where prisoners predominated, leased convicts were a highly significant part of the labor force in the coal industry in these neighboring states. Indeed, the regional development of the Lower South's coal and iron industry as a whole demonstrates the degree to which rapid development rested on the ability of southern capitalists to use the penal system to recruit the core of their productive labor force.[3]

I

In a remarkable presentation before the National Prison Association in 1897, T.J. Hill, general manager of the state-run convict coal mines in East Tennessee, outlined for the NPA delegates the considerable contribution prison labor had made to the development of the southern

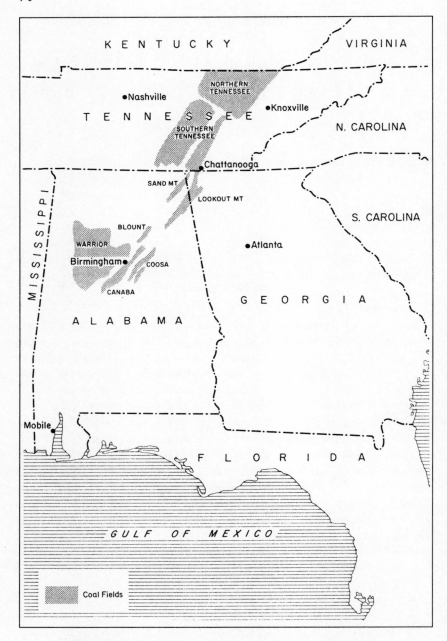

Figure 4.1 Coalfields of Tennessee, Georgia and Alabama

Source: H.H. Chapman, *The Iron and Steel Industries of the South* (University, Ala.: University of Alabama Press, 1953).

coal industry over the past two decades. Appropriately, Hill began by noting the compatibility of "industrial conditions" and the desired penal reform of "concentrat[ing] the convicts in large bodies at healthful locations about the coal mines." The permanent nature of the coal camps, Hill argued, represented a vast improvement over the temporary and mobile convict camps that prevailed when convicts had been leased to railroads in the immediate aftermath of the Civil War. This penal "reform" was made possible by the fact that "a strong effort was ... being made to develop the iron and coal industries of [Alabama and Tennessee]," development impeded by the difficulty of labor recruitment. Hill reminded his audience that during the 1870s "it was a practical impossibility to get our free native people, either white or black ... to work in the mines." As a result, the states agreed to lease convicts to the coal operators.[4]

Hill believed that much of the industrial development in East Tennessee and northeast Alabama could be traced to this decision to begin mining operations with forced labor. The use of convict miners "made possible the rapid development of the wonderful natural resources of the two states" and "gave an impetus to the manufacturing interests of the entire South, which could not otherwise have been possible, for at least many years." He left no doubt that "the enforced employment of so many laborers in the mines" led directly to the growth of "branches of manufacturing, dependent on the coal mines for fuel," thus providing employment to free workers, attracting capital, and providing a sturdy industrial infrastructure.[5]

Such structural benefits of forced labor extended to the creation of an entirely new industrial labor force as well. "The occupation of mining has been opened up to the negro," Hill proclaimed, "although his entry into the craft has been principally through the rugged gates of the penitentiary." The convict lease thus served as a prime means of proletarianization for a black population "mostly from the agricultural districts [who] had not been taught trades." Hill claimed that convicts who worked in the mines frequently found employment as miners upon their release. For blacks this was a decided benefit, he said, since "the negro is practically barred from all higher branches of the mechanical arts," but "the released negro convict, if a skillful miner ... finds ready employment at fair and equal wages."[6]

Thus Hill argued that forced labor developed resources "impossible of development by free labor"; proletarianized a black labor force otherwise mired in agricultural labor and the legacy of slavery; and, far from competing with free labor, provided "employment to additional free labor" by stimulating industrial growth, especially in the iron industry

Table 4.1 Coal, Coke and Pig-Iron Production in Alabama, Tennessee and Georgia, 1880–1900

	Coal (bituminous) (1000 tons)			Coke (1000 tons)			Pig iron (1000 tons)		
	USA	Ala./Tenn./Ga.	%	USA	Ala./Tenn./Ga.	%	USA	Ala./Tenn./Ga.	%
1880	4,178	104	2.5	3,338	229	6.9	4,295	175	4.1
1884	7,373	340	4.6	4,874	543	11.1	4,589	367	8.0
1890	11,132	494	4.4[a]	11,508	1,524	13.2	10,271	1,247	12.1
1900	21,251	1,243	5.8	20,533	2,660	13.0	13,789	1,576	11.4

Note: [a] It is worth noting that 45% of the coal produced in these states was used in coke production, as compared to 13.8% of the US total.

Source: United States Department of the Interior, US Geological Survey, *Mineral Resources of the United States*, 1883–84, 1889–90, 1891, 1900.

which depended on cheap and readily accessible coal and coke for fuel.[7] By Hill's account, it would appear that there was indeed a "Prussian Road" to the modern South; but it did not run through the cotton fields of the black belt. Instead, it paved the way for dramatic industrial development in an arc sweeping southwestward from Knoxville to Birmingham. Industrial penal labor, not sharecropping, represented the crucial relation of production on this distinctive southern path to modern capitalism. In fact, Hill was correct: the recruitment, control, and proletarianization of black labor for the regional development of the Deep South's coal and iron industries in the years 1870–1900 was closely linked to the convict lease system. The largest coal mines in the region, at the base of the operations of the most successfully vertically integrated enterprises, relied on convicts as the core of their labor force.

Despite a shortage of capital, rudimentary technology, weak markets, a poor labor supply, and competition with a predominant agricultural sector, a significant industrial complex did develop in isolated pockets of the New South. While the region always remained "underdeveloped" relative to northern states, and failed to keep pace particularly *after* the turn of the century, the period 1870–1900 still showed incredibly rapid industrial development in several southern states. Considering that the South began the last three decades of the nineteenth century with a practically nonexistent industrial base, the development of the southern coal and iron industry – always the structural key to industrial growth in any modern economy – was nothing less than extraordinary, even compared to the pace of industrial expansion north of the Mason–Dixon line during the same period. There is no need to dispute the "colonial economy" thesis – indeed, the corporations in the forefront of southern coal and iron development eventually found most of their capital in the hands of Yankees – to show that even without adequate home markets the industrial base of Georgia, Tennessee and Alabama sustained significant growth between 1870 and 1900 (see Table 4.1). Between 1880 and 1900 coal and coke production from these three states multiplied fivefold, and pig-iron output tripled. By the turn of the century, these states produced 6 per cent of the nation's bituminous coal, 13 per cent of its coke, and 11 per cent of its pig iron. The peak of this development, measured by production levels of coal, coke and pig iron, occurred in the mid 1890s; in 1896 these three states together produced 19 per cent of US pig iron, and twice that proportion of open-market pig iron not destined for steel production.[8]

It is more than ironic that the supposedly antibourgeois Redeemer regimes that came to power in the wake of Radical Reconstruction embraced William Kelley's notion that "iron and coal are the most potent agents of civilization." The leaders of the New South oversaw the successful attempts to build an industrial infrastructure, even while they refused to repudiate entirely their erstwhile "peculiar system of labor." During the 1870s and 1880s numerous geologists, investors, politicians, boosters, and observers waxed eloquent over the enormous potential of the untapped resources lying under the southern tip of the Appalachian chain. Once they made this region accessible by rail lines, its advocates claimed, the proximity of bituminous coalfields, iron-ore deposits, and limestone "flux" would make of the mountain districts of Tennessee, Alabama, and Georgia "a region of coke-made iron on a scale grander than has ever been witnessed on the habitable globe." Noting the imminent arrival of the "iron horse, with his civilized shriek" in the rich iron-ore beds and coal fields of East Tennessee, the state commissioner of agriculture and mining had visions of "a chain of fiery [iron] furnaces ... that will illumine the whole eastern margin of the Cumberland Table-land" and heard "the eternal whir and buzz of machinery." Indeed, as railroads cut through the heart of the Alabama coal basins they "attracted the attention of capitalists, and in a few years the iron and coal industries on these great lines of railroads increased with astonishing rapidity," according to an observer in the mid 1880s. By 1886, when Kelley traveled to Tennessee, Alabama and northwest Georgia, he enthusiastically reported that the burgeoning iron and mineral industries of the region were a great success, and held up this emerging industrial base as the best hope for the progress of the New South.[9]

The suddenness of this development was remarkable. A crude and fledgling iron industry had developed in this part of the South in ante-bellum years, but was virtually destroyed by the ravages of military encounters. Since the antebellum iron industry primarily relied on charcoal as fuel, rather than coke, large-scale development of the coal-fields did not accompany the construction of furnaces. Coal was mined in the region on a small scale, but by individuals rather than corpora-tions. These "local" coal banks, easily accessible without heavy invest-ment, often provided fuel for a resident blacksmith. Not a single "captive mine" – that is, a coal mine owned by a larger industrial enterprise with extensive fuel needs, such as an iron producer, railroad, or rolling mill – existed in Tennessee, Alabama, or Georgia before the Civil War.[10]

Thus, by the early 1870s the coal and iron industries of the Appa-lachian escarpment remained practically undeveloped. For example, Alabama produced *no* coke-fueled pig iron until 1876, and only 20,818 tons of charcoal-fueled iron in that same year. In 1870, only 13,200 tons of coal were removed from Alabama's immense field; and coke production did not begin in the state until 1880. But in an astonishingly brief period of time Alabama built an integrated coal and iron complex of coke-fueled furnaces, attributable to the unique contiguity of coal, ore and limestone in the Southern Appalachian chain.[11] By 1890 Alabama produced 4.1 million tons of coal; 1.1 million tons of coke; and 718,383 tons of pig iron. The US Geological Survey for 1890 remarked that "in no other State have such rapid strides been made in the production of coal as in Alabama during the past decade," and that same year the US Census Office enthusiastically reported that the growth of the Alabama coal industry since 1880 "has been almost phenomenal." This coal was transformed into fuel for iron production, and by 1895 Alabama had twenty iron furnaces "in blast," surpassed only by Ohio and Pennsylvania.[12]

The story was no less dramatic in the mountains of East Tennessee. In 1870 the state produced only 133,418 tons of coal; by 1890 this figure had increased to 2.2 million tons. By 1880 the state was ranked third in US coke production. And in the same period the production of pig iron in Tennessee multiplied over sevenfold. One corner of southeast Tennessee, the "Chattanooga District," boasted nineteen blast furnaces by 1884. There had been just two such furnaces in the area in 1872.[13]

Yet the susceptibility of southern iron furnaces to economic downturns revealed structural inadequacies in the region's evolving industrial base, and even enthusiasts expressed some reservations. The violent fluctuations in the business cycle that punctuated the 1870s, 1880s, and 1890s with depressions struck the pig-iron industry – and thus the market for southern coal, coke, and ore – particularly hard.[14] From 1873 to 1878, 80 per cent of southern iron furnaces shut down for a time, and the financial panic of the mid 1870s "almost swept the southern iron investments out of existence."[15]

James Swank, president of the American Iron and Steel Association, believed that southern states had to meet at least two conditions in order to make the postwar iron industry a stable success. First, rolling mills and other home markets for pig iron would have to be established in the South. And second, production could be cheapened by further substituting mineral fuel – bituminous coal and coke – for charcoal. Swank found the growth of the local coke industry and the opening of southern coal mines encouraging. Still, he questioned the quality of the fuel, and suspected that furnaces were sometimes built "in advance of the development of neighboring coke-producing coal deposits."[16] The poor quality of raw materials was also noted by southern mining engineer William Phillips. "In Alabama," Phillips complained, "we have ores of a moderate content, and they must therefore be mined at a low cost." In addition, the thin and irregular coal seams in the southern fields made efficient mining difficult. When added to the cost of shipping finished products such as rolled iron to northern and western markets, these constraints could appear insurmountable.[17]

Nevertheless, the most militant advocates of industrialization in the New South tended to overlook these objective constraints on development and sang the praises of the contiguous mineral fields without hesitation. Not so the "labor problem," which for boosters and detractors alike served as the focus for explanations of the industrial South's economic travails. The "labor problem" frequently served as shorthand for racist assumptions about the "regularity" of free black labor. As late as 1903, in his survey of the US iron and steel industry, Henry Campbell of the Pennsylvania Steel Company noted that "one of the great drawbacks [for this industry] in the South is the labor question." In the "absence of a white population trained to industrial pursuits," southern industrialists had to "depend upon the negro, and the colored man has had no education in this line of work," Campbell moaned. He attributed the alleged deficiencies of black labor to the legacy of slavery, agricultural labor, and paternalism. In the prevailing racist view of the day, he believed that blacks were not "a saving provident, hard-working people," and complained that they "will work only long enough to get a little cash, whereupon they quit work and live in idleness upon their earnings." The result, he claimed, was both an appallingly high rate of labor turnover and a lack of labor discipline, since "a summary discharge has no terrors, as living [in the South] is cheap and their wants are few."[18]

As Campbell recognized, labor turnover and instability, rather than cost, were southern industrialists' greatest lament. "Without convicts," one Alabama coal superintendent complained in 1884, "we have to depend on free negroes to do the tramming, driving & dumping [of coal]. If the weather is cold, or if there is a funeral, a marriage or a circus in the neighborhood they are rarely in place." He expressed hope that "when this class of labor becomes familiar with the requirement of mining & learns the importance of regularity it will be more reliable." Similarly, when the US Senate investigation of relations between labor and capital visited the Birmingham District in the 1880s, J.W. Sloss, owner of the Sloss Iron Works in Birmingham (and a lessee of convicts) complained that to work his furnaces with free labor he needed 269 men, but his monthly payroll averaged 569. "That is one of our troubles here. The irregularity of labor," he told the senators. "We cannot do our work as effectively or thoroughly as if we had a regular force of men." Sloss claimed to rely heavily on black labor for his furnace workers, drawn from all over the deep South; "a moving, restless, migratory class," Sloss remarked, "quite different from the farm or plantation negroes," who, he erroneously believed, tended to stay put. Of course he overlooked the fact that his black workers had most likely been agricultural laborers who had failed to do just that.[19]

Often the workers at Sloss's furnace would leave on a Saturday without giving notice and fail to return the following week. The consequences of this uncertainty could be disastrous; if the company could not find replacements the furnace might have to be shut down, potentially doing expensive damage to the plant. Sloss calculated the average time put in by each of his employees as fourteen days per month; "no contract restrains them" from this fickle behavior, he bitterly concluded. Similarly, the superintendent of the Eureka iron works in Alabama testified that the "class of colored people that have grown up to manhood since emancipation we find the most unreliable of all."[20] Such "unreliability," of course, expressed black workers' understanding of mobility as one of the most important aspects of freedom. Their consistent refusal to meet the demands of industrial labor discipline derived from their recent experience of emancipation, and matched the response of rural peoples' initial encounters with industrialization in many societies.

The regular operation of iron furnaces also depended on a steady and predictable supply of coal and coke from the South's mines, and some southern coal operators believed that in the mines "convict labor [was] more reliable and productive than free labor" and that "the convict accomplishes more work than the free laborer." Convicts were "forced to work steadily [and] their output may be depended upon," went the rationale. With free labor, white or black, "how [is] the operator or producer ... going to know how much coal or coke he is going to produce in the year or in the month if some of the miners work 10 days, some 15, some 12, and some 20 days in the month," complained Birmingham coal operators. "In [Alabama's] Birmingham district," testified Shelby Harrison, an investigator for *The Survey*, "most of the large companies have to keep from 50 to 75 per cent larger number of negroes on the pay roll than they expect to be working from day to day." On the other hand, when they used convicts, "300 men, for instance, go to sleep at night, and 300 men get up the next day and are ready for work," and this was for 310 days a year. "[Convict labor] is regular. I was told by a number of employers that that was one of the greatest things they liked about it," Harrison concluded. The assured labor of convicts allowed select mines to achieve certainty of production

levels, making their contracts with furnaces and other industrial enterprises particularly secure.[21]

To be sure, mine operators also looked to convicts because of the
cheapness of their labor. One iron-furnace operator told the US Senate
committee that "we have the raw materials for making iron as abundant
and as accessible and as cheaply got at ... as we could ask; ... we could
only reduce the cost of iron by reducing the price of labor" in the
South. Some coal mine operators who paid "an excessive royalty ... for
the coal in the ground" to northern capitalists "worked the mines on
the cheapest plan" they could. This could be achieved by reducing the
pay scale of free miners; if the workers threatened to strike in the face
of this reduction, the company could bring in convicts leased from the
state.[22] Similarly, unstable southern markets and poor coal quality forced
coal operators to reduce their mining costs, and this also instigated
strikes by free miners.[23] Convicts in a company's coal mine helped
operators overcome these constraints and saved them money. For
example, in the Pratt mines in Alabama in the 1880s free miners dug
about four tons of coal a day, and were paid 50 cents per ton, for a
daily wage of about $2; but a "first-class" convict miner cost the
company only $19 a month. Directly comparing the cost of their own
free and convict labor, including the expenses of convict hire, food,
clothing, and guards, Birmingham's Coalburg Coal and Coke Company
calculated that they raised convict coal for $0.96 a ton, while free labor-
mined coal cost them $1.05 a ton. Coal operators in Tennessee who
worked both convict and free labor also found the former less costly. In
1882 the Tennessee Coal, Iron, and Railroad Company (TCI) worked
convicts for $1.10 per day, while free labor cost them $1.75.[24]

The cost advantages of forced labor in coal mining had indirect
effects as well. The US Bureau of Labor estimated that the wages of
free miners were reduced 10 to 20 per cent in areas where convicts
were also used to mine coal. The "mine owners [in Alabama] say they
could not work at a profit without the lowering effect in wages of
convict-labor competition," the Bureau reported in 1886. And, naturally,
in its attacks on convict competition the United Mine Workers (UMW)
union pointed to the comparative cheapness and lowering of wages as
prime evils of the lease. "Miners working near the mines where convict
labor is employed are working at lessor [sic] rates than they would if
they had no convicts around them," proclaimed the UMW Journal.[25]

But, ultimately, comparative costs proved less significant to New
South capitalists than the contrast between a fixed cost paid to the state
for a predetermined amount of long-term forced labor and an unpredictable labor cost subject to the uncertain supply of reluctant

proletarians or wage negotiations with organized workers. "In regard to the difference between convict labor and free labor, there is no material difference," when all factors are considered, J.A. Bartamm informed the director of the Coalburg Coal Company. Instead, convicts proved advantageous because "they act as a check on free labor, in keeping down strikes"; "you can always depend on a certain amount of work done each day"; and "they can be forced to do work which it would be very hard to get free labor to do." Even when the cost of leasing and maintaining convict labor approached the cost of free labor, the problems of labor recruitment, training, discipline, turnover and consistency were reason enough to use forced labor in the South's coalfields.[26]

Keeping the cost of production down, competing successfully for labor with the agricultural sector, and maintaining stable labor relations were imperative because of the less readily removed shackles on the growth of the southern iron and coal industry. But reduction of labor costs and an increase in "reliability" had limits imposed by free workers themselves, who were "ready to stop work for the most trivial reasons," in a coal operator's words.[27] Precisely at this point in the productive process, particularly in its earliest stages and at its resource base – the coal mines – convicts played an important role in the development of southern industry. Reliance on a convict labor force leased from the state eliminated the problem of labor turnover and unpredictability; the desire to limit uncertain operating costs in weakly established enterprises reinforced the tendency to seek bound labor. Convict labor resolved the problem of maintaining rapid growth in the face of the extreme industrial vulnerability that plagued capitalist enterprises in the postbellum South.

II

In the coalfields of West Virginia, Illinois, and Kentucky a "judicious mixture" of migrant southern blacks, immigrants, and native whites, often helped coal operators dominate their labor force.[28] But in Alabama, Tennessee, and Georgia, they recruited another layer to the segmented labor market. In the Deep South, many coal operators relied on the lease system as a method of forced proletarianization. African-American convict miners – particularly long-term prisoners – made up the core of an industrial working class that could not maintain agrarian work habits, could not quit before developing industrial skills, could be used as a reserve army of labor, and frequently filled the ranks of free miners after their release. "Work in the mines gives [black convicts] a proficiency at a kind of labor by which they can earn a far better livelihood than before conviction," claimed R.H. Dawson, Alabama's Chief Inspector of Convicts.[29]

From the outset the convict lease system's supposed ability to forge a black industrial working class from a peasantry was marshaled as a defense and justification for forced labor. As Tennessee debated the merits of convict coal mining in the early 1870s, the Nashville *Republican Banner* heartily endorsed the convict lease, maintaining that "when [the convicts] have served their time out, they are schooled miners, and may continue in that pursuit." Two decades later, T.J. Hill agreed that "with kind treatment and proper instruction a large percentage of [black convicts] soon became excellent workmen." In the 1880s a convict at the Pratt mines in Alabama told the US Senate committee on capital and labor that about 250 ex-convicts still worked for the company, and the prison warden defended convict leasing by pointing out that Alabama's black workers earned only $8 a month on a plantation, but after being released from the convict mines an ex-prisoner could earn up to $3 a day as a free miner. "Of the men who have been discharged from [the penitentiary mines] with a good record for good conduct, nearly all have staid [*sic*] in the mine," claimed the warden. "There can be no question that convicts produce more after than before conviction," an Alabama house committee investigating the convict mines proclaimed.[30]

Even amidst the complaints about the unreliability of black labor, some detractors could not help but remark that "the colored laborers [in Birmingham] are making a good deal of money, especially our ex-convicts." This did not always result in labor docility, however. One group of ex-convicts struck for higher wages in 1882. "I do not know that they have [labor unions], but whether they have or not, they act in concert," a mine manager proclaimed. Alabama's inspector of convicts decried the fact that in the mines "the ex-convicts are most blatant about the rights of free labor [to be unhindered by convict competition], forgetting that had they never been convicts, they would never have been miners."[31]

Free miners and other critics of the convict lease in Alabama also remarked on this process of state-sponsored forced proletarianization. "If you don't like common labor or farming you can go to the State warden of the prison and get a suit of striped clothes and be appointed a coal miner," "Dawson" wryly remarked in a letter to the *National Labor Tribune*. Free workers at times attributed the dangerous conditions and frequent explosions in Alabama's mines to the "ignorant" labor of the convicts, who were "generally recruited from the cotton fields of

Table 4.2   Race of Convict Miners in Alabama, 1898

	State convicts		County convicts		Total	
	no.	%	*no.*	%	*no.*	%
TCI						
white	63	8.7	8	2.5	71	6.7
black	664	91.3	318	97.5	982	93.3
Sloss						
white	16	7.1	29	9.2	45	8.3
black	208	92.9	286	90.8	494	91.7
Total						
white	79	8.3	37	5.8	116	7.3
black	872	91.7	604	94.2	1476	92.7

Source: Alabama, *Second Biennial Report of the Board of Inspectors of Convicts, 1896–1898* (Montgomery, Ala.: State Printer, 1898), p. 19.

South Alabama." This form of "recruitment" sprang from the "fee system," critics claimed, which perpetuated the "crying evil of convicting men for offenses in order that deputies and court officials ... may get their fees." Many of the prisoners at the Coalburg mines, for instance, had been sent there from every county in the state for petty offenses. "I do not wish it to be understood that I in any way approve of a man committing a wrong," cautioned black UMW organizer R.L. Davis after a trip to Birmingham, "but in Alabama they will for the most trivial offense give you a term at Coalburg or Pratt mines, and especially if it happens to be a dusky son of Ham."[32]

The criminal justice system thus provided a steady stream of blacks from the cotton belt to the Birmingham District. Many of these men, convicted of petty offenses that challenged the rigid racial proscriptions of agricultural districts, spent time in the mines for court costs long beyond their original sentences. In 1890, for instance, Hale County had twelve convicts at the coal mines, convicted of petty larceny, carrying a concealed weapon, failing to perform a contract, and poisoning a mule, among other crimes. Greene County, also in the heart of Alabama's black belt, sent ten convict miners to Birmingham that same year for assault and profanity, cruelty to animals, petty larceny, and "false pretenses and removing mortgaged property." This last crime brought a sentence of two years, and an additional year mining coal to pay for the costs of prosecution.[33] Such convictions helped planters maintain control over agricultural workers, even while they provided a new source of labor for Alabama's industrial entrepreneurs. For these involuntary recruits to the mines often remained in Birmingham.

Indeed, according to the mine managers in the Birmingham District up to half of the convicts who learned how to dig coal while incarcerated obtained jobs in the trade upon release. Given the steadily increasing percentage of African-Americans in the coal mines from 1880 onward – by 1898, Davis estimated, 70 per cent of the free miners in the Birmingham District were black – there may be some truth to this, since blacks made up over 90 per cent of the convict force in Alabama's mines (see Table 4.2).[34] In its investigation of the Birmingham District in 1910 the US Immigration Commission attributed a "steadily increasing supply of efficient, steady and trained negro miners" over the last few decades to Alabama's convict lease system:

> after the convict has worked in the coal mines for several years he has learned a trade thoroughly. Not only does he become a trained miner, but owing to the system of rigid discipline and enforced regularity of work, he becomes through habit a steady workman, accustomed to regular hours. When his term [in prison] ends he almost invariably ... continues to be a coal miner for the reason that he does not know how to do anything else, and because he has been taught to do one thing well and to earn a good wage.

The commission estimated that 50 per cent of the African-American coal miners in Birmingham were ex-convicts.[35] The convict camps thus may have proved to be a peculiar and especially brutal training ground for a crucial component of the South's industrial labor force.

Men like R.L. Davis, and other UMW organizers, recognized convict labor as "hurtful to the white and colored miner alike" in driving down wages and breaking strikes, and knew that mine owners liked forced labor because it could not be organized. But another significant impact of forced proletarianization was the increase in labor supply and creation of a reserve army of labor through the steady "unnatural" influx of ex-convicts into the coal fields. Thus the *UMW Journal* complained that "all of [the convicts] are coal diggers when set free, and sometimes take the place of honest, practical miners, and not one in every twenty ... saw a coal mine until convicted." "Jefferson County [Birmingham] seems to be the selected dumping ground of the state," complained "Observer," and convicts remained there after serving time, not only "bringing them into competition with free labor as convicts [but] filling up this county with ex-convicts from all over the state." Free miners objected to the "pouring loose on this community hordes of ex-convicts," which made it an undesirable place for miners to live and work, and gave mining districts a bad reputation.[36]

Whites voiced many of these complaints, and the fact that the ex-convict workers were black aided the coal operators in perpetuating the racial tensions so inimical to organization in the Birmingham District, despite Davis's best efforts to bring black and white miners together in opposition to convict labor. If belied by occasional sympathy for the victims of the convict lease, or rare attempts to organize them, the association of ex-convicts, cheap labor, and black strikebreakers was a powerful one in the minds of white miners. Even in Kentucky, it was suggested, "nonunion camps are all black men, and they are constantly recruited from the convict camps of Tennessee and Alabama."[37]

But convict labor was not simply a wedge used in response to southern industrial boosters' complaints about an inefficient labor market; it also made a significant contribution to economic development of the region. The key factor in the successful operation of southern pig-iron furnaces in the 1880s and 1890s was the use of locally produced coke as fuel; the crucial element in the production of southern coke was consistent access to cheap bituminous coal. The most successful coal and iron enterprises in the region vertically integrated their production of pig iron by stoking their furnaces with their own coke, coke which had been produced with coal from their own captive mines. Coerced mine labor lay at the center of this productive process. Convicts appear in the South's first large-scale captive coal mines; in the most productive mines in each lessee's holdings, and indeed in the region; and in the mines with the largest concentration of mine laborers in the Deep South. Finally, convicts labored for the most successfully integrated southern mineral companies, those that generally weathered the frequent depressions, swallowed up competitors, defeated challenges by organized labor, and moved into the vanguard of southern industrial growth.[38]

III

By the 1880s local observers agreed that the coal and iron resources of Tennessee, Alabama, and Georgia were "destined to revolutionize the iron manufacture of the country," while admitting that "the important factor in the question of the cheap production of iron is prison labor." No less an authority than Yankee industrialist Edward Atkinson predicted that "the centre of the iron and steel industry of the future will be within a radius of 100 miles from the highest peak ... in the heart of the Southern Appalachian chain."[39] Hoping for ever-increasing industrial growth, the mine inspector of Tennessee pointed out in 1883

that "cheap coal and cheap coke are now the needs of our iron manufacturing enterprises," and that "from large operations doing a great
business on a small margin of profit can only be expected [production
of] cheap coal."[40] In the 1880s the largest coal mining and coke-smelting
operations in the area were the Pratt and Coalburg mines in Birmingham, the TCI mines at Tracy City, Tennessee, the Knoxville Iron
Company mine in the Coal Creek District of Tennessee, and Joseph
Brown's Dade County coal mines in northwest Georgia. Each of these
enterprises used convicts for a significant portion of their labor force,
both in the mines and at their coke ovens, and provided fuel for iron
furnaces in Knoxville, Chattanooga, and Birmingham.[41]

Tennessee Coal, Iron and Railroad's Tracy City mines, for instance,
described in 1883 as "the largest single mining operation in [Tennes-
see]," leased convicts for two-thirds of their 933-man labor force. In the
early 1880s, the company operated four coal mines, six hundred coke
ovens, three iron furnaces, and twenty-three miles of rail line. It rested
on $3 million of capital, most of it held in New York City.[42] By 1893
TCI, which produced 60 per cent of the value of all coal and iron
products in Tennessee and Alabama, could boast that it had become
the "largest producer of bituminous coal and pig iron for the open
market [that is, non-steel production] of any company in America."[43]
In addition to its own integrated enterprise, TCI supplied fuel to
railroads, cotton mills, oil mills, rolling mills, foundries, and cotton
compresses all across the South. By 1898 the company planned to erect
a steel plant with a projected daily capacity surpassed only by Andrew
Carnegie's massive Homestead works in Pennsylvania.[44]

The development of this vast southern industrial empire can be
traced to the first convict coal mines opened in Tennessee, which
provided the raw material for the development of coke and then iron
production in the 1870s and 1880s. Located about twenty miles northwest of the Tennessee, Alabama and Georgia border, in 1870 the Tracy
City mines shipped only 47,110 tons of coal and 668 tons of coke.[45] But
large-scale corporate mining and coke production was inaugurated in
the New South the following year, when Colonel Arthur S. Colyar
decided to lease one hundred convicts from the state and put them to
work in the Tracy City mines. Three years later, in 1874, these mines
produced nearly half of the state's coal output, and the Bureau of
Agriculture stated that "the coal in [Grundy] County is now at the very
foundation of commerce and manufacturing, and by means of the
capital and enterprise which it has developed, many other industrial
interests have taken a new start."[46] In eight months of 1869, working
the mines with free labor, TCI had made a profit of $7,379.42; between

May 1871 and May 1872, with a convict labor force in place, the same mines earned the company $58,456.66. By 1873, TCI sold coal produced for 4.28 cents a bushel at the price of 9.24 cents.[47]

Convicts, it turned out, produced a very high proportion of "slack" coal (that is, fine or broken bits of coal, as opposed to "lump" coal), suitable only for stoking coke ovens. One internal report on the Tennessee mines suggested that the proportion of slack coal in convict mines measured as high as 46 per cent, twice that common in free labor mines.[48] In general, the more dependent a mine operation was on convict labor, the more likely it was to coke a high proportion of its own coal in subsidiary ovens.[49] Indeed, one of the reasons TCI built 120 coke ovens in 1873 was to provide an outlet for its convict-mined slack coal, which proved difficult to sell on the open market. The company then expanded to pig-iron production which would rely on the Tracy City coke for fuel.[50]

The growth of TCI's coke facilities was a prominent feature of the company's expansion, and was closely linked to the erection of the Chattanooga Iron Company blast furnace nearby, in 1873. This pig-iron furnace also relied on coke purchased from the Dade County convict mines and coke ovens across the state line in Georgia, and employed twelve hundred men.[51] By 1876 Tennessee's state geologist claimed that Tracy City coal had been "mined more extensively than any other in the state.... It makes excellent coke, which is used extensively in the manufacture of pig iron, and in rolling mills," he boasted. TCI shipped coke to Alabama, to Chattanooga, and to the Rising Fawn and Bartow furnaces in northwest Georgia for pig-iron manufacture.[52]

The success of these mines should come as no surprise, for Colonel Colyar, president of TCI in the early 1870s, was quite explicit about the distinct advantages he saw in forced labor. In June 1870 the Nashville *Republican Banner* had suggested that the state purchase the then-struggling coal mines from Colyar and work its convicts there, in order to provide cheap fuel for other industrial enterprises in the area. With a steady supply of inexpensive coal, the *Banner* believed, "manufacturing enterprise and capital will flow into the state." Furthermore, "if the scarcity of fuel is attributable to the scarcity of labor" in East Tennessee, convict labor could provide the ideal solution. Rather than competing with free (white) labor, convict workers in the mines would stimulate manufacturing and increase the opportunities for employment, drawing the state's population into the industrial sector, the newspaper claimed.[53]

But Colyar himself went one better than the *Banner*, by suggesting that the state provide him with the convicts while he maintained ownership of the mines. Iron and coal production in Tennessee were "in their incipiency," but "having absolute control of the [convict] labor ... [will] make it a certainty that the labor can be profitably used," Colyar insisted. Best of all, he argued, with convict labor "you remove all danger and cost of strikes, which is a big [cost] item in the production of coal in this state." The cheaper and steadier labor of convicts would provide less expensive coal for all the state's people, including its free workers, Colyar concluded.[54] By the end of 1872 Colyar again wrote to the paper, unabashedly proclaiming that "this noticeable speck of enterprise ... is especially due to the convict labor system adopted by the company," and the success of the Tennessee coal trade was the "result of a steady and uniform system of labor" made possible by coercion.[55]

Throughout the 1880s TCI continued to expand its operations in Tennessee, purchasing an iron furnace in South Pittsburgh from a failing British company in 1882, and then preceding to open up the nearby Inman ore mines with a convict labor force. With the security of convict-produced coke from Tracy City and the iron ore from the Inman mines, TCI erected two additional furnaces at South Pittsburgh; these three furnaces, with a daily capacity of 125 tons of pig iron each, were the largest in Tennessee.[56] TCI became Tennessee's dominant coal company, operating thirteen of the state's sixty-six coal mines by 1891, and was responsible for over 20 per cent of the state's coal output even within a vastly expanded industry. Tracy City's coke ovens alone in 1892 produced 132,541 tons of the state's total of 334,508 tons of coke, far surpassing all competitors; the company's furnaces produced nearly one-third of the state's pig iron.[57]

Convicts continued to lie at the heart of this integrated production of coal, coke and iron. By the 1890s, with the industry in full blast in Tennessee, TCI worked 400 convicts at Tracy City mining coal and stoking coke ovens, 275 more convicts at their Inman ore mines, and more than 100 convicts who replaced striking free workers at the recently acquired Oliver Springs mines.[58] The company's position of strength soon allowed it to cross the border and buy up some of the most promising companies in Alabama's coalfield. When Tennessee reclaimed its convicts and placed them in a state-owned mine in 1896, coal production at Tracy City declined 25 per cent, but TCI had already shifted the bulk of its operations to Birmingham, where the convict lease proved more secure.[59]

Coal and iron development in Alabama closely paralleled that of East Tennessee; the original mines, the most productive mines, and the mines most central to industrial integration were the ones that successfully concentrated, monopolized, and exploited convict labor. In 1874

Alabama's Commissioner of Industrial Resources could still complain that "coal mining in this state ... can only be considered at this time in the merest dawn of its infancy," with only 40,000 tons mined in 1873 – easily surpassed in the 1880s by a single convict mine. By 1885, the year before TCI bought into the Alabama field, the state mined 2.2 million tons of coal, 401,000 tons of which were dug by convicts.[60] In large measure this "new era in the coal business of Alabama" could be attributed to the Pratt Coal and Coke Company, which opened mines six miles from Birmingham in 1879. By 1886 Pratt's four mines produced 622,940 tons of coal. Two of these four mines were worked entirely by 506 convicts; indeed, the Pratt Company was the primary lessee of both state and county convicts in Alabama. Essentially, its coal mines were the main branch of the state's penitentiary.[61]

The Pratt Coal and Coke Company, later to become TCI's Alabama division, was the creation of one of the postbellum South's most notorious capitalist entrepreneurs, Henry F. DeBardeleben. Contemporaries described the ruthless DeBardeleben as "the most successful organizer of great industries who, probably, ever lived in Alabama," as well as "one of the wealthiest men in the South." Even the United Mine Workers acknowledged "King Henry" as "the great 'developer' of the coal and iron industry of Alabama," but pointed out that "he is also well known ... to be among the first employers of convict labor in the mines." DeBardeleben initially benefited from his close association with antebellum industrialist Daniel Pratt.[62] But this New South entrepreneur brought together the crucial elements of outside investors, cheap coal from captive mines, coke ovens, iron furnaces dependent on his own fuel, and forced labor. This combination lay at the heart of Birmingham's industrial growth, and the "Magic City" became in turn the most significant example of industrial development in the Lower South. By 1898, with conversion to steel production on the horizon, Alabama's inspector of mines and industry looked back over two decades of rapid industrial development and correctly concluded that "the Birmingham District owes more to the Pratt mines for its existence than any other agency," mines which continued to work nearly one thousand convicts.[63]

The most dramatic leaps in the levels of coal production – and consequent investment in blast furnaces – in Alabama coincide with the large-scale use of convict labor in the 1880s by the Pratt Company and its main competitor in the Birmingham District, the Sloss Company mines at Coalburg. These two companies together monopolized Alabama's convict lease by the end of the 1880s, and consequently established the region's most sophisticated integrated coal, coke and iron facilities.[64] Above all, DeBardeleben's initial demonstration that cheap coal for coking purposes was available in the Birmingham District "induced other capitalists to invest at Birmingham in blast furnaces and rolling mills."[65] A coke-fueled iron furnace had been put in blast during the war, but "the experiment was not continued" because of the absence of a steady supply of coal; in the New South, convict labor solved this problem.[66]

Recognizing the potential for cheap iron production, DeBardeleben and his original partner, James W. Sloss, purchased 30,000 acres of the Warrior coal field, adjacent to the fledgling city of Birmingham, in 1878.[67] The Pratt Company opened its first mines in 1880 and 1881 – Slope No. 2 and Shaft No. 1 – with approximately 110 convict miners leased from the state.[68] On 23 November 1880, DeBardeleben put into blast the city's first iron furnace, fueled steadily by coked coal from his convict mines. This furnace supplied pig iron to the Birmingham Rolling Mills, which by 1888 was the city's largest employer in manufacturing, with nine hundred workers. With the southern market "growing more exacting, requiring for steam purposes a clean coal, with more lump and less fine coal," the Pratt Company came to rely more and more on convicts, who by lack of skill or dearth of effort produced the finer coal more appropriate for coking.[69]

With an assured, virtually limitless, and adjacent source of mineral fuel, Birmingham industry boomed from 1880 onward.[70] In the four years after the Pratt mines began to ship coal, eight new major industrial concerns were founded, bringing rolling mills, furnaces, and additional mining companies to the district. Many of these industries relied directly on convict-mined coal, and in fact were founded or encouraged by DeBardeleben and Sloss themselves, as outlets for their product. The Pratt Coal and Coke Company grew apace, as did the related pig-iron industry in the area. By 1886 developed industry in Birmingham included over $5 million of "active capital engaged in the manufacture of pig iron," and between 1880 and 1890 the amount of capital invested in Alabama blast furnaces rocketed from $2.7 million to $15.7 million.[71]

When absorbed by TCI in 1886, Pratt Coal and Iron was "the largest coal company in the South," and its force of convicts maintained half of the company's daily coal output.[72] Consequently, on its accession to power in the Birmingham District, TCI moved to secure a guaranteed force of six hundred convicts for ten years, paying $18.50 a month for a "first class" miner, who was required to produce four tons of coal daily. Given that in 1889 free coal miners in Alabama earned on average $2.15 per day, and worked about sixty days less than convicts during the course of a year, TCI obtained from the state a steady labor force at a good saving, even with the cost of maintaining the convicts.[73]

Despite its efforts at monopolization, the Pratt/TCI nexus of coal and iron production was not the only industrial concern in Alabama able to place convicts at the base of its productive process. During the 1880s the company led by James W. Sloss underwent a similar trajectory. Sloss, who was instrumental in bringing together Alabama's plantation and industrial interests, was encouraged in 1881 by DeBardeleben to start his own furnace company in order to widen the local market for the rapidly expanding production of Pratt coal and coke. With "the promise of cheap coal from the Pratt mines," Sloss established the Sloss Furnace Company and erected two blast furnaces and some coke ovens ten miles north of the city. Then, in 1886, Sloss sold out to northern capitalists, and effected a consolidation capitalized at $3 million to create the Sloss Iron and Steel Company. Significantly, in this reorganization the company acquired its own captive convict mines in the district, severing its dependence on coal from its main competitor, TCI.[74]

These were the mines at Coalburg, owned since 1882 by the Coalburg Coal and Coke Company, Alabama's second largest lessee of convicts. In their first two years the Coalburg mines went from a production level of 125 to 4,000 tons a day, and sold coal to railroads, iron works, cotton mills, stock yards, and water works, in Atlanta as well as Birmingham. The Pratt Company, and then TCI, leased the majority of Alabama's *state*, or felony, convicts. But the Coalburg Coal Company – and subsequently Sloss Iron and Steel – recruited much of their prison labor from the pool of convicts sentenced in Alabama's county courts, in surrounding Jefferson County and across the state in nine other counties. Often these misdemeanor convicts were sentenced for court "costs" or fines they were unable to pay. Before the consolidation in 1886, Coalburg worked 192 convicts in two of its four mines, which overall produced 186,000 tons of coal – second only to the Pratt mines. By 1889, having acquired additional county convicts, the Sloss Company worked 320 convicts at its Coalburg mines, and production expanded as the number of prisoners continued to grow.[75]

Yet these short-term prisoners "just from the cotton fields" did not always prove to be expert miners, and often served out their sentences before learning the necessary skills of a coal miner. Thus, like its competitors, the Coalburg company quickly discovered the necessity of finding a market for the "slack," cokeable coal produced by inexperienced convicts. "It is imperative that a market be found for the coke made from the fine coal," the superintendent of the mines wrote in 1885. Together, the use of convicts, soft coal, and thin coal seams produced coal suitable only for coke ovens; if not coked, one-fourth "of the out-put of the mines is put in the waste bank," he declared. He urged the company to build more coke ovens and acquire furnaces in order to use this coal.[76]

By 1892 the Sloss Iron and Steel Company furnaces, fueled by the Coalburg coal and coke, produced 175,000 tons of pig and foundry iron annually – again, second only to TCI.[77] And, much as TCI was built upon the conglomeration of numerous coal mines, coke ovens, and blast furnaces, so too did the Sloss Company form the nucleus of ever larger concentrations of capital by absorbing smaller competitors and, in turn, merging with others itself. In great measure these corporations' strength can be attributed to the steady access to the cheap fuel that lay at the base of their industrial pyramid. As the scale of production swelled, convict labor guaranteed "a certain supply of a definite amount of coal."[78] In Alabama's mineral district by the turn of the century, TCI's only serious rival was the recently consolidated Sloss–Sheffield Steel and Iron Company, which operated 7 blast furnaces, 1,500 coke ovens, and 5 coal mines – including the original two convict mines at Coalburg, now together working over five hundred convicts at hard labor.[79]

Clearly convict-mined coal helped provide the necessary fuel for the initial exploitation of the Deep South's iron ore and the creation of a significant pig-iron industry. By the mid 1890s, in fact, after a special investigation Canadian Customs barred the importation of pig iron from twenty-three furnaces in Alabama and Tennessee because it was produced "under the taint of prison labour" by reliance on convict-produced coal and coke.[80] This "taint" persisted even when convicts represented only 10 to 15 per cent of the mine labor force in Alabama, as they did in the 1890s (although by 1897, 26 per cent of all coal miners in the Birmingham District were prisoners).[81] Indeed, as the *Southern Miner and Manufacturer* had pointed out in 1884, "the introduction of convict labor [in Tennessee] displaced some miners, but being *reliable* it developed the mines to such an extent" that even with five hundred convicts working the mines far more positions were eventually created for free workers.[82] As with operations in Tennessee, the Pratt Company and then TCI found that with business placed on a sound basis with convict-supplied coal they were able to expand by opening free labor mines as well; by 1890 Alabama had 1,310 convict miners and 5,665 free miners. Even so, an examination of production levels in the Pratt mines from 1880 to 1898 indicates that forced labor continued to be significant when surrounded by free mines. Over this eighteen-year period the total output of the three convict mines at Pratt – the third was opened in 1894 during a strike – was 7 million tons, or 47 per cent of the total output of the ten mine openings worked by the company during these years.[83]

Thus, in addition to being the first mines opened, the convict mines were also consistently the most productive mines in DeBardeleben's and then TCI's empire.[84] More importantly, this was the coal that stoked TCI's 806 coke ovens in the Birmingham District. Between them TCI's two convict mines alone produced nearly 10 per cent of Alabama's coal by 1893, even though the state then boasted sixty-five coal mines. In part this could be attributed to the unusually large labor force that the convict lease helped the company place in and around these mines – five hundred each in 1893, two hundred more employees than any other mine in the state. And in part this high level of production was due to the length of the working year for the convicts, 310 days, a regimen unmatched by any free labor mine.[85] The state average in 1893 was only 237 days, curtailed in part by idleness occasioned by the closing of several Birmingham furnaces.[86] Needless to say, convict mines remained open in such periods of economic downturn, while operators laid off free miners.

Like TCI, the Sloss Company worked its Coalburg convicts in only two of its eleven mine openings in the Pratt seam. These two mines, however, had 200 and 180 unfree miners respectively, who worked over 300 days a year; thus they were the largest and most continuously operated mines owned by Sloss. The two convict mines, Coalburg No. 4 and No. 9, produced 31 per cent of the company's coal in 1893. All told, the four convict mines in the Pratt seam produced 14.4 per cent of Alabama's total coal in 1893, and their adjacent coke ovens supplied over one-fourth of the state's total – second only to Pennsylvania in its magnitude.[87]

Thus in the lower Appalachian coalfield not only were convicts located in the first mines opened, but these convict mines continued to outstrip all others in production, were relied upon to keep furnaces in blast during strikes, and kept operating during economic slowdowns. They also lay at the heart of the largest companies' ability to integrate and consolidate their operations on a massive scale. Indeed, in the southern states, as elsewhere, conglomerations of industrial enterprises into ever-larger and dominant corporations marked the period 1880–1900.[88] Unlike the rest of the nation, however, this process was closely tied to the availability of forced labor.

IV

Corporate consolidation was closely related to another characteristic of the Deep South's coalfield during the 1880s and 1890s, also similar to national trends. Nationwide, the coal industry was noted for labor strife, strikes, and violence; as the US Geological Survey complained in its 1889 report, "strikes are of almost constant occurrence [in the coal industry] in one part of the country or another," due to the miners' refusal to accept wage cuts when "the state of the market renders a curtailment of mining expenses necessary." Alabama and Tennessee were no exception, much to the coal operators' distress. During the 1890s industrial development, rural dislocation, urbanization, and economic depression swelled the available free labor pool in the South and exacerbated conflict between labor and capital in the region. Even though in sheer numbers convict labor appeared to decline in importance as southern industry expanded its free labor operations, forced labor remained crucial to the patterns of labor strife and industrial integration in the New South even into the twentieth century.[89] Rapid industrial development in a poorly developed and capital-scarce region depended on stable labor relations; disputes between labor and capital threatened to impede production or scare away desperately needed capital investment. Thus southern coal operators placed convict labor at a key point in the industrial process in order to ensure a predictable supply of coal, and to keep iron furnaces in blast during strikes or labor unrest.

Despite T.J. Hill's suggestion that convict labor "was a benefit instead of a detriment to the larger class of free labor," in the South over twenty coal strikes in opposition to convict labor were recorded between 1881 and 1900. Where convicts and free miners worked in the same vicinity, they "[did] not come in contact without friction," TCI admitted in its annual report. The pages of the *UMW Journal*, which began publication in 1891, were filled with denunciations of convict leasing in the mines: black and white miners alike recognized that prisoners were used "to prevent the spread of organization and as an 'effectual preventative' during a strike." "Free men cannot contend and strike in a state that the largest coal output is worked by convict labor," complained a UMW district organizer in Alabama in 1895, in the wake of the failed strike of 1894.[90]

The union's antagonists readily agreed with this observation. DeBardeleben himself told the Alabama General Assembly that "convict labor competing with free labor is advantageous to the mine owner. If all were free miners they could combine and strike and thereby put up the price of coal," he pointed out, "but where convict labor exists the mine owner can sell coal cheaper." He also noted that in the absence of labor troubles, the operator – and presumably the state's industries that relied on cheap coal – benefited from "the certainty of filling his contracts." This reason for using convict labor persisted into the

Progressive Era, when one investigator of industrial conditions in the Birmingham District told the US Congress that "one peculiar advantage [of convict labor] which the employers admit is that it gives them a club over organized labor. Whenever there is a strike, the convict mines go on turning out coal regularly," he noted. "So long as coal is mined here by convicts the mine workers will never close this district," predicted industrialist James Bowron in 1923, more than three decades after the UMW's first attempts to organize the Alabama field.[91]

From the beginning the most successful coal operators had recognized the potential for labor control embodied in convict labor. As Arthur S. Colyar, the progenitor of TCI, remarked in 1872, "to put on foot successful mining operations in Tennessee with two strikes a year was impossible.... This has been remedied by convict labor."[92] With forced labor, a supply of cheap fuel was secure and delivery certain. "Those dependent on coal have no such security anywhere [else]," he boasted. The convict mines in Tennessee were the "only mines in the United States free from strikes," and this fact would certainly attract capital and manufacturing enterprises to the region. In this respect the Tennessee mines would prove a sharp contrast to the Pennsylvania coalfields, which were wracked by class conflict, Colyar assured investors. "The reason given for the high price of coal in all northern cities is the uncertainty of labor to mine it," the colonel proclaimed. "Using our convict labor in the very commencement of our mining operations ... we may avoid the conflict between labor and capital which has made the immense mines of Pennsylvania a boiling cauldron under the commerce of the nation," he concluded melodramatically.[93] Other observers also favorably contrasted southern coal mining with the northern industry. "The condition of the coal trade in the North has been clearly portrayed by the almost constant strikes and disputes between employers and employed.... while here [in Alabama] there has been no interruption in the production of coal," remarked the editor of a Philadelphia newspaper during a trip South in the 1880s, pointing to the successful use of convicts as one of the reasons for labor peace.[94]

Such peace was short-lived. The great coal and iron boom of the 1880s was followed by new challenges to the southern industry in the 1890s: increased competition, a deep depression and a sharp drop in the price of coal and iron, the pressing necessity to convert iron production to steel, and labor conflict on a massive scale, particularly as miners' organizations made inroads in the Alabama field and corporations attempted to cope with the drop in prices.[95] Access to convict labor proved a crucial asset for the corporations that weathered these crises, by providing flexibility during economic downturns, helping to defeat labor's challenge, and allowing TCI and Sloss to consolidate power in the Birmingham District and convert to steel production.

Convicts proved significant to labor conflicts in several ways during the 1890s. First, rather than cut tonnage rates to cope with diminishing coal markets, a company might curtail production by laying off its free workers, and maintain its convict mines at full production levels. One of the main grievances miners in Tennessee voiced about convict labor was that, "in dull times, when orders [for coal] were slack, free labor was made idle, while convicts were compelled to perform their tasks." The *UMWJ* concurred that "when trade is slack, the convict works and the free miner stays at home. When cars run slow in the mine, the convict gets his usual quota while the free miner remains a looker on."[96] Second, in the event of a strike a company with convicts could continue to produce coal, which in turn could be used to meet contracts or stoke their own furnaces – avoiding the costliest damage of a strike to integrated coal and iron production, the taking of a furnace out of blast. "In case of strikes," TCI assured stockholders in its annual report for 1890, "[the convicts] can furnish us enough coal to keep at least three of the Ensley furnaces running."[97] In frequent instances convicts actually entered the mines in direct response to a strike, effectively replacing the free labor force in a particular mine for good or opening a new mine altogether.[98]

A shift from free to convict labor might also occur as a lockout, in order to enforce a wage cut or a speed-up, or to break an *anticipated* strike. Fearing that free miners planned a walkout at the end of 1890 in order to renegotiate their wage scale and join the newly formed UMW, TCI president Alfred Shook advised his general manager, G.B. McCormack, to prepare to break the strike. "Bank *every* furnace you can," he told "Mac," and "seal up the [coke] ovens." During the lockout the company should "put all convicts on coal, in whatever mines are best," and then sell the coal to "railroads, rolling mills, [and] other large customers." Moreover, if "there is any trouble between the [free] miners and the convicts," then "the state of Alabama should protect you with the strong arm of the law." Indeed, the prison warden warned that "there is some talk of the miners trying to extricate the convicts," but assured that "if they should attempt such a thing I will give them a warm reception." The other danger was that of miners "working on the convicts to induce them not to do extra work during the strike," but the warden could guard against that as well. "By this means you can certainly whip the strike in 45 days," Shook assured McCormack, and within two weeks the strike indeed appeared to be "whipped" and the company expected a 10 to 15 per cent wage cut. "This strike has done more to put off the day when convicts will be taken out of [the mines] than anything that could have been done," remarked one of Alabama's prison inspectors presciently at the close of 1890.[99]

A similar strategy used the following year in Tennessee had far less beneficial results, however, when free miners took militant action to insure that "they would no longer be forced to compete ... with men who had by their criminal acts forfeited the right to liberty."[100] In fact, the notorious "convict war" of East Tennessee in 1891 and 1892 was a direct result of attempts by mine operators to replace free workers with convicts, a shift induced both by layoffs and strikes.[101] In the first instance, with a glutted coal market, some operators curtailed production by shutting down their free labor mines and maintaining their convict mines, where labor was a predetermined cost fixed by the state. Alternatively, following disputes over wage rates or the weighing of coal (a notorious means of extracting surplus from miners), miners would stage a walkout and then find themselves replaced by convicts and locked out.[102] "Not content with using convicts in their own mines," the *UMWJ* complained, the lessees "have adopted a hiring-out system, so that when miners sought to improve their position convicts would be supplied to the [other] operators for the purpose of further crushing their workmen" in the Tennessee field.[103]

Within the space of thirteen months, Tennessee's coal miners attacked five convict camps, including TCI's Inman ore mines and, of course, Tracy City, on three different occasions. Miners first struck the Tennessee Mining Company mines at Briceville in mid July when the company rejected their request to have a worker weigh the coal (a "checkweighman"). "Convicts from Coal Creek were sent to fill the places of the striking miners," the *UMWJ* reported, and the miners responded by driving the convicts from the mines by force.[104] When the legislature subsequently failed to abolish convict leasing, the miners planned and executed "the final attack on the convict camps and the release of the prisoners." Free miners spared TCI's mines until August 1892, when they finally burned the convict camp at Tracy City to the ground, and set the convicts free. "There has been much dissatisfaction among the miners of Tracy City because of the lease system, which allows the bulk of the labor to be done in the mines by convicts," the *UMWJ* somewhat drily remarked. In fact, as the miners' paper had pointed out before, in Tennessee the convict question had ultimately "resolved itself into a contest of labor against capital."[105]

The anti-convict labor insurrections in the Tennessee coalfield were so severe that in 1892 the upheaval was held responsible for the 15 per cent reduction in coal output suffered by the state that year. Arthur

Colyar himself prematurely proclaimed that "when the Tennessee Coal and Iron Company gives up its lease it will never again employ convict labor." In an internal report the company noted that "we have sustained the most serious losses by reason of the 'Convict troubles' ... which resulted in the actual destruction of much valuable property, the temporary stoppage of our works, the increased cost of the material produced by convict labor, and the general demoralization [that is, assertiveness] of all our labor." This alone was a powerful admission of how central forced labor was to TCI's operations. "We have not been able to 're-establish' the standard of labor or the quality of coal and coke" since the miners released the convicts, the report claimed. The company's iron furnaces "suffered from the use of inferior coke," the report concluded.[106]

Despite the turmoil, the state returned the convicts to TCI only two weeks after their release in 1892; by 1893, on the eve of a general strike by free miners, TCI operated two large new convict mines to supplement the Lone Rock mine at Tracy City, with an additional 185 convicts. By 1896, just prior to the abolition of convict leasing in Tennessee, convicts working in two mines continued to produce 73 per cent of Tracy City's coal, while convict coke-oven workers made 90 per cent of the division's coke. Tennessee did abolish the convict lease, but the miners' violence and suppression by the militia severely weakened the fledgling UMW in the Tennessee field, by the union's own admission.[107]

The same economic forces that generated violent opposition to convict labor led to "a strike of unusual dimensions" in the spring of 1894, one that affected the entire Appalachian bituminous field, from Pennsylvania to Alabama. In response to unilateral wage cuts instituted by the coal operators, 150,000 coal miners were called out of the mines by the national UMW on 26 April 1894, and the strike lasted most of the summer. But in Tennessee and Alabama the convict mines continued to produce coal – and turn a healthy profit, as coal became scarce and prices began to rise while the labor costs in convict mines remained fixed.[108] In Tennessee, for example, all the miners in the Coal Creek District went out on strike, but "the striking miners dislike very much the idea of the convicts turning out from twelve to eighteen cars of coal a day while they are on strike." In Tennessee the strike was short-lived; the most productive companies relied on their convicts, and held out.[109] In Alabama, convict labor in key productive sectors during this period of intense class conflict also proved essential to the survival and renewed dominance of the industry by the Birmingham District's most powerful corporations.

"Me thinks I hear the bugle sound ..., and the Tennessee war is being tried at Pratt City and Coalburg and every man is on his way and soon the convicts are loose and the stockade is burning," wrote "Cromwell" in the *UMW Journal* at the commencement of the 1894 upheaval.[110] Despite this fantasy call to arms, the Birmingham District did not experience a direct attack on convict mines as Tennessee had two years earlier, even though the 1894 walkout in Alabama led to an increased reliance on convicts.[111] Just prior to the strike, TCI petitioned the state to increase the amount of coal they could require their convict force to produce. And as soon as the miners quit work, the company requested extra convicts to open a third convict mine to supply coal to the district's furnaces and industries during the strike. "The expense of starting up the third mine ... will make it an unprofitable transaction," the company confessed, "except for the advantages we may indirectly gain in the settlement of the labor troubles."[112]

Although this particular request was denied, TCI did open a third convict mine in the Pratt field in 1894 and increased the number of convicts under its control to 1,138. The Sloss Company maintained its convict force at nearly six hundred workers.[113] Furthermore, production at the convict mines increased in 1894 by 31.7 per cent, while as a result of the strike the state's overall production dropped below 4.4 million tons, a decrease of nearly 1 million tons (17.2 per cent) from 1893. Thus during the year in which Alabama coal operators faced their greatest challenge since the opening of the field, forced labor mined 24 per cent of the state's coal, a substantial increase over the 14.4 per cent of the previous year.[114] As the US Geological Survey reported at the end of 1894, in the Alabama mines "where convict labor is employed, the convicts continued to work while the free labor was out [on strike]." Thus, while the Pratt mines lost 1,500 workers to the strike, TCI could continue to supply coal to its coke ovens and fuel to the furnaces it intended to keep in blast. Similarly, the Coalburg mines reported that their convict force worked 310 days of 1894 – the most in the state – but that their free labor worked only 170 days that year.[115]

The Tradesman, a southern industrial trade journal, noted in the early weeks of the strike that "the fact that there are about 1,000 convicts at the Pratt mines and 600 at Coalburg who mine coal has been the main factor in preventing a stoppage of production," since only 735 free miners remained at work in Alabama's mines. In fact, the journal hinted that the strike could be interpreted as a lockout. Due to the business depression, the operators preferred to idle most of their mines and furnaces, and keep only their convict force at work at a fixed labor cost so low they could afford it, even as coal and iron demand plummeted.

As the Alabama House reported, "when coal is short in sales the convicts continue their usual output, while the free miners are stopped."[116]

Evidence from company records also suggests that what was a strike
nationally, in Alabama may have been a lockout made possible by
convict labor. A full month before the UMW's strike call, one of TCI's
directors advocated a lockout in order to institute a 25 per cent wage
cut. Henry F. DeBardeleben suggested that all the convicts be moved
to the company's Blue Creek mine, "mining coal enough there for all
the furnaces and closing down the other mines." Another group of
convicts could be moved from Pratt to Blocton mines, and "the men
thrown out of work there [at Blocton] would be told they could get
work at Pratt at a reduction of about 25 per cent." By June 1894,
Alabama's miners recognized that "the miners of Alabama came on
strike one week prior to [the national UMW] ... because we were forced
to it by trickery on the part of our employers," and that their strike was
threatened "because of the hundreds of convicts we have that fill two
of the largest and best mines in this section of the country."[117]

By the end of the summer the strike was broken, and TCI and Sloss
emerged from the period of labor turmoil and economic depression in
a stronger position than ever to dominate the region's coal and iron
market. With the state's assumption of convict mining in Tennessee at
the end of 1895, TCI continued to pour resources into its Alabama
holdings where the lease remained secure. In 1897 TCI's eighteen mines
produced 47.4 per cent of Alabama's coal, and their three convict mines
provided one-fourth of the company's total output. Convicts still made
up 40.1 per cent of TCI's labor force at the Pratt mines, and 36 per
cent of the Sloss Company's total coal mining force. And at this time,
when Alabama produced 35 per cent of all pig iron used in the country's foundries, mills and pipe-works (production uses excluding steel
plants), TCI's 2,250 ton *daily* output represented half of the state's production of this crucial industrial product.[118]

After 1898 TCI began the long-overdue conversion to steel production, fulfilling Alfred Shook's prediction that "as soon as the labor troubles are settled in the South, an active start looking to the manufacture
of steel will be made at or near Birmingham."[119] Indeed, before the
onset of the economic crisis and subsequent labor conflict, Shook had
written to Arthur Colyar, extolling the past two decades of development while warning that it would be for naught without advancing to
accommodate steel production. From the Tennessee and Cumberland
watersheds, through north Georgia, down into Birmingham, coal and
pig iron had lain at the heart of the plateau's successful growth, Shook
observed. "Without this development," he insisted, "the whole country

from Roanoke Va.... down to Chattanooga and Birmingham ... would today be practically what it was when the war closed. It has given employment ... compelled railroad systems to extend their lines," provided a market for timber and farm produce, and built schools, churches, villages, towns and cities. Yet, Shook maintained, the future was in steel, and unless the South entered this market, its economy would be left behind. "If we are forced to stop the development of our yet practically untouched mineral fields for want of a [local] market, then the growth of our iron industry must stop," Shook concluded.[120]

Given the many obstacles to industrial development in this region, the rapidity of economic progress made in the last quarter of the nineteenth century was remarkable. Southern capitalists pressed on in the face of weak and volatile markets, inferior resources, competition with vastly superior northern enterprises, and a labor force alternately unwilling to meet the demands of industrial discipline and militantly insistent upon its rights. In economic if not moral terms, the achievements of these entrepreneurs are far more striking than their failures. Yet the very constraints these men faced encouraged them to turn to forced labor for rapid capitalist development. The corporations in the forefront of the South's coal and iron industry relied on convicts to recruit a "reliable" labor force, to build their enterprises, to integrate production, to consolidate corporate control, and to crush the labor organization that was the inevitable result of the creation of a southern industrial proletariat.

These same powerful corporations were in the vanguard of the twentieth-century southern steel and cast-iron products industries as well, and the full advent of a modernized industrial base in the Birmingham region did nothing to eliminate the use of forced labor. In 1902 the Sloss–Sheffield Steel and Iron Company moved all of the convicts from Coalburg to its new Flat Top mines, with a projected capacity of over 1,000 tons of coal per day, and two hundred coke ovens which would provide "ample supply" for the company's seven furnaces. This improvement was "absolutely necessary both from an economic standpoint and in order to guarantee operations in face of bad weather, railway disasters, strikes, or other contingencies," the company's annual report confided. "The idea is to make the company independent in the matter of raw materials"; with such independence, Sloss–Sheffield became a major supplier of pig iron to the region's pipe foundries.[121] By 1909 the Flat Top mine produced 434,750 tons of coal with a workforce of 425 convicts – an astonishing level of productivity by any standards.[122]

Tennessee Coal and Iron, the corporation that first opened a small convict mine at Tracy City in 1871 and brought steel to Birmingham at the century's end, could boast by then that "the company is entirely self-contained, producing from its own land its iron ores ... and the coal, converting [it] into coke in its own ovens, producing its pig iron in its own blast furnaces, and converting the same into steel in its open hearth furnaces." TCI sold its 23 coal mines, 18 ore mines, 3,000 coke ovens, 16 blast furnaces, and 8 open-hearth steel furnaces to US Steel in 1907, for $49 million; the national conglomerate continued to use convicts to mine its coal.[123] The company continued the struggle to "obtain steady and efficient labor," and suffered a 400 per cent employee turnover rate among its free workers.[124] In 1912 the Birmingham complaint that "the local supply [of labor] is inadequate ... [because] the Negroes, who in the mines and furnaces constitute more than 50 per cent of the working force, do not appear to be dependable" could still be heard.[125] TCI's new management tried to stabilize the workforce with improvements in housing, sanitary conditions, and other welfare measures, but still found itself embroiled in bitter labor disputes.[126] George Crawford, the new president of TCI after the US Steel takeover, did not immediately extend his progressivism to the convict labor question. "The chief inducement for the hiring of convicts was the certainty of a supply of coal for our manufacturing operations in the contingency of labor troubles," he continued to insist as late as 1911.[127] By that time the three largest producers of coal in Alabama were TCI, Sloss–Sheffield, and the Pratt Consolidated Coal Company; these corporations also owned the largest convict mines in Alabama.[128]

US Steel's southern division corporate hagiography, published in 1960, was dedicated to the nineteenth-century founders of TCI and the South's steel industry. The corporation recognized that Tennessee Coal and Iron's "earlier years, and in fact its first half century, marked a period of adversity which many times threatened its collapse." It was duly noted that the fact "that TCI survived to become the South's major steel producer is tribute enough to those daring pioneer businessmen who time and again risked their capital and their standing as industrialists to pull it back from the brink of disaster." Yet if the New South industrialists thus "typically represented the American spirit of free enterprise and business venture," this account failed to note that they often relied on penal slavery to help build industrial capitalism in Dixie.[129]

Joe Brown's Mines

Joe Brown, Joe Brown,
he's a mean white man
he's a mean white man
I know, honey he put
them shackles around
around my leg.
                    African-American work song,
                Georgia, recorded in the 1920s, thirty
                years after Joseph E. Brown's death[1]

In Alabama and Tennessee, even those enterprises in the vanguard of southern coal production at times found themselves constrained by the contradictory nature of convict labor. In the history of convict mining in Tennessee there are hints of the tensions embodied in the use of forced labor. Not all operators expressed satisfaction with the productive capabilities of convicts. When the owners of the Monitor mine replaced their locked-out miners with convicts in 1891, precipitating the riots of that year, they found it required 170 prisoners to replace their 125 free workers, and that production levels still declined even with this larger labor force. Similarly, TCI was accused by a fellow mine operator, who subleased convicts from them to replace strikers, of sending him "a class of poor convicts, such as should never be sent to the mines," which cut into his production levels. He complained that he could get only two-and-a-half tons of coal from each of them a day, instead of the expected four.[2] In Alabama, as well, despite the advantages they provided, convict workers were understood to be limited by "the want of skill and adaptability to mine work." "A large number worked in the mines [are] wholly unfit for the work," the Alabama House reported in

1897. The legislators estimated that only about one-sixth of the prisoners working in Alabama's mines were "first class convicts" who could meet a four-ton daily task.[3]

Indeed, the effort to extract this task from the convicts and to get the state to "upgrade" the class of their laborers continuously vexed Alabama's coal operators. Reporting that 248 "darkies" had been punished in a single month at the Coalburg mines, a convict inspector urged that the company "should remove the difficulty of an unjust task which apparently made it necessary for [the warden] to punish them." But the warden claimed that "he has to try and get what the officers [of the company] demand and yet he knows that the demand is more than the convicts ought reasonably be required to get." Another problem at Coalburg was that the company upgraded the men to second-class (requiring a three-ton task) "before they were competent coal cutters." "One reason they have urged was the short terms of the men [that is, county convicts] and the necessity for allowing them to *raise* them as rapidly as possible," the inspector noted. As a result, "by a large majority the whipping is by one way or another for failure to get the task." Of course, as another inspector informed the governor, "it is very natural for a man who expects to get his pay out of the labor of the convict to want him tasked to his utmost capacity." Convicts complained that they received whippings for "failure to get task," "not working," or "not loading" even when there were not enough cars available in the mine. One prisoner desperately wrote to an inspector that he "had a contrayery mule to Drive & i could not make time with him & i was punished for it i could not do any more if i could i would."[4]

Moreover, as we have seen, convicts appeared to many to be sloppy workers, capable mostly of digging "slack," or broken, powdery coal, good only for coking. Most "lump" coal produced by convicts was of poor quality and size; one operator complained that "we have lost standing in various markets from the employment of this class of labor." Whether this was due, as some claimed, to lack of skill and experience, merely indifference, or outright sabotage, coal operators quickly discovered that "convict labor and clean mining do not go together." The chief engineer of the Tennessee state-run mines noted that under the lease a convict's task included laying track, propping the roof, blasting, mining coal, loading cars, and pushing them to the entry, all of which was done with a noted lack of enthusiasm. "The evils resulting from this are found to be badly laid track, badly set props, and, as a rule, twice as many [props] as needed, coal not mined at all, but simply shot to pieces, and finally loaded up with all the slate, sulphur, and other refuse at hand" in order to make the task. The only way to combat this was whipping, which did not appear to be effective. Finally, as a last resort to defend themselves against exploitation, convicts would even go on strike or set fires in the mine.[5]

Furthermore, while convict labor made an industrial take-off possible, it also may have contributed to the long-term stagnation of the Deep South's heavy industry after the turn of the century. It has been suggested that the inability of the southern iron and steel industry to modernize fully its plant with labor-saving technology was related to the availability of cheap black labor, particularly for furnace work in the Birmingham District.[6] This short-sightedness may have also been linked to the reduced labor costs at the convict coal mines that supplied southern furnaces with fuel. And like the furnaces it stoked, the coal industry itself was slow to modernize; the mines of the Deep South lagged far behind those in the West Virginia and Pennsylvania fields in the adoption of coal-cutting machinery. Undoubtedly, reliance on forced labor made it less imperative to take advantage of technological advances designed, in part, to subvert free labor's control of the productive process.[7]

But perhaps the most fundamental contradiction of convict labor was rooted in its most salient advantage: the capitalization of labor costs. Elimination of the uncertainty of free labor also curtailed the capitalist's freedom to dismiss labor when it became superfluous. Even in the earliest days of convict mining TCI had discovered the potential dangers of fixed labor costs. Arthur Colyar, the man who first capitalized on the potential of convict leasing, temporarily lost his control of the company in the Panic of 1873, because of his indebtedness to the convict contractor who worked the labor. And even in the depression of 1894, from which TCI emerged stronger than ever, of the 536 convicts at the Tracy City mines, 185 were idle in the winter of 1894-95, while the company paid for the lease and for their support. "I think the convict system is injurious to employers of convicts, for in case of low price of coal they are compelled to sell coal at any price to keep going, regardless of cost," testified an Alabama convict lessee during the depths of the depression of the 1890s.[8]

Structural impediments to economic development, and the sensitivity of southern industry to larger market trends, were compelling factors in southern capitalists' turn to convict labor. The region's industrial weaknesses typified an "underdeveloped" economy subject to a form of "modernization" dependent on outside capital and markets; repressive or coercive labor relations often accompany this phase of development. Paradoxically, however, the very instability of nascent southern industries made firms with too heavy an investment in forced labor potentially vulnerable to swings in the business cycle. A fixed labor cost could be a serious liability when production had to be halted because of a lack of markets. Moreover, when coal and iron prices dipped, the need to *increase* production without increasing operating costs became that much greater; but the output and efficiency of convict workers were limited by their lack of skill and their own efforts to resist exploitation. Corporal punishment could only extract so much labor before it precipitated resistance, revolt, or state intervention on the convicts' behalf.

Thus the same factors that made bound labor expedient carried with them its most serious limitations. Firms that maintained a balance of forced and free labor – the former operating as a predictable and fixed cost and driven to meet a set task, the latter allowing the flexibility of wage reductions, rent increases in company housing, or lay-offs – could successfully exploit convict labor. But companies that temporarily capitalized their entire labor cost in the form of forced labor, as those in Georgia did, found themselves dependent on the state for their labor supply, in charge of workers who required a unique level of coercion, and vulnerable to the market forces unleashed by industrial capitalism. For these entrepreneurs the results of dependence on forced labor in an industrializing free labor economy were considerably more ambiguous.

Of the several enterprises that attempted to use Georgia's postbellum penal system as a mechanism of labor recruitment and control, the Dade Coal Company appeared to be the most successful. As the state in the 1870s sought a solution to the convict problem that would combine "permanency, character, force, and [be] self-sustaining," long-term labor in the coal mines appeared to be the most promising system. The Dade coal mines offered several advantages, from the state's point of view. Convicts were consolidated in a large force, in a single location, from which escapes were infrequent; the lessees were financially secure, had invested a large amount of capital in their enterprise, and desired a long-term lease of the "worst desperadoes as may be assigned to us." "A degree of healthfulness, appropriate discipline and security against escape" supposedly made the mines the ideal location for convict labor. In his 1875 report, Georgia's principal keeper concluded that the Dade Coal Company's initial experience with convicts "demonstrated the adaptability of this species of labor to the purposes of mining," and he later repeated the contention that the Dade mines were the "best managed portion of the Georgia penitentiary." For the convicts, however, the Dade mines would prove to be a "Southern Siberia," a brutal introduction to modern industrial labor discipline, and the site of their most active day-to-day resistance to their plight.[9]

In contrast to the explosion of development in neighboring states,

This bank of coke ovens in northwest Georgia, central to Senator Joseph E. Brown's integrated production of coal, iron ore, and pig iron in the 1890s, was stoked by convicts confined at Cole City. (*Georgia Department of Mines, Mining and Geology Records, Georgia Department of Archives and History*)

Joseph Brown's Rising Fawn pig-iron furnace. Free workers carried out the skilled furnace work; convicts supplied the raw material from adjacent iron mines and the nearby Dade coal mines and coke ovens. (*Georgia Department of Mines, Mining and Geology Records, Georgia Department of Archives and History*)

Chattahoochee Brick Company convicts were detailed to help construct the Whittier Cotton Mills, built in 1885–96 near this major convict camp owned by the former mayor of Atlanta. (*Atlanta History Center*)

After 1900 the seasonal boom in naval stores encouraged many turpentine producers in south Georgia and north Florida to exploit short-term convicts. This Florida convict "scrapes" a pine tree for resin. The original caption reads: "No dry clothing provided after long hours in swampy woods. Not a good pair of shoes in camp."
(*US Department of Agriculture, Office of Public Roads, RG30, National Archives Still Pictures Branch*)

A Georgia road gang in Rockdale County in 1909, shortly after the abolition of convict leasing in Georgia. This may have been the first graded road in the county. The telephone lines as well suggest the chain gang's affinity with the modernization of the rural South. (*Vanishing Georgia Collection, Georgia Department of Archives and History*)

Convicts dig clay for a sand–clay road near Eastman, Georgia, in 1910. The original caption notes: "Entire cost of keeping these men 36¢ a day." (*US Department of Agriculture, Office of Public Roads, RG30, National Archives Still Pictures Branch*)

Another Georgia chain gang in 1915, this one near Brunswick, a section of lowcountry Georgia with an active good roads movement and an African-American majority. Note the leg shackles in which the men work. (*US Department of Agriculture, Office of Public Roads, RG30, National Archives Still Pictures Branch*)

This 1920 posed photograph of a Georgia convict camp suggests one of the ironies of the abolition of leasing: the gradual increase in the proportion of whites sent to the chain gang. In virtually no other social institution of the time would Georgia's whites and blacks come into such intimate contact. Of course the seating arrangement in the photo reflects the futile attempt at segregation even in a prison camp. (*Vanishing Georgia Collection, Georgia Department of Archives and History*)

These cruel portable steel cages proved an essential "innovation" for the transient nature of convict road work in Georgia after 1908. The original caption for this 1910 photograph reads: "Desperate convicts locked in these cages at night. The one on the right holds 20 men, the other holds 12 men." (*US Department of Agriculture, Office of Public Roads, RG30, National Archives Still Pictures Branch*)

Working on the road made flight appear within reach, but every convict camp had its notorious bloodhounds. These dogs have treed an escaped Georgia convict, in a photo taken in 1910. The large number of attempted escapes from the chain gang testified to the continued brutality of Georgia's penal system. Between 1910 and 1930, for example, over 6,000 convicts made a break for freedom – on average about 10 per cent of all felony prisoners each year. More than half were recaptured. (*US Department of Agriculture, Office of Public Roads, RG30, National Archives Still Pictures Branch*)

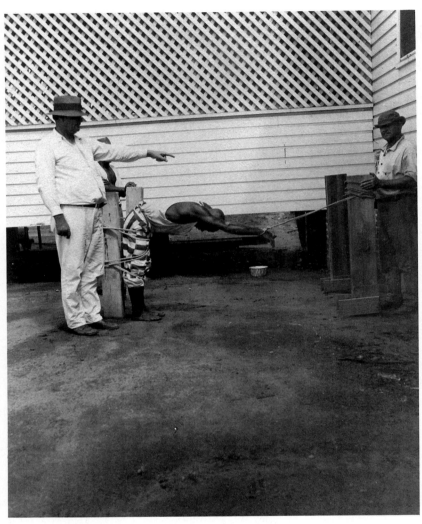

In the 1920s whipping was "officially" abolished in Georgia's convict camps. But other tortures – known euphemistically as "restricted movement" – were devised for those attempting to escape, for refusing to work, cursing, fighting, and "impudent talk." This picture was taken in 1931 by the radical journalist John Spivak, who sought to expose the horrors of Georgia's penal system in his 1932 novel *Georgia Nigger*. (*John Spivak Papers, Syracuse University Library*)

coal output in Georgia never grew much beyond 400,000 tons per year. Production rose to 372,740 tons by 1893, fluctuated after that, and peaked at 417,000 tons in 1903.[10] Similarly, the labor force never increased much beyond its core of convicts, though these exceeded eight hundred in the 1890s.[11] The postwar extraction of bituminous coal from Georgia's relatively small field clearly depended on the labor of the state's convicts, since after 1876 virtually all of the coal miners in Georgia were unfree. Nevertheless, there is no doubt that "Joe Brown's mines," and the convict mines in adjacent Walker County which opened in 1892, made a significant contribution to Georgia's postbellum economy. Coal from these mines provided fuel for the state's rapidly expanding railroads, especially the Western and Atlantic; energy to power the Atlanta Rolling Mill, the city's largest postbellum employer, and other developing industries; and after being coked in the Dade Coal Company's ovens, stoked Brown's Rising Fawn pig-iron furnace in Dade County, as well as the Chattanooga Iron Company's furnace across the river in Tennessee.[12]

The ceiling on coal production in Georgia was primarily a result of the limited nature of the state's mineral deposits. Yet the very fact that the capitalist entrepreneurs who attempted to develop the industry there never abandoned a nearly complete reliance on forced labor effectively demonstrates the contradictions of this labor form in isolation. Limited productivity and the dangers of a capitalized labor force in an era of economic uncertainty inhibited the development of Georgia's coal and iron industry. The convict mines of Tennessee and Alabama helped the most powerful coal companies in those states weather the depression of the 1890s; but in Georgia the unfortunate Dade Coal Company went into receivership, in large measure because of its overreliance on convicts.

Where the tail end of the Appalachian chain cuts through the northwest corner of Georgia lie two isolated, rural counties, Dade and Walker. Known in the nineteenth century as the "independent state of Dade," even today, while little over seventy-five miles from Atlanta, and only twenty-five miles from Chattanooga, this sparsely populated area has remained relatively immune to the modernizing forces of the New South. Cut by a series of parallel ridges, the countryside alternates between long narrow valleys and the broad vistas visible from the flat tops of Lookout and Sand mountains. To the side of the mountain roads the traveler can still find the tailings from coal and iron mines, a few abandoned shafts, the concrete flume of a coal washer, and the beehive-shaped ovens which prepared coke for the blast furnaces of Rising Fawn and Chattanooga.[13] Ironically, the antebellum labor relations of this region that would boast the largest concentrations of convict labor after the war, were atypical. Dade County, future site of the Dade Coal Company, had the lowest concentration of slaves in Georgia in 1860, with only 297 bondspeople in a population of 3,000. Only forty-nine slaveholders resided in the county. This upcountry county had no plantations, of course. Zachary Gordon, an absentee slaveholder, owned the largest number of slaves in Dade County – thirty-two. Described as "the operator of coal mines in northwest Georgia," Gordon also owned the "Gordon Cole [*sic*] Bank," evidently worked by his slaves in 1860, but left abandoned by 1870. These were the mines resurrected by Joseph E. Brown and his business partners with convict labor in the 1870s and 1880s.[14]

More significant than prewar coal mining in northwest Georgia was the development of small-scale pig iron furnaces, which in this early period relied for fuel on charcoal rather than bituminous coal and coke. On the eve of the Civil War, furnaces in this region employed over six hundred "operators and laborers," five hundred of whom were free whites, but came to rely increasingly on slave labor during the conflict. Mark A. Cooper – one of the proponents of convict leasing in 1866 – was one of Georgia's more prominent iron entrepreneurs of this era, and believed wholeheartedly in the possibilities of southern industrialization based on coal and iron ore deposits. Despite some success, however, northern competition, lack of access to rail lines and markets, and reliance on charcoal for fuel made this nascent antebellum industry weak. Military destruction came as the final blow in the 1860s, and "lack of capital for reconstruction and operation of the works, shortage of skilled labour, and a general pessimism about the future of the section" hampered immediate postwar recovery.[15]

But even Redemption, and its ostensible hostility to industrial progress, did nothing to dampen the persistence of the enthusiastic promoters of development of this region. To the contrary, shortly after taking office in 1872, Democratic governor James M. Smith received a letter from a geologist at the Georgia Polytechnic Institute, heaping lavish praise on the mineral resources of north Georgia, and encouraging their exploitation. The geologist William G. Atkinson envisioned all the classic indicators of economic growth flowing from the "exhaustless [*sic*] supply of coal which in Dade and Walker counties awaits the attention of leading men." Industrialization would follow the European and northern pattern, he believed. Development of the region would, he suggested, "throw into Georgia millions of dollars" and "also rapidly double her population, by the opening of portals to the European immigration tide." Moreover, "the effect of this outpouring flood of fuel supply, and its lifegiving impetus to the manufactures of all kinds" was illustrated by "the examples of England and Prussia – and, nearer by, Pennsylvania, New York, and Ohio."[16]

The earliest postwar systematic survey of the state's mineral resources followed soon thereafter, carried out by state geologist George Little. Little emphasized the need for awareness among Georgia's citizens and urged local initiatives for development, since "wealthy [northern] speculators already are buying up mineral lands at *agrarian* prices." An investor from Baltimore, for instance, had recently purchased mineral lands that promised to yield $60,000 annually for a mere $400. Yet he also lamented the fact that he found "poor men" searching for fuel in the region's coal banks, and stressed the need to supplant independent diggers with locally based integrated firms committed to full exploitation of the rich coal and contiguous iron deposits of Lookout Mountain, which "afford the greatest abundance of ore for iron furnaces."[17]

One such firm, founded by a Georgian who Atkinson and Little surely would have considered a "leading man," was already in existence in 1874, and in fact supplied "a large portion of the fuel of [Atlanta]."[18] This was the Dade Coal Company, and its allied corporation, the Georgia Iron and Coal Company, both chartered by the newly "redeemed" state legislature in February 1873, with tax-exempt status.[19] By 1889 these companies formed the nucleus of a large trust, the Georgia Mining, Manufacturing and Investment Company, organized to preserve the charters of six separate corporations. The closely guarded charters were "very valuable and could not ... be duplicated in the State of Georgia" after the 1877 Constitution, which put an end to legislative corporate charters for mining or manufacturing companies.[20]

Together the six companies of the trust formed an interlocking complex of coal mines, coke ovens, iron-ore pits, railheads, and iron furnaces, all under the direction of Joseph E. Brown and his son Julius. Northern capital, supplied by Jacob Seaver of Boston, was instrumental in the development of this conglomeration, and the corporation's general manager, J.W. Hoffman, lived in Philadelphia. Coal and coke were produced by the Dade Coal Company and the Castle Rock Coal Company, which together held 18,000 acres of prime land on Lookout Mountain, worked 346 coke ovens, and by 1889 shipped nearly 150,000 tons of coke and coal. The Georgia Iron and Coal Company and the Bartow Iron and Manganese Company worked 17,000 acres of land with "some of the most valuable brown hematite ore" in fifteen ore banks in northwest Georgia, and shipped 44,080 tons of iron in the same year. Much of this ore, and all of the coke from the company's ovens, was used in the iron furnaces of the Walker Iron and Coal

Company, in Rising Fawn, Georgia, and by the Chattanooga Iron Company just over the border in Tennessee, together turning out over 44,000 tons of pig iron in 1889. Both of these pig-iron production facilities were also part of the Browns' industrial fiefdom. Because of these companies, by the mid 1880s Georgia ranked sixth in the nation in coke production. From 1 May to 30 September 1889, these six companies made a profit of $49,201.13; in November 1889 alone, the return was $9,146.59. The stockholders anticipated further expansion, given that the Georgia Mining, Manufacturing and Investment Company boasted $5 million in authorized capital, $1 million of which had already been paid in.[21]

Shortly thereafter, in 1891 and 1892, a rival firm sprang up on the other side of Lookout Mountain, in adjoining Walker County. This was the Durham Coal and Coke Company, owned by James W. English, former mayor of Atlanta and president of the Chattahoochee Brick Company, the city's largest brickyard, which was worked by a large force of convicts and was "a potent factor in [Atlanta's] prosperity." "Captain" English, with no roots in the antebellum elite, was one of the prominent New South capitalists who believed "that the future progress and prosperity of the South, especially of Georgia, depends to a great extent on manufacturing." With the advent of the Durham mines, and their subsidiary coke ovens in the valley at Chickamauga, coal production in Georgia increased from 215,000 tons in 1892 to 373,000 tons by 1893.[22]

The elements of industrial progress in this corner of the New South appear typical of postbellum capitalist development in the region: the initial penetration of rail lines; a combination of local political power with outside capital; legislative corporate charter; vertical and horizontal integration; diversified investment; and the link between rural extractive industry and burgeoning urban growth, whose manufacturers, in the case of Atlanta, benefited from access to a cheap fuel supply.[23] But Brown and his partners, and their competitors in the Georgia coal fields, departed from the capitalist model of economic development in one important respect. Rather than rely on in-migration to a remote corner of the Georgia mountains, or the begrudging labor of dispossessed tenant farmers, both the Dade Coal Company and the Durham Coal and Coke Company used the state's penal system to recruit and retain the essential component of their labor force.

Like Joseph Brown, James English had many financial and industrial interests, including a piece of the three penitentiary "companies" that served as a conduit from the courts to the states' railroad and turpentine camps, brickyards, and of course, coal mines. Between them, by 1894, the two coal mining companies in Georgia controlled 970 of the

state's convicts, with 840 working the mines and 130 more in subsidiary
iron-ore and pig-iron production. This was 45 per cent of all the convicts
leased by the state, and the 550 convicts in the Dade coal mines was
by far the largest concentration of bound laborers in Georgia at the
time.[24]

Convict leasing in the New South is commonly regarded as a continuity of or replacement for slavery.[25] Yet this form of penal labor
developed under conditions specific to the birth of southern industrial
capitalism, and was accompanied more by flexibility and contradiction
than a fully developed world-view compatible with a specific mode of
production. The persistent racial assumptions borne by a slave society
accommodated the use of the postbellum penal system to recruit and
exploit black labor, it is true. Unlike antebellum slaveholders, however,
postwar beneficiaries of the convict lease had no "way of life" bound
up with dependence on convicts, no *particular* commitment to forced
labor, other than that of the capitalist's balance sheet of investment,
production and profit. For the lessee the convicts were merely "machines
for whose rental a certain price is paid." Thus Brown and his partners
were content to use free or bound labor to suit different purposes in
the production process, and to respond to varying economic conditions,
fluctuations in the labor market, tractability of their hired labor force,
and structural imperatives. When incorporated in 1889, for instance,
the Bartow Iron and Manganese Company was explicitly authorized
"to employ convict or free labor to do its work," and such flexibility
was characteristic of initial efforts to employ labor in the area's coal
and iron industry.[26]

Once they raised capital and obtained legislative charters, Brown
and his partners faced the task of recruiting a labor force. In the 1870s
northwest Georgia was an unpromising region from which to draw a
large proletarianized workforce. Out of a population of 3,080 in Dade
County in 1870 there were only 496 males aged 18 to 45. Most of the
small African-American population worked as farm laborers, though
there were 23 black railroad workers in the county (15 of them from
other states). As for whites, there were 29 railroad hands and only 6
men listed as miners in 1870. The county had only a handful of residents
engaged in "manufacturing" at all, mostly in small enterprises such as
flour mills and blacksmith shops. Indeed, in 1870, the entire state of
Georgia had only 8 iron furnace workers and 192 miners who dug
gold, marble, slate and granite.[27] Moreover, unlike the Piedmont
counties to the southeast, Dade's agricultural population remained relatively insulated from the spread of the cotton economy and the accompanying increase in tenancy that prised so many southerners from the

land and drove them to mine and mill in the latter part of the nineteenth century. Even by 1890, 62 per cent of Dade County's farms were
still cultivated by owners rather than tenants (the state-wide average
was 46 per cent), and a negligible number of acres in Dade were planted
in cotton.[28]

Nevertheless, the turn to convict labor was not merely a response to
labor unavailability. Although the districts surrounding Brown's Cole
[Coal] City mines in 1880 had only twenty-four free workers employed
at the mines, elsewhere in the county the Dade Coal Company did rely
on free labor – for the time being. The furnace and ore mines at Rising
Fawn employed about 260 men. Of the over two hundred free men
who worked at the furnace, 172 were black, many of them born in
Virginia, the heart of the antebellum iron industry.[29]

Indeed, the Rising Fawn division of the Dade coal and iron complex
provides an interesting illustration of the interpenetration of free and
forced labor. Erected initially in 1874 by "New York capitalists," the
furnace went into receivership within two years, despite its proximity to
a major rail line and deposits of limestone, ore and coal. Apparently
the company had trouble procuring an adequate supply of coal and
coke for fuel (perhaps because Joseph Brown withheld it, since he
bought them out in 1876).[30] This early effort at pig-iron production
relied on free labor, much to the company's misfortune, since when the
furnace shut down in 1876, 136 workers filed liens for back pay worth
over $8,000.[31]

Upon taking over the company, Brown and his Tennessee partner
James C. Warner (who was also connected with TCI) continued to use
free labor, both in the adjacent ore mines and at the furnace itself,
where the majority of workers were black. A steady supply of fuel was
no longer an obstacle to production, of course, since coal from Brown's
convict mines six miles up the rail line was readily available. But in
1884 Brown acquired seventy-five extra convicts, and rather than placing
them in the coal mines he replaced the free workers at the Rising Fawn
iron-ore mines. Having received only a few days notice of this event,
the workers at the mines "have taken bitter exception and are in a state
of excited discontent," reported the Atlanta Constitution. "Some ... are
said to be counseling resistance by force to the work of supplanting
them with felons," but nothing came of it.[32]

But of course only a portion of the workforce was "supplanted by
felons," since free labor continued to do the generally more skilled
work of operating the blast furnace, while the company confined
convicts to mining the raw material, "work[ing] underground in exca-
vations blasted out through rock and slate." "We run the furnaces on

free labor entirely, except when they won't work," claimed J.R. Brock, superintendent of the Rising Fawn works. This circumstance, however, was not infrequent; "sometimes at pay-day [the free workers] won't come out at all," complained Brock, and convicts had to fill in to keep the furnaces running.[33]

Certainly the substitution of convicts for free workers was controversial, but lessees frequently deflected criticism of convict labor by appeals to a clever conflation of race and skill level. James English, owner of the Durham mines, claimed that he was "opposed to convict labor being worked in competition with skilled white labor," and used his convicts only in the turpentine, mining, and brick industries and "similar work that a white man cannot and will not perform." The lease, which concentrated prisoners in these industries, was touted by whites as the best penal system available, because it was "adapted" to the prison population in Georgia — "ninety per cent of them being common negro laborers."[34]

Black critics of the lease, however, were well aware that "black laborers are continually displaced in such industries as brick-making, mining, road-building etc." A meeting of the Conference of Colored Men of Georgia declared it "a crime to have chain gang labor compete with and throw out of work the honest citizens of the state." Unfortunately, "the desire to make the labor of criminals pay" meant ignoring competition with free labor "unless the free laborers are white and have a vote." Interestingly, the one southern industry in which convicts were almost never worked was textiles; not only would this entail competition with free white labor, but on the occasions when free and convict labor were worked in tandem black men would be placed in proximity with white women, an absolute taboo.[35]

Coal mining, on the other hand, was an industry with both a high skill level and an ambiguous racial designation. As blacks began to supplant whites in the southern mines, often as strikebreakers or convicts, the dignity of such labor was correspondingly devalued. Thus the *Tradesman* of Chattanooga could argue in 1894 (the year of the widespread bituminous coal strike) that "coal mining is coarse and brutalizing work for a white man to do. [But] it is an employment that rather raises the dignity of negro labor, than lowers it." By this logic prison labor in the mines could even be elevated to the realm of reform and rehabilitation, as it occasionally was. "A large proportion of [convicts] are persons who have never formed habits of industry," complained the principal keeper. Thus, it was "wise to provide systematic labor for convicts.... Regular labor for the convicts ... tends, at least, to the formation of habits that may materially aid them at their release."

Once mining was defined as "negro work" and thus lost its ideological status as "skilled" labor, convict competition with free labor in the mining industry vanished as a social concern (except, of course, among the miners themselves). Thus the Georgia prison commission could remark that, while in the North convicts competed directly with skilled workers, in the South "their competition is entirely with unskilled labor, which can succeed as well at one pursuit as at another." Furthermore, the supposed shortage of labor in the South lessened the problem of competition with free labor. "So great is the demand for common labor in such industries as the convicts are engaged in and the laborers so scarce, that no one has ever been known to go unemployed because of such competition," rationalized the prison commission.[36]

Despite the willingness to use free labor in some aspects of production, from the beginning the acquisition of convict labor and development of Georgia's coalfield were closely intertwined. The coal at the Durham mines was coked below the mountain, at Chickamauga, and James English relied on a convict force – most likely transferred from one of his railroad projects in the area – to run a rail up the mountain in 1891 to connect the ovens and the mines, before he worked the prisoners in the mine.[37] For his part, Joseph Brown was quite explicit about his labor needs when he bid for convicts in 1874. He informed the governor that he was willing to pay $10 per convict per year for "a fair average lot." On the other hand, if the Dade Coal Company was permitted to "select such as are the best adapted to the purposes for which they are leased," he was willing to pay $26 a head. His bid stated that the company "desire[d] the convicts to be used as miners, in its coal mine ... and as railroad track hands, and as laborers, in dumping coal, running coke ovens, and other matters connected with the mining and shipment of coal," including building iron furnaces in which to smelt pig iron.[38]

"The best adapted" prisoners for the mines and coke ovens apparently were those with the longest sentences. If one of the problems with free labor was, in the words of the principal keeper, that it was "constantly changing employment and becomes skilled in none," it would be foolish to reproduce this turnover problem by working short-term convicts in the mines. Historically, under systems of penal labor, "valuable workers whose maintenance and training involved considerable expense must be retained as long as possible," and Georgia was known for its lengthy prison sentences.[39] Lessees with heavy permanent capital investments, such as coal and iron mines, prized long-term convicts, despite the discipline problems these prisoners might entail. By law, in the lease authorized in 1876 all convicts sentenced to over five years were automatically destined for the Dade Coal Company. And when the Dade mines received part of their quota of long-term convicts from a camp on the Marietta and North Georgia Railroad, the railroad contractor complained bitterly that these experienced workers were replaced by "feeble and sickly short-term convicts, unable to do any real service, and which were a burden."[40]

Of course the result was an ever-increasing number of long-term or life-sentence prisoners in the mines, since each year these convicts were sentenced but rarely discharged. Thus by 1882, 56 of the 315 convicts held by the Dade Coal Company had been sentenced for life, and an additional 186 were condemned to work for the company for ten years or more. Of the lifetime labor force all but 6 of the 56 were black; 28 had been convicted of murder, 11 of arson, 3 of burglary or robbery, and 3 of bestiality. Another 11, all black, were sent to the mines for life for "rioting" in Dodge County. Interestingly, 38 of these convicts sent to labor in the mountains were from plantation-belt counties, where they had most likely been agricultural workers. The state also claimed to have an interest in sending these convicts to the mines. As the mine superintendent pointed out, "the worst criminals in the state went to his mines, on account of the convenience of the mines to protect them and keep them there." And certainly, since these convicts worked underground, escape was less likely than in railroad camps or in the turpentine woods, where work was out in the open. "The men labor during the day one-quarter mile under the ground," noted the principal keeper assuredly. "In the evening they come out on the chain, and are guarded into their quarters, which cuts off every avenue of escape."[41]

But as with most advantages of convict leasing, the use of long-term convicts carried with it a less desirable result. The danger posed by this labor force was frequently cited as the reason for the need for strict discipline in the mines. "At these camps are a large per cent of the long term and most desperate criminals who require strict government to keep them under subjection," the assistant principal keeper reported to the governor in 1886.[42] Yet, while this was undoubtedly true, it is worth noting that of the 186 convicts with sentences of ten years or more, 86 were guilty of burglary, and 20 had been convicted of other property crimes, such as larceny, horse stealing, or forgery. Of these, 34 were from the plantation belt (33 of them black), and 35 came from urban counties such as Fulton (Atlanta), Richmond (Augusta), and Chatham (Savannah), all of them black. African-American convicts always far outnumbered whites in the coal mines; in 1880, for instance, of the 371 convicts at the Dade mines, 340 were black. African-Americans sent to work in the mines from the growing cities or the tightly controlled plantation belt, for lengthy terms for property crimes, exemplified the lease's simultaneous function as a mechanism of labor recruitment and social control of the black race.[43]

Whatever they were sentenced for, long-term or permanent convicts were desirable because, as in Alabama and Tennessee, the elimination of the problem of turnover and labor uncertainty at the source of raw materials proved most seductive for Georgia's lessees. Given all the other impediments to southern industrialization, the ability to command a large stable labor force at a price negotiated with the state gave capitalists a powerful incentive to lease convicts. Even Joseph Brown's northern investor almost immediately discovered the benefits of having a fixed labor force, at low cost, at the company's disposal. A few months after Brown had successfully obtained convicts from the state in the lease of 1874, Jacob Seaver complained that the company had already invested too much capital in the mines without adequate return, due to the low prices commanded by pig iron. He suggested that they "stop and wait untill [sic] we could realize something for our outlay ... [and] reduce our expenses to its lowest possible limits." When demand picked up again Seaver believed the firm ready to produce three hundred tons of coal daily, "without incurring much extra expense with the convict labor."[44] This particular strategy would return to haunt the company during the depression of the 1890s, however, when they could no longer command a satisfactory price for their coal and iron, but were unable to discharge their large convict labor force.

Under the Penitentiary Act of 1876, the Dade Coal Company became "Penitentiary Company No. 1," and thus obtained the right – and the obligation – to acquire a proportion of all the state convicts for twenty years (1879–99) for its portion of a fixed cost of $25,000 annually. (Penitentiary Companies 2 and 3, which represented other lessees, would also contribute their share of this fee, in proportion to the number of convicts they held.) Under this unusual arrangement, as long as business was good it was in the company's interest to increase the number of convicts it held, since they paid a fixed cost for the lease, not for convicts per capita. By 1896, the principal keeper estimated that the Dade Coal Company's lease expenditure for six hundred convicts had been reduced to only 3 cents a day per convict.[45]

The combination of a fixed cost, negotiated once for the last two decades of the century, and a long-term guarantee of labor that could gain experience, was particularly advantageous in the production of coal and coke that undergirded Georgia's postbellum iron industry. The coal deposits in northwest Georgia were defined by two characteristics: thin and irregular seams, which made mining expensive and unpredictable, and a high carbon content, which made the coal ideal for coking, the key step in the integration of coal mining with efficient pig-iron production.[46] Thus if the coal could be dug cheaply and consistently by convicts, it could then be used to produce coke and pig iron. The combination of soft coal and forced labor in the Georgia mines led to a very high proportion of "slack" coal in the company's output, but this was perfect for stoking coke ovens.[47] Thus Georgia consistently converted a larger percentage of its coal product to coke than other states did; during the 1880s very little of the state's coal went to the open market, but instead served as the basis for vertically integrated iron production. By 1884 two-thirds of all the coal from the Dade mines went directly to the company's three hundred coke ovens three miles down the mountain from the mines. In 1889, when 73 per cent of Georgia's coal was used to make coke, West Virginia, for example, coked only 15 per cent. Even as the market for Georgia's coal increased and broadened this trend continued, so that in 1900, 46 per cent was still used in coke production.[48]

This meant, however, that Georgia's pig-iron industry was extremely dependent upon the convict coal mines if it was to keep up production, and, in turn, that the mines had a restricted market. Essentially other branches of the Georgia Manufacturing and Mining Company "purchased" the Dade Coal Company's coal and coke. Consequently the convicts used to dig coal, stoke coke ovens, and mine iron ore became structurally indispensable to these enterprises, and indeed to Georgia's small but growing industrial infrastructure. Moreover, the labor process had to be constant, so that there would always be enough coal to feed the coke ovens, which would go cold if production halted or slowed. "It requires the working of a certain system to get the coal there and have it there," claimed one manager, and forced labor assured the company of a constant supply. As Julius Brown pointed out, the company's iron was sold by contract in advance, and the production of coal and coke by the convicts was essential to their ability to meet these contracts. The Georgia Mining, Manufacturing Company insisted that "the labor of the convicts has been secured for the operation of its coal and iron properties which ... are so situated that they can be worked with greater advantages by convict than free labor." To lose the convict lease (as they were in danger of doing in the 1890s), they argued, would "suspend the entire operation of all the properties."[49]

Even after the company's assets passed into the hands of another company after the turn of the century, convict labor still lay at the heart of this industrial complex. When pressed, the lessees were quick to argue that they were unable to operate at all without recourse to compulsory labor. "The convicts are employed in the operation of the [Georgia Iron and Coal Company's] iron furnace in Dade County, and of its iron mines in Bartow county, in which places the procurement of free labor is practically impossible," insisted a lessee in a legal petition to retain a group of subleased convicts. Moreover, "the transportation of labor to said points, from other points, is wholly impracticable, owing to the scarcity of labor throughout the entire country," the company claimed. "If the convicts are removed," the petition concluded, "it will cause the shutting down of said operation." "Free labor is exceedingly scarce and difficult to get" even with the help of four labor agents, complained the lessee. "Inasmuch as those portions of properties worked with convicts are operated in conjunction with other portions, and the cessation of work at one place will necessitate cessation of work at other places," leased convicts were the essential component of successful and continuous production in Georgia's coal and iron business.[50]

Convict labor appeared ideal to the lessees not only because of its constancy, but because, unlike free labor, it could be moved around at will like other factors of production, such as capital, technology or managerial expertise. "The lessees interchange their convicts at their convenience, employing a number of them for an indefinite time at other places," remarked the penitentiary physician. When he found in 1892 that the Dade Coal Company "had a much larger number of convicts than [they] could find profitable work for," since the Rising Fawn furnace had been shut for repairs, Julius Brown hired fifty convicts out to the Liberty Brick Company, where "they could be worked at greater profit than they can at the mines" for $100 per annum. Similarly, when J.W. Hoffman discovered the convicts had mined enough iron ore for the Rising Fawn furnace, and that the coal mines were "limited by being shorthanded," he transferred twenty "long-term men" back to the coal mines.[51]

Such flexibility was effective within the confines of the lease system itself, but much to their dismay the Browns discovered it had a limit, one prescribed by their obligation to maintain the convicts for the state even when they had no use for their labor. For the same tightly integrated operation that made forced labor essential to production also left the Dade Coal Company extremely vulnerable to fluctuations in the price of pig iron, which dropped precipitously in the depression of the 1890s. Despite the apparent advantage of flexibility, the structural dependency on forced labor proved a liability in this event.

The initial optimism of the Georgia Mining, Manufacturing Company in 1889 turned out to be unwarranted, for in the six years succeeding its incorporation the Browns' operations posted a loss of

$80,000, and Julius Brown privately complained in 1895 that "times are entirely too hard to go into any enterprises now. I was foolish enough to go into one years ago and have lost heavily by it." The Georgia Mining, Manufacturing Company subsequently went into receivership, was reorganized as the Southern Mining Company, and eventually fell into the hands of Joel Hurt, a real-estate developer in Atlanta, and Joseph Brown's successor as one of the wealthiest entrepreneurs of the Gate City. Hurt renamed the enterprise the Georgia Iron and Coal Company, and continued to use convict labor. Like many other firms in the region, the shaky nature of the Browns' enterprise was exposed by the economic crisis of the last decade of the nineteenth century. But in the final analysis Julius Brown insisted that it was the fixed costs of the convict lease that proved fatal to the company.[52]

Placing the Georgia Mining, Manufacturing Company in receivership in January 1895, the Fulton County Superior Court remarked that "for several years past the [company], owing to the condition of the country, has been operating its works at a heavy loss." The court also noted that the company was "largely in arrears with its [free] laborers, owing them $25,000 and more," and Julius Brown himself complained privately that "the labor will not work until their past debts are paid." "Unless I can provide for labor the whole organization is liable to break up.... There are threats of strikes among the [free] laborers and unless I can satisfy them we cannot conduct operations," he told the court. Keeping the furnaces in blast with his *free* labor was so crucial because the company was "compelled to work the mines in order to work the convicts. We cannot sell coke or coal and are compelled to burn it in order to produce a merchantable product [that is, pig iron]." Privately he informed a potential supplier of emergency funds that, "I must start Rising Fawn furnace," and he wrote his general manager that "if the laborers come to their senses we will start both furnaces [Rising Fawn and Chattanooga], if they do not we will operate one – if they do not do that we will operate none ... [and] simply turn the convicts back to the State and close up the whole business."[53]

The problem for Brown, however, was that as the appointed receiver part of his task was "to provide means for the care and keeping of the convicts" leased to the enterprises held by the Georgia Mining, Manufacturing Company. Thus, in attempting to reorganize the company he desperately wrote to Jacob Seaver in May 1895, pointing out that "we owe the State for nearly all the convict rental last year and the rental due this year ... and the State is pressing us for payment."[54] More damaging still to the company's financial prospects was the fact that during the period of receivership, since they could not be discharged like free labor, and had to be fed, clothed, housed, and cared for, the convict force represented a huge drain on resources. Selling goods to free labor through the company stores yielded a *profit* of 25 per cent for the Georgia Mining, Manufacturing Company; from 24 January 1895 to 30 September 1896 the company earned over $28,000 this way, one of the few areas in which it was in the black, since the overall losses in this same period amounted to $14,500. In contrast, at the convict mine the Dade Coal Company spent $82,552.59 to maintain the captive labor force, including $19,557.97 for guards, $31,660.30 on food, $9,583.62 on clothing, $1,982.62 for medical care, and over $12,000 paid to the state for this privilege. Over this eighteen-month period the Dade Coal division lost $34,000.[55] Such losses were due to the combination of low iron prices, the consequent drop in the demand for coal, decreased output, and the heavy expenses of maintaining a full force of convicts.[56] Brown claimed that he and the other stockholders of the company "sacrificed their own interest to take care of the convicts." He later argued that "if he had not been compelled to care for the convicts, the properties under his control could have been shut down when it was not profitable to operate them."[57]

Of course much of this crisis was brought on by the belief that the company's continued access to forced labor when good times returned was essential for its survival, even if at the time the convicts appeared to be a severe burden. While struggling to remain solvent, when writing to a banker friend for financial help, Brown pleaded "the Legislature will soon be in session and we will have trouble about the convicts" unless the company was effectively reorganized.[58] Indeed, the predictable result of these financial difficulties was that when a legislative committee visited the mines in December 1895 they found the prison camp "in the very worst condition," and complained that "the convicts are actually being starved and have not sufficient clothing." This was clearly due to the company's strained finances, since maintenance of the convicts was one of the few reducible costs. But since production was still necessary, the convicts were treated "with great cruelty" in order to get them to continue to work. The pouring of water into the convicts' nostrils and lungs had replaced whipping as the torture of choice, perhaps because it did not incapacitate the already weakened prisoners for labor; the convicts "could go [back] to work right away" after the water treatment, unlike whipping which made them sore.[59]

The consequence of the legislators' report was a full-blown investigation of the Dade mines ordered by Governor Atkinson in 1896, which resulted in the revocation of the lease, the confiscation of four hundred convicts, and the abolition of the Cole City, Rising Fawn, and Bartow

Iron convict camps. Thus the denouement for the Georgia Mining, Manufacturing Company was bankruptcy *and* loss of its convict lease; nevertheless the organization that supplanted it and took over its holdings, Joel Hurt's Georgia Iron and Coal Company, remained equally committed to forced labor in the mines. In 1902 the Prison Commission was still able to report that the three coal mines in Georgia "employ convict labor only."[60]

The reorganization of Georgia's coal and iron industry coincided with the state's reorganization of the penal system. In 1897 the General Assembly passed an Act authorizing a new convict lease to begin in 1899. This time, however, convicts could not be leased for more than five years, subleasing (the reletting of leased convicts to another company by the original lessee) was permitted, and convicts were to be bid for on a per-capita basis.[61] From the point of view of the lessees and the state this was essentially an economic rationalization of the system, which could allow more flexibility than had the previous twenty-year fixed lease. The lessees no longer would have to pay for convicts they did not need, and could sublease them if the price of coal dropped; the state could increase its revenue from the system with each conviction.

With economic recovery after 1898 came an increase in the price of commodities produced by convicts. This increase, coupled with the opening of the lease to bidding wars and subleases, demonstrated the "value of the [convict] labor under the new law." The 1899 price of $96 per convict per annum (in the coal mines) was soon eclipsed by subleases worth $174, and the lease of 1904 cost lessees $225 for each convict, as free labor became ever more difficult to recruit and retain in a time of prosperity. Capitalists complained bitterly that the "increase in wages makes it possible for [the negro] to earn as good a living as the majority of them want by working two or three days in the week," and thus were willing to pay the high cost of convict labor because of its steadiness.[62]

Examining forced labor from a comparative perspective, Tom Brass has pointed out that the customary defense of coercive labor relations, a "shortage" of freely sold labor, is as much an ideological as a material condition. The notion of a "labor shortage" is "applied by employers not to an absolute unavailability of labour-power ... but to a situation where market forces permit the free workers that do exist to operate as (and reap the benefits from being) a proletariat."[63] Thus the ability of free workers to withhold their labor, to quit, to go on strike, to demand back wages, to change jobs, or to work sporadically conditioned the "necessity" of obtaining convict workers.

Like their rivals in Alabama and Tennessee, Georgia's coal and iron producers initially turned to forced labor because of the "unreliability" of free labor in an already tenuous southern industry. "The [Dade Coal] company has had to get more convicts on account of the scarcity of free labor," noted a local newspaper in 1891. "Then where is there room to complain of hard times when labor is scarce at such liberal wages as that company pays?," the paper continued. But indeed, as Georgia's prison commission itself remarked, when times appeared good for free labor the demand for convicts increased, since "ordinary free labor ... become[s] scarce, high, insufficient and unsatisfactory, necessarily creating a steady increase in the value of convict labor." When wages were high enough, free labor became "unsatisfactory and unreliable, working in no case more than five days in the week, and frequently less." This problem could be particularly acute in the mining industry, concentrated in rural, isolated and mountainous areas with a long tradition of self-sufficiency and labor independence. "A miner is like a bird. He goes and comes. Here today and somewhere else tomorrow," the doctor at the Durham mines claimed.[64]

It was this very demand for steady labor that increased the value of forced labor in boom times; indeed when the price of convict labor was high, as it became in Georgia by the turn of the century, "no advantage accrue[d] to the contractor employing such labor, except that his supply is more constant and reliable." Despite its cost, this was the moment when a bound labor force appeared most attractive to enterprises frustrated by increasing labor mobility. The obverse, however, was also true. When prices for commodities such as coal, brick, or naval stores slumped, companies begged to be "relieved of their leases."[65] This exposed the key difference between free and forced labor in the unstable southern economy: free labor could be dismissed at will, but the fixed nature of forced labor was a potentially disastrous overhead cost for the lessees, who were obligated by the state to carry the cost of maintaining the prisoners. A lessee's convict camp was, after all, a branch of the state penitentiary. But this contradiction also suggests a significant rationale for forced industrial labor in the New South; whatever obstacles to labor mobility remained in agriculture, in the industrial sector the southern labor market threatened to operate freely. From the vantage point of the struggling southern capitalist this was precisely the problem, and convict labor was the solution.

By making convict labor more responsive to economic conditions and fluctuations in the free labor market, the changes instituted in Georgia's convict lease in 1897 may have served to lessen the tension between the lessees' obligation to serve the state as a penitentiary and their desire to do business. But the result was exacerbation of the other great contradiction of the convict lease, that between penal function and labor exploitation. Even as the risks of reliance on bound labor were reduced, the expense of obtaining forced labor approached the cost of free labor. This consequently increased the lessees' desire to extract a maximum amount of labor from the prisoners, inevitably leading to resistance and even state intervention on the convicts' behalf. For the state, the lessee, and the prisoner alike this conflict had always shaped daily life in Joe Brown's mines, and on occasion escalated to full confrontation.

"Goin' to Take My Time":
Convict Resistance, Punishment
and the Task System

The captain holler hurry,
Goin' to take my time.
Say captain holler hurry,
Goin' to take my time.
Say he makin' money,
And I'm trying to make time.
Say he can lose his job,
But I can't lose mine.
                    Convict work song[1]

In Atlanta in mid July 1886, the talk of the black community was the
mutiny of the convicts who worked at Joe Brown's Dade County coal
mines and coke ovens. On 12 July, 109 prisoners refused to go to work
and barricaded themselves inside their quarters. The convicts insisted
that they would not return to work until the "squad boss" who supervised their labor and meted out punishment was dismissed, until the
quality of their food was improved, and until corporal punishment was
abolished at the camp. The principal keeper of the penitentiary, John
Towers, quickly traveled from Atlanta to isolated Dade County, where
he was informed by the strike leaders that those three demands had to
be met, or they "would have to be brought out dead." Towers reportedly
replied to the rebellious convicts: "then you will be brought out dead."

In fact, Towers did wire Governor McDaniel that he feared it would
be necessary to "shoot three or four [convicts] before they surrender."
The governor suggested that Atlanta's militia, the Gate City Guard,
could be sent to quell the mutiny. But he and the principal keeper
decided it would be best to starve out the convicts. The prisoners had
hoarded rations so that they could maintain their premeditated strike,

but by the morning of the third day Towers believed that half of them were willing to capitulate and leave the stockade. By late afternoon on 14 July he was able to telegram to Atlanta that the "mutiny [is] over [we] are taking them out as fast as irons can be put on ... glad we did not have to kill any."[2]

Later, in his annual report for 1886, Towers suggested that the "mutiny" had been "under the control of a few leaders" who threatened to kill any convicts who went back to work. He did note, however, that the convicts referred to their action as a strike, and "alleged several causes in justification of it." But in his report the principal keeper remained adamant that "there was no good reason at all for the mutiny," and even hinted darkly that there was "some outside instigation." Yet the legislative committee that visited the Dade County convict camps that December found that the convicts had several justified complaints about the vicious and arbitrary behavior of their "whipping boss," Killpatrick. In fact, the committee recommended to the governor that he replace Killpatrick. This, of course, had been the principal demand made by the striking prisoners six months earlier.[3]

In many ways this incident differed little from most industrial conflicts of the late nineteenth century in the defiant nature of the workforce, the potential for violence, and the intervention of the state on the side of capital. But the revolt of these convicts also illustrates some of the more significant features of the industrial convict labor system of the New South. On the one hand, it appears that the company had a great deal of latitude in coercing its bound labor force. There was a legal basis for punishing those workers who did not meet the pace of work, a pace set by the imperatives of the lessee and sometimes backed up by state power. On the other hand, extraction of labor from the prisoners had limits imposed by the convicts themselves, and even by the state, which played the contradictory role of final enforcer of discipline and yet ultimate protector of the convicts' welfare.

These tensions became most evident on the rare occasions of outright concerted convict mutiny against the lease system. Indeed, at least four "convict revolts" occurred in Georgia between 1886 and 1892, though the one in 1886 most resembles a strike. There were rumors of a strike, and then an actual mutiny, in December 1886 and January 1887 at the Rising Fawn furnace in Dade County; a mass escape attempt at the Dade Coal mines in June 1891; and a revolt of convicts at the Walker County coal mines in April 1892.[4] But an examination of the daily work experience of convicts in Georgia's coal and iron complex also reveals constant conflict over the level of exploitation of prison labor, a day-to-day struggle inherent in the structure of the work and

the penal system. At the "point of production" this conflict was embedded in the task system of labor which prevailed in the convict mines;
and in the penal system itself, at issue was who regulated the pace of
convict work, the state or the lessee.

As we have seen, Georgia's coal and iron industry turned to forced
labor because "unreliable" free labor made this factor of production
too uncertain. But, given the structure of the coal industry in the "hand-
loading era" of mine operations, the difficulties of maintaining a consistent, well-trained labor force were compounded by management's
inability to exercise control over the labor process itself. In the 1880s
and 1890s, as the market for bituminous coal expanded and competition
stiffened, mine operators attempted simultaneously to reduce costs and
boost production. But because the prevailing form of wage payment in
the coal industry was based on unsupervised piece-work – compensation by the ton mined – the notorious "miner's freedom" hewed from
this system severely constrained management's ability to gain the upper
hand in the struggle for control over production. Mine labor at the coal
"face" took place far from the eyes of management, in underground
"rooms" connected to a central mine shaft which ran into the hillside.
The free coal miner operated essentially as an independent artisan who
worked his "room" by cutting the coal, blasting it loose, and loading it
into a car which he pushed to the main shaft so that it could be hauled
to the surface. Each miner attached a numbered identification tag to
his cars so his tonnage could be counted, and he was paid for the
number of one-ton cars he sent out of the mine. In addition a miner
was responsible for so-called "dead work" – clearing debris, timbering
the rooms to prevent cave-ins, and laying the track that took the loaded
cars from face to mine head. "The principal characteristic of the hand-
loading era," contends one of its most astute scholars, "is that management did not directly control the pace of production."[5]
    Because of the lack of managerial supervision of labor, the tonnage
system was the only way to regulate the pace of production; but the
advantage in this case frequently fell to the miner, who insisted on his
right to leave the mine when he felt he had dug enough coal for the day.
By the late nineteenth century, the miner's retention of this customary
right became increasingly "incompatible with the managerial need to
plan, to coordinate, and to control the labor process for maximum
profits."[6] But if management could not directly control the pace of labor,
there were other weapons available in the attempt to discipline the labor
force. The flip side of a piece rate, of course, is management's ability to
manipulate the pay rate in order to increase production. In addition to

cutting the price paid per ton, mine owners extorted profit from their employees by cheating them on the weighing of the coal, and by forcing them to purchase supplies, food and shelter from the company at inflated prices. These methods frequently resulted in bloody and prolonged strikes, and sometimes in the replacement of free miners by convicts.[7]

Convict mine operators, however, found a novel way not only to subvert the miner's control embedded in the tonnage system, but to turn it to their advantage. With free labor, a wage relation based on a piece-price system allowed miners to contend for control over production. But convict labor transformed the work into a task system that could apparently push labor extraction to its utmost limits, precipitating a different kind of struggle. The fixed nature of his labor force allowed the lessee to bypass the obstacles of labor recruitment, retention and negotiation, but this was a double-edged sword. Without the incentive of wages, or the threat of dismissal, convicts had no internally compelling reason to work at all, and their main object was to avoid labor as much as possible.[8] In the absence of a free market in labor, a wage relation, or even a patina of paternalism, the extraction of industrial forced labor in the postbellum period thus took on a special character, mediated by the task system. Convicts were commanded to produce a predetermined quantity of coal each day, or suffer corporal punishment.

The task system that prevailed in convict mines had more in common with its predecessor under slavery than it did with the piece-price system that frequently represented the entering wedge of capitalist labor relations in a free labor society. Antebellum task work did much to shape the slave labor regime in certain agricultural sectors where it was appropriate, particularly rice culture on the Carolina and Georgia coasts. The relative absence of supervision this form of labor entailed may have permitted some slaves to carve out a uniquely autonomous sphere for themselves, allowing them to define the pace of work and the allocation of tasks, to profit from paid overwork, and even to obtain property.[9] The benefits of the task system were also supposedly prevalent in industrial slavery, where slave ironworkers could earn pay for work they did beyond the task; "the pervasiveness of the 'task system' with its built-in provision for cash bonuses emerges in retrospect as the distinguishing feature of black labor organization outside the agricultural realm," one historian has claimed. Yet the most thorough study of industrial slavery rejects the notion that task labor increased the slave's ability to control his own labor; instead, it is seen as one of the driving mechanisms of labor exploitation.[10] Within a society that denied blacks ownership of their own labor power, perhaps task work allowed slaves to recoup some of their expropriated labor; but in a post-emancipation society supposedly committed to the sanctity of free labor relations, when wedded to the convict lease the task system became the ultimate form of labor extraction that capitalists sought and failed to obtain from free workers.

Task work also had a penal rationale. When Cecil Rhodes began using convicts in the DeBeers diamond mines in South Africa during the 1880s they labored only on surface workings, "since only there could complete surveillance be enforced."[11] This was in marked contrast to labor in Georgia's coal mines where no real surveillance or supervision of the convicts was possible, which made for a rather unique penal system to say the least. "We were absolutely taken away from the guards when we entered the mines," testified one convict.[12] Thus the task system was more than an instrument of labor extraction, but also the primary means to enforce the punishment of hard labor itself. Not meeting the task would result in a whipping, and to meet the task required steady work throughout the day.[13] "No punishment shall be administered to a convict," proclaimed the Georgia Prison Commission, "except in cases where it is reasonably necessary to enforce discipline or *compel work or labor by the convicts*."[14] This subordination of all penal functions to the single goal of labor extraction gave convict leasing its unique character as a particularly brutal penal system.

The task system of labor exploitation that prevailed in the coal mines made labor and punishment dependent on one another. The lessee had made an investment in his labor force, and his sole interest lay in maximizing the profit from that investment. Of course, as defenders of the lease pointed out, it was also supposedly in the lessee's interest not to overwork his fixed labor force. Convict labor did amount to slavery, one defender conceded, but "[the lessee's] interest leads him to make the most of it.... Thus the sensible proprietor would serve his own interest by not overtaxing his labor," just as capitalists paternalistically looked out for their free labor, obviating the need for an eight-hour day. "A convict, like a mule, must be fed if you expect paying results from his labor," noted an inspector of convict camps.[15] These proscriptions were often honored in the breach.

Georgia's black community had no doubt about the accompanying racial ideology that informed the decision to lease convicts. Because of the legacy of slavery, "the black workman existed for the comfort and profit of white people.... Consequently, for a lessee to work convicts for his profit was a most natural thing," noted a participant in a conference on "negro crime" at Atlanta University in 1904. This view of labor dovetailed with a penal ideology, since "these convicts were to be punished, and the slave theory of punishment was pain and intimidation."[16]

Ironically, in Georgia the task system initially developed as a concession to the convicts working in Joseph Brown's mines. After the convicts complained about the rigor of labor in the mines in 1874, tasks were instituted and rewards tendered for work done beyond the set task.[17] This opportunity for the convict to cross, from one hour to the next, the threshold from uncompensated slave to wage worker might be regarded as one of the few benefits prisoners might reap from the system. One convict in the Alabama mines, for instance, claimed that he could finish his five-ton task by nine in the morning, and then "cut five or six tons for myself at 40 cents a ton."[18] Even at this unlikely Stakhanovite pace, however, this convict would receive only $2 for ten tons of coal; the equivalent amount of pay for free labor, at 60 cents a ton, would be $6. Moreover, at least in Georgia's mines, convicts received their pay in scrip, redeemable only at the prison commissary. As in industrial slavery, cash incentives beyond the task "were not a step towards emancipation, but rather a technique ... of control."[19]

Like piece-work payments for free labor, the convict's task could be adjusted. "If they found a man could dig a task and get through with it by three or four o'clock in the evening they would increase it, and fix it so that he couldn't get out at that time," one ex-convict testified.[20] And what the company could provide the company could take away. Frustrated with the low productivity of the convicts at the Dade mines in 1893, Julius Brown reported to the stockholders that "I have not been able to get as satisfactory work out of this division of the property as I had hoped.... I have ordered payments of extra compensation for convicts entirely shut off ... we [are] not running a summer resort hotel for criminals."[21]

Historians of slave labor have made a strong case for the impact the organization of task work had on slave life and culture in the Lowcountry. And certainly the "miner's freedom" embodied in tonnage payments was one of the most significant factors shaping the lives of free coal miners, before mechanization restructured their work. So, too, were the actual conditions of convict life shaped by the necessity of making their "task." Yet, while there may be much to say for the relative autonomy antebellum slaves could exercise in the time they preserved beyond their task, when they finished digging coal for the company convict miners were briefly transmuted into proletarians (if they chose to remain at work) or idle prisoners (if they returned to the stockade), not independent peasants, artisans or property owners. Perhaps "overwork" compensation allowed convicts to purchase extra tobacco, and it certainly stoked the gambling that constituted one of their few available leisure-time pursuits. But, as workers, the main motivation "to get out the daily amount of coal [was] to save them from the punishment to be inflicted by the whipping boss."[22]

When convicts arrived at the Dade Coal mines, the "boss" greeted them and introduced them to their work with these words: "Now boys, I don't want to have to punish you. I want you to get your task done. If you get your task done everything will be all right. I want to get along all right and I want to treat you boys right, and if you get your task done, we will never have any trouble."[23] The ease or difficulty with which this could be accomplished was a common point of scrutiny in the routine grand-jury and legislative investigations of the convict camps that passed for oversight of the lease system.[24] Evaluations of the labor regimen varied wildly from year to year, investigation to investigation, and mine to mine. Joseph Brown, not surprisingly, insisted that company officials required only "moderate work" of the convicts in his mines. A special legislative committee that visited Coal City in 1881 noted that "the convicts are worked at tasks in the mines, and are not overworked." And the Dade County Grand Jury in 1897 reported that "we find that the convicts can easily accomplish their daily tasks."[25]

Yet the same grand jury the following year remarked that "some [convicts] complained that their tasks were too heavy, while others said they could complete their tasks in the allotted time." "We think the men are overtasked, owing to the small vein of coal where they work," concluded the grand jury convened in 1901.[26] The legislature as well was not always uncritical of task work. In 1890 the House Penitentiary Committee visited the Dade mines. Notwithstanding the fact that mine superintendents expected their visit, the committee reproached the company for the conditions they found at the convict mines. They took the unusual step of actually going underground "to see the kind of work and the amount required of each man," which they found "an experience never to be forgotten." In order to obtain the set task, "the men [were] working in such places as rendered it necessary for them to lie on their stomachs while at work, often in the mud and water, in bad ventilation." "We condemn in the strongest terms the rule that requires each man to mine a given quantity of coal daily or receive ... punishment," this committee concluded.[27]

Such condemnation went unheeded. Eighteen years later, in the investigations that culminated in the abolition of the lease and convict mining in Georgia, legislators regarded the task system as one of the prime instruments of cruelty under the existing penal system; "the possibilities of the cruel treatment of the convicts in regard [to the task] are limitless," was the overwhelming conclusion of the 1908 investigators.[28] The 1908 committee remarked that at the mines there were "an unusually large number of whippings ... for 'shortage on tasks' and 'slate in coal'." The convicts at the Durham mines "were given very heavy tasks and were punished severely if they failed to get through with the tasks," an ex-convict testified. Noting that a squad of fifty convicts had been transferred from a brickyard, where they had worked quite satisfactorily, to the mines, where they suddenly received frequent whippings for "idleness" and "failure to get tasks," the committee resolved that the labor expected of convict miners must be unreasonable. "Men, even convicts, are not going to 'idle' or fail to get their tasks, week after week, when they know a whipping is certain, if the tasks are fair, reasonable and within their ability," they concluded.[29] Even the whipping boss, who was authorized to punish the convicts, admitted that "there is a great deal of difference in digging coal than in making brick."[30]

Task work for convicts in coal mining was defined by two factors unique to this particular industry. First, the ability of a convict to meet his task depended on a host of factors, over none of which he or the company had much control. "The reasonableness of these tasks depends largely on the size of the vein [of coal], the conditions under which mining is carried on, on the expertness of the particular operator, on the amount of 'propping' to be done [to prevent accidents]," claimed one observer, not to mention the amount of slate in the coal, the distance a miner's "room" might be from the main shaft, and the availability of cars to fill. This habitual uncertainty of the industry was one of the reasons mine operators turned to coerced labor in the first place. But the notorious variability of mine work made fair tasking incompatible with a system of labor based on punishment; the "idea of an arbitrary [that is, fixed] task is preposterous," testified E.D. Brock, warden at Coal City.[31] Yet the second factor of mine work – the impossibility of direct supervision of recalcitrant convicts spread out miles apart underground – made task work an absolute necessity.[32] The determination of the task, and whether it could be "reasonably" obtained, was the main arena of conflict in the mines. Shaped by this question were the conditions of labor and safety; the convicts' attempts to resist forced labor and avoid punishment; and the question of ultimate sovereignty over the convicts and their labor.

Like free miners, convicts worked in rooms off a main shaft, down which ran a track for the coal cars loaded by the prisoners at the coal face. The convict would dig about ten feet under the coal face and then blast the coal loose with shot powder.[33] He would then load a car with the loose coal, being careful (or not so careful) to pick out the worthless slate, and push it back to the main shaft. This work entailed digging coal lying down or on one's knees, due to the thinness of the coal seams (sometimes as narrow as eighteen inches, and rarely thicker than four feet). This work was often done in water, in a dark tunnel six to eight feet wide, illuminated only by the convict's head lamp, which frequently dripped oil in his eyes and overcame him with fumes.[34]

According to the coal operators, several criteria were taken into account in determining a convict's allotted task under these conditions, including the width of the seam in his "room." Tasks were supposedly even "purposely placed lower than they would otherwise have been" to create an incentive for paid overwork.[35] Free miners in southern Appalachia during the "hand-loading era" might produce between four and six tons of coal daily, though even here racism might influence the coal operator's judgement. "A good white miner ... can take about six tons of coal per day," one mine owner told the US Industrial Commission, but blacks were supposedly less willing to increase their output in order to increase their wages. "If he can make 55 cents a ton cutting coal [the black miner] does not care to work more than four days in the week," he claimed. In practice most of the evidence points to a relatively inflexible similar task of four or five tons for convicts, which many prisoners struggled to meet.[36]

After about twelve beatings for the crime of "shortage," a convict's task might be reduced; even so, one ex-prisoner testified, 40 per cent of the convicts in one mine were unable to finish their task by night-fall.[37] Convict miners testified that many of them could not even take the time to eat, for fear that they would fall behind and not make the task in time. Basic hygiene went by the board as well, since keeping their beds, bodies, and clothing clean required the convicts' time, and time was money to the lessees.[38] Above all, as the investigating committee in 1908 pointed out, punishment was inflicted in any case, without much regard for the ability of the convicts to meet the task. Indeed, recent arrivals to the Lookout Mines were always whipped right off, in order to "break them in," much as antebellum slaves had been "seasoned."[39] "Did they whip them much for not working?", one convict was asked during an investigation. "Not much," he replied sardonically. "They did not whip them much for not working, they whipped them for not working as much as they wanted them to."[40] When confronted with evidence of this sort of treatment, one state prison official responded that "a negro can't get along without it." Significantly, the leather strap used to punish convicts for failure to work at the pace set by the company was known colloquially as a "negro regulator."[41]

Mine safety was a frequent casualty of the enforced pace of work. Again, like free miners, in addition to their task convicts had to perform the mine's "dead work," most significantly the timbering of their tunnels and rooms to prevent falls of slate. Prisoners labored in places "where they are liable to be crushed to death at any moment," and accidents in the convict mines occurred frequently. Convicts were killed or badly hurt by the coal cars, by explosions, by pick wounds, and most frequently "mashed by slate," "injured by slate," or "killed by slate fall." Between 1888 and 1894, there were over one hundred injuries in the Dade Mines (where at the time about five hundred prisoners were at work), fifteen of them fatal. This fatality rate of approximately one death per 100,000 tons of coal mined far exceeded the 1896 West Virginia rate of 200,000 tons in bituminous mining, for instance, and it compared unfavorably to what the US Geological Survey later called the "year in which the darkest record was made in the history of the [coal] industry," 1907, when only 145,000 tons were mined for every worker who lost his life.[42]

In the convict mines, a large proportion of the recorded casualties were attributable to cave-ins. Naturally, investigators tended to blame the convicts rather than the lessees for this carnage. The mines were "as safe as well can be," reported the Dade County Grand Jury in 1897. "We find that the accidents that have occurred was [sic] by the carelessness of the convicts themselves," the jurors concluded. One guard at the mines estimated that there was at least one casualty from falling slate each month, but similarly attributed this to convict negligence or incompetent timbering. One of the prison commission members – an ex-slaveowner who admitted he had never entered the mines, and had no idea what a reasonable task might be – blamed the mines' poor safety record on the carelessness of *black* convicts. He falsely claimed that "you never see a white man mashed up" from a slate fall. In truth, however, the relatively few injuries sustained by white convicts were clearly due to their paucity and their assignment to less dangerous work outside of the mines, not their alleged skill as miners.[43]

According to the black convicts themselves, any "carelessness" was dictated by the requirements of labor rather than their alleged racial characteristics. A convict had a certain number of tons to produce on pain of punishment, so "he would not take the time to brace the slate and it fell on him," testified one prisoner. "The men could not take the time to timber [the mine roof] properly or they would not finish their task," another concurred. As a result "men were continually getting their legs [and] arms broken or their body bruised up in some way."[44] The 1908 investigation noted at the Durham Mines "a large percentage of cases in the hospital resulting from accidents in the mines, from falling slate," and linked this explicitly to the pressure to make the task.[45]

Table 6.1   Labor-related Punishment, Cole City Convict Mines, 1901–1904

Month	No. punished	Labor-related (on same day)[a]
October 1901	27	14 (5, 4, 4)
November 1901	52	44 (8, 7, 5)
December 1901	35	28 (7, 7, 4)
January 1902	30	13 (6)
February 1902	26	15 (7,6)
March 1902	31	15 (7,6)
April 1902	10	4 (3)
May 1902	26	9 (4, 3, 2)
June 1902	25	15 (5, 3, 3)
July 1902	17	10 (5, 2, 2)
August 1902	16	13 (6, 5)
September 1902	17	8 (4, 3)
October 1902	30	19 (6, 5, 4)
December 1902	39	15 (4, 4)
January 1903	31	12 (4)
February 1903	32	7
March 1903	36	15 (8)
April 1903	56	36 (5, 5, 3, 3)
May 1903	51	41 (9, 8, 4, 3, 3, 3)
June 1903	53	34 (9, 7, 4, 4)
July 1903	54	39 (15, 9, 6)
August 1903	23	14 (5, 4)
September 1903	43	35 (8, 5, 3)
October 1903	31	21 (5)
November 1903	53	27 (5, 4)
December 1903	28	15 (3)
January 1904	39	18 (6, 4, 3)
February 1904	14	3
March 1904	19	12
Total	944	551

Note: [a] Includes "Idleness," "Short on Task," "Slate" (i.e. loading too much slate with coal), and "Doctor" (i.e. feigning sickness). There were between 100 and 150 convicts at Cole City in this period; see Prison Commission, *Reports*.

Source: Monthly Reports of Convicts Punished ("Whipping Reports"), Vol. 1, Cole [*sic*] City Camp, 1901–1904, Records of the Prison Commission, Records of the Board of Corrections, Georgia Department of Archives and History.

Of course, the convicts were not helpless in the face of this mechanism of labor extraction. As we have seen, there is evidence of sporadic "mutinies" which might on occasion revolve around the prisoners' treatment at the hands of the whipping boss. In another instance, convicts in the Durham mines advocated a strike to protest ventilation and gas problems that were so bad, according to the warden, that "if [the] mine was situated in any of the states where mining laws were enforced it would be immediately closed."[46] Convicts would also knock out timbers on purpose in order to cause a cave-in, so that a day could be taken out from the task to clear a room of debris.[47]

But less drastic methods of "day-to-day" resistance could be adopted. One common method convicts used to cheat the whipping boss was to load slate at the bottom of a car in order to make the task more quickly. This practice was particularly irksome to company officials, since they had trouble selling coal mixed with too much slate. "It injures the class of coal in every respect," lamented one whipping boss.[48] In addition to frequent punishment for "shortage," "idleness," "slate," and other designations referring to resistance to the task, the "whipping reports" also show beatings for "feigning illness." This practice, known among convicts as "betting the doctor," was a popular means of avoiding work altogether and "beating the company out of a day's work."[49] Severe discipline was meted out on a regular basis for these various methods of circumventing the task, as the records kept by the whipping bosses indicate. At the Dade mines, for instance, between 1901 and 1904 fully 58 per cent of the nearly one thousand whippings administered were for such labor-related infractions (the rest were for fighting, gambling, or general "disobedience"). Frequently these violations involved more than one prisoner, suggesting the possibility of collusion, at least on a small scale (see Table 6.1).[50]

The task system was open to manipulation in other ways as well. One convict pointed out that, while he was able to make his task "in a good reasonable place," others fell behind, not least because "a heap of times the men would get behind by loading [coal] for other fellows." This aided convicts less able to keep up with the work, either because of their physical condition or because, as one convict complained, "the boss man ... put me in a place that I couldn't hardly get my task." "If they have [a task] of five cars [i.e. five tons] maybe they might load two or three cars, and some other fellow would load two, and that would make his task," one convict revealed. If tasks were set weekly, as they sometimes were, this sort of mutuality was extended to convicts who had eight to ten cars left to load at the end of the week; but it also appears to have been provided to the mines' "gal boys," or known homosexuals.[51]

In other cases, "some of the men that cannot get the amount of coal required of them are paying other men that get their [own] task [done] to help them," a grand-jury investigation noted. Aid might even be extended to convicts weakened by punishment and thus unable to meet their task. But if the mine boss discovered such collusion, the helper's own task would be increased in order to fill his available time. Another trick the convicts discovered was to switch numbers or car tags, in order to get credit for cars filled by other prisoners, though it is not clear that this practice was always by mutual agreement. Certainly desperation to make the task and avoid punishment led to predatory behavior at times. For instance, when the distance between the coal face and the main shaft was extensive, convicts would pilfer coal from another's car as it rolled past, in order to help make up their own task. In Alabama mines, where "an able-bodied man and a worthless one are worked together as partners," this "buddie" system sometimes led to violence when the weaker member of the pair fell behind on his share of the task.[52]

The ongoing struggle between convicts and their masters over the extraction of labor was overlaid with another conflict, that between the lessees and the state. From the point of view of the state, the lessees bought only the *labor* of the convicts, and in exchange incurred the responsibility of caring for their bodies. Joseph Brown himself acknowledged that convicts were not owned like slaves, and that the lessees only "have a property in the labor of the convicts." The unusual contract relationship among lessee, convict, and state was well-expressed by Georgia's Supreme Court:

> Of course a [leased] convict is not property. He is a human being and the State owes to him the same duty that it would owe to any other human being under the same unfortunate circumstances.... His labor, however, during his term of service, is a property right which may be the basis of a valid contract.

Even criminals "are certainly entitled to something like humane treatment," the House Committee on the Penitentiary concluded, "and it is the duty of the State to see that they receive it."[53]

Four decades of convict leasing in Georgia were punctuated by repeatedly futile attempts by the governor, the principal keeper, the penitentiary physician, the legislature, and various investigating committees to suggest the lessees meet their obligation to maintain humane conditions, "so far as [it] might be consistent with the working of the convicts."[54] The penitentiary physician naively submitted in 1888 that convicts could be "the healthiest class of people in the state" if given a regular diet, regular hours of work, and regular labor. But poor food, inadequate shelter and clothing, overzealous punishment, and above all labor that was too exacting had led to high rates of sickness and mortality, he observed.[55] The state made a constant and fruitless effort to limit the hours of labor for the convicts, and to prohibit labor on Sundays altogether. In 1875, in a notice sent to the lessees, the principal keeper emphasized that the lease contracts restricted labor to ten hours a day; later, hours were "regulated by the length of the day," with forty minutes allowed for meals.[56] Despite these restrictions, the actual labor done during a day was left to the lessee – and ultimately the task – to determine. Completion of the task superseded any working of convicts by the hour; thus did the lessees and their labor supervisors "carry out the custom" of getting all the work they could from the convicts.[57]

Despite the stricture against Sunday labor at the convict camps, there was also plenty of evidence that the lessees persisted in working their prisoners seven days a week.[58] The ostensible reason for this practice in the coal and iron industry was that the coke ovens and iron furnaces could not be allowed to cool down, because returning them to optimum temperature would be costly and time-consuming. In the mines, removing slate and doing other dead work could be done by convicts on Sunday.[59] "In operating all blast furnaces," claimed the superintendent at Rising Fawn, "it is absolutely necessary that as much work should be done on Sunday as on any other day. Some times the company runs short of free labor ..., and then we are forced to put on a few convicts to fill up their places."[60] Despite the objections by grand juries and legislative committees to this work, the president of one iron company insisted that the principal keeper of the penitentiary himself had "granted these irregularities upon the ground that they were necessary to the successful operation of the iron furnaces."[61]

Moreover, as with overwork, convicts were paid (usually in scrip) for their extra work on Sundays, and the lessees claimed they were glad to volunteer for the labor.[62] Some prisoners, however, testified that they were told to do the extra work or incur punishment. One legislative committee discovered that "the convicts claim that if they don't work willingly [on Sunday] for whatever is offered them they are required to work anyhow and receive for their work whatever their employers choose to give them." The investigative committee in 1908 "utterly reject[ed] the belief that there can be much 'volunteering' among convicts. They can hardly be called 'free agents' and there can be such anomaly as an 'unwilling volunteer' in a convict camp," the committee concluded. They felt such extra work should be done by hired free labor.[63] Privately, Julius Brown acknowledged to his stockholders that there was one compelling reason for asking prisoners to 'volunteer' to drain the mines of water on Sundays: "it could be done much cheaper by convicts than by free labor." He claimed that the convicts were glad to do this work, but this was probably because he had just abolished pay for work beyond the task during the week.[64]

When Governor John B. Gordon launched an investigation into the convict camps in 1887, the penitentiary physician who so passionately believed that good treatment would lead to healthy convicts was encouraged. The doctor hoped the investigation would force the contractors to be more solicitous of the convicts' welfare. This particular intrusion into the world of the convicts was unusual, for it was instigated in part by a plea for help written to the governor by a prisoner.

> [W]e gete hafe ar nufe to eat [and are] drive out ind the rind [rain] + Beet all but to death ... we ar knok don with stick + is stomp with feet the print of Capt. C.C. Bingham [the whipping boss] Butes ar all in our head ... we no that we ar in prison But we don't think that it is yr. rule for them to Do us that way,

complained this desperate convict. He claimed that some convicts had been beaten to death, and went on to beg that the governor "send sum on ell [some one else] to Be on us."[65]

Indeed, the inquiry that followed led to the arrest of the whipping boss at this camp, Captain Bingham, who "inhumanly whipped the convicts" under his charge, according to the report by the assistant principal keeper.[66] Notwithstanding a report by the lessees that "the convicts ... are becoming more disobedient and difficult to manage because of the investigation now going on as to the treatment of the convicts," Governor Gordon and the penitentiary officials found the lease companies responsible for "excessive whipping and in some cases ... unreasonable and excessive labor," and threatened to cancel their contracts. Gordon, who had once leased convicts himself, claimed that while once a necessary "expedient," the convict lease had now outlived its usefulness. In the end, however, the governor merely levied a fine of $2,500 on the penitentiary companies, which was paid under protest, and did nothing to abolish a system that benefited some of his closest political cronies.[67]

These sorts of sporadic investigations and slaps on the wrist were commonplace, and derived from the political power of the lessees and the loose and inefficient system of oversight that prevailed under Georgia's twenty-year lease law (1879–99). E.T. Shubrick, assistant principal keeper, and one of the more humane and conscientious prison officials to watch over the "welfare" of the leased convicts, confessed that due to "unavoidable causes" it was impossible for him to visit every far-flung convict camp in the state – fourteen in 1878, twenty-six by 1896. Yet he cheerfully gave them all clean bills of health anyway.

The penitentiary committee of the Georgia House of Representatives, which inspected the Dade mines in 1890, admitted that "it was very evident that our visit was not unexpected" and that "preparations had been made to give everything connected with the camp as good an appearance as possible." Moreover, fear played a part in obscuring conditions at the convict camps. "The convicts are very shy of visitors, and are afraid to expose the treatment received at the camp.... They knew that ... they would be at the mercy of their 'bosses'" when an investigation was finished. As the convict who wrote Governor Gordon indicated, when the principal keeper visited the camp the prisoners were afraid to report honestly on their daily travail, because if they did the whipping boss would "all mos kill ous when he is gond."[68]

When challenged over hours of labor, lack of food and water, or poor hygiene and medical care, the lease companies insisted that "it is in the highest interest of [a lessee] to keep his men in perfect physical condition in order that their labor may be productive and remunerative." The notion that care for the convicts was "dictated by considerations of interest as well as humanity" even led to the extravagant claim that "the sanitary regulations [at the Dade mines] are very *beneficial* to the health of the prisoners" (emphasis added). The optimistic principal physician agreed that he thought the lessees, "recognizing the fact that the continuous labor of well men is more profitable than the prolonged idleness of sick ones," were willing to follow his hygienic recommendations.[69]

Failing this defense, the lessees at best admitted a lapse in their own supervision of their lower-rank personnel, laying blame on their subordinates, the whipping bosses.[70] At worst, they and their defenders fell back on what a historian of southern African labor calls the racist "board and lodging myth." Confronted with the abysmal conditions endured by early-twentieth-century mine workers in southern Rhodesia, the defenders of the industry proposed that African workers benefited from the food, housing and medical care provided by the mining companies. The Rhodesian Chamber of Mines claimed that for these beneficiaries of colonialist labor policy conditions were "vastly better than the natives have been accustomed to at their own kraals."[71] So, too, did the defenders of Georgia's convict camps constantly compare the prisoners to the "ordinary negro laborer." In one instance, one even used "the old rule to give a darkey three and a half pounds of meat and a peck of meal a week" as a touchstone for the amount of food provided to the convicts. "What a contrast to the diet of the European peasant," crowed another defender of leasing, echoing the pro-slavery arguments of an earlier generation. The convicts "are in far better condition than ninety-five per cent of them were before conviction, and, in fact, than a large majority of honest laborers in any community in the state," boasted the prison commission. When asked to compare the convicts to "their own race outside of the Penitentiary," another observer felt that "as a rule they are decidedly better fed, better clothed, better slept, better doctored, better housed and better preached to than those outside."[72]

As was customary, these views were bolstered by the powerful assumptions of African-American racial inferiority that underlay all white discussions of the black laborer, forced or free, in the postbellum South. "The convicts fare better [than free black workers], as regards health because they are controlled; they are made to be regular in their habits and they are better fed and fed with more regularity," a former principal physician claimed. "You know the difficulty of all the race everywhere, when they are at their daily labor, in keeping them cleanly," replied the indomitable Joseph Brown to one of the detractors of conditions in his mines.[73] Yet when one of Georgia's few remaining black legislators, W.H. Styles, visited Brown's mines in 1892 he justly concluded that "if there is any hell on earth, it is the Dade coal mines, where these poor unfortunate creatures are so inhumanely treated.... [The] food is too scanty for the hard labor they have to do." The penitentiary committee of which Styles was the only black member observed the exact same conditions, but reported to the legislature that "the convicts are just as well provided for and treated as the present system of working them will admit." The committee remarked approvingly, however, that "the whites and negroes have separate sleeping quarters."[74]

The sporadic and piecemeal state oversight and investigations that permitted some of the worst abuses in the convict camps were not the only forms of control over penal labor available to the state. As early as 1881, after a legislative investigation turned up numerous "existing evils in the penitentiary system," the investigative committee concluded that "humanity and justice require that the state appoint an officer at each camp to stand between the convict and lessee."[75] But until 1897, in the absence of the daily presence of state officials at the convict camps, the lessees retained what they justifiably regarded as their most significant privilege: "being charged with the management of these convicts we must insist upon the right of naming the men who shall control them."[76] This facet of lessee control was crucial for the maximum extraction of labor, because it allowed the company leasing the convicts, not the state, to define and oversee the pace of work – the task – and mete out punishment for the failure to meet it.

The authority of the company to compel labor resided in the person of the whipping boss. In response to the legislative recommendation in

1881, the state ostensibly controlled punishment by approving the appointment of the men authorized to administer whippings at each camp.[77] In practice, however, this whipping boss was nothing more than a loyal employee chosen by the lessee, and might even be the same person responsible for the overall direction of the enterprise which utilized forced labor. "Whipping Bosses are not the Agents of the State," Governor Gordon acknowledged in concluding his 1887 investigation.[78]

The lessees vigorously defended the prerogative of designating the whipping boss as a necessary component of maintaining "discipline" at their camps. The "superintendent of labor and convicts" at the Dade coal complex in 1889, for instance, wrote to his employer, Joseph Brown, that the appointment of an additional whipping boss was necessary because of the increase in the number of convicts under the company's control. "I believe under the law these appointments are made by the company or lessee and endorsed by the Penitentiary officials and the Governor," he informed Brown, who sent the note on to Governor Gordon. Two years later the Browns sought yet another whipping boss for the "Slope" mines division of Dade, with the suggestive reminder that "the convicts there are hard to control." "You will remember that is the camp where the insurrection was last June," Julius Brown warned Governor Northen pointedly. "The uniform practice in the Executive Office since the lease has been ... that the individual lessee having control of the convicts should name the Whipping Boss," Brown told Governor Atkinson in 1896 when his desired appointments were being held up. "Serious trouble is apprehended at the Mines, unless some one has authority to impose punishment," he added ominously.[79]

On occasion the governor might revoke a whipping boss's commission in instances of egregious mistreatment of convicts, drunkenness, or other lapses, as Governor Gordon did in 1887.[80] But when directly challenged in their personnel decisions, lessees were quick to defend their supervisory claims. After being told by Governor Northen that the references for his whipping boss were unacceptable, Julius Brown somewhat petulantly retorted "I did not know that your rule was to require endorsers personally known to you or [the principal keeper] in making these appointments. I supposed that if they were reputable citizens of standing in the county that that was all that was required." And meeting resistance to a requested transfer of a whipping boss the following year, Brown angrily rebuked the governor: "have I not the right to make changes in my employees when and where I please, or do you insist in my keeping any special one employed?"[81]

Indeed, it was this very power of appointment of the whipping boss that the state sought to reclaim upon reorganization of the penal system and the lease in 1897. Under the "Act to create a prison commission" of that year the whipping bosses were transformed into deputy wardens. The power to punish prisoners was placed in the hands of these men now supposedly wholly employed by the state, rather than by the lessees of convict labor. By this law a three-member prison commission replaced the principal keeper, and was granted "complete management and control of the state convicts," including the right to "regulate the hours of their labor [and] the manner and extent of their punishment" through direct appointment of the supervisory personnel at the convict camps.[82]

Although this same law also authorized a new five-year lease of the convicts, to begin on 1 April 1899, the new prison officials disingenuously insisted that this reorganization eliminated state leasing of prisoners in Georgia, since the convicts were never removed from the state's direct control. Under the "lease system" of the past two decades, the prison commissioners proclaimed in 1900, "the state not only sold the labor of the convicts, but parted with their custody and control" as well. Since the wardens – or whipping bosses – were "dependent for their positions and wages upon the lessees, the State's interest and the welfare of the convicts were made subservient to the interest of their employers, [which was] profitable results from the convict labor." This statement was an admirably accurate critique of Georgia's postbellum penal system, but the subsequent assertion that "the new system is [in] no respects a lease system," because "the state through its own officers and employees [is] controlling and working [the convicts]," was a less penetrating observation. Indeed, in its report the previous year, the prison commission had listed as one of the warden or deputy warden's primary duties to "require the performance of good and faithful labor by the convicts for the employer." Despite the fact that the terms "lease," "hire," "bidder," and "paying ... for the annual labor of the convicts" (perhaps "labor" was the operative word here) were all explicit in the new act, the prison commission boldly proclaimed that "there is no lease law in Georgia, nor a lease system, nor lease contracts." The US Bureau of Labor, however, in its report on convict labor in 1905, had no doubt that Georgia was one of the states that still leased convicts.[83]

Even if it did not exactly eliminate convict leasing, theoretically this new form of direct oversight of convict labor represented a vast improvement. Now standing between the lessee and the convict worker was a state officer charged with looking out for the prisoners' welfare on a daily basis, as well as enforcing discipline. The state took from the convict the right to sell his labor power, but now reserved for itself control of his person.[84] But even this reform proved unable to over-come the basic contradiction of penal labor in Georgia: the enforce-ment of discipline remained congruent with the extraction of labor, and thus in the lessee's interest, not the state's. There continued to be room for considerable ambiguity – to put it charitably – in the warden's ultimate allegiance in a convict mine, an ambiguity that the lessees did their best to exacerbate. For if the prisoners "fail[ed] to secure these tasks or have too much slate in the coal, on the complaint of the mining bosses they [were] whipped by the State's Officers." But the "mining boss or foreman, an employee of the lessee, fixes the task and decides if it has been obtained or if there is too much slate in it."[85]

When the lessees had direct control over the position of whipping boss, they effectively conjoined management of an enterprise, maximum labor extraction, and penal authority. After the "reform" of 1897 they found methods to obtain similar results. Sometimes the lessee would simply propose that the prison commission name his own superintend-ent as camp "warden," and he could then continue to direct the labor and punish the convicts, now ostensibly under the aegis of the state.[86] Most blatantly, the lessees simply paid wardens and guards a salary in addition to what they received from the state in their official capacity, sometimes as much as 150 per cent more. This extra money was "simply paid to keep these wardens from becoming cross wise with the Company," one beneficiary claimed. The legislature and the prison commission readily admitted that the low salaries tendered to peni-tentiary personnel contributed to this practice. "We wardens can look out for ourselves," testified one recipient of the dual salary. During the 1908 investigation of the convict system this cooptation was more than once described as "customary" in the convict camps.[87]

The lessees and wardens, with feigned innocence, protested that the payments were for "rendering services." "They doubtless were," scoffed the 1908 investigating committee. The convicts had no problem with such fine points: "the [lessee] paid large sums of money to the deputy warden of the state who was located at the works and thus ... made [him] its agent and employee and not the employee of the state," claimed a prisoner in a lawsuit against his former captor. With dis-arming candor, Joel Hurt, who after 1900 operated the coal and iron mines that had previously belonged to the Browns, was quite blunt about the reason for the extra compensation and dual appointments: it enabled him to get more work out of the convicts.[88]

Thus, even after the state asserted its absolute right to limit the amount of labor done by the convicts, the lessees managed to subvert this control. Their ability to do so revolved around the continuation of

Table 6.2 Productivity in Coal Mining, 1880–1910 (bituminous tons raised per miner per day worked)

	USA	Ga.	Ala.	Tenn.	W.Va.
1880	1.90	1.17	0.71	1.78	1.97
1890	2.56	1.72	1.77	1.62	2.66
1891	2.57	0.64			
1892	2.72	1.67			
1893	2.73	1.48			
1894	2.84	1.60			
1895	2.90	0.99	2.25	2.21	3.05
1896	2.94	1.10			
1897	3.04	1.37			
1898	3.09	1.63			
1899	3.05	1.36			
1900	2.98	1.90	2.34	1.90	3.36
1901	2.94	1.54			
1902	3.06	1.76			
1903	3.02	2.05			
1904	3.15	1.96			
1905	3.24	1.63	2.69	2.20	3.74
1906	3.36	1.62			
1907	3.29	1.71			
1908	3.34	1.51			
1910	3.46	1.73	2.91	2.65	3.94
Mean	2.96	1.53			

Source: USGS, *Mineral Resources of the United States*, 1883–1910. Statistics necessary to calculate productivity are not available for 1881–89 or 1909.

task work, and was particularly effective in coal mining, where direct supervision of penal labor – by state or lessee – remained impossible. Neither the state inspectors nor the wardens permanently at the camps made any pretense of examining the interior of the mines to determine what a "reasonable task" might be.[89] Nevertheless, the deputy wardens "punish[ed], frequently and severely, on the report of an employee of the lessee that some task has not been accomplished, without actual knowledge of the severity of the task, or the conditions under which imposed." The company's "mine boss" set the task, measured the coal, and decided if it had been met – and then the state's overseer whipped on his recommendation. The warden "generally took the word" of the boss in this matter.[90] Regarding the underground work of mining coal itself, below the earth's surface "the state had no jurisdiction over us," testified one convict.[91]

In some instances this procedure was simplified. One deputy warden who had been simultaneously "employed" by the lessee as a superintendent of labor claimed that, while he might set the task in his capacity as a company man, he made his decisions on punishment only when wearing his hat as warden for the state of Georgia. At another camp it was said that the warden and the superintendent "have no trouble" with each other – they were the same man![92] Such subterfuge did not always suffice, however, for despite these ruses the question of labor and punishment led to occasional friction between lessees and state officials. James English, lessee of convicts at the Chattahoochee brickyard and investor in the Durham coal mines, firmly believed that the wardens should work the convicts to the advantage of the contractor, who, after all, had paid for the labor. "The State's representative [is there] simply to see the negroes give [the lessee] reasonable labor," he claimed. But the legislative committee investigating the lease suggested that the warden "ought to be taking care of convicts, instead of bossing them." For their part, the wardens saw their role as "look[ing] after the work for [the lessee] and the state." The lessees complained that the state did not get enough work from the prisoners; some wardens, however, found unreasonable the labor requirements they were asked to enforce.[93]

Joel Hurt was particularly disgruntled because the warden at one of his convict camps would not always whip prisoners for "the lack of work." When confronted by the prison commission or a legislative committee about the apparently excessive tasks required in his mines, Hurt retorted that "miners are tasked everywhere" and "the [prison] commissioners don't pose as expert miners." Hurt complained that at the end of the day his convicts broke into song, singing "Promiseland," and that "men ought to be worked so hard they couldn't sing." He demanded that the state officials at his mine use discipline to get more work out of his bound labor force. The chairman of the prison commission, Judge Joseph S. Turner, insisted that "the contractors only buy the labor," which the state had a right to limit in the interest of humane treatment. Yet Judge Turner also admitted his belief that "when convicts work, I think they necessarily have to do the same work free men would do"; in fact, the prison commission determined if the contractor was provided with "reasonable labor" in the mines by comparing convict output to free labor.[94]

Despite the fact that the most ardent defenders of convict leasing claimed that prisoners could do twice the work of free labor, this comparison suggested otherwise. The relative efficiency and productivity of convict workers, especially in mining, is open to dispute. True, the pace

Table 6.3 Annual Days Worked in Bituminous Coal Mining, 1890–1908, 1915

Year	US average	Ga.	Ala.	Tenn.	W.Va.
1890	226	313	217	263	227
1891	223	312			
1892	219	277			
1893	204	342			
1894	171	304			
1895	194	312	244	224	195
1896	192	303			
1897	196	304			
1898	211	298			
1899	234	302			
1900	234	278	257	242	231
1901	225	291			
1902	230	312			
1903	225	298			
1904	202	222			
1905	211	270	225	222	209
1906	213	279			
1907	234	262			
1908	193	261	222	209	185
1915	203	197	223	220	208

Source: United States Geological Survey, *Report on the Mineral Resources of the United States*, 1900, 1901, 1905, 1908, 1910, 1915.

of work at English's Chattahoochee brickyard, for instance, was believed to be so brutal that "not a class of [free] white labor in Georgia ... could stand it a week," and the company's productive capacity reflected this fact. And the prevailing attitude about race, labor, and penal discipline among prison officials and lessees in the South was "that more work is done by a colored convict than by the average colored free laborer."[95] But coal mining was a fairly skilled occupation, in which convicts intent on resisting labor might have limited productive capability, whatever their "reliability." A harsh criminal justice system provided some solutions to this problem; as we have seen, coal operators preferred long-term convicts in the mines because long sentences offered "an unusual opportunity for training the convicts for skilled labor."[96] Yet despite the faith in forced labor shown by the lessees and despite the control they exercised over convict labor with the task system, raw data indicate that the daily tons of coal raised per man in Georgia (where nearly all miners were bound workers) consistently fell below the national average. Indeed, over time, Georgia's convicts produced only *half* the coal dug per man in states where free labor pre-dominated (see Table 6.2).[97]

This consistently low mining productivity and its relationship to convict labor can be understood in two ways. Although Georgia's mines almost always recorded more days worked annually than any other state in the nation (see Table 6.3),[98] convict labor still may have been woefully inefficient, due to the lack of skill, training and, of course, resistance to an enforced task. At times the lessees expressed their mounting frustration with this labor, particularly as productivity steadily increased in other coalfields. "I have not felt during the year that we have gotten as much work out of these convicts at the Mines as we ought to have done," Julius Brown complained to the Dade Coal Company's stockholders in his 1893 report. "I have complained to the Superintendent.... I have notified him in very positive terms that these matters must be remedied," he reassured them. Apparently the situation did not improve. In the 1896 investigation of the Georgia Mining, Manufacturing Company the general manager admitted that the "amount of coal for [the] number of men employed – was not coal enough. It was nothing in proportion to the amount of coal gotten out in other mines with the same number of men." Remarking on a decrease of 40 per cent in coal production in Georgia over this period, the US Geological Survey also noted that the number of miners and days worked had not decreased proportionally. The USGS directly attributed this to the employment of convicts in the mines. After the turn of the century the Geological Survey continued to suggest that "the apparently low average of efficiency [in Georgia's coal mines] is explained by the fact that state convicts are employed to a considerable extent ..., and these in the large majority of cases have for experience as coal miners only the periods of their incarceration." Alternatively, however, low productivity can be understood as the very reason for reliance on forced labor in the first place. That is, the geological and topographical constraints on the area's coal production – coal seams "not sufficiently thick and regular for profitable working" – made mining with free labor an unprofitable proposition in Georgia, for capital and labor alike.[99]

The marked increase in US mining productivity at the century's end, attributable to technological developments such as mechanized coal picks, was not duplicated in Georgia's mines, but this fact is similarly ambiguous. By 1900, 25 per cent of the nation's bituminous coal was mined by machine, and a decade later the figure was 41 per cent. But mining machines were not used at all in Georgia until 1905 because reliance on cheap forced labor inhibited the incentive to modernize.

"As a large part of the work in [Georgia's] mines is done by convicts," the US Geological Survey reported in 1905, "mining machines have not been introduced."[100] But whether the continued lag and then widening gap in productivity was a constraint on profits in a highly competitive industry, or whether these mines could be profitable at all *without* forced labor remains an open question.[101]

The post-convict leasing demise of Georgia's mining industry, however, lends credence to the latter suggestion. A decade after the removal of the last convicts from the mines in April 1909, Georgia's coal output had decreased to 66,000 tons, from a peak of over 400,000 in 1903. This negligible production was supposedly due to "the lack of men." Coal and capital were certainly available. In 1907 the Georgia coalfield had an estimated remaining productive capacity of at least 600 million tons, and in 1911 a $10 million mine-company consolidation subsumed Georgia's Durham mines.[102] The decline in production had begun in 1908, when coal output dropped 27 per cent, from 362,401 to 264,822 tons. This was followed the next year by a further decline of 20 per cent, to the lowest output in two decades.[103] The US Geological Survey believed that "the decrease in both 1908 and 1909 was due to the withdrawal by the state of the convicts who were employed as miners ... and to the inability of the operators to secure enough [free] labor to keep the mines up to capacity." The related production of pig iron in Georgia – 10 per cent of the South's production in 1880 – also met its demise; by 1909 there were no iron furnaces in blast left in the state.[104]

After 1899 the problem of low mining productivity was coupled with a new constraint as the price for leasing convict labor increased dramatically, almost reaching the cost of free labor. Before that date, under the twenty-year lease, lessees had paid a fixed price to the state. As the number of convicts increased, the actual cost for each one was reduced by the 1890s to approximately $10 per annum. But when the lease was renewed by the act of 1897, over fifty companies bid for convicts per capita, at an average price of $100 per annum for each convict. After 1900 prices for coal, iron, lumber, brick and naval stores – all produced by convicts – began to rise, and in an increasingly competitive labor market convict lessees continued to bid up the price of acquiring forced labor. By 1904 the coal companies paid between $225 and $250 a year for each prisoner they brought to the mines.[105] As a result of this increased cost, the lessees likely sought to increase the recalcitrant prisoners' output in order to maintain profitability. But the result of this was the eruption of one of the central contradictions exposed by the task system, that between state protection of the convicts' welfare and their status as state-created slaves. This contradiction explains some of the increasing tension over the control of the pace of work, which helped lead in 1908 to the abolition of the lease in Georgia.[106]

Ultimately the viability of convict labor rested not only on structural factors, but on the degree to which productive forced labor could be made compatible with the penal rationales of custody and punishment. For convict coal mining to be profitable, prisoners had to be made to work. The brutality of convict leasing derived from the prisoners' dual identity as objects of correction and of production; its limits were defined by the convicts' struggle against complete enslavement, and the state's resulting willingness to enforce the notion that "there is or should be a difference in the life of a prisoner and that of a slave."[107]

"Bad Boys Make Good Roads": From Convict Lease to Chain Gang

Bad boys make good roads.
> Georgia folk saying

They point with pride to the roads you built for them,
They ride in comfort over the rails you laid for them.
They put hammers in your hands
And said – Drive so much before sundown.
> Sterling Brown, "Strong Men"[1]

"On account of the convict employment, strikes are of rare occurrence" in Georgia's coal industry, the US Geological Survey reported in 1900. And on the eve of the abolition of leasing eight years later, the USGS could still report that "little interference by labor troubles is experienced" in Georgia's mines.[2] Thus, the 1910 strike and "riot" of the Italian immigrant miners who replaced the convicts at his mines must have come as a rude awakening to James English, Jr.

Southern capitalists unable or unwilling to obtain free labor or convicts frequently turned to peonage or contract immigrant labor to extract maximum labor in minimum time.[3] In Georgia after the turn of the century, continued widespread white dissatisfaction with black labor found new expression in a renewed call for immigration. A correspondent to the editor of the Atlanta *Constitution* despaired of the labor situation "unless something is done by the people of our State ... to do away with the existing conditions of labor, especially the loafing negro labor.... [T]here is only one remedy, and that is a systematic campaign to induce to locate in our midst Immigrants of the better class," he wrote. "This will gradually force the negro out of this section," he hoped, "or put them to work, and only in this manner can the important question [of labor] before our Manufacturers and Farmers be solved," he concluded.[4]

With the abolition of convict leasing in 1908, James English, Jr., the heir apparent to the fortune built up by his father with convict labor at Atlanta's Chattahoochee Brick Company, tried this "remedy" in his Durham coal mines. Apparently he failed to obtain workers of the "better class." Almost exactly one year after turning over his convicts to the state, English hired a group of forty-five Italian miners and arranged to pay them as a group through their *Padrone* or labor agent.[5] Unfortunately the *Padrone* made off with the first month's payroll and "left for parts unknown." Not receiving their pay, and English refusing to compensate them for the loss, the miners went on strike, threatened to kill English if he set foot on his property, and vowed to keep the mines for themselves for five years, having "taken charge of the property and ... [begun] running things to suit themselves." They refused to let the "native miners" work the mines as well.[6]

English responded by calling on his friend Governor Joseph M. Brown – son of the convict lessee, Joe Brown – who obligingly sent troops to Walker County to remove the immigrant workers from the mines. The militia arrived at Durham, captured the rebellious miners, and put them on a guarded train to Chattanooga with the proviso that they would not be prosecuted if they stayed away from Durham. Thanking Brown for his prompt response, English assured the governor he felt "confident that but for your timely aid rendered in calling out the militia, the property of the Company would have been seriously damaged."[7]

This dramatic episode was followed by an official protest by the Italian government, whose ambassador noted that one-third of the men on strike were Americans, not Italians. The Atlanta Federation of Trades also criticized English and Brown for their handling of the matter, suggesting the question of the miners' purloined pay should have been settled in court. "There was no real need of the military," the Federation concluded. Even the aide Brown sent to the mining district to investigate reluctantly reported that he "found the sentiment of the citizenry [near the] mine almost of the unanimous opinion that there was no real danger and the calling of the troops [was unnecessary]."[8]

In a speech to the legislature justifying his action, Governor Brown defensively remarked: "experience with this class of Italians in other states ... demonstrates the necessity of caution and promptness in dealing with them in a turbulent mood."[9] In a bizarre coda to this event, Brown received a letter from the superintendent of the Durham mines with suggested rationales for the military intervention, including the view that the "Italians were not driven out of Georgia in the interest

of Jim English," but in the interest of "white miners" who could now
return to work. "Make sure whether the American miners were white
or negroes, so as to shape the language accordingly," his correspondent
cautioned.[10] Presumably such drastic state action would appear illegiti-
mate if carried out on behalf of African-American workers. As for James
English, Jr., the following year he sold his coal mine operation in a
consolidation financed by a "New York capitalist."[11]

The transition from convict to free labor in Georgia in 1909 was not
nearly so traumatic at the English family's other major enterprise, the
Chattahoochee Brick Company (CBC), located by the clay banks on the
outskirts of Atlanta. Nevertheless, the experience of this operation after
the abolition of leasing illustrates the very good reasons for its twenty-
year reliance on forced labor. The CBC, which had relied almost entirely
on a force of 175 convicts for over two decades to produce up to 200,000
bricks daily for many of Atlanta's new buildings, struggled to adapt to
the sudden necessity of recruiting a free labor force after 1908.[12]

This convict brickyard, the largest brick producer in the state, had
long been notorious for putting free labor out of work in the industry.
As early as 1886 the US Bureau of Labor observed that "the brick-
making industry around Atlanta, formerly employing about 600 hands,
has been broken up almost entirely by convict-labor competition."
Indeed, 30 per cent of Georgia's brick production in 1886 relied on
convicts – more than any other state. Other brick operators complained
that they, too, had to lease convicts in order to compete with English's
firm. And, of course, Georgia's embryonic labor movement contended
that convict labor at the brickyard "takes that much work out of the
hands of that much free labor."[13]

Despite the complaints of the labor movement, as the termination of
the lease approached Chattahoochee Brick's management expressed
doubt about their ability to make do with labor freely given by Atlanta's working men. In June 1908, with agitation against the lease in full
swing, the company's general manager, Harry English, informed the
stockholders that he did "not know ... whether arrangements could be
made to operate the plant with free labor." Arguing that, "should we
have to abandon the convict lease entirely ... we would not be able to
produce these brick at as little cost," he recommended holding surplus
brick inventory until prices rose.[14]

When Georgia's legislature abolished the lease that September, the
company began to plan for the difficult transition to free labor,
scheduled for 1 April 1909. The meeting opened with "Capt. [James]
English call[ing] attention to the fact that the present convict lease for

labor expires on March 31st, 1909." Harry English began his report by noting grimly: "it is quite evident now that this plant will have to be operated in the future with free labor," and urged action "with the view of the possibility of this plant being closed down." Since the convicts would be removed in three months, he recommended that the company "manufacture all of the brick we can possibly produce between now and the expiration of the present convict lease ... and by that means accumulate as large a reserve [of brick] as possible" while waiting for a price increase. After 1 April, he noted, they could begin to hire free labor or the "plant could remain idle with very little cost attached." But due to a persistent slump in the price of brick, he suggested "it might be advisable for us to keep the plant idle after the expiration of our present convict lease."[15]

What this plan to operate the plant at full capacity for ninety days running meant for the convicts can only be imagined. Although there is no direct evidence that the convicts' daily task was increased, English's report was adopted, and the company's output for January to March 1909 surpassed 7.8 million brick – nearly 18 per cent more than the average output for this quarter over the previous four winters. This tendency to "get as much labor from these leased convicts as their strength will allow" was common in the waning days of the lease, according to Atlanta's labor newspaper, the *Journal of Labor*. Contractors knew "that the time is short when this thing of bartering and trading for human souls will be stopped."[16]

This calculated attempt to maximize the productive capacity of forced labor before its termination was also shaped by the anticipated changes – and cost increases – a shift to free labor would entail. Back in June 1908 the general manager of the Chattahoochee Brick Company had realized "it will be necessary to make some arrangements whereby the [free] help can secure quarters near the plant ... [and] improvements will have to be made if free labor is employed as the plant is located some seven miles from the City [of Atlanta]." Despite the frequent assertion that the convicts enjoyed living conditions on a par with that of free labor, English recognized that free labor would refuse to inhabit former prison barracks, and the brick company would "have to erect suitable quarters for such labor, at considerable expense." After all, free workers "would hardly be willing to occupy buildings heretofore occupied by prisoners," he pointed out as he struggled to recruit labor in May 1909.[17]

The problem of housing, however, was merely one of many new conditions brought on at the Chattahoochee brickyard by the prospect of managing free labor. Immediately after giving up their 164 convicts to the prison commission, the company began to repair its machinery,

Table 7.1   Brick Production, Cost and Profit, Chattahoochee Brick
Company, 1900–1910

	Product (*1,000*)	Cost (*$/1,000*)	Labor (*$/1,000*)	Price (*$/1,000*)	Profit (*$/1,000*)
With convict labor					
1900–01	30,037	3.85	0.69	5.80	1.95
1905–06	30,833	4.70	1.19	5.76	1.06
1906–07	32,225	4.83	1.20	7.26	2.43
1907–08	32,722	4.67	1.15	6.68	2.01
1908–09[a]	28,215	4.25	1.16	5.62	1.37
With free labor					
1909–10	16,156	6.56	1.98	6.19	−0.37

Note: [a] 10 months.

Source: Annual Statements, Brick Yard Account, 1900–1910, Folder 2, Box 1, Financial Records, Chattahoochee Brick Company Records, Atlanta History Center. Statements are from 1 June to 31 May, except 1908–1909, which is 1 June to 31 March, the last ten months of the convict-lease.

and planned to "put the plant in good condition and ready [it] for the manufacture of brick" with a new labor force. But, it was admitted, productive capacity now depended "very largely upon our ability to get the right kind of labor." After an April in which production was entirely suspended, the general manager reported that he needed 160 laborers, but appeared unsure if this was realistic. "We do not know ... whether or not we can always keep that number satisfied out at the works, situated as it is, remote from town," he cautioned the board of directors. In May 1909 the company's output dropped to 870,450 brick, only 27 per cent of the output with forced labor the previous May.[18]

At the next meeting Harry English confessed that "on starting the manufacture of brick [after the lease] it was difficult to get reliable labor, even at higher wages than the same class of labor was receiving in the City." Many workers applied, and came out to the works, but "they became dissatisfied." "They did not like the work, nor the accommodations ... [and] they wanted pay for each day's work each night that they might buy food supplies," English complained. Unlike convicts, free labor unhappy with the conditions at the brick works could "vote with their feet" and choose to work elsewhere. Even after three years, company officials still suggested that "free labor [was] found unsatisfactory and quite different from convict labor. The convicts worked from sun-up to sun-down while free labor worked from 6 to 5 o'clock and only worked when they wanted to," the stockholders complained. Worse still, "employees at the plant were being arrested and annoyed by the County Police," and the company had to make bond for "[a] negro and let him go back to work."[19]

Due to the difficulties of recruiting a stable free labor force, production over the first year after the removal of the convicts continued to lag. From June 1909 to June 1910 the Chattahoochee Brick Company manufactured only 16 million brick, far below the annual 30 million normally produced with forced labor. In no single month during that year did output exceed 1.6 million brick, a level to which production had not sunk since February 1903. In addition, production costs zoomed to $6.56 per thousand brick, while during the last ten months of the lease they had been $4.25; convict labor had cost $1.16 per thousand in 1908–09, while its free labor replacement cost $1.98 during the first year of the new labor system. In 1909–10 the company sold brick for $6.19 per thousand, for a 37 cent loss per thousand despite the price increase. This was a sharp drop from the $2.43 profit in 1906–07, $2.01 in 1907–08, and even $1.37 during the final year of the lease as brick prices dropped to $5.62 per thousand (see Table 7.1).[20]

In fact, over the next three years the company sustained losses of over $50,000 while adjusting to the new form of labor.[21] Higher labor costs took their toll, but in part this deficit was also due to a host of new capital expenditures occasioned by the shift to free labor, improvements that had been unnecessary with convict labor. In May 1909, for instance, James English announced to the board of directors that "to protect the Company against the loss resulting from personal injuries and accidents he had taken out employer's liability insurance," hardly required with a bound labor force. A year later he finally agreed to spend $8,000 to build twenty-five "cottages" to house the labor force. These were completed in December 1910, and designated as "negro" dwellings. Nevertheless, the fact that "the old convict camp was not adopted to the free labor system" continued to plague the enterprise.[22] Other improvements included the purchase of new clay banks, the construction of a tramway to transport the clay convicts used to move by wheelbarrow, and, most significantly, a steam shovel to dig the clay from the river bank. James English emphasized that, with the company's new dependence on free labor, this mechanization was more than a convenience; "the steam shovel was a labor saver: ... it required now only three men to do the work where formerly from 22 to 25 men were required," he reported enthusiastically.[23]

Despite the slow recovery, the initial losses, and the persistent doubts, once such improvements were made the company eventually became profitable on a free-labor basis. The same report that noted the three-year decline in profits also happily indicated that much of the loss was recouped in a mere three months in the latter part of 1912. By 1914 the CBC was clearly back on its feet, as Harry English informed James English that "the condition of the company is good," and boasted that in August and July 1914 alone output reached an astronomical 8.5 million brick. Nevertheless, despite the $1.60 per thousand profit, he did remind the president that "these results have been accomplished over a heavy increased cost as compared with previous years during [the] convict lease system."[24]

"Organized labor in Georgia has for years fought the pernicious convict lease system," boasted Atlanta's *Journal of Labor* as it finally saw these efforts bearing fruit with the abolition of the lease in 1908.[25] On the eve of the removal of the convicts from private labor camps in 1909 the *Journal* insisted that the transition would be painless, an overly optimistic prediction, given Chattahoochee Brick's subsequent difficulties. Of the twenty felony convict camps in the state, "not a single one of them ... contemplates retiring from business with the expiration of the lease system, and practically all of them have completed arrangements for the immediate substitution of free labor," labor's newspaper claimed. Indeed, this was the main goal of the labor movement's ongoing struggle against leasing, carried on "not only in the name of humanity ... but also on behalf of the working men ... of Georgia who emphatically insist that the criminals of the state should not be put into competition with free labor." For these opponents of the lease, abolition meant that, "with the removal of the convicts from labor in the coal mines, brick yards, saw mills, and turpentine camps, employment will be afforded to nearly 2,000 free laborers, in places which have heretofore been filled exclusively by convicts."[26]

Organized labor emphasized competition with free labor as the problem with the lease more than other reformers, but they joined a growing consensus when they "demanded that the convicts be placed upon the public roads." Along with the other opponents of convict leasing – farmers who desired improved transportation, Georgia's club-women and penal reformers, the black and white press, Progressive legislators, capitalists who could not obtain convicts, and, above all, partisans of the good roads movement – they "believe[d] the best interest of the state and the public at large will best be served if convicts are made to do public duty on the roads," where they could work "without producing unfair competition with anyone."[27] Opposition to the lease did include a protest "against this foul wrong upon the convicts themselves" and popular outcry over "punishments, abuses, and suffering ... inflicted upon the convicts which were unjustified, unmerciful, cruel and in-human."[28] Yet, as the black newspaper the Savannah *Tribune* pointed out, crusading reformers were "intensely interested in the welfare of the [few] white convicts ... but not a word is said of the cruelties inflicted upon hundreds of poor colored prisoners." The paper noted that they had "been telling about the blot of Georgia's penitentiary system" for years "but slight attention was paid to what we said."[29]

Indeed, whether the county chain gangs that supplanted the lease system after 1908 mitigated the plight of the black convict is severely open to doubt. Coy and Earl Hicks, sent to the Worth County chain gang in 1912 for liquor selling, quickly discovered that "the negro in [southeast] Georgia is still in a manner a chattell." They had pleaded guilty to the charge because "with a white man swearing positively that they had sold liquor" they faced certain conviction. Their sentences were appealed at the behest of "a respected and successful [white] farmer." The Hicks, father and son, had a good reputation among local planters as hard workers, their attorney claimed, and should only have to pay a fine. Similarly, Horace Hammond, a black man who had worked nineteen years under the convict lease in the Dade Coal mines on a murder charge, found himself in 1916 sentenced to work Coweta County's roads for twelve months. Hammond had asked C.H. Newton to give him a ride home, and offered to pay him $4 when they got there. Unable to produce the money upon arrival, he was hauled into court for "cheating and swindling" and fined $80, which he could not pay. Hammond made his escape from the chain gang after two weeks. These men undoubtedly saw little difference between a county chain gang or a stint in the mines.[30] In Georgia after 1908 the futile effort to reconcile labor recruitment, racial control, and infrastructural develop-ment with a rational and humane penal policy merely shifted from the private to the public sector.

"Please, reader, do not read this chapter unless you can steel your heart against pain," cautioned Frank Tannenbaum in his 1924 exposé of conditions in southern prison camps. The catalog of officially sanctioned horrors introduced by these words bore a strong resemblance to George Washington Cable's indictment of convict leasing in *The Silent South*, published four decades earlier. Nearly a decade after Tannenbaum's book appeared, in response to the revelations of Robert Burns's *I am a Fugitive from the Georgia Chain Gang!*, the *Nation* proclaimed that "no [fugitive] ought to be delivered to Georgia as long as it persists in its inhuman and barbarous chain gang system." Yet the brutal regime endured by African-Americans working the southern roads in the 1920s and 1930s, so forcefully described by Tannenbaum as one of the "darker phases" of the South, was actually conceived as a model of regional reform and progress, the direct result of the abolition of convict leasing. The chain gang of mostly black convicts working the roads of the Deep South came to exemplify the brutality of southern race relations, the repressive aspect of southern labor relations, and the moral and economic backwardness of the region in general.[31] But when it originated, the penal road gang was regarded as a quintessential southern Progressive reform. Its advocates promoted this reform as the embodiment of penal humanitarianism, state-sponsored economic modernization and efficiency, and racial moderation.

The Progressive Era elements of convict road work are particularly clear in their close relationship to the great wave of early-twentieth-century southern reform known as the "good roads movement," which successfully melded agrarian discontent and urban Progressivism. The attempt to improve southern roads initiated "the closer binding of the common interests of the farmer and the merchant," in the words of Georgia's Progressive Era governor, Joseph M. Brown. "The South is today enjoying an era of prosperity and expansion," wrote the Director of the US Department of Agriculture's Office of Public Roads (OPR) in 1910. "Its manufacturing industries are being enlarged; its railroads are being extended, and its agriculture is ... opening up to new possibilities." "But in order for this growth to continue," he warned, "it will be necessary that the roads of the South be improved." In concert with state and local "good roads" associations across the South, this federal agency promoted a modern transportation network as the answer to southern social and economic woes.[32]

The good roads movement spearheaded by the OPR accommodated many interests, which can conveniently be lumped together under the rubric "modernizers." Its rural legions included farmers who wanted easier and cheaper access to local markets (in the 1890s the People's Party advocated good roads), as well as advocates of stable but modern agrarian life who sought to improve school and church attendance, stem rural out-migration, and (somewhat paradoxically) decrease rural isolation. This group was joined in the South's growing cities by urban boosters and working men who desired cheaper goods supplied from the hinterland, and thus favored road improvement. Throughout the South, capitalists and merchants who sought an improved transportation network, and railroad owners who naively regarded roads as state-financed trunk lines that would increase their freight, also supported this reform movement. Finally, the good roads movement was promoted by a new class of southern technocrats: civil engineers working either in state geological surveys or the Office of Public Roads itself, who wanted to apply their expertise to the modernization of the South's economy.[33]

North Carolina, for instance, had one of the most active good roads movements in the South. After 1900, under the aegis of its directors, Joseph A. Holmes and his successor, Joseph Hyde Pratt, the state Geological Survey was virtually converted into the main propaganda arm of the North Carolina Good Roads Association (NCGRA). Holmes and Pratt were also national leaders of the good roads movement.[34] Under their leadership, and armed with the legitimacy provided by the state Geological Survey, good roads advocates in North Carolina attacked the state's notorious "mud-tax" of frequently impassable highways on three fronts: labor, finance, and expertise. This entailed abolishing the statute labor system; increasing local revenue through taxation or debt to finance road work; and providing localities with professional engineering and construction advice. In each case the provision of convict labor became a key component in overcoming obstacles to their vision of southern progress and their goal of building a modern transportation infrastructure.[35]

The first battlefront was the region's archaic statute labor system. "The antebellum style of 'working' the public highways, which generally prevails, is about as well suited to the purpose as were the old militia musters to the development of actual soldiers," a speaker informed the first NCGRA annual convention in 1902. Indeed, by 1904 only ten of North Carolina's one hundred counties had entirely abandoned the feudal system of "warning out" all able-bodied road hands for four or five days of work a year on the local roads. In Georgia, only 8 of 137 counties had done away with this so-called "labor tax" by 1904, and the value of conscripted labor across the state that year still exceeded the cash taxes collected for county road work. Not surprisingly the corvée was hopelessly ineffective. "If there is a pernicious law or custom in our state," proclaimed Governor Carr of North Carolina, "I believe it is the old system of working roads. The average road hand goes on the road with the purpose not to work."[36]

Thus, from its earliest days in the 1890s the good roads movement recognized that an ambitious program of highway expansion demanded a large and efficient labor force, and that the statute labor system was wholly inadequate to the task. Joseph A. Holmes wrote to the Director of the US Office of Public Road Information that "the abandonment of the old system of compulsory road labor" by free men, and its replacement by "a system of road work by [cash] taxation, and the use of convict labor in road building is [an] essential feature of any system for the improvement of public roads." At its founding convention the NCGRA pursued this course; "we urge a more extended use of convict labor in road building in North Carolina," they resolved. Holmes himself seconded the resolution.[37]

Holmes liked to recount publicly a boyhood "anecdote" in order to dramatize the need for a disciplined and regular workforce on the South's roads. He suggested that conscript road work was more of a social event than anything else; the "custom" was that when the crops were laid by, a few dozen men and boys would "spend a few days working the roads." Fifteen of them would assemble in the morning, bringing whatever tools they had at hand. By noon, perhaps twenty men would be at work, and half a mile of dirt road would be graded. Then, of course, it was time to stop for lunch. During this two-hour break – it was usually a hot day, after all – the road hands discussed politics and hunting, swapped stories, and talked of everything "except how to build good roads." By 3:30 a handful of men returned home; at 4:30 a handful more. By the end of the day, Holmes concluded, the road gang had removed some stones, covered others, filled a few mud-holes, and "had played two dozen games of marbles, and several rounds of 'knucks' and 'mumble-the-peg'." "We made the most of the social feature of the occasion," he informed his audience, "doing as little work as we thought could be made to answer the purpose."[38]

Certainly the antiquated statute labor system of road work casts some interesting light on the much-vaunted neighborliness of nineteenth-century southern social relations. As one correspondent from Davidson County, North Carolina complained to the state commissioner of labor, "the people are disposed not to work the roads if they can help it.... The hands are always neighbors of the overseer; he therefore hates to enforce obedience to his orders [and] the overseers and road hands are neighbors of the [county] supervisors, and they know that to enforce the law would be to create hard feelings among their neighbors, and they neglect their duty."[39] "Everybody in our county wants a good road. But there is no one that wants to work the road," reported one Low-country good roads advocate.[40] Moreover, county road overseers frequently complained about their chronic inability to procure a steady or reliable supply of conscript labor. Either it was too hot, or the hands lived "too scattering," or too few showed up, or their time was up before the work was completed, or labor demands for crops took precedence.[41] "I have heard farmers say they had rather pay five dollars road tax than loose [sic] a days ploughing when in a push by having the road overseer take all his hands away," one correspondent informed Holmes.[42]

Road work was also fraught with class tensions, which agrarian dissidents such as the Populists easily might exploit. Those whites without property, and unable to pay the cash to commute their labor, resented working the roads for the benefit of landowners more dependent on commerce.[43] In a 1900 survey of attitudes about the state roads, Holmes frequently received the likes of the opinion that "capitalist and wealthy men own most of the land. And the poorer classes do not take much delight in working and making roads that would be worth more to the capitalist and the landowner than it would be to themselves.... It is nothing but right that those who derive the most benefit from good roads, should contribute the larger share.... Hurrah for the taxation system," this yeoman concluded. "I dont think that any law is just which requires labor alone to make and repair the public roads," seconded a correspondent from Watauga County. "I think there should be some sistem [sic] of taxation so that capital should help to keep up the roads," he recommended.[44] Road engineers in the field encountered "firm opposition to the system of conscript labor as old, inadequate, unequal and therefore unjust."[45] "By taxation the burden is made proportionately equal and just," one of Holmes's correspondents insisted.[46] And in a public speech to a good roads meeting, the North Carolina Commissioner of Agriculture confirmed the "folly, absurdity and injustice of a road system which attempted to force the keeping up of the roads upon those who had little interest in their condition, and letting go scot-free the property of the county."[47]

Unfortunately, "the property of the county" often resisted any increase in *ad valorem* taxation for road improvement, and instead pressed for more rigorous enforcement of the road conscript laws, or new "laws that would give [the] J.P. more jurisdiction ... to fine the guilty and turn them over to towns for Public Road improvement."[48] One irate correspondent suggested that in order to get more work from the hands the number of days required should be increased to ten, and nonpayers of the poll tax should be required to work it out on the road, "so that the idlers who are good for nothing can be made to bear part of the burden." Then, and only then, would increased taxation be acceptable to property-holders.[49] These sentiments obviously indicated receptivity to convict labor, preferably black, as a resolution to the bitter class tensions among whites.

One interim solution, however, was for counties to collect the commutation tax paid by citizens in lieu of their required labor, and then use this money to hire men to work the roads. But these funds proved difficult to collect or insufficient, "it being the general agreement that since they are paying [property] taxes for keeping the roads they have no further duties in relation to the maintenance of public roads."[50] Even when counties found the financial means to hire labor, it could be difficult to recruit. "I would have worked some [roads] last week," one road overseer reported contritely, "but could not get any [hired] hand[s] ... hands are rite hard to get owing to the busy season." Roads were best worked "during hot, dry months and not during winter," noted one of Holmes's correspondents, but "our roads have no attention during summer ... , we wait until crops are 'laid by' and fall rains set in." As a result, "the roads are made nearly impassable," he complained. When sufficient hired labor could be had, the road hands were hardly more efficient than the reluctant conscripts they replaced. A delegate to one of the earliest North Carolina Good Roads conventions pointed out that half of a hired labor force would not return for a second week of work after they had been paid off. "You can get more work out of convicts than you can of hired labor," he proclaimed.[51]

If both conscript and hired labor appeared unreliable, convict labor proved the ideal solution. In order to create a public demand for better roads, the reformers felt, good roads would have to be constructed without straining local fiscal resources or alienating taxpayers. "The best plan to insure this," insisted one advocate, "is to concentrate our efforts that all convicts shall be employed on the roads ... so that the people can see the results and the benefits to accrue."[52] Faced with the necessity of replacing statute labor, and anxious to demonstrate the benefits of good roads to tightfisted voters, Holmes and his supporters saw North Carolina's forced labor pool as an immense resource at their disposal. Thus the North Carolina Highway Commission, established in 1902 at the behest of the good roads movement, noted in its first report that "the value of [convict labor] is not to be underestimated, and the state in its present condition can not otherwise obtain" labor for the improvement of its roads. Counties that normally could not "afford to employ the labor necessary to build permanent good roads, can, by the use of convicts, largely reduce this expense, and it is in this way quite an inducement for them to undertake the work."[53]

As progress was made, good roads enthusiasts pointed to convict labor as a key component of the change sweeping the southern trans- portation network. "The old labor system is gradually giving place to the more modern, more enlightened, and more practicable system of improving roads by taxation," reported the US Department of Agricul- ture in 1904. As a result, "the number of convicts employed at road building in the different states has steadily increased ... and the use of the convict force has done much to help along the movement for good roads in all [the South]," the report continued, because "its employment has cheapened the cost of road building." "The use of convict labor has been the beginning and the basis of the modern road building in the southern states," Joseph Holmes bluntly informed the North Carolina Good Roads Convention in 1902.[54]

North Carolina, while in the forefront of the good roads cause, was no exception. Wherever enthusiasm for good roads in the South reigned, there was a corresponding attack on convict leasing and a call for the state to put the convicts to work on the roads instead. The good roads movement quickly became "identified with the movement to take the prisoner out of the cell, the prison factory, and the mine to work him in the fresh air and sunshine." Georgia was an early convert to this gospel. "The substance of the work of several of the last Georgia road congresses was to pass resolutions to the effect that the convicts should be worked upon the roads," noted an observer in the 1890s.[55] Because of its vast pool of convicts, Georgia eventually provided other states with a compelling illustration of what could be accomplished with forced labor once it was controlled by the state.[56]

Georgia's own state Good Roads Association was formed in December 1901, at the behest of the national Office of Public Roads; "any white citizen upon payment of dues may become a member," read its by-laws.[57] But as early as 1894, O.H. Sheffield, a civil engineer at the University of Georgia, had produced a study for the OPR on "the improvement of the road system of Georgia." Sheffield emphatically rejected the statute labor system, and insisted that "through the employment of convicts on the public roads is offered a rational solution of the road question."[58] At the time, however, because the state's two thousand felony convicts were leased, only misdemeanor convicts under short sentences were available for public county road work. Georgia gradually expanded the cast of the legal net that captured prisoners for the use of county chain gangs instead of the private lease camps; in 1903, for example, the legislature gave counties the option of requisitioning for road work state felony convicts with less than five-year sentences to supplement their misdemeanor county prisoners. But the felony convict labor force was not completely mobilized for road work in Georgia until the state abolished convict leasing in 1908.[59]

This exemplary Progressive reform has been presented both as a response to humanitarian outrage stirred up by the press and as a corrective to the declining economic rationality of convict leasing, as the cost of the lease increased.[60] But such noble sentiments as "the punishment [of convicts] ought not to be at the hands of a private party who may be tempted by the exigencies of business ... to make punishment either more or less" were not given political expression until reformers could agree upon an alternative for the convict lease. After all, as the Savannah *Tribune* had pointed out, the revelations of cruelty were hardly news, even to white Georgians; the lessees had endured nearly forty years of adverse investigations. But with the help of Georgia's labor movement the campaign for good roads finally provided an acceptable alternative. In the southwestern states (Texas, Mississippi, Louisiana, Arkansas) state penal farms were the preferred "Progressive" alternative to leasing, while some border states shifted to the industrial factory contract-labor model of the penitentiary recently abandoned in the North. But road work prevailed in the southeast, where it was most appropriate to that region's emerging political economy.[61]

Southern good roads advocates harnessed convict labor to characteristic Progressive methods and beliefs. By attacking the statute labor system, they championed efficiency. Moreover, road improvement was financed with modern forms of state-generated revenue, either increased tax assessments or debt in the form of local bond issues. And road-building could not go forward without the intervention of experts; localities were provided with professional engineering and construction advice, often under the aegis of the federal OPR. Many of the engineers who worked and wrote for the OPR were from the South, and were employed in state bureaucracies as well as the federal government. William L. Spoon, Joseph A. Holmes, Joseph Hyde Pratt, and P. St. Julien Wilson all fit this profile, for example. The penetration of the federal bureaucracy by southerners during the Progressive Era, and their impact on race relations at the national level, is a full story in itself. But as historians of southern Progressivism have noted, many southern reform movements of this era were also oriented toward the "rationalization" of race relations. And in the realm of Progressive ideas about race, the good roads movement and the champions of penal reform found common cause.[62]

Remarking on the extraordinary revelations of the 1908 investigation of the convict lease that preceded its abolition in Georgia, the southern reformer Alexander McKelway pointed out that a witness "would frequently speak of a convict as a 'nigger,' when it was found that he meant a white man." Such confusion was readily understandable, given that nine-tenths of the state's prisoners were black. It also reveals, however, the intimate association in the mind of the white southerner of the "social death" imposed on the convict with the enforced status of the black race more generally. In an effort to redeem the white convict from this association, the most racist defenders of the lease had complained that it "lays on the Caucasian a dreadful grief, which the

African does not feel" because it brought the races into close contact. Indeed, it was rationalized, this effective deterrent was the explanation for the small proportion of whites in the penal system. These attitudes informed the anticipation of some penal reformers that, with the abolition of leasing, white prisoners would be remanded to a central penitentiary, while blacks would work the public roads in chains, since their "moral standard[s] [are] not lowered by this form of publicity."[63]

But it would be a mistake to understand McKelway's support for the elimination of leasing as merely an attempt to rescue a handful of whites from its indiscriminate brutality. Southern Progressives applauded the abolition of the convict lease because this reform also advanced what they believed was their "moderate" racial agenda for African-Americans. The shameful lease and double standards of justice lacked legitimacy as a legal sanction, and thus encouraged "absolute indifference of the negroes to the punishment of the criminal," Progressives claimed. By removing brutality and corruption from the penal system, men like McKelway hoped to encourage "the negroes ... to aid in the detection of the criminal and his delivery to justice."[64] For Progressives, overt racial repression and brutality were counterproductive. Instead, social progress for the South and the nation as a whole depended on well-ordered race relations and the firm control – and protection – of what they regarded as a childlike race.[65]

Thus disfranchisement, segregation, and prohibition were all promoted as supposed "reforms" to check the chaotic tendencies of southern race relations and to protect against the feared "moral and physical reversion" of what nearly all whites believed was the inferior race.[66] In Georgia, in the wake of the 1906 Atlanta race riot, these were the "accomplishments" of Progressive governor Hoke Smith's administration, which also oversaw the abolition of convict leasing, placing blacks in something of a quandary. The Savannah *Tribune*, for instance, confronted the dilemma of wanting to excoriate Smith for depriving blacks of the vote while congratulating him for ending the convict lease.[67] Unfortunately, in the latter instance, the substitution of the public chain gang for the private lease mobilized the power of the state to reproduce what white Progressives understood to be the benign paternalism of antebellum slavery. When it came to the south's "criminal class" – synonymous, in the minds of white reformers, with "the negro" – the chain gang thus could operate as a form of state-sponsored *noblesse oblige*. Just as the vicious and arbitrary mob would be replaced by the strong but fair arm of the law, the greed of the convict lessees would be supplanted by the reformatory power and interest of the state, they held. As one northern penal reformer noted, "the convict on the road is the slave of the state," and slaves had always labored faithfully for kind masters, he believed.[68]

In a striking update of the pro-slavery argument presented before the Southern Sociological Congress in 1913, Georgia legislator Hooper Alexander explained how progressive penology and modern racial paternalism went hand in hand. Antebellum slavery had itself been a "reform" made necessary by the racial burden left to the colonies by the African slave trade, he claimed. This burden required governmental action, but "domestic slavery was an expedient for discharging that duty by contract." In other words, slavery had been nothing more than the privatization and alienation of the state's natural function of racial control; and slave labor was merely the slaveowner's just compensation for carrying out this function at his own expense. So, too, in the wake of emancipation Alexander saw the convict lease as an analogous private means to carry out the public end of coping with the freed slaves' "natural" criminal tendencies. He admitted, however, that in contrast to the peculiar institution the convict lease did not prove beneficial for blacks. Nevertheless, he concluded, "the evil was far worse than the sufferings of the convict," as bad as those might have been; for convict leasing both competed with free labor and represented "the shirking of government duty."[69]

Ultimately, Progressive reformers relied on the chain gang to reclaim what they saw as the state's "government duty" simultaneously to constrain and uplift the black race; unfortunately, in the process the "sufferings of the convict" were ignored. The good roads movement looked to the state to provide a labor pool; but the chain gang, which the state used to supply the manpower for road improvement, perpetuated rather than eradicated one of the "darker phases of the South." In fact, the most ambitious pre-New Deal effort to nationalize and modernize the isolated rural South depended on one of the region's most viciously racist local institutions. For Progressive Era chain gangs had their origins in some of the *worst* prison camps found during the era of leasing, those reserved for petty criminals sentenced in county or municipal courts for misdemeanors.[70] Under Georgia's lease system, unless they were subleased, long-term felony convicts generally worked in large groups for heavily capitalized private industries, including the "largest lumber business in the South," George V. Gress's convict-worked sawmill in Wilcox County. But alongside this system coexisted a parallel, shadowy network of county and municipal road gangs and isolated, marginal turpentine and lumber camps, which worked small groups of short-term misdemeanor prisoners. Post-1908 chain gangs in Georgia had their origins in this archipelago of misdemeanor convict camps, which numbered over fifty by the turn of the century.[71]

Many of the convicts in these original misdemeanor camps were sentenced to between thirty days and one year for petty crimes such as gambling, carrying a concealed weapon, drunkenness, fighting, disorderly conduct, loitering, and vagrancy. The Bibb County, Georgia road camp, for instance, drew its labor force from the summary convictions meted out by the Macon city recorder's court, which in March 1904 alone sent 124 men and 25 women to the county chain gang for a total of 6,751 days of labor. Some 56 of these convictions were for drunkenness, 40 for disorderly conduct, 18 for fighting, 12 for loitering, another 12 for violating city ordinances, 4 for reckless driving or riding, 2 for throwing rocks, and 1 simply for "suspect." Dan Johnson was given six months on the roads for "suspect loitering." Henry Jamison, an African-American whose habeas corpus challenge to the chain gang later reached federal district court, in a few minutes before Macon's recorder was "sentenced to pay a fine of Sixty Dollars, or ... to serve a term of Two Hundred and Ten days in the County Chain Gang" for drunk and disorderly conduct "in Barracks" (the police station). Macon's recorder's court heard between eighteen and fifty cases like this daily.[72]

Although the list of sentences imposed in Macon is not broken down by race, the Bibb County sheriff testified in federal court that of 180 state, county, and municipal convicts on the county roads, only 10 or 12 were white. Some of the black convicts were Macon's porters, seamstresses, and launderers, or laborers at the city's cotton presses. But only one-fourth can be located in the city directory at all, suggesting that large numbers were transients or rural blacks from the surrounding county who visited Macon only to be caught in its daily dragnet. Savannah's black newspaper noted a similar procedure of labor "recruitment" in that city's municipal court. Observing that labor was needed for a new city drainage project, the *Tribune* asked sarcastically "will word be sent to the recorder and the judge of the city court for these extra men?"[73]

These misdemeanor convicts on the roads were worked by the county authorities; but others were leased to private interests just as the state felony convicts were. Rural misdemeanants faced a cruel experience in isolated turpentine camps, sawmills, and other enterprises with short-term or seasonal labor needs, especially in south Georgia. The Donalson Lumber Company, in Decatur County, for example, leased thirty-nine convicts (thirty-seven of them black) for its turpentine business in 1899. Twenty-six of these bound laborers had been convicted of larceny, and these convicts were drawn from the courts of six different nearby counties. E.J. Smith's turpentine camp in Berrien County had twenty-nine black convicts from its own court, all except one males between the ages of fourteen and thirty-seven, two-thirds of them unable to read and write. They had been sentenced for gaming, larceny, carrying a concealed weapon, and "running away." Eight of them were at the camp for the second time; one man was serving his fifth sentence there. During the month of May 1900, eleven of these convicts were whipped to "enforce work."[74]

County-court clerks, sheriffs, and judges gladly leased these convicts out, often in an attempt to collect their fees and costs. The recorded minutes of the Colquitt County Court in 1894, in south Georgia turpentine country, include "sales" of convicts charged with carrying a concealed weapon, and unable to pay a fine, to Grier Brothers' turpentine camp for "twenty-four dollars, the highest offer made by any chain gang." In the same county in 1903, Will Boyd received five months at a lumber camp for stealing an axe; in Wilcox County an unspecified "misdemeanor" could mean twelve months of "hard labor" for the Ocmulgee Brick Company.[75]

> Thought I heard – huh!
> Judge Pequette say – huh!
> Forty-five dollars – huh!
> Take him away – huh!

went a work song sung by African-American convicts in Georgia.[76]

Turpentine farm operators in particular sought this bound labor force because of the fluidity and the constraints of their production process. They often tapped pine trees in forests on leased land, making it necessary "for the production to continue until the [land] lease is expired" even if the market price of naval stores went down. The important "box-cutting" that exposed the pine resin could only be done in the winter months, and was carried out by a task system of labor, readily adaptable to forced labor. Workers would then have to return to the forest in the summer to "chip" the trees to get at the turpentine. This highly destructive method of extraction produced diminishing returns each season, and eventually required a new virgin stand of timber to remain profitable. Finally, turpentine operators using free labor recruited transient black workers, many drawn from out of state, who prized their mobility. With convicts, however, employers "know just where to find their men when they want them, which is something of an item in a country where the help is mostly niggers," one observer noted. The combination of labor uncertainty, production on a narrow margin, destructive methods of extraction, seasonality, geographic mobility, and

Table 7.2 Distribution of Georgia Misdemeanor Convicts by Work,
1898–1908

	Forest[a]		Farm		Roads		Other[b]		Total
	no.	%	no.	%	no.	%	no.	%	
1898	305	16.6	141	7.7	1,388	75.7			1,834
1899	616	25.8	273	11.5	1,495	62.7			2,384
1900	613	25.0	346	14.1	1,469	59.9	23	0.9	2,451
1901	660	32.5	236	11.6	1,092	53.8	43	2.1	2,031
1902	643	29.0	175	7.9	1,256	56.6	147	6.6	2,221
1904	502	25.6	99	5.0	1,297	66.0	66	3.4	1,964
1905	590	25.8	82	3.6	1,597	70.0	67	2.9	2,283
1906	503	24.6	51	2.5	1,410	69.0	79[c]	3.9	2,043
1907	559	24.3	75	3.3	1,650	71.8	14	0.6	2,298
1908	495	20.4	54	2.2	1,871	76.9	12	0.5	2,432

Notes: [a] Includes turpentine, sawmills, cutting wood and crossties.   [b] Mining ore and coal, brickmaking.   [c] Includes 57 on railroad work.

Source: Prison Commission, *Report*.

isolation encouraged many turpentine operators to look to the county courts for their labor supply.[77]

For all these same reasons, convict camps in the turpentine woods were remote, temporary, and rudimentary. The living conditions, food, and work regimens by task in these camps and those in the related lumber industry were absolutely the most severe in Georgia, even though they punished the state's most petty criminals. Many of these backwoods camps operated entirely without state sanction or oversight, as indifferent as it was. These so-called "wildcat" camps – twenty-four were discovered in an 1897 investigation – were technically illegal, but appeared immune to efforts to stamp them out. Wildcat convict camps had 598 prisoners in 1897; of these, 570, or 95 per cent, were black. "The average penal camp of the State penitentiary is a heaven compared to the agony and torture suffered by misdemeanor convicts in many of these joints of suffering," concluded the state's investigator.[78]

County commissioners who wanted to improve their roads had frequently to compete with both wildcat and official local turpentine and brickyard camps for the misdemeanor labor force (see Table 7.2 for distribution), especially when wages for free labor rose and "the loafing negro has things going his way and goes from place to place" (in the words of a turpentine operator). When wages were high, a stable, cheap labor force was at a premium, and the demand for leased convicts

Table 7.3 County Road Improvement and Convict Labor in Georgia, 1901

	Counties	
	using convicts (n = 25)	no convicts (n = 112)
Road mileage	9,570	36,342
% of mileage in state	20.8	79.2
Miles graded	1,379 (14.4%)	467 (1.3%)
% of graded in state	74.7	25.3
Miles surfaced	505 (5.2%)	58 (0.2%)
% of surfaced in state	89.7	10.3
Total improved	1,884 (19.7%)	525 (1.4%)
% of improved in state	78.2	21.8
Black population >50%	18 counties (72%)	48 counties (43%)
Median black population %	62.2%	41.1%

Source: Georgia Geological Survey. *A Preliminary Report of the Roads and Road-Building Materials of Georgia*, Bulletin No. 8 (Atlanta, Ga.: State Printer, 1901), and US Dept. of the Interior, US Census Office, *Twelfth Census of the United States, 1900*, Vol. 1, *Population* (Washington, DC: GPO, 1901), pp. 533–34.

increased. As one local black critic of south Georgia justice pointed out in 1904, "there is such a demand down in South Georgia for turpentine hands and sawmill hands" that blacks "are given the full extent of the law on the weakest evidence," so that turpentine operators could "buy them for their labor" in court. Entrepreneurs who sought a bound labor force were often thwarted, however, because rising wages also enabled blacks to pay fines for misdemeanors, rather than serve their sentence of hard labor, thus *decreasing* the pool of short-term convicts just when operators needed them. The Georgia Prison Commission reported in 1901, for instance, that in prosperous times, when the price of cotton was high, black laborers hauled before local courts for misdemeanors – or their white patrons on the plantations – could come up with the cash for fines. This, the commissioners claimed, restricted the available pool of misdemeanor convicts.[79]

In Colquitt County, for example, the local grand jury (which convened twice a year) constantly prodded the county commissioners to "make arrangements for working the misdemeanor convicts of the county on the public roads." The commissioners themselves acknowledged that there was "a good deal of complaint ... in regard to the public roads of the county being in bad shape." Yet at the same time the grand jury noted that in September 1903 there were thirty convicts at work at the Allen & Holmes turpentine camp; the following year they reported that twenty convicts were found at Mallets and Gray's sawmills. In 1905 the county was able to get nine convicts for its road crew, but by 1907 the grand jury still complained that "we found [only] two convicts and are informed that in about two weeks they both will be released and the chain-gang will have no inmates.... We would recommend that some Means be provided to increase the number of convicts," they concluded. Three years after the statewide abolition of leasing, however, the grand jury reported that thirty convicts – twenty-nine of them black – worked Colquitt County's roads. "As a whole," the grand jury concluded in 1911, "the Public roads of the County have been greatly improved during the past few years."[80] But until 1908 the tension over the distribution of county misdemeanor convicts persisted despite the dubious legality of misdemeanor leases.

Counties that established chain gangs on a regular basis showed a marked improvement in their roads, and gradually misdemeanor convicts were put on the county chain gangs instead of being leased. By 1908, 77 per cent of Georgia's misdemeanants worked on the roads (see Table 7.2). Because Georgia's county courts were overly concerned with punishing African-Americans' efforts at labor mobility, as well as their alleged social transgressions, the racial composition of the misdemeanor chain gangs was even more lopsided than the penitentiary, with 95 per cent of the convicts being black. "The crime for which Negroes are most strictly held to account [in this county] is that of breaking contracts," reported one correspondent from the black belt to Atlanta University's 1904 conference on "negro crime." This was compounded by the fact that few black misdemeanants could pay the fines which supported sheriffs, county judges, and court officials. White men often paid fines for blacks, noted another correspondent to the conference, "in order that he can tie him. This is what some of them call controlling labor."[81]

Significantly, the first counties in Georgia to draw on this pool of black labor for their roads were not just those with the best roads; geographically they cut a swath through the state's black belt of plantation districts, where African-Americans were concentrated, racial subordination and control were essential to agriculture, and good roads benefited large landholders (see Figure 7.1). It is also interesting to note that almost all the counties of the "terrible tenth" congressional district, the stronghold of Georgia Populism, established chain gangs before 1900. The Populists had both opposed convict leasing and supported

174

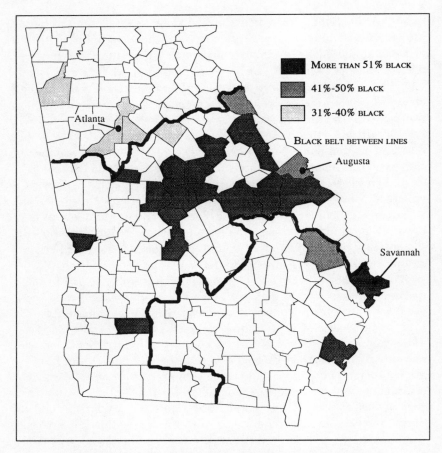

Figure 7.1   Racial Composition of Georgia Counties
with Chain Gangs, 1901

Source: Georgia Geological Survey, *A Preliminary Report on the Roads and Road-Building Materials of Georgia*, Bulletin No. 8 (Atlanta, Ga.: State Printer, 1901); *Numan v. Bartley, The Creation of Modern Georgia* (Atlanta, Ga.: University of Georgia, 1983), for black-belt counties; US Department of Interior, US Census Office, *Twelfth Census of the US*, Vol. 1, *Population* (Washington, DC: GPO, 1901), pp. 533–4. Map by Dean Hansen.

good roads. Counties with growing urban areas, where social control of a black working class cut loose from plantation "discipline" meshed with commercial expansion, were also pioneers of the chain gang. By 1901 only 25 of Georgia's 137 counties worked convicts on the roads, but these counties, with only 21 per cent of all roads in the state, boasted 90 per cent of the state's surfaced roads and 75 per cent of the graded roads. Indeed, in the 112 counties that relied on statute labor or hired free labor to work the roads only 1.4 per cent of the roads were improved; in the counties with chain gangs the comparable figure was 19.7 per cent (see Table 7.3).[82]

Frustrated Georgia county commissioners who could not acquire convicts complained to the state geologist in 1901 that "we use only statute labor, and our roads are poorly worked." This same correspondent concluded: "I am satisfied that we can never have good roads until they are worked by direct taxation, and the use of the Chain gang." In counties with convicts, such as Richmond, it was reported that "we find them the most satisfactory labor for the roads, and the very best disposition to make of the convicts." Generally, those counties that reported a recent adoption of the chain gang noted that "the roads during this time [since using convict labor] have been greatly improved." Atlanta and surrounding Fulton County, commercial hub of the Progressive South, had the state's most modern road system in 1901. Misdemeanor convicts had worked the roads there since 1876, when a local judge noticed their impassable condition, and "to ameliorate these conditions ... organized the first chain-gang."[83]

Apparently the use of misdemeanor convicts on the roads was popular, as Georgia's law of 1903 which made felony convicts with sentences of less than five years available to the counties suggests. Any county which "work[ed] their misdemeanor convicts upon the public roads" could petition the prison commission for these felons to add to the growing pool of misdemeanor prisoners doing road work. Thus even before the convict lease was abolished in 1908, leasing had been eroded by road work, and nearly 50 per cent of Georgia's entire forced labor pool worked on the state's roads (see Table 7.4).[84]

The abolition of convict leasing in 1908 placed nearly five thousand felony and misdemeanor convicts, 91 per cent of whom were black, in the hands of the state to be worked on the roads. Georgia's counties immediately clamored for their apportionment of forced labor, and state officials anticipated the beneficial results of the new penal system.[85] Ten days after the General Assembly passed the legislation ending leasing, Governor Hoke Smith proudly informed the US Office of Public Roads that "we are about to inaugurate upon a broad scale the improvement

Table 7.4   Felony and Misdemeanor Convicts on Georgia Roads, 1904–1908

	Felony (on roads)		Misdemeanor (on roads)		Total (on roads)		%
1904	2,315	(573)	1,964	(1,297)	4,279	(1,870)	43.7
1905	2,280	(573)	2,283	(1,597)	4,563	(2,170)	47.5
1906	2,344	(571)	2,043	(1,410)	4,387	(1,981)	45.2
1907	2,464	(574)	2,298	(1,650)	4,762	(2,224)	46.7
1908	2,564	(615)	2,432	(1,871)	4,996	(2,486)	49.8

Source: Prison Commission, *Report*, 1904–08 (1 June of each year).

of our roads in Georgia," a project made possible by the large pool of forced labor suddenly at the state's disposal. And when he boasted of his administration's record in his legislative address the following year, Smith pointed to the end of the convict lease as a prime example of Progressive reform. "[A]ll the convicts … are now at work upon the public roads of the State," he told the General Assembly. "As a result of placing the convicts upon the public roads an enthusiasm has been aroused throughout the entire state for good roads," he concluded.[86]

During the subsequent years Georgia's penal reform was touted as a great success, not least by the prophets of southern progress and economic modernization, who insisted that "good roads and prosperity are synonymous."[87] Legislative committees continued to visit convict camps, and remarked approvingly that "the magnitude of the work being done in Georgia by the convicts, and the results being accomplished, are almost beyond conception." In a single year alone, the legislature claimed, convicts had "graded and made permanent" six thousand miles of road and "to some extent permanently improved" another fifteen thousand miles. This was made possible because "with little or no inconvenience [the convict] accomplishes double as much in a day as a free laborer."[88] Georgia's prison commission, whose three members were delegates to the National Good Roads Convention in 1912, was equally enthusiastic. In 1911 the commission reported that convicts worked the roads in 135 of Georgia's 146 counties, which were "getting real benefit out of the convicts on their highways." The state geologist, while noting that the eleven counties without chain gangs – all in the Upcountry, with negligible black populations – "have no improved roads," claimed that in the rest of the state convicts built twelve miles of good roads each day. In counties with chain gangs, prisoners were "constructing annually more than twice the number of miles of improved highways than [Georgia] had when our present convict system was put into effect," according to this state official. "It is only a matter of time when our good old state of Georgia will lead the entire United States in the matter of good roads," boasted the prison commissioners.[89]

This may have been an idle boast, but other observers confirmed the rapid improvement in Georgia's transportation infrastructure. *Southern Good Roads* magazine, the mouthpiece of the good roads movement, ran several editorials praising Georgia for "throw[ing] off the shackles [of the lease] and ... building more good roads than any other state in the South," and urged other southern states to follow suit by taking the convicts "in the penitentiaries, on farms, in factories and mines, or ... leased out to contractors" and putting them on the roads. Good roads enthusiasts pointed to the immense increase in the taxable value of property in Georgia wherever new or improved roads penetrated, and looked to the state as an example of the benefits derived from a comprehensive road-building program with convict labor.[90]

Rhetoric and boosterism aside, the number of miles of surfaced road and the percentage of roads improved in Georgia did increase dramatically once convicts began to work on the highways. In 1904 not even 3 per cent of the state's 57,000 miles of roads was surfaced with gravel, stone, or sand-clay. By 1909, when all the convicts were placed on the roads, the state had 82,000 miles of road, 7.27 per cent of which was surfaced, although only five miles were laid in bituminous macadam, the most modern road surface. Five years later, however, the percentage of surfaced roads had at least doubled to 15.5 per cent, and was, in one estimate, over 25 per cent; by 1914, fourteen Georgia counties had between 200 and 300 miles of surfaced roads. Over 300 miles were now surfaced in bituminous macadam, according to one estimate, and Georgia's 13,000 miles of surfaced rural roads by the end of 1915 surpassed that of all other southern states, and indeed ranked fifth in the United States.[91]

Generally speaking, after the abolition of convict leasing in Georgia, the counties with the most miles of improved roads were the counties with the largest force of convicts, both their own misdemeanants and the felony prisoners they acquired from the state prison commission. The roads of Clarke County, home of the University of Georgia (whose civil engineering department was in the forefront of the state's good roads/convict labor movement), for example, benefited from ten thousand man-days of forced labor between April 1913 and April 1914, provided by as many as sixty-six black and twelve white convicts. In

1909, only 30.6 per cent of this county's roads were surfaced; by 1914 the figure was 57.2 per cent, surpassed by only a handful of counties in the state. "The county is remarkable for its system of public roads, which are among the best in the state," one student of rural life in Clarke County remarked. Only fifteen years earlier the superintendent of Clarke's public roads had vowed to employ misdemeanor convicts in road work, complaining that "it is well nigh impossible to have [conscripted] farm-hands do good work, because they are untrained and the overseers ... allow them to kill time."[92]

Clearly statewide success in road improvement was in great measure due to the labor of the convicts, which was held by its advocates to be superior to free labor. Forced labor was cheap and reliable. The Georgia Senate estimated that convict labor cost "less than half what free labor would cost." Moreover, unlike free labor, convicts were "absolutely dependable so far as numbers are concerned," according to a report by the OPR. "Plans for work can be made in advance with a sure knowledge that the anticipated number of laborers will be on hand to execute them," which had been impossible with the inefficient statute labor system. This regularity of labor allowed the road overseer to "develop the maximum efficiency of each man to an extent which is not possible with shifting free labor," the OPR concluded. Thus convict labor combined the "great advantages of regularity, of being under perfect control, and of being operated at about 60 per cent of the cost of ordinary labor."[93]

In short, promoters of convict road work saw the same economic advantages in forced labor that the convict lessees had before them; the OPR even helped build "object lesson" roads with convict labor in the South, and studied the cost of these projects to demonstrate their superior efficiency. According to its advocates, "convict labor is far more easily controlled" than statute or even hired labor. "You take the average built free man and put him on the public roads and work him hard for ten hours a day, and he will strike for higher wages," claimed William L. Spoon, a road engineer. "The convict," on the other hand, "is forced to do regular work and that regular work results in the upbuilding of the convict, the upbuilding of the public roads, and the upbuilding of the state," he proclaimed.[94]

Spoon, at least, reminded the good roads movement that the chain gang was meant to be progressive in the area of penology as well as economic development. With all its racial connotations, "bad boys make good roads" became a folk aphorism in Georgia, but penal reformers believed that "bad men on bad roads make good roads while [work on] good roads make[s] good men."[95] After all, as the reformer Alexander

McKelway told the American Prison Association in 1908, with the abolition of leasing in Georgia "the retributive idea of punishment is giving place at last among us to the reformatory idea."[96] Humanitarian and rehabilitatory penal conditions were not merely attributed to state – as opposed to private – control of convict labor, but to the very character of labor on the roads. The cult of the "strenuous life," the frequent conflation of the physical and moral spheres in the Progressive Era, was applied to penal labor, especially in the South. "Life in the convict road camp ... is more conducive to maintaining and building up the general health and manhood of the convict than where he is confined behind prison walls," opined *Southern Good Roads* magazine. The Director of the US Office of Public Roads used a "poem," supposedly written by a convict in Virginia, to illustrate the prisoners' own alleged preference for "open air work."

> Oh! take me back to the convict camp,
>   Put me to work on the grade;
> I like the scent of the canvas tent
>   And the bunk the Sargeant made.
>
> Just take me out of this pesky jail,
>   To the camp, and God's fresh air;
> Away from this shack, where the small gray-back,
>   Skiddoos through my uncut hair....
>
> Oh! take me back to the village of tents,
>   I am sick of this prison cell;
> I'm an old Hobo, but think I know
>   When I strike a good hotel.
>
> Please take me back, today if you can,
>   Just forget about your fee;
> I've been there once, and served six months,
>   And the road man's jail suits me.[97]

This sort of ditty was meant to imply that on the roads the convict worked at a "healthful occupation" which simultaneously improved his character and paid his debt to society. "Even if against his will [the convict] is taught to know what it means to be healthy, cleanly, industrious and orderly, he will have reached a higher standard of living by reason of his experience on the convict force," suggested one defender of the South's convict camps. The supposedly invigorating and rewarding experience of outdoor labor was even contrasted to the alienation of penitentiary factory labor; "although the convict's labor [on the roads] may be of very great benefit to the state, it also is of benefit to the convict himself in that it brings to him the realization he cannot grasp in the prison-shop grind, that he may be of real importance in life as a producing agent," insisted the US Office of Public Roads. Joseph Hyde Pratt, one of the most persistent advocates of the chain gang, admitted that despite the fear of competition with free labor "the state should try to train the prisoner to some useful occupation." On the roads, he claimed implausibly, convicts will be "trained as expert day laborers and can give good value for money received."[98]

The enthusiasm of the good roads movement for the chain gang was not confined to the South, but "it was in the South that convict road labor became so popular that it threatened to displace all other penal systems," according to one historian. During the Progressive Era, observers attributed this in part to climate – outdoor labor was possible year round in the South; but the factor of race was more significant than sunshine. Most of the convicts in the South, of course, were African-Americans. Road work was frequently defended as particularly appropriate to southern conditions because blacks were perceived as suited to the heavy, unskilled labor it required, and the discipline of coerced outdoor labor was perceived as beneficial to blacks. Good roads advocates at the national level, as well as the regional and local levels, advanced these racial rationales for the chain gang. "Personally, I favor the employment of convicts [only] in the Southern States in the building of public roads," a federal road engineer wrote privately in 1912, "as in this section of the country the convicts are largely made up of negroes, who are benefited by outdoor manual labor, and whose moral standard is not lowered" by working in chains in public. "The negro is accustomed to outdoor occupations ... [and is] experienced in manual labor," claimed the assistant director of the US Office of Public Roads, and he "does not possess the same aversion to working in public ... as is characteristic of the white race."[99]

The compatibility of penal labor and road improvement was thus deemed unique in the South, where, in the words of OPR engineers, "the human material dealt with is so radically different from that of the other sections." The racialist defense of the chain gang received the imprimatur of the national OPR, which fifty years after emancipation argued that convict road work in the South was racially, penologically and economically progressive because "the negro of criminal tendency is compelled by the chain-gang to live a regular and healthful life," and "fear of punishment produces a respectful attention to the orders of the overseer, and a willingness to do more work than money would induce him to perform."[100] Thus, with federal collusion, the reform of the South's penal system left its basic function of racial and labor discipline intact.

Racial ideology, Progressive penology, and the goal of economic modernization were reconciled in the realm of political economy. As in the past, on the road gangs forced black labor was "recruited" for the most "progressive" sector of the southern economy. Only now, penal reform, the desire for improved transportation, and the archaic nature of statute labor for road work led to the abolition of the lease and the use of convicts on the roads, in Georgia and elsewhere. This transformed the work regime of convicts, but also, more significantly, the relationship between forced labor and the economy. "The people should demand that their criminals be worked on the roads.... The state should receive the profit of their labor, and not a few individuals," was the battle cry against convict leasing in a region with modern iron furnaces and ancient dirt roads.[101]

As the most prominent penal reform in the early-twentieth-century South, the convict road gang was touted as a healthy (literally) alternative to the practice of leasing state and county convicts to coal mines, turpentine farms, brickyards, and railroads. But by wresting the convicts from the hands of the New South's capitalist entrepreneurs, the state abandoned its role as a recruiter and seller of forced labor, labor used for capital accumulation and the exploitation of the South's resources in primarily extractive industries. Instead, the state became the direct exploiter of that labor in an effort to build and maintain a transportation infrastructure which might contribute to the expansion of the manufacturing, consumer, and commercial sectors.

Just as that earlier system of forced labor was driven primarily by the dictates of political economy rather than humane penology, so too was the decision to remove the South's forced labor pool from the hands of private enterprise and give it to the "people" in the interest of a more public notion of economic development. "The convict is as much the property of the state as the slave before the war was the property of the slave owner," wrote one reformer. "The state is his real master and as such is not only responsible for his well-being, but for the productivity of his labor to the end that the community at large may be served." Road work in particular was held up as penal labor "for the common welfare." Since the criminal had offended the community, his hard labor "belongs to all the people"; on the South's roads, "instead of building to the interests of private parties [the convict] is building to the interest of all the people," declared believers in the chain gang.[102]

After 1908 Georgia was considered a "banner" state in road-building, but one of the "most backward in its penological development," writes a historian of southern penal reform. In fact the very success of the state's road-expansion program depended upon its brutal penal conditions. With such an overwhelming emphasis on the economic benefits of forced labor it should come as no surprise that for the convicts themselves the difference between the chain gang and the convict lease proved negligible. This was especially true because the convicts were now scattered in hundreds of county road camps subject to little state oversight, the very problem that had plagued the misdemeanor lease and road camps which served as the precedent for the "progressive" chain gangs that so resembled them. Even after the transition from the convict lease to the chain gang, investigators and convicts complained about poor food and sanitation, relentless labor, and brutal punishment in the state's isolated road camps, where felons and misdemeanants worked together in chains. Georgia's prison commission rules were ignored, claimed one convict on the Hall County chain gang in 1912, and convicts were forced to work under horrendous conditions as a result. The bosses of the gang "have got a whole lots of Rules of they own," he complained to the governor, "so they can get [to] Beat a man half to [death] Every Day." In words reminiscent of long-forgotten desperate pleas to the state executive by leased convicts, another black chain gang prisoner wrote: "[I] have Been Beat + treated wor[se] than if I was a Dog." Perhaps conditions in such convict camps were more modern because "a convict overseer ... [now] rides about in an auto- mobile and uses a strap handwide *studded with brass nails to flog convicts.*"[103]

In North Carolina, another pioneering state in convict road work, chain gang convicts complained to the governor in 1920 that "we are beat up like dogs ... they work us hard and half feed us [and] beat us with shovel and stick." They added that "we cannot make it for the food." Another group of black convicts wrote that "they are whipping right on. We can't get water but one time a day. We cant live." Reports of mass beatings and shootings on the Wayne County chain gang also reached the governor, through the importunities of a "respectable colored woman" in the community. From Johnson County, Wiley Woodard, a black convict, admitted that he "made a mistake" but insisted that this "does not call for the management of this camp to treat me and my race as dogs because he has been mislead [*sic*] regard- ing the law." Woodard pointed out that road work at his camp was "at the point of a gun and threats of [the] lash." An independent observer of North Carolina's chain gang wrote the governor that even though "the State may be getting some good roads out of this system" the chain gang should be terminated, for "it savors too much of slavery times."[104]

Muckraking accounts of southern chain gangs from the 1920s, 1930s, and even late 1940s reveal persistent common features of this unique penal system. Convicts labored, ate, and slept with chains riveted around their ankles. Work was done "under the gun" from sun-up to sundown, shoveling dirt at fourteen shovelfuls a minute. Food was bug-infested, rotten, and unvarying; "rest" was taken in unwashed bedding, often in wheeled cages nine feet wide by twenty feet long containing eighteen beds. Medical treatment and bathing facilities were unsanitary, if available at all. And, above all, corporal punishment and outright torture – casual blows from rifle butts or clubs, whipping with a leather strap, confinement in a "sweat-box" under the southern sun, and hanging from stocks or bars – was meted out for the most insignificant transgressions, particularly to African-Americans who remained the majority of chain gang prisoners.[105]

"The Act of 1908 [abolishing the lease] contemplated humanitarianism as the basis of the management of the State's convicts in the infliction of punishment," proclaimed the Georgia Senate Penitentiary Committee in 1912, and "convicts are not [*sic*] longer considered an object of merchandise." Yet the committee also warned that "in some instances the county authorities appeared to exercise a property right over the convicts." Do not "adopt the plan of farming the men out to individual counties," a Georgia penal reformer warned Alabama's governor in 1913, "do not let public exploitation take the place of private exploitation." Indeed, public control and supervision did not alter the desire of whites to use the penal system to exploit black labor. The prison commission reported in 1912 that "the [county] authorities are doing their utmost to properly care for the convicts in their charge and at the same time get the maximum amount of work for their roads." Yet humanitarian, as opposed to economic, progress was impossible "as long as [the state] puts the emphasis on road work, instead of reclamation of the prisoner," noted the Prison Association of Georgia.[106]

After 1908 the extraction of labor continued to define the conditions of life for Georgia's convicts, much as it had in both private camps and on public misdemeanor road gangs before the abolition of leasing, and white racial beliefs continued to justify the practice. It had always been common knowledge in white Georgia that "men sentenced [to the chain gang] for crap shooting, gambling, burglarizing stores ... ain't used to work.... They will not do a good day's work unless they whip them," one prosecutor claimed. "Without some method of punishment, why, we would not be able to get much work" out of the convicts insisted the boss of the Bibb County chain gang in 1904. Convicts on this chain gang complained that "generally they were whipping some one mighty near all the time" and that "if you don't work like fighting fire all the time you are whipped, [by] a man standing over you with a big strap."

Such treatment was selective, however. The guards "did not whip the white people at all while I was out there," testified one convict. "[White convicts] fare very well, but the colored people catch it shore [*sic*]."[107]

This persistent notion that blacks would only work effectively under the threat of punishment was the ideological basis of penal labor in the South, and the greatest continuity between the convict lease and the chain gang was this racialist view of labor. Moreover, the "reformed" southern penal system continued to play a dual role, not only enforcing labor discipline through direct coercion of its unfortunate recruits but also through imminent threat to its potential victims. The road gang was a highly visible, and economically beneficial, means of social control of rural African-Americans, who were habitually castigated by powerful whites for their alleged reluctance to enter and remain in the agricultural labor market. In a revealing comment on the highly developed chain gang system he observed in Georgia, one road engineer remarked that

> the most striking effect of the convict camp on the roads is its effect on the free labor in producing abundance of labor on the plantations. The prompt arrests for loitering, gambling and other petty offenses with a short sentence on the chain-gang has a wholesome effect on a race that are not noted for either industry or thrift.

The chain gang thus represented one more link in the chain of dependence and coercion shackling African-Americans who sought alternatives to sharecropping and plantation labor.[108]

Similarly, black convicts were deemed desirable for road work because "you can control the convict and make him work while you have practically no control of the free [black] labor," which allegedly did not respond properly to the inducement of wages. Free black labor was regarded by whites as deficient because "a nigger is born happy, and he is going to stay that way if possible," wrote an itinerant Office of Public Roads engineer to his superior in Washington, when asked to compare free and convict labor. "So as soon as any money is earned, it is spent in dissipation ... and the next morning [you] find him disqualified for work," he complained. "If you hire that kind of a nigger [for road work], he won't do much and you can't make him." He voiced a preference for forced labor, because "the convict is kept in his place, sleeping at night.... Nature has no mortgage on him, the only one is the shackle he wears. And as long as that is on him, he must obey."[109]

Another OPR agent who travelled across the South, James Abbott, made similar observations, but with a more critical eye. "Wherever they use convict labor on roads in the South it is nearly all colored, and they control them with the lash," he wrote with disgust. Visiting the Mecklenburg County road camp in North Carolina (widely regarded as the model for convict road work), Abbott reported that "the man in charge told me that it would be impossible to work colored convicts successfully without plenty of corporal punishment," the same belief that had shaped conditions under the convict lease. "This would never do with white men," he observed without irony, for "public sentiment would not tolerate it, and it would bring odium to the good roads cause." Recounting with horror his recent investigations of southern road gangs, Abbott suggested that in these county convict camps

> [the negro's] condition is more deplorable than it ever was in antebellum days. They beat him and torture him and do all manner of evil things to him. It often happens there that a negro convict working on the road invites the bullet of a guard as a desirable alternative and desperate relief from a condition to which death is preferred.

Abbott, unlike most advocates of good roads, recognized that this form of progress in the South was based on a single terrible tradition: on the roads, as in the railroad camps, coal mines, turpentine forests, and brickyards before, "the negro convict is a slave."[110]

Penal reform – the abolition of convict leasing – and the good roads movement were inseparable components of one particular attempt to bring the South into the twentieth century. Because effective road construction, improvement, and maintenance in the South was almost always associated with the use of convicts, the very process of modernization remained dependent on one of the South's apparently ineradicable claims to distinctiveness: forced black labor. With the help and encouragement of federal intervention, the progress embodied in a modern transportation network and the tradition of unfree black labor proved symbiotic. In this instance, the humanitarian pretensions of southern Progressivism were fatally undermined by its antidemocratic, racially intolerant, and labor-repressive character. The substitution of the public chain gang for the private convict lease did not sweep away these antimodern tendencies in the region, but rather reconciled them with the advent of modernity.[111]

8

Epilogue:
Forced Labor and Progress

> There is no document of civilization that is not at the same time a document of barbarism.
> Walter Benjamin, "Theses on the Philosophy of History"[1]

Diverse forms of forced labor have been found in many societies, under many conditions. Slavery and penal labor both existed in the ancient world. Serfdom shaped much of the character of premodern European social relations, and persisted well into the nineteenth century in Eastern Europe and Russia. As European societies shook off the last vestiges of feudalism, forced labor was carried to the New World, in a vast arc encompassing both the highlands and plantations of the Americas. In colonial Africa as well, European domination brought with it forms of coercive labor new to a continent that had long known indigenous slavery; and labor relations in industrialized South Africa under apartheid were clearly shaped by colonial strategies of labor extraction up until yesterday. Finally, Stalin's Gulag, and the Nazi labor and extermination camps, stand as horrific examples of forced labor in the modern world.

Bound labor has not always been associated with the fully developed chattel slavery oriented toward market production that gave the antebellum American South, for example, a distinctive character. In various guises this form of labor has both preceded and followed in the wake of chattel slavery. Forced labor has even developed in societies where the New World's peculiar form of ownership of one person by another, rationalized by bourgeois property relations, was unknown. Consistent features of this form of labor have included the collusion of the state, penal servitude as an enforcer of work, and intensification and expansion during periods of rapid economic development or transformation.

Coercive labor relations frequently aim to control a population reluctant to enter wage labor relations freely, and encourage the consequent proletarianization of these recalcitrant recruits to the "free" labor market. The beneficiaries of this process often justify its harshness as necessary and efficacious discipline for this emergent working class. In advanced societies such labor coercion has even been legitimized by resort to the ultimate expression of capitalist free labor relations, the contract. And when not controlled by individuals, forced labor has frequently been concentrated by the state on public works – pyramids, waterworks, and roadways.

Involuntary servitude has also been reserved as the fate for conquered combatants in war, for indigenous peoples in the New World and Africa, and for races deemed "inferior" by Europeans (and those of European descent) or Aryans. Its victims include both "enemies of the people," and those declared "criminal" by a judicial rationale derived from enlightenment principles and bourgeois social relations. Everywhere, as the criminologist Thorsten Sellin has argued, slavery and punishment have been an inseparable dyad, in advanced as well as primitive societies. Indeed, as the "right" for individuals freely to dispose of their labor power as they saw fit (within the dictates of the market) increasingly came to define capitalist social relations, as it began to in the New South, the revocation of that right became the ultimate sanction. In putatively "modern" societies, where citizens value the rule of law, that right can only be limited by legal procedures restrained by, for example, constitutional legality. The Thirteenth Amendment to the US Constitution expresses this bargain succinctly. But wherever the historical legacy of racialism has been conjoined to the identification of penal sanction with enslavement, as it was in the postbellum South, and really in the United States as a whole, the results for a society's vision of equality and labor have been profoundly destructive. This has been true even – perhaps especially – when forced labor contributed to economic development.[2]

One of the persistent themes of American history has been an abiding faith in progress and development; and one of the persistent themes of southern history has been the necessity for federal intervention to extend the benefits of progress to the nation's less "developed" region. Whether carried out by the Union Army, carpetbaggers, northern capital, technocratic "experts," the judiciary, or, today, the forces of postindustrial economic change, this process has frequently revolved around the inseparable issues of labor and race. Free labor triumphed over slavery in the Civil War, but in their effort to reshape the South it was the original prophets of a New South, the

Reconstructionists, who fastened the convict-lease upon the region's former bondspeople, as Hoke Smith took pains to remind the legislature when his administration finally abolished the system in Georgia.[3] And it was those ersatz defenders of southern tradition, the Redeemers, who invited northern capital to help them reap the benefits of forced labor, as they developed the South's extractive sector. Finally, as a wave of Progressive reform brought an end to the convict lease, it was the federal agents of progress, the civil engineers of the US Office of Public Roads, who helped articulate and exploit the enormous contribution of the South's black forced labor pool to yet another vision of a New South.[4]

This continual correspondence between the forces of modernization and the perpetuation of bound labor was no anomaly. Even chattel slavery in the Americas was a crucial component in the historical development of capitalism.[5] The various extreme forms of labor coercion and control that supplanted slavery in the modern world continued to demonstrate a "progressive" quality; rather than constituting an "archaic" obstacle to capitalist development, destined to be swept away by modernity, unfree labor has frequently been an essential element in the accumulation process that made that development possible.[6]

In the postbellum South, at each stage of the region's development, convict labor was concentrated in some of the most significant and rapidly growing sectors of the economy. Initially southern prisoners worked on the railroads, laying the indispensable infrastructure for nineteenth-century economic development. Then, as southern capitalists turned to the rapid development of the region's exploitable resources, convicts played a key role in the increasing vertical integration of extractive industries which required large concentrations of steady, predictable, controllable – i.e. proletarianized – labor. When the inflexible cost of this capitalized labor force became a detriment during sudden economic downturns, convict labor proved adaptable to other uses, particularly in seasonal and migratory extractive sectors, such as the lumber and turpentine industries. Finally, as many white southerners tired of the persistent underdevelopment that helped make unfree labor compatible with the exploitation of the region's raw materials in the first place, the chain gang came to replace the convict-lease as the dominant form of penal labor in the twentieth-century South.[7] This decisive shift from private to public exploitation of forced black labor marked the triumph of the modern state's version of the social and economic benefits to be reaped from bound labor, in the name of developing a more healthy, less dependent, "progressive" economy. Thus, from Reconstruction through the Progressive Era the various uses of convict labor coincided with changes in the political economy of southern capitalism. In each case the impetus to harness forced labor to the project of infrastructural development and economic growth came not from those who yearned for the social and economic order of the slave South, but from the region's most ardent advocates of progress, who sought to reconcile modernization with the racial caste system.

Robert Elliott Burns's *I am a Fugitive from the Georgia Chain Gang!*, published in 1932, and the subsequent hit movie based on his book, cast a national spotlight on Georgia's horrendous penal system during the Depression era. Burns's focus on governmental corruption and ineptitude, his inaccurate portrayal of Georgia's penal system as a holdover from a discredited past, and the popular format of an adventure story against the odds all fit well with the country's mood in the early years of the economic crisis. The outcry occasioned by Burns's first-person account of the horrors of working the roads on a Georgia chain gang can only be considered ironic, however. Burns himself was a businessman, not an ardent social reformer following in the footsteps of George Washington Cable, Rebecca Latimer Felton, or Frank Tannenbaum, all of whom had earlier exposed the barbarity of southern punishment.[8] Moreover, his story competed with contemporaneous attacks on the southern chain gang by writers considerably to his left.[9] Nevertheless, Burns's account painted a grim and convincing portrait of a penal system governed by capricious cruelty, alternately beset by bureaucratic indifference and corruption, and driven by the desire to wring from felons their "debt" to the state in the coin of relentless hard labor on county roads.

Of course, *I am a Fugitive* pointed to another paradox as well: Burns was white. If penal reform in Georgia had done nothing to ameliorate the plight of the convict, what *did* begin to change with the advent of the chain gang was the racial composition of Georgia's convict force. Indeed, during the 1920s, the era in which Burns's narrative was set, Georgia's prison system became truly biracial for the first time in its history. Black critics of the convict-lease had long attributed the state's reluctance to punish whites to the system's brutalities and its association with slavery.[10] In 1908, when convict-leasing came to an end in Georgia, there were only 322 white prisoners in a white population of 1.4 million. This incarceration rate of 23 prisoners per 100,000 whites was absurdly low by any historical standards. But if nearly 90 per cent of the state's felony convicts were black when the chain gang was instituted, two decades later 27 per cent of the prisoners were white, and the absolute number of white convicts had increased to 916.[11]

Contradictions abound in this transformation. In a state increasingly committed to segregation from cradle to grave, black and white convicts worked the roads together, chained to one another in full view of the public. Although its advocates initially deemed the chain gang especially appropriate for blacks, the abolition of leasing actually accommodated the criminal justice system to punishing white lawbreakers, since it diminished the hesitation of juries to mete out prison sentences to whites. Yet, at the same time, the resulting increased visibility of white prisoners began to erode the public faith in the benefits and justice of penal labor. The national horror which greeted Burns's tale cannot be divorced from the fact that this particular victim of the chain gang had white skin. Indeed in 1931 and 1932, an almost identical but far less celebrated case of suffering, desperate escape, and fugitive life was recounted by a black Georgian, Jesse Crawford, who with the help of the National Association for the Advancement of Colored People suc-cessfully defeated Georgia's attempts to extradite him from Michigan, whence he had fled.[12]

Despite the scandal generated by *I am a Fugitive*, the southern convict road gang, like its predecessor the convict-lease, eventually began to succumb to economic and social forces which redefined the place of penal labor in the South's political economy, rather than to the renewed clamor for humanitarian penal reform. Even as early as World War I, the US Department of Agriculture noted that demobilization would create unemployment which could be partially contained by road work for the jobless. Indeed, in the 1920s southern states began to discover that in hard times road work might be necessary as a form of *relief*, partly because "idle [negro] labor ... is liable to produce a very acute and dangerous situation," but also for the benefit of unemployed whites. In Georgia, in 1922, a state highway engineer, W.R. Neel, reported that he was "receiving letters ... asking why we do not start [road] work and give relief to so many unemployed people who are actually suffering throughout the state."[13]

During the Great Depression, which hit the South particularly hard, the full realization dawned that "the more prisoners that are worked upon the roads the less opportunity is given citizens ..., many [of whom] formerly worked upon highways [and] are now seeking relief from the Welfare Agencies." In 1931 a Georgia congressman, noting that "convicts are being used on the construction of some federal aid roads" in Georgia, angrily enquired of the Bureau of Public Roads, "what benefits may be derived from road construction in the relief of un-employment where the funds appropriated are used in the maintenance of convict labor?" The Bureau promptly replied that federal emergency appropriations to the states for road work as unemployment relief carried the explicit rider that "the use of convict labor on emergency Federal aid projects is prohibited."[14]

This represented quite a change. Prior to the 1930s, besides the persistent advocacy – and even supervision – of convict road work by federal road engineers, in practice the most telling example of federal encouragement for the chain gang had been the willingness to accede to the demands of southern states that the region's counties be allowed to use convict labor as a matching contribution to federal grants-in-aid for road improvement.[15] Since the passage of the Federal Road Aid Act of 1916, "a very considerable amount of highway work financed in part by Federal aid has been performed by convict labor in Georgia," the head of the US Bureau of Public Roads admitted in 1930. Increasingly, however, after that year bankrupt and impoverished southern counties found they could no longer afford to maintain even the most rudimentary chain gang, and remanded their convicts to the state authorities. Combined with the growing importance of federal relief funds mandating that "no convict labor shall be employed on the project" and the consequent growth of a free labor road force, these fiscal and political constraints began to erode the importance of county chain gangs to the state's economy.[16]

Thus it was that in penology, as in so many other areas, the New Deal and Great Depression began the final assault against the "southern way of life." Gradually, over the past sixty years, the chain gang has disappeared from the South's roads, and most southern prisons have conformed to the model prescribed by modern penology: huge penitentiaries which serve primarily as warehouses for society's permanently displaced and disemployed (former) citizens. Modern prison life, in the South now as in the rest of the United States, is defined by a numbing, brutal inactivity, an "enforced idleness," which ironically even in the 1930s one historian of prisons thought to characterize as worse than the forced labor then prevailing on the southern chain gangs.[17]

Rather than "hard labor," today's prisoners do "hard *time*." But this, too, like its predecessors, reflects some fundamental facts about race and political economy in America. Racial disproportion is the most striking continuity in the history of southern, and indeed US, prisons. In Georgia, where today perhaps a quarter of the state's population is African-American, blacks make up 60 per cent of the prison population. The United States has one of the highest incarceration rates in the world; but for African-Americans, more than half of those imprisoned in the United States, this rate is far higher still.[18] African-Americans have always invoked the experience of enslavement and imprisonment – and escape – as powerful metaphors for injustice and the struggle

against it. References to the Middle Passage, plantation slavery, the
convict-lease, the chain gang, and the penitentiary abound in African-
American folklore, song (especially work songs), and literature.[19] Today,
the words "Parchman" and "Angola," the penal colonies of Mississippi
and Louisiana respectively, still carry a chilling resonance for many
African-Americans.[20] Not only in the South, but in the USA as a whole,
there is still no separating the question of punishment from the matter
of race; and punishment has always been related to labor, both forced
and free.

The status of work outside of penal institutions, as much as labor
exploitation on the inside, has always shaped the nature of convict labor.
Historically, a labor economist points out, in the United States "the
[racial] duality of the criminal justice system evolved in tandem with
the [racial] duality of the labor market"; in other words, penal systems
have both defined African-Americans as a "criminal" class and helped
channel their labor into the least rewarding sectors of the economy.
One result of southern convict labor, for instance, was the degradation
of labor in industries in which prisoners were concentrated; since these
also happened to be the same industries with high concentrations of
free black workers fleeing the agricultural labor market, this tended to
exacerbate the southern association of the least desirable forms of non-
agricultural labor with a racially subordinated class.[21] The convict-lease,
the chain gang, and the modern penitentiary have all reflected *and*
reinforced African-Americans' location – or lack of it – in the American labor market.

In the postbellum South, at least until the Depression, perhaps until
the postwar period, the criminal justice system served to exploit unfree
black workers in order to help industrial capitalism through its develop-
mental stages, and to terrorize free black workers into silent, if bitter,
acceptance of their subordinate role in the economy and society. Not
even northward migration, new (if temporary) opportunities in the labor
market, the civil-rights struggles and partial victories, and the growth
of the newest New South, the Sunbelt, have been able to dissolve the
historical bonds of race, labor markets, poverty, and punishment. As
capitalism has entered its advanced, or postindustrial, stage many
African-Americans have essentially been shunted out of the labor market
altogether. This recently created enormous surplus labor pool is no
longer the object of exploitation, but simply of social control; prisons
can keep young, unemployed blacks "permanently out of the labor
market," and those lucky enough to hold minimum-wage jobs can be
thankful they are not in prison. When race was associated with
compulsion, punishment emphasized compulsory labor and proletarian-

ization; when it is associated with idleness, punishment means restraint and control of a de-proletarianized "*lumpen*" class. For today, when structural unemployment, deindustrialization, and social dislocation have their most dramatic impact on the African-American community, incarceration is often the fate reserved for the so-called "black underclass," the chronically disemployed who populate the nation's penal colony.[22]

In an era defined by radical attempts to dismantle state functions, criminal justice facilities stand as a striking exception. When it comes to building and staffing new prisons, state legislatures abandon all pretense of fiscal restraint, and engage in what one trenchant analyst has fittingly dubbed "carceral keynesianism."[23] The expansion of the "prison-industrial complex" provides jobs for the rural unemployed even while it siphons off the urban "underclass" from America's terminally ill cities. If and when the prison boom proves too costly, a new movement is afoot in this post-welfare-state era: the privatization of punishment.

Contemporary privatized convict labor – usually compensated, at best, with a sub-minimum wage – appeals in particular to the service sector, arguably the most "progressive" sphere of today's economy, and appears suited to the imperatives and rhythms of postindustrial production. "Private sector involvement in prison-based businesses offers specific advantages to companies with specific labor needs," remarks a 1985 National Institute of Justice report on this burgeoning form of penal labor, without irony. "Some general benefits can accrue to virtually any company that agrees to employ prisoners," the report continues.

> The principal economic benefit is free use of space and utilities. Some personnel cost savings can be realized by employing prison labor, primarily because employer-paid health insurance coverage is not required. [Nor, of course, are any other benefits.] ... Prison labor is attractive to the employer with seasonal labor needs, who can fine-tune labor costs much more precisely, and with *much less risk of losing workers*, with a prison labor force than with non-prisoner workers. Prison labor is also attractive to companies with shift demands that are difficult to fill ... and to companies with short-term product manufacturing cycles followed by long idle periods.

Of course many prisoners are "willing" to work under any conditions, when the alternative is the deadening idleness and monotony of prison life.[24]

Another study of privatization commissioned by the Department of Justice notes the "potential political concern" that prisoners might organize labor unions in order to improve their working conditions. But this concern is quickly dismissed; the study reports that "states are allowed to prohibit collective bargaining and other union activity of prisoners, and federal law prohibits convicted felons from holding union office." And in the event of a legal objection to this form of labor subordination and exploitation,

> these restrictions are likely to withstand constitutional challenge, since the 13th Amendment allows involuntary servitude as a punishment for crime and may thus attach some of the characteristics of slavery to prisoners – including prohibitions on slave organizations.[25]

In the most barbaric regimes of the twentieth century the modern state nullified free labor by arbitrary and summary means. Simply belonging to a group or class of individuals stigmatized by the state or the ruling class – "natives" in Portuguese Africa or the Congo, Jews in the Reich, Kulaks in Stalinist Russia – limited or extinguished altogether the right to be free from enslavement. Remarkably, this contradiction of modernity – under the rule of law and otherwise – has almost always been in the interest of progress, and not just rhetorically so. The "liquidation" of the Kulaks as a class may have been "progressive" only in the minds of Stalin and his commissars, but their labor in the camps and mines of the Gulag made a significant contribution to the shock industrialization that helped fend off the German attack in the 1940s. As for the Nazis, their absolute negation of moral progress provided a slave labor force for Germany's most highly developed sectors of a modern industrial complex. In fact, it was the Nazi state that most completely adapted forced labor to the mass forms of industrial labor and organization – in chemicals, armaments, automotive, rubber, electronics – that resemble what we today regard as modern production.[26]

The southern penal system cannot be directly equated with the Gulag (though at least one left-wing social critic in the 1930s thought otherwise) or with Auschwitz (though at least one southern historian has done so).[27] Yet these comparisons serve to emphasize the compatibility of forced labor with ideals of progress, both economic and moral, though the latter was usually true only in the minds of its advocates. Nor do I think that southern convict labor, unlike the chattel slavery that preceded it, constituted a full "mode of production," a set of social relations arranged to extract labor that defined the character of the entire society.[28] But it was a significant "hybrid form" of labor particularly appropriate to an underdeveloped region seeking, through rapid economic advancement, to fully enter the capitalist world while pre-serving a racial caste system.[29] More than one social critic has observed that "the way prisons are run and their inmates treated gives a faithful picture of a society, especially of the ideas and methods of those who dominate that society."[30] As the most extreme incarnation of southern labor relations, convict labor in the New South – and, indeed, well into the twentieth century – testified to certain fundamental and persistent facts about the postbellum southern social, economic, and racial order.

Long after the abolition of slavery, race continued to define one's place in the labor market: blacks' prescribed "place" in southern society was to toil for the benefit of whites, and whites believed African-Americans would only freely give their labor under compulsion. If the actions of the freedpeople themselves demonstrated otherwise, this only encouraged reliance on forced labor. For nearly a century after emanci-pation, whites tailored the region's system of punishment to fit this model of social relations. Moreover, the penal regime was repeatedly shaped by the prevailing political economy. When wedded to the project of accelerated economic development under adverse conditions, the South's brutal system of forced labor reconciled modernization with the continuation of racial domination. The convict-lease and its succes-sor, the chain gang, serve as potent reminders of historical tendencies that much of the rest of the world has been made well aware of: that progress is not necessarily progressive for all peoples, and that the bearers of modernity frequently carry with them its antithesis.

Notes

Abbreviations

ADAH	Alabama Department of Archives and History, Montgomery, Alabama
AHC	Atlanta History Center, Atlanta, Georgia
BPL	Birmingham Public Library, Department of Archives and Manuscripts, Birmingham, Alabama
GDAH	Georgia Department of Archives and History, Atlanta, Georgia
GPO	Government Printing Office
NA-WNRC	National Archives, Washington National Records Center, Suitland, Maryland
NCGS	North Carolina Geological Survey
OPR	Office of Public Roads, US Department of Agriculture
RG	Record Group
SHC	Southern Historical Collection, University of North Carolina, Chapel Hill, North Carolina
SRC	Southern Railway Collection, Virginia Polytechnic University, Blacksburg, Virginia
UGA	University of Georgia Library, Special Collections, Athens, Georgia
USDA	United States Department of Agriculture
USGS	United States Geological Survey

Preface

1. *New York Times*, 13 September 1994; US Department of Justice, Bureau of Justice Statistics, *Bulletin: Prisoners in 1993*; Jerome G. Miller, "Hobbling a Generation: Young African American Males in Washington, D.C.'s Criminal Justice System," National Center on Institutions and Alternatives, April 1992.

2. David J. Rothman, "The Crime of Punishment," *New York Review of Books*, 17 February 1994, pp. 34–8; Michael Tonry, *Malign Neglect: Race, Crime, and Punishment in America* (New York: Oxford University Press, 1995); Bureau of Justice Statistics, *Bulletin: Prisoners in 1993*; Jerome G. Miller, "Search and Destroy: The Plight of African American Males in the Criminal Justice System," Fall 1993, p. 10; National Council

on Institutions and Alternatives, "Hobbling a Generation: Young African American Males in the Criminal Justice System of America's Cities," September 1992.

3. For good surveys of southern convict labor, see Matthew J. Mancini, *"One Dies, Get Another": Convict Labor in the American South* (Columbia: University of South Carolina Press, forthcoming); Mildred C. Fierce, *Slavery Revisited: Blacks and the Southern Convict Lease System, 1865–1933* (Brooklyn: Africana Studies Research Center, 1994); Edward L. Ayers, *Vengeance and Justice: Crime and Punishment in the 19th-Century American South* (New York: Oxford University Press, 1984), pp. 185–222; Dewey Grantham, *Southern Progressivism: The Reconciliation of Progress and Tradition* (Knoxville: University of Tennessee Press, 1983), pp. 128–32; Dan T. Carter, "Politics and Business: The Convict Lease System in the Post-Civil War South," (M.A. thesis, University of Wisconsin, 1964); Hilda Jane Zimmerman, "Penal Systems and Penal Reform in the South Since the Civil War," (Ph.D. dissertation, University of North Carolina, 1947).

4. Some recent examples of this kind of study include W. Fitzhugh Brundage, *Lynching in the New South: Georgia and Virginia, 1880–1930* (Urbana: University of Illinois Press, 1993); James C. Cobb, *The Most Southern Place on Earth* (New York: Oxford University Press, 1993); Mark V. Wetherington, *The New South Comes to Wiregrass Georgia, 1860–1910* (Knoxville: University of Tennessee Press, 1994); Edward L. Ayers, *The Promise of the New South: Life After Reconstruction* (Oxford: Oxford University Press, 1993); Jacqueline Jones, *The Dispossessed: America's Underclasses from the Civil War to the Present* (New York: Basic Books, 1992); John Cell, *The Highest Stage of White Supremacy: The Origins of Segregation in South Africa and the U.S. South* (Cambridge: Cambridge University Press, 1982).

5. Savannah *Tribune*, 18 December 1897; 7 December 1895; the *Tribune* was one of Georgia's leading African-American newspapers.

6. Georgia General Assembly, *Journal of the House of Representatives*, 1892, p. 655; Rebecca Felton, "The Convict System of Georgia," *The Forum* 2 (January 1887), pp. 484–90.

7. Lawrence Langer, *Admitting the Holocaust: Collected Essays* (New York: Oxford University Press, 1995), p. 3. For the most thorough treatment of convict life in the nineteenth-century South, see Mary Ellen Curtin, *"Enclosed in a Shell of Self-Importance": Black Prisoners in the New South, 1870–1900* (Charlottesville: University Press of Virginia, forthcoming).

8. Joseph E. Brown to Rebecca L. Felton, 28 July 1883, Folder 1; 3 December 1885, Folder 2; 29 July 1885, Folder 3; 18 January 1886, Folder 4; 13 October 1887, Folder 5; 13 December 1889, Folder 7: all in Box 2, Rebecca Lattimer Felton Collection, UGA.

9. "Two Candidates a Generation Apart in Contest for Atlanta Mayor," *Washington Post*, 4 August 1989, p. A3.

Chapter 1

1. Antonio Gramsci, *Selections from the Prison Notebooks*, edited and translated by Quintin Hoare and Geoffrey Nowell Smith (New York: International Publishers, 1971), p. 276.

2. C. Vann Woodward, *Origins of the New South, 1877–1913* (Baton Rouge: Louisiana State University Press, 1951), p. 14.

3. Margaret Mitchell, *Gone With the Wind* (New York: Warner Books, 1993), pp. 753, 779.

4. George P. Rawick, *The American Slave: A Composite Autobiography*, supp. 1, Vol.

6 (1) MS (Westport, Conn: Greenwood, 1977), p. 2.

5. Henry Hatcher file, Box 54, Applications for Clemency, Executive Department Papers, GDAH.

6. The best description and summary of the various systems of nineteenth-century penal labor in the United States is found in US Bureau of Labor, *Convict Labor*, Second Annual Report of the Commissioner of Labor, 1886 (Washington, DC: GPO, 1886), pp. 371–96; see also Glen A. Gildemeister, *Prison Labor and Convict Competition With Free Workers in Industrializing America, 1840–1890* (New York: Garland Press, 1987), on the organization of convict labor in the North.

7. Matt Mancini, "'One Dies, Get Another': How to Think About Convict Leasing," paper presented at the Annual Meeting of the Southern Historical Association, 8–11 November 1989, copy in author's possession.

8. Eric Foner, *Nothing But Freedom: Emancipation and Its Legacy* (Baton Rouge: Louisiana State University Press, 1983) is an excellent brief exploration of this struggle; see also Joseph P. Reidy, *From Slavery to Agrarian Capitalism in the Cotton Plantation South: Central Georgia, 1800–1880* (Chapel Hill: University of North Carolina Press, 1992), pp. 136–60, 215–41.

9. For the dilemma this duality posed for the South's landed elites, see Steven Hahn, "Class and State in Postemancipation Societies: Southern Planters in Comparative Perspective," *American Historical Review* 95 (February 1990), pp. 75–98.

10. Steven Hahn, *The Roots of Southern Populism: Yeomen Farmers and the Transformation of the Georgia Upcountry* (New York: Oxford University Press, 1984); Lacy K. Ford, "Rednecks and Merchants: Economic Development and Social Tensions in the South Carolina Upcountry, 1865–1900," *Journal of American History* 71 (September 1984), pp. 294–318; Numan V. Bartley, *The Creation of Modern Georgia* (Athens: University of Georgia Press, 1983); Jacquelyn Dowd Hall, et al., *Like a Family: The Making of a Southern Cotton Mill World* (Chapel Hill: University of North Carolina Press, 1987), pp. 4–43; Foner, *Nothing But Freedom*; Gavin Wright, *Old South, New South: Revolutions in the Southern Economy Since the Civil War* (New York: Basic Books, 1986); Harold D. Woodman, "Post-Civil War Agriculture and the Law," *Agricultural History* 53 (January 1979), pp. 319–37.

11. David Brion Davis, *Slavery and Human Progress* (New York: Oxford University Press, 1984); Hahn, "Class and State in Postemancipation Societies," pp. 76–7.

12. Robert S. Cotterill, "The Old South to the New South," in George B. Tindall, ed., *The Pursuit of Southern History: Presidential Addresses of the Southern Historical Association*, (Baton Rouge: Louisiana State University Press, 1964), p. 238; Alexis de Tocqueville, *Democracy in America*, edited by J.P. Mayer and Max Lerner, 2 vols (New York: Harper and Row, 1966), pp. 312–33, 344–5; Twelve Southerners, *I'll Take My Stand: The South and the Agrarian Tradition* (New York: Harper and Bros, 1930); Eugene D. Genovese, *The Southern Tradition: The Achievement and Limitations of an American Conservatism* (Cambridge, Mass.: Harvard University Press, 1994); John Shelton Reed, *The Enduring South: Subcultural Persistence in Mass Society* (Chapel Hill: University of North Carolina Press, 1986); Shearer Davis Bowman, *Masters and Lords: Mid-19th-Century U.S. Planters and Prussian Junkers* (New York: Oxford University Press, 1993), p. 109.

13. Woodward, *Origins of the New South*; Sheldon Hackney, "Origins of the New South in Retrospect," *Journal of Southern History* 38 (May 1972), pp. 191–216; C. Vann Woodward, *Thinking Back: The Perils of Writing History* (Baton Rouge: Louisiana State University Press, 1986), pp. 59–79. On the continuity and change debate, see Dan T. Carter, "From the Old South to the New: Another Look at the Theme of Change and Continuity," in Walter J. Fraser and Winfred B. Moore, eds., *From the Old South to the New: Essays on the Transitional South* (Westport, Conn.: Greenwood Press, 1981),

pp. 23–32, which offers some cautionary remarks about overreliance on this dichotomy. The most recent synthesis of postbellum southern history, Edward L. Ayers, *The Promise of the New South: Life After Reconstruction* (New York: Oxford University Press, 1992), explicitly measures itself against Woodward.

14. Jonathan M. Wiener, *Social Origins of the New South: Alabama 1860–1885* (Baton Rouge: Louisiana State University Press, 1978); also Lewis Nicholas Wynne, *The Continuity of Cotton: Planter Politics in Georgia, 1865–1892* (Macon, Ga.: Mercer University Press, 1986); Barrington Moore, Jr., *Social Origins of Dictatorship and Democracy: Lord and Peasant in the Making of the Modern World* (Boston: Beacon Press, 1966).

15. Dwight B. Billings, Jr., *Planters and the Making of the "New South": Class, Politics and Development in North Carolina, 1865–1900* (Chapel Hill: University of North Carolina Press, 1979), p. 223. For a summary of the use of the "Prussian Road" model in both German and American historiography, see Bowman, *Masters and Lords*, pp. 103–11.

16. Moore, *Social Origins of Dictatorship and Democracy*; Billings, *Planters and the Making of the "New South"*; Wiener, *Social Origins of the New South*; Jonathan Wiener, "Class Structure and Economic Development in the South, 1865–1955," *American Historical Review* 84 (December 1979), pp. 970–92, and Harold D. Woodward's comment, ibid., p. 998; Jonathan Wiener, "Review of Reviews: Barrington Moore's *Social Origins of Dictatorship and Democracy*," *History and Theory* 15 (1976), pp. 146–75.

17. Eugene D. Genovese, *The Political Economy of Slavery: Studies in the Economy and Society of the Slave South* (New York: Vintage, 1967), pp. 206–7.

18. Moore, *Social Origins of Dictatorship and Democracy*, pp. 153, 149.

19. Woodward, *Thinking Back*, p. 70; Wiener, *Social Origins of the New South*; Wiener, "Class Structure"; Jay Mandle, *The Roots of Black Poverty* (Durham, N.C.: Duke University Press, 1978) for underdevelopment argument.

20. See Lawrence Powell, "The Prussians are Coming," *Georgia Historical Quarterly* 71 (Winter 1987), pp. 638–67; and James C. Cobb, "Beyond Planters and Industrialists: A New Perspective on the New South," *Journal of Southern History* 54 (February 1988), pp. 45–68, for excellent summaries of the change/continuity debate.

21. Wright, *Old South, New South*, p. 49. Michael Wayne, *The Reshaping of Plantation Society: The Natchez District* (Baton Rouge: Louisiana State University Press, 1984) is an important exception to the focus on continuity based on individuals; Wayne demonstrates both "persistence" and the transformation of the means planters used to maintain economic dominance. See Harold Woodman's work for the most consistent insistence that the transition to free labor was of paramount importance, e.g. "Sequel to Slavery: The New History Views the Postbellum South," *Journal of Southern History* 43 (November 1977), pp. 523–54; "Post-Civil War Agriculture and the Law," *Agricultural History* 53 (January 1979), pp. 319–37; "How New Was the New South," *Agricultural History* 58 (October 1984), pp. 429–45; and his contribution to John B. Boles and Evelyn Thomas Nolen, eds., *Interpreting Southern History: Essays in Honor of Sanford W. Higginbotham* (Baton Rouge: Louisiana State University Press, 1987). Woodward, in *Thinking Back*, pp. 74–5, brushes off his critics by pointing out the importance of New South class position over Old South ties.

22. Powell, "The Prussians are Coming," p. 641; Woodman, comment on Wiener, "Class Structure," p. 998; Hahn, "Class and State in Postemancipation Societies."

23. Michael O'Brien, "The 19th-Century American South," *The Historical Journal* 24 (September 1981), pp. 751–63, p. 762; see also Bowman, *Masters and Lords*, pp. 103–11.

24. Jonathan Wiener, "Reconsidering the Wiener Thesis," comment given at the Organization of American Historians Meeting, April 1991, Louisville, Kentucky, in author's possession.

25. Billings, *Planters and the Making of the "New South"*, pp. 96–113, 219–21, 223 (quotation); see also Philip J. Wood, *Southern Capitalism: The Political Economy of North Carolina, 1880–1980* (Durham, N.C.: Duke University Press, 1986) for a similar analysis of the North Carolina textile industry.

26. Powell, "The Prussians are Coming", pp. 640–41, for this observation; Mandle, *Roots of Black Poverty*, for a coherent exposition of the relationship between a plantation "mode of production" and underdevelopment.

27. For the relevant historiography, see, e.g., Wiener, *Social Origins of the New South*; Mandle, *Roots of Black Poverty*; Cobb, "Beyond Planters and Industrialists"; Wright, *Old South, New South*; Roger Ransom and Richard Sutch, *One Kind of Freedom: The Economic Consequences of Emancipation* (Cambridge: Cambridge University Press, 1977); Woodman, "Sequel to Slavery."

28. The work of Ralph Shlomowitz offers the most undiluted faith in the triumph of the market and free labor relations in the South, in the Chicago School of economics style; see, for a good example, "'Bound' or 'Free'? Black Labor in Cotton and Sugarcane Farming, 1865–1880," *Journal of Southern History* 50 (November 1984), pp. 567–96. Joseph D. Reid, Jr., Robert Higgs, and Stephen J. DeCanio also trumpet the hegemony of the free market; e.g. Reid, "Sharecropping as an Understandable Market Response: The Postbellum South," *Journal of Economic History* 33 (March 1973), pp. 106–30; Higgs, *Competition and Coercion: Blacks in the American Economy, 1865–1914* (Cambridge: Cambridge University Press, 1977); DeCanio, *Agriculture in the Postbellum South: The Economics of Production and Supply* (Cambridge, Mass.: Harvard University Press, 1974); Woodman, "Sequel to Slavery," provides the best summary and critique of the work of these cliometric economic historians. Surprisingly, this approach has diminished during the 1980s. Wiener, *Social Origins of the New South*, and Mandle, *Roots of Black Poverty* emphasize nonmarket factors in the shaping of southern labor relations. Wayne, *Reshaping of Plantation Society*; Wright, *Old South, New South*; and Ransom and Sutch, *One Kind of Freedom*, are three examples of balanced assessments that account for market and nonmarket (if one accepts such a distinction) forces.

29. Robert Higgs, comment on Wiener, "Class Structure," p. 997.

30. James C. Cobb, *Industrialization and Southern Society, 1877–1984* (Lexington: The University Press of Kentucky, 1984), p. 2.

31. John Cell, *The Highest Stage of White Supremacy: The Origins of Segregation in South Africa and the U.S. South* (Cambridge: Cambridge University Press, 1982); Jacqueline Jones, *The Dispossessed: America's Underclasses from the Civil War to the Present* (New York: Basic Books, 1992); W. Fitzhugh Brundage, *Lynching in the New South: Georgia and Virginia, 1880–1930* (Urbana: University of Illinois Press, 1993); James C. Cobb, *The Most Southern Place on Earth* (New York: Oxford University Press, 1993); Mark V. Wetherington, *The New South Comes to Wiregrass Georgia, 1860–1910* (Knoxville: University of Tennessee Press, 1994); Ayers, *Promise of the New South*.

32. This theoretical approach is derived from Barbara J. Fields, "The Nineteenth-Century American South: History and Theory," *Plantation Society in the Americas* 1 (April 1983), pp. 7–27, esp. pp. 8, 22, 24–5, who in turn draws heavily on dependency theory and Marxist analyses of the transition from feudalism to capitalism.

33. Wright, *Old South, New South*.

34. Fields, "The Nineteenth-Century American South," p. 25. On black labor mobility in the New South, see William Cohen, *At Freedom's Edge: Black Mobility and the Southern White Quest for Racial Control, 1861–1915* (Baton Rouge: Louisiana State University Press, 1991).

35. Gavin Wright's interpretation in *Old South, New South* advances this point forcefully.

36. Wright, *Old South, New South*, p. 52.

37. Ibid., pp. 41, 44–6, 55, 60; p. 52 for quotation.

38. See James C. Cobb, "Making Sense of Southern Economic History," review of Gavin Wright, *Old South, New South,* in *Georgia Historical Quarterly* 71 (Spring 1987), pp. 53–74.

39. Cobb, "Beyond Planters and Industrialists," p. 60; Cobb, *Industrialization and Southern Society,* p. 17.

40. Stanley Greenberg, *Race and State in Capitalist Development: Comparative Perspectives* (New Haven, Conn.: Yale University Press, 1980), pp. 133–4.

41. Ibid., pp. 395–6.

42. Cell, *The Highest Stage of White Supremacy.*

43. Holland Thompson, "Effects of Industrialism upon Political and Social Ideas," *Annals of the American Academy of Political and Social Science,* issue on "The New South" 35 (January 1910), pp. 134, 142; Holland Thompson, *The New South: A Chronicle of Social and Industrial Evolution* (New Haven, Conn.: Yale University Press, 1919), p. 8.

44. The best single account of the convict lease is Edward L. Ayers, *Vengeance and Justice: Crime and Punishment in the 19th Century American South* (New York: Oxford University Press, 1984), pp. 185–222. While Ayers acknowledges the contribution of convict labor to economic modernization in the New South, he insists that the lease eroded the "moral authority" (p. 208) of the region's elite. Dewey Grantham, *Southern Progressivism: The Reconciliation of Progress and Tradition* (Knoxville: University of Tennessee Press, 1983).

45. Fletcher M. Green, "Some Aspects of the Convict Lease System in the Southern States," in Fletcher M. Green, ed., *Essays in Southern History* (Chapel Hill: University of North Carolina, 1949), p. 121.

46. N. Gordon Carper, "The Convict-Lease System in Florida, 1866–1923," (Ph.D. dissertation, Florida State University, 1964), pp. 218–65; Green, "Some Aspects," p. 121; E. Merton Coulter, *Georgia, A Short History* (Chapel Hill: University of North Carolina Press, 1960), pp. 414–16; E. Merton Coulter, *James Monroe Smith, Georgia Planter: Before Death and After* (Athens: University of Georgia Press, 1961), pp. 64–92; Hilda Jane Zimmerman, "The Penal Reform Movement in the South During the Progressive Period, 1890–1917," *Journal of Southern History* 17 (November 1951), pp. 462–92; A. Elizabeth Taylor, "The Origin and Development of the Convict Lease System in Georgia," *Georgia Historical Quarterly* 26 (June 1942), pp. 113–28; Taylor, "The Abolition of the Convict Lease System in Georgia," *Georgia Historical Quarterly* 26 (June 1942), pp. 273–87.

47. O. Nigel Bolland, "Systems of Domination After Slavery: The Control of Land and Labor," *Comparative Studies in Society and History* 23 (October 1981), pp. 591–619, p. 616n.

48. On road expansion and the modernization of the South, see Howard Preston, *Dirt Roads to Dixie: Accessibility and Modernization in the South, 1885–1935* (Knoxville: University of Tennessee Press, 1990). Georgia Geological Survey, *A Second Report on the Public Roads of Georgia,* Bulletin No. 24 (Atlanta, Ga.: State Printer, 1910); *A Third Report on the Public Roads of Georgia,* Bulletin No. 28 (Atlanta, Ga.: State Printer, 1912); American Highway Association, *The Official Good Roads Year Book of the United States* (Washington, DC: AHA, 1913), p. 390.

49. Georgia Prison Commission, *Annual Report,* 1908–09, Table 2; "Chaingangs in Georgia," Men and Religion Bulletin No. 61, attached to Philip Weltner to Emmet O'Neal, 14 July 1913, Governor's Papers, Administrative Files, Box 97 (Convict Department), ADAH; Robert Elliot Burns, *I am a Fugitive from the Georgia Chain Gang!* (New York: Vanguard Press, 1932); John O'Connor, ed., *I am a Fugitive from a Chain Gang* (Madison: University of Wisconsin Press, 1981).

50. Burns, *I am a Fugitive,* p. 57.

Chapter 2

1. Charles L. Purdue, Jr., Thomas E. Barten, and Robert K. Phillips, eds., *Weevils in the Wheat: Interviews with Virginia Ex-Slaves* (Bloomington: Indiana University Press, 1980), pp. 266–7; Jim Watkins file, Box 127, Executive Department Papers, Applications for Clemency, GDAH; G.G. Flynt file, Box 41, Applications for Clemency, Executive Department Papers, GDAH.

2. W.E.B. Du Bois, ed., *Some Notes on Negro Crime, Particularly in Georgia*, Ninth Conference for the Study of Negro Problems (Atlanta, Ga.: Atlanta University Press, 1904), pp. 5–6; Letter to the Editor, New York *Freeman*, 13 March 1886; Savannah *Tribune*, 16 May 1903; 2 April 1892; 23 April 1892; 8 August 1908.

3. US Bureau of Labor, *Convict Labor*, Second Annual Report of the Commissioner of Labor (Washington, DC: GPO, 1887), p. 3.

4. Ibid., pp. 4, 287, 372, 379, and pp. 152–8, Table VII. See also Glen A. Gildemeister, *Prison Labor and Convict Competition with Free Workers in Industrializing America, 1840–1890* (New York: Garland Press, 1987) for an excellent discussion of convict labor in the context of nineteenth-century industrialization.

5. US Bureau of Labor, *Convict Labor*, pp. 4, 387, 296.

6. Ibid., p. 81.

7. See John Dittmer, *Black Georgia in the Progressive Era* (Urbana: University of Illinois Press, 1977), p. 89. The criminologist Thorsten Sellin in particular, in *Slavery and the Penal System* (New York: Elsevier, 1976), pp. 145–76, blames the southern convict lease on slavery; his work is an extended argument that points to the frequent convergence of slavery and forms of punishment throughout history.

8. Edward L. Ayers, *Vengeance and Justice: Crime and Punishment in the 19th Century American South* (New York: Oxford University Press, 1984), p. 192; see also Christopher R. Adamson, "Punishment After Slavery: Southern Penal Systems, 1865–1890," *Social Problems* 30 (June 1983), pp. 555–67, for this view from a functionalist sociological perspective. For an early articulation of this position, see Dan T. Carter, "Politics and Business: The Convict Lease System in the Post-Civil War South," (M.A. thesis, University of Wisconsin, 1964).

9. Robert S. Starobin, *Industrial Slavery in the Old South* (New York: Oxford University Press, 1970); Clarence L. Mohr, *On the Threshold of Freedom: Masters and Slaves in Civil War Georgia* (Athens: University of Georgia Press, 1986), ch. 5; Raimondo Lurraghi, *The Rise and Fall of the Plantation South* (New York: New Transactions, 1980); Ronald L. Lewis, *Coal, Iron and Slaves: Industrial Slavery in Maryland and Virginia, 1715–1865* (Westport, Conn.: Greenwood Press, 1979), and *Black Coal Miners in America: Race, Class and Community Conflict 1780–1980* (Lexington: The University Press of Kentucky, 1987), ch. 1. Lawrence N. Powell, "The Prussians are Coming," *Georgia Historical Quarterly* 71 (Winter 1987), p. 664, perceptively remarks that if there was a "Prussian Road" to industrialization in the South it is found in the Confederacy. Lurraghi's book offers an argument akin to this view.

10. Mohr, *On the Threshold of Freedom*, p. 151.

11. Starobin, *Industrial Slavery*, pp. 173–6.

12. Ibid., pp. 123–4.

13. James M. Russell, *Atlanta 1847–1890: City Building in the Old South and the New* (Baton Rouge: Louisiana State University Press, 1988), pp. 55, 254–5; Mohr, *On the Threshold of Freedom*, pp. 121, 126 on Lemuel Grant.

14. Russell, *Atlanta 1847–1890*, pp. 82–3, 100–108, 115.

15. Starobin, *Industrial Slavery*, p. 145.

16. Lewis, *Black Coal Miners*, p. 11.

17. US Bureau of Labor, *Convict Labor*, pp. 76, 90, 98–100; *Report of the Principal*

Keeper of the Penitentiary of Georgia from October 20, 1884 to October 20, 1886, Prison Commission Records, Records of the Georgia Board of Corrections, GDAH, pp. 4–7 (hereafter cited as Principal Keeper, *Report,* followed by the year). See also Principal Keeper, *Report,* 1874, pp. 6–8; 1868, p. 9.

18. Orlando Patterson, *Slavery and Social Death: A Comparative Study* (Cambridge, Mass.: Harvard University Press, 1982), pp. 44–5.

19. For three examples drawn from different eras, see H.H. Tucker, "Prison Labor," in American Prison Association, *Proceedings of the Annual Meeting,* 1886 (Chicago: Donnelley and Sons, 1887), pp. 245–64; Fred H. Wines, "Colored Criminals," in National Conference of Charities and Correction, *Proceedings,* 1903 (Boston: G.H. Ellis, 1904), pp. 444–7; George Herbert Clarke, "Georgia and the Chain Gang," *Outlook* 82 (13 January 1906), pp. 73–9.

20. Ayers, *Vengeance and Justice,* p. 70; see also Fletcher M. Green, "Some Aspects of the Convict Lease System in the Southern States," in Fletcher M. Green, ed., *Essays in Southern History* (Chapel Hill: University of North Carolina Press, 1949), p. 114, for the same point. Alternatively, for an emphasis on the contrasts between antebellum northern and southern prisons, see Blake McKelvey, *American Prisons: A History of Good Intentions* (1936; reprint, Montclair, N.J.: Patterson Smith, 1977). In Georgia's case the Milledgeville Penitentiary was quite similar to northern institutions. For the antebellum history of the Georgia Penitentiary, see James C. Bonner, "The Georgia Penitentiary at Milledgeville 1817–1874," *Georgia Historical Quarterly* 55 (Fall 1971), pp. 303–28. The principal keeper summarized this history for the legislature in his *Report* for the years 1872–73, pp. 10–22, and again in 1877–78, pp. 1–4.

21. E.T. Hiller, "Development of the Systems of Control of Convict Labor in the United States," *Journal of Criminal Law and Criminology* 5 (July 1914), pp. 241–69. By 1914 only Florida (1923), Alabama (1928), and North Carolina (1933) had yet to abolish the private working of convicts. See Sellin, *Slavery and the Penal System,* pp. 152, 157, 160.

22. Hiller, "Systems of Control," pp. 242, 245, 257; also Gildemeister, *Prison Labor and Convict Competition,* pp. 19–41, 225–55.

23. Hiller, "Systems of Control," pp. 242, 248, 268–9. See also Georg Rusche and Otto Kirchheimer, *Punishment and Social Structure* (New York: Columbia University Press, 1939), for the classic Marxist penological view that "every system of production tends to discover punishments which correspond to its productive relationships" (p. 5). For another interesting theoretical discussion of nineteenth-century American penology, see Christopher R. Adamson, "Toward a Marxian Penology: Captive Criminal Populations as Economic Threats and Resources," *Social Problems* 31 (April 1984), pp. 435–58, which argues that "variations in labor supply and the business cycle" determined the degree to which criminals were seen as a "threat" to capitalist accumulation or as a "resource" whose forced labor could contribute to accumulation (p. 438). In the postbellum South ex-slaves were treated by the penal system as a threat *and* a resource (pp. 449–50).

24. Gildemeister, *Prison Labor,* pp. iii, 17; see also Enoch C. Wines and Theodore Dwight, *Report on the Prisons and Reformatories of the United States and Canada* (Albany, N.Y.: Van Benthuysen and Sons, 1867), p. 248.

25. Hiller, "Systems of Control," pp. 248–50.

26. Principal Keeper, *Report,* 1872–73, pp. 18–19.

27. Ibid., pp. 19–21.

28. For a comparison of northern and southern penitentiaries, see Ayers, *Vengeance and Justice,* ch. 2, esp. pp. 67–9. For the role of the "merchant-capitalist" in expanding penal labor in northern prisons, see John R. Commons et al., *History of Labour in the United States,* Volume 1 (1918; reprint, New York: Macmillan, 1946), pp.

344–6.

29. Principal Keeper, *Report*, 1852–3, p. 11; 1859–60, p. 3. See Ayers, *Vengeance and Justice*, pp. 61, 295 n. 57; and Peter Wallenstein, *From Slave South to New South: Public Policy in Nineteenth-Century Georgia* (Chapel Hill: University of North Carolina Press, 1987), p. 80, for the absence of blacks in the Georgia penitentiary.

30. US Department of the Interior, Census Office, *Compendium of the Ninth Census (June 1, 1870)* (Washington, DC: GPO, 1872), pp. 534–5, for 1850 figures on Massachusetts and Georgia. Michael S. Hindus, *Prison and Plantation: Crime, Justice and Authority in Massachusetts and South Carolina, 1767–1878* (Chapel Hill: University of North Carolina Press, 1980), p. xxvii, is the comparative study that suggests the irrelevance of the penitentiary in a plantation society. See Ralph Betts Flanders, *Plantation Slavery in Georgia* (Chapel Hill: University of North Carolina Press, 1933), pp. 254–79; Eugene D. Genovese, *Roll, Jordan, Roll: The World the Slaves Made* (New York: Random House, 1972), pp. 632–5; and Philip J. Schwarz, *Twice Condemned: Slaves and the Criminal Laws of Virginia, 1705–1865* (Baton Rouge: Louisiana State University Press, 1988), for non-incarcerative punishments of slaves.

31. Ayers, *Vengeance and Justice*, p. 67; Principal Keeper, *Report*, 1852–53, p. 7; Bonner, "Penitentiary at Milledgeville."

32. Principal Keeper, *Report*, 1852–53, pp. 4–5; for the principal keeper's offer to lease the penitentiary in the 1850s, see *Report*, 1872–73, pp. 19–20.

33. Principal Keeper, *Report*, 1856–57, p. 2; 1877–78, p. 6.

34. Principal Keeper, *Report*, 1856–57, p. 2; 1857–58, pp. 2–3.

35. Principal Keeper, *Report*, 1861–62, p. 29; Bonner, "Penitentiary at Milledgeville," p. 316; *Report*, 1877–78, p. 6.

36. Alan Conway, *The Reconstruction of Georgia* (Minneapolis: University of Minnesota Press, 1966), p. 12; Isaac Wheeler Avery, *The History of the State of Georgia from 1850 to 1881* (New York: Brown and Derby, 1881), pp. 308–9, 317; Ayers, *Vengeance and Justice*, p. 186.

37. William T. Sherman, *Memoirs of General William T. Sherman, Written by Himself*, 4th edn, 2 vols (New York: Charles Webster, 1892), Vol. 2, p. 188 (23 November 1864); Conway, *Reconstruction of Georgia*, p. 46; Ayers, *Vengeance and Justice*, p. 187.

38. Hiller, "Systems of Control," pp. 254–5.

39. See Eric Foner, *Reconstruction: America's Unfinished Revolution, 1863–1877* (New York: Harper and Row, 1988), ch. 1, for an excellent treatment of the industrial growth and class conflict brought on by the Civil War.

40. Georgia General Assembly, *Acts and Resolutions*, 1866, p. 153.

41. On antebellum penitentiaries, race, and punishments for slaves, see Ayers, *Vengeance and Justice*, ch. 2; Hindus, *Prison and Plantation*; Schwarz, *Twice Condemned*. On the contradictions of law in slave society, see Genovese, *Roll, Jordan, Roll*, pp. 25–49.

42. George Washington Cable, *The Silent South, together with the Freedman's Case in Equity and the Convict Lease System* (1883; reprint, New York: Charles Scribner's Sons, 1907), p. 179; Tucker, "Prison Labor," p. 248.

43. Cable, *The Silent South*, p. 179.

44. Gildemeister, *Prison Labor*, pp. 79–82.

45. Wines, "Colored Criminals," p. 445.

46. Principal Keeper, *Report*, 1868, p. 4.

47. Ibid., pp. 18, 9.

48. Georgia General Assembly, *Proceedings of the Joint Committee Appointed to Investigate the Condition of the Georgia Penitentiary* (1870; reprint, New York: Arno Press, 1974), p. 8; Principal Keeper, *Report*, 1869, pp. 14–19. A manuscript of the 1870 investigation is available in Box 3, Legislative Investigations, Joint and Special Committees, Legislative Papers, GDAH.

49. Howell Cobb, Mark A. Cooper, and John A. Fitten to Charles J. Jenkins, "Report of the Committee on the Location of the Penitentiary," 2 November 1866, Box 53, Governor's Incoming Correspondence, Executive Department Papers, GDAH, pp. 4, 7 (hereafter cited as "Report of the Committee"); Principal Keeper, *Report*, 1872–73, p. 21; Principal Keeper, *Report*, 1869, pp. 14–15.

50. James C. Scott, "Everyday Forms of Peasant Resistance," *Journal of Peasant Studies* 13 (January 1986), pp. 5–35; James C. Scott, *Weapons of the Weak: Everyday Forms of Peasant Resistance* (New Haven, Conn.: Yale University Press, 1985); Alex Lichtenstein, "Theft, Moral Economy, and the Transition from Slavery to Freedom in the American South," in Stephan Palmié, ed., *Slave Cultures and the Culture of Slavery* (Knoxville: University of Tennessee Press, 1995); Joseph P. Reidy, *From Slavery to Agrarian Capitalism in the Cotton Plantation South: Central Georgia, 1800–1880* (Chapel Hill: University of North Carolina Press, 1992), pp. 222–7, 240 (quotation). See also Eric Foner, *Nothing But Freedom: Emancipation and its Legacy* (Baton Rouge: Louisiana State University Press, 1983), pp. 57–65; Steven Hahn, "Hunting, Fishing and Foraging: Common Rights and Class Relations in the Postbellum South," *Radical History Review* 26 (Fall 1982), pp. 37–64.

51. A.C. Walker to Gen. D. Tilson, 24 November 1865, Unregistered Letters Received, ser. 632, Georgia Assistant Cmr, Records of the Bureau of Refugees, Freedmen, and Abandoned Lands, RG105, National Archives, Washington, DC.

52. *Appling v. Odom*, 46 Ga. 584 (1872).

53. Gerald Jaynes, *Branches Without Roots: Genesis of the Black Working Class in the American South, 1862–1882* (New York: Oxford University Press, 1986), pp. 141–57; Harold D. Woodman, "Post-Civil War Southern Agriculture and the Law," *Agricultural History* 53 (January 1979), pp. 319–37.

54. Conway, *Reconstruction of Georgia*, p. 56; Daniel Novak, *The Wheel of Servitude: Black Forced Labor After Slavery* (Lexington: The University Press of Kentucky, 1978), p. 7; US Prison Industries Reorganization Administration, *The Prison Labor Problem in Georgia* (Washington, DC: GPO, 1937), pp. 3–4. For more on misdemeanor convicts in Georgia, see Chapter 7, below. See General Assembly, *Acts*, 1865–66, pp. 231–3 for the law reducing twenty-one different felonies to misdemeanors, including rape, hog stealing, larceny from the house, and receiving stolen goods.

55. Principal Keeper, *Report*, 1868; *Reports*, 1852–62; "List of the names of the Convicts in the hands of Grant, Alexander & Co., on the 1st day of January, 1870, together with their Ages, Counties from which they came, Crimes, When Received, and Length of Sentence," in Principal Keeper, *Report*, 1869, pp. 14–19. The law defining burglary was passed in the following session, General Assembly, *Acts*, 1866, pp. 151–2.

56. "Report of the Committee," pp. 15–16.

57. Ibid.

58. Ibid., p. 1.

59. Such a critique of Georgia's penitentiary was not unprecedented, however; see Ayers, *Vengeance and Justice*, p. 66, for an example.

60. Numan V. Bartley, *The Creation of Modern Georgia* (Athens: University of Georgia Press, 1983), pp. 29, 33; William J. Northen, *Men of Mark in Georgia*, Vol. 2 (Atlanta, Ga.: A.B. Caldwell, 1912), p. 207.

61. "Report of the Committee," p. 2.

62. Ibid., pp. 8–10.

63. Ibid.

64. General Assembly, *Acts*, 1865–66, pp. 37–8; Bonner, "Penitentiary at Milledgeville," p. 321. This Act, passed in March 1866, was the first postwar legislation to address the convict problem. It also permitted local Justices to "hire out"

convicts to "contractors on the Public works" in their county. It is unclear if this Act applied only to misdemeanor convicts or felony convicts as well.

65. "Report of the Committee," pp. 4–5, 10–13.

66. See Mohr, *On the Threshold of Freedom*, pp. 153–4, for Mark Cooper's background; General Assembly, *Acts*, 1866, p. 115, for incorporation of the Iron and Mining Company of Dade County; see Chapter 5, below, for a full discussion of the Dade Coal Company. On the chameleon-like Brown, see Derrell C. Roberts, *Joseph E. Brown and the Politics of Reconstruction* (University: University of Alabama Press, 1973); and Joseph H. Parks, *Joseph E. Brown of Georgia* (Baton Rouge: Louisiana State University Press, 1977).

67. Governor Charles Jenkins's letter of transmittal to the General Assembly, 12 November 1866, Box 53, Governor's Correspondence, GDAH.

68. Jenkins to the General Assembly, 12 November 1866; and "Report of the Committee," pp. 2–3, both in Box 53, Governor's Correspondence, GDAH.

69. On changes in the criminal justice system after emancipation, and its focus on blacks, see Ayers, *Vengeance and Justice*, pp. 168–9, 175–6, 179, 184.

70. Bonner, "Penitentiary at Milledgeville," p. 321; Principal Keeper, *Report*, 1877–78, p. 6, shows $18,000 appropriated for the penitentiary in March 1866, when Jenkins was governor, none in 1867, and $20,000 appropriated in October 1868 under the Republican regime.

71. General Assembly, *Acts*, 1866, p. 216.

72. "Report of the Committee," p. 11.

73. General Assembly, *Acts*, 1866, p. 155.

74. Ibid., pp. 121–2; Principal Keeper, *Report*, 1877–78, p. 6.

75. Bonner, "Penitentiary at Milledgeville," p. 321.

76. US Congress, House of Representatives, *Hearings before the Committee on Investigation of the United States Steel Corporation* (Washington, DC: GPO, 1912), p. 2985.

77. For example, Foner, *Reconstruction*, esp. pp. 28–9, 234–6, 525.

78. Conway, *Reconstruction of Georgia*, p. 62.

Chapter 3

1. Bertolt Brecht, *Selected Poems*, translated by H.R. Hays (New York: Harcourt Brace Jovanovich, 1975), p. 109.

2. Quamly Walker file, Box 125, Applications for Clemency, Executive Department Papers, GDAH.

3. On Republicans and railroads, see Mark W. Summers, *Railroads, Reconstruction and the Gospel of Prosperity: Aid Under the Radical Republicans, 1865–1877* (Princeton, N.J.: Princeton University Press, 1984); Eric Foner, *Reconstruction: America's Unfinished Revolution 1863–1877* (New York: Harper and Row, 1988), pp. 379–92; Peter Wallenstein, *From Slave South to New South: Public Policy in Nineteenth-Century Georgia* (Chapel Hill: University of North Carolina Press, 1987), pp. 170–82; on the eventual collapse of southern railroad investments, see John F. Stover, *The Railroads of the South: A Study in Finance and Control* (Chapel Hill: University of North Carolina Press, 1955).

4. Elizabeth Studley Nathans, *Losing the Peace: Georgia Republicans and Reconstruction* (Baton Rouge: Louisiana State University, 1968), pp. 225, 227. This view is obviously in accord with C. Vann Woodward's in *Origins of the New South, 1877–1913* (Baton Rouge: Louisiana State University Press, 1951).

5. Jacquelyn Dowd Hall et al., *Like a Family: The Making of a Southern Cotton Mill World* (Chapel Hill: University of North Carolina Press, 1987), ch. 1; Jonathan M. Wiener, *Social Origins of the New South: Alabama, 1860–1885* (Baton Rouge: Louisiana

State University Press, 1978), pp. 192–4; Philip J. Wood, *Southern Capitalism: The Political Economy of North Carolina, 1880–1980* (Durham, N.C.: Duke University Press, 1986), pp. 22–31, 39–43.

6. *Hamby and Toomer v. Georgia Coal and Iron Co.*, "Exhibit A," File A-29476, Box 510, Supreme Court Case Files, Office of the Clerk, Records of the Supreme Court of Georgia, GDAH; US Industrial Commission, *Report on Relations and Conditions of Capital and Labor*, Vol. 7 (Washington, DC: GPO, 1901), pp. 482, 550; Physicians Report, 1 December 1896, Box 43, Governors' Papers (Convict Bureau Reports), ADAH.

7. W.E.B. Du Bois, ed., *Some Notes on Negro Crime, Particularly in Georgia* (Atlanta, Ga.: Atlanta University Press, 1904), pp. 16, 38, 43, 46.

8. Principal Keeper, *Report*, 1873, 1877–78.

9. Clarence L. Mohr, *On the Threshold of Freedom: Masters and Slaves in Civil War Georgia* (Athens: University of Georgia Press, 1986), p. 141.

10. Mark A. Cooper, Howell Cobb, and John Fitten to Governor Charles Jenkins, "Report of Committee on Location of the Penitentiary," 2 November 1866, Box 53, Governor's Incoming Correspondence, Executive Department Papers, GDAH, pp. 10–11.

11. Georgia General Assembly, *Acts*, 1866, pp. 121–2.

12. Memorandum from General Thomas Ruger to Principal Keeper of the Penitentiary, 29 April 1868; Copy of Agreement between General Thomas Ruger, Principal Keeper, and William A. Fort, 21 April 1868, both in Box 54, Governor's Correspondence, GDAH.

13. S.F. Stephens to General Thomas Ruger, 20 May 1868; Ruger to Stephens, 23 May 1868, Box 55, Governor's Correspondence, GDAH.

14. Principal Keeper, *Report*, 1877–78, p. 4; A. Elizabeth Taylor, "The Origin and Development of the Convict Lease System in Georgia," *Georgia Historical Quarterly* 26 (March 1942), p. 114.

15. Principal Keeper, *Report*, 1877–78, p. 4.

16. On the Army and the Freedmen's Bureau role in enforcing labor, see Daniel Novak, *The Wheel of Servitude: Black Forced Labor After Slavery* (Lexington: The University Press of Kentucky, 1978), pp. 9–11; William S. McFeely, *Yankee Stepfather: General O.O. Howard and the Freedmen* (New Haven, Conn.: Yale University Press, 1968), esp. pp. 149–65; Foner, *Reconstruction*, pp. 153–70, which emphasizes contract ideology. On whipping, see Georgia General Assembly, *Proceedings of the Joint Committee to Investigate the Condition of the Georgia Penitentiary* (1870; reprint, New York: Arno Press, 1974), pp. 6–7, 71 (hereafter cited as *Proceedings to Investigate*, 1870); Michael S. Hindus, *Prison and Plantation: Crime, Justice and Authority in Massachusetts and South Carolina, 1767–1878* (Chapel Hill: University of North Carolina Press, 1980), pp. 99–100, 145–6. Novak points out that the lease was instituted by military commanders in other southern states as well.

17. Alan Conway, *Reconstruction in Georgia* (Minneapolis: University of Minnesota Press, 1966), p. 156; Georgia Executive Minutes, 24 July 1868, p. 144, GDAH.

18. Michael Perman, *The Road to Redemption: Southern Politics, 1869–1879* (Chapel Hill: University of North Carolina Press, 1984), pp. 32–4; on Bullock, see Russell Duncan, *Entrepreneur for Equality: Governor Rufus Bullock, Commerce, and Race in Post-Civil War Georgia* (Athens: University of Georgia Press, 1994).

19. Wallenstein, *From Slave South to New South*, p. 172.

20. Numan V. Bartley, *The Creation of Modern Georgia* (Athens: University of Georgia Press, 1983), p. 56.

21. *Letter from his Excellency Governor Bullock of Georgia, in Reply to the Honorable John Scott...* (Atlanta: n.pub., 1871), Newberry Library, Chicago; *Address of Rufus B. Bullock*

to the People of Georgia. A Review of the Revolutionary Proceedings of the Late Repudiating Legislature, October 1872 (n.p., n.pub.), Newberry Library, p. 13; Bartley, *Creation of Georgia*, p. 72; Nathans, *Losing the Peace*, pp. 207–12; Wallenstein, *From Slave South to New South*, pp. 173–8; and Georgia General Assembly, *Report of the Committee to Investigate the Bonds Issued or Negotiated Since July 4, 1868* (Atlanta, Ga.: State Printer, 1872); Stover, *Railroads of the South*, p. 61. See Summers, *Railroads and the Gospel of Prosperity*, for the definitive treatment of the southern railroad boom during Reconstruction.

22. Wallenstein, *From Slave South to New South*, pp. 173–6; Carter Goodrich, "Public Aid to Railroads in the Reconstruction South," *Political Science Quarterly* 71 (September 1956), pp. 407–42; Summers, *Gospel of Prosperity*, pp. 32–4; Foner, *Reconstruction*, p. 379 for a brief but perceptive discussion of the link between the "gospel of prosperity" and railroad construction.

23. Conway, *Reconstruction of Georgia*, pp. 14, 35; Thomas C. Bryan, *Confederate Georgia* (Athens: University of Georgia Press, 1953), pp. 116–17.

24. Conway, *Reconstruction of Georgia*, p. 38, drawing from the 31st Report of the Central Railroad of Georgia.

25. Jonathan McLeod, "Black and White Workers: Atlanta During Reconstruction," (Ph.D. dissertation, University of California, Los Angeles, 1987), p. 50; Stover, *Railroads of the South*, p. 57; Sir John Kennaway, *On Sherman's Track, or the South After the War* (London: Seely, Jackson and Halliday, 1867), p. 52.

26. Foner, *Reconstruction*, pp. 138–40; Leon F. Litwack, *Been in the Storm So Long: The Aftermath of Slavery* (New York: Vintage, 1979), pp. 292–304.

27. Stover, *Railroads of the South*, pp. viii, 97.

28. General Assembly, *Acts*, 1870, p. 360, for "financial embarrassment."

29. Nathans, *Losing the Peace*, pp. 58, 118–20; Perman, *Road to Redemption*, pp. 32–4, 44–5. Perman argues that the emphasis placed on internal improvements strengthened the hand of the centrists in the Republican Party.

30. Bartley, *Creation of Georgia*, p. 71.

31. Atlanta *Daily New Era*, 17 November 1866, quoted in Conway, *Reconstruction of Georgia*, p. 104. See also Nathans, *Losing the Peace*, pp. 44–5, for Joseph E. Brown's role in seeking comprehensive economic development for the state.

32. Wallenstein, *From Slave South to New South*, pp. 174–5; General Assembly, *Acts*, 1866, pp. 128–9, 119–35.

33. Wallenstein, *From Slave South to New South*, pp. 174–7; Goodrich, "Public Aid to Railroads," p. 417; Stover, *Railroads of the South*, p. 82; General Assembly, *Acts*, 1868, pp. 141–5; 1869, pp. 147–55; 1870, pp. 273–378.

34. Stover, *Railroads of the South*, p. 25; Summers, *Gospel of Prosperity*, pp. 134–5. US Department of the Interior, Census Office, *Preliminary Report on the Eighth Census:1860* (Washington, DC: GPO, 1861), p. 222; US Department of the Interior, Census Office, *Report on the Agencies of Transportation in the United States*, Tenth Census (1880), Vol. 4 (Washington, DC: GPO, 1883), p. 307.

35. *Letter from his Excellency Governor Bullock of Georgia*, pp. 13, 16; General Assembly, *Acts*, 1869, p. 152; 1866, pp. 127–8; 1868, pp. 141, 144. Also Wallenstein, *From Slave South to New South*, pp. 174–7; Goodrich, "Public Aid to Railroads," pp. 417–23.

36. Summers, *Gospel of Prosperity*, pp. 186–7, 217. Labor cost is from the Alabama and Chattanooga Railroad, in Alabama, which ran close to the Georgia line. Northeastern Alabama and northwestern Georgia, where the first railroad work with convicts was done, were economically quite similar regions in any case. On the Marietta and North Georgia, see R.E. Barclay, *The Railroad Comes to Ducktown* (Knoxville: n.p., 1973), pp. 155–71.

37. The mileage estimate is pieced together from General Assembly, *Proceedings to Investigate*, 1870; US Census Office, *Agencies of Transportation*, 1880; General Assembly,

Acts, 1866–71; and *Poor's Manual of Railroads* (New York: H.V. & H.W. Poor, 1868–72).

38. Principal Keeper, *Report*, 1868, pp. 4–5; 1877–78, p. 4. Due to name changes I cannot locate mileage figures for the Georgia and Alabama Railroad. In general, linking particular railroads with bonds and convict labor is often difficult, due to frequent name changes and/or inconsistency in name usage in legislative acts, US Census documents, the 1870 investigation of the convict lease, and the reports of the principal keeper. What follows is what I can link with certainty using a combination of these sources.

39. General Assembly, *Acts*, 1869, p. 152; US Census Office, *Agencies of Transportation*, 1880, pp. 349, 352.

40. James M. Russell, *Atlanta 1847–1890: City Building in the Old South and the New* (Baton Rouge: Louisiana State University Press, 1988), pp. 55, 165.

41. Mohr, *On the Threshold of Freedom*, pp. 140–41.

42. *Proceedings to Investigate*, 1870, p. 75; Russell, *City Building in the Old South and New*, pp. 165, 254–5; Kenneth Coleman and Charles Stephen Gurr, eds., *Dictionary of Georgia Biography*, 2 vols (Athens: University of Georgia Press, 1983), Vol. 1, pp. 362–4. The *Dictionary* concludes that while unreknowned, "[John T.] Grant should be remembered for his pioneering efforts in the construction of Georgia railroads" (p. 364).

43. Principal Keeper, *Report*, 1868, pp. 4–5, 8–9. There is some discrepancy in the number of convicts reported in 1868. The principal keeper noted that the railroad contractors were quite lax in reporting to him the convicts they received (*Report*, p. 7). See *Proceedings to Investigate*, 1870, pp. 15–16, for copies of the contracts made in 1868 and 1869.

44. Principal Keeper, *Report*, 1868, p. 9.

45. Principal Keeper, *Report*, 1869, pp. 6, 9.

46. *Proceedings to Investigate*, 1870, pp. 15–16.

47. Ibid., p. 76.

48. Ibid., pp. 111, 117 (quotation), 139, 143, 155.

49. Principal Keeper, *Report*, 1869, p. 6; *Proceedings to Investigate*, 1870, pp. 50, 75, 164.

50. General Assembly, *Acts*, 1868, p. 141; Wallenstein, *From Slave South to New South*, p. 175; Stover, *Railroads of the South*, p. 25.

51. General Assembly, *Acts*, 1868, p. 141; *Poor's Manual of Railroads*, 1868, p. 222; 1870, p. 50; 1871, p. 470.

52. See Captain Christopher's report of his investigation of the Macon and Brunswick in *Proceedings to Investigate*, 1870, p. 111.

53. Enoch C. Wines, *The State of Prisons and of Child-Saving Institutions in the Civilized World* (Cambridge, Mass.: J. Wilson & Son, 1880), p. 191.

54. Wallenstein, *From Slave South to New South*, p. 176; Mark V. Wetherington, *The New South Comes to Wiregrass Georgia, 1860–1910* (Knoxville: University of Tennessee Press, 1994), pp. 47–62; General Assembly, *Acts*, 1866, pp. 127–8; Rufus Bullock to the Atlanta *Constitution*, 9 June 1885, reprinted in *Georgia's Repudiated Bonds: Letters from Ex-Governor Bullock to the Constitution Newspaper* (Atlanta: James Harrison and Co., 1886), p. 24.

55. Principal Keeper, *Report*, 1868, p. 5; *Proceedings to Investigate*, 1870, pp. 143, 152, 158, 115; US Census Office, *Agencies of Transportation*, 1880, pp. 348–51; *Poor's Manual of Railroads*, 1868, p. 315; 1870, p. 415.

56. Wallenstein, *From Slave South to New South*, p. 174.

57. General Assembly, *Acts*, 1869, pp. 149–52. The fifty-miles-per-year stipulation was later removed.

58. Principal Keeper, *Report*, 1870, p. 63; H.I. Kimball to Rufus B. Bullock, 5

June 1871, reprinted in *Address of Rufus Bullock*, p. 39; US Census Office, *Agencies of Transportation*, 1880, pp. 349, 516; *Poor's Manual of Railroads*, 1870, p. 115; 1871, p. 351.

59. General Assembly, *Acts*, 1868, pp. 143–4.

60. Ibid.

61. *Proceedings to Investigate*, 1870, p. 157.

62. US Census Office, *Agencies of Transportation*, 1880, pp. 348–9; Principal Keeper, *Report*, 1870; 1872–73, p. 4; *Poor's Manual of Railroads*, 1870, p. 433; 1871, p. 435; 1872, p. 574.

63. Atlanta and Richmond Railroad, *Annual Report, 1874*, SRC, p. 3; Report to Stockholders, 12 June 1872, Atlanta and Richmond Railroad, Correspondence, SRC.

64. General Assembly, *Acts*, 1870, pp. 360–61.

65. *Proceedings to Investigate*, 1870, p. 134; Wallenstein, *From Slave South to New South*, p. 177; General Assembly, *Acts*, 1870, pp. 360–61; US Census Office, *Agencies of Transportation*, 1880, p. 353.

66. Principal Keeper, *Report*, 1868, pp. 8–9.

67. *Proceedings to Investigate*, 1870, pp. 56, 78, 108, 153.

68. Ibid., pp. 17, 89, 143.

69. Ibid., pp. 141, 198.

70. Ibid., p. 143.

71. Ibid., pp. 143, 166, 182, 187.

72. Ibid., pp. 155, 166, 149, 106; see also Transcript of Record, City Court of Atlanta, 3/4 July 1893, *Chattahoochee Brick Company* v. *Braswell*, Case File A-18146, Box 293, Office of the Clerk of Court, Supreme Court Case Files, Records of the Supreme Court of Georgia, GDAH, p. 9, for a convict's testimony on the dangerous nature of this work.

73. *Proceedings to Investigate*, 1870, p. 152 (quotation); see also pp. 121, 145, 185.

74. Ibid., pp. 32, 136.

75. Ibid., p. 187.

76. Ibid., p. 90.

77. Ibid., e.g., p. 141.

78. Ibid., pp. 78–9, 197.

79. Ibid., pp. 6–7, 78.

80. Ibid., pp. 66, 71.

81. Ibid., p. 116; see Captain Christopher's full report, pp. 110–16.

82. Ibid., p. 197.

83. Principal Keeper, *Report*, 1877–78, p. 11.

84. *Proceedings to Investigate*, 1870, p. 159.

85. Ibid., pp. 55, 123, 185, 197.

86. E.g., ibid., p. 123.

87. Ibid., pp. 141–2.

88. Ibid., p. 156; Principal Keeper, *Report*, 1877–78, p. 11. Principal Keeper, *Reports* for the years 1854–62 show seventeen deaths over these nine years; in contrast, in 1868 alone there were sixteen deaths on the railroads, although the number of convicts who passed through the penal system was fewer than the period 1854–62. Principal Keeper, *Report*, 1868, p. 8.

89. *Proceedings to Investigate*, 1870, pp. 106–7.

90. Ibid., p. 115. Grant claimed that he worked both convict and free labor, though I can find no evidence of the latter. It is possible that his firm hired free workers to lay track after the convicts graded the road bed, but I have been unable to locate a payroll book or similar evidence that might demonstrate this.

91. *Proceedings to Investigate*, 1870, p. 169.

92. Barclay, *Railroad Comes to Ducktown*, p. 166.

93. *Proceedings to Investigate*, 1870, p. 134.

94. Ibid., p. 143.

95. Ibid., pp. 196-9; Edmund L. Drago, *Black Politicians and Reconstruction in Georgia* (Baton Rouge: Louisiana State University Press, 1982), pp. 63, 71-2.

96. Principal Keeper, *Report*, 1869, pp. 8-10.

97. Principal Keeper, *Report*, 1870, pp. 6-8.

98. Petition to General Assembly from Citizens of Richmond County, 2 September 1870, "Convicts" Subject File, Box 64, File II, Central Research Section, GDAH. Unfortunately, there is no indication of the race of the petitioners.

99. *Georgia's Repudiated Bonds*; General Assembly, *Acts*, 1871, pp. 25-6, for the "Redeemers'" first lease act. Nathans, *Losing the Peace*, pp. 222-7, esp. p. 224; Woodward, *Origins of the New South*, ch. 1; Wallenstein, *From Slave South to New South*, part 3, all emphasize the essential *continuity* of Reconstruction and Redemption.

100. Georgia Executive Department, Executive Minutes, 17 July 1872, p. 389, GDAH; Georgia General Assembly, *Journal of the Senate*, 1872, p. 139; A. Elizabeth Taylor, "The Origin and Development of the Convict Lease System in Georgia," *Georgia Historical Quarterly* 26 (March 1942), p. 116.

101. Principal Keeper, *Report*, 1877-78, p. 6.

102. Principal Keeper, *Report*, 1868, pp. 8-10.

103. Principal Keeper, *Report*, 1870, p. 8; General Assembly, *Acts*, 1871, pp. 24-6; Principal Keeper, *Report*, 1872-73, pp. 23, 25.

104. *Proceedings to Investigate*, 1870, p. 182; for a similar opinion, see testimony of John Harris, State Senator, ibid., p. 132.

105. Principal Keeper, *Report*, 1872-73, pp. 9-10, 25.

106. Ibid., pp. 9-10, 25, 38.

107. On black crime in postbellum Georgia, see Albert Colbey Smith, "Down Freedom's Road: The Contours of Race, Class, and Property Crime in Black-Belt Georgia, 1866-1919" (Ph.D. dissertation, University of Georgia, 1982), p. 254 for quotation. Also see Edward L. Ayers, *Vengeance and Justice: Crime and Punishment in the 19th Century American South* (New York: Oxford University Press, 1984), especially pp. 168-9, 175-6, 179, 184; Eric Foner, *Nothing But Freedom: Emancipation and Its Legacy* (Baton Rouge: Louisiana State University Press, 1983), pp. 58-60; Vernon Lane Wharton, *The Negro in Mississippi, 1865-1890* (Chapel Hill: University of North Carolina Press, 1947), pp. 237-8, for that state's infamous "pig law."

108. See, e.g., "List of Convicts in the Georgia Penitentiary," in Principal Keeper, *Report*, 1872-73, pp. 28-36.

109. Principal Keeper, *Report*, 1875, p. 14; 1876, p. 8.

110. Principal Keeper, *Report*, 1876, pp. 7, 16; H.H. Tucker, "Prison Labor," in American Prison Association, *Proceedings of the Annual Meeting*, 1886 (Chicago: Donnelley and Sons, 1887), pp. 260-61.

111. Solicitor General of Newton County to Governor Northen, 12 June 1891, Nathan Bailey file, Box 4, Applications for Clemency, Executive Department Papers, GDAH; Principal Keeper, *Report*, 1876, p. 7.

112. Savannah *Tribune*, 23 February 1895; 8 August 1908; Principal Keeper, *Report*, 1876, p. 16. In 1870, seventeen deaths were recorded; from April 1872 to April 1873, twenty-six; in nine months of 1874, forty; and during 1875, forty-nine; *Report*, 1870-1875.

113. On the broad economic impact of railroads, see Mark W. Summers, *Gospel of Prosperity*, pp. 300-301; on the Upcountry, see Steven Hahn, *The Roots of Southern Populism: Yeoman Farmers and the Transformation of the Georgia Upcountry, 1850-1890* (New York: Oxford University Press, 1983), pp. 145-6, 177-8. See also David F. Weiman, "The Economic Emancipation of the Non-Slaveholding Class: Upcountry Farmers

in the Georgia Cotton Economy," *Journal of Economic History* 45 (March 1985), pp. 71–93, 84–5; David F. Weiman, "Urban Growth on the Periphery of the Antebellum Cotton Belt: Atlanta, 1847–1860," *Journal of Economic History* 48 (June 1988), pp. 259–72, 271. Also Stover, *Railroads of the South*, p. 58; Russell, *City Building in the Old South and the New*, pp. 242–4, 248. See also W.W. Finley, "Southern Railroads and Industrial Development," *Annals of the American Academy of Political and Social Science*, issue on "The New South," 35 (January 1910), p. 99, for a retrospective view that railroads made it possible to develop Georgia industry based on raw materials. For mileage figures, see Stover, *Railroads of the South*, p. 61, and US Department of the Interior, Census Office, *Report on the Transportation Business in the U.S. at the 11th Census: 1890*, part 1, *Transportation by Land* (Washington, DC: GPO, 1895), p. 4.

114. Summers, *Gospel of Prosperity*, p. 301; Carter Goodrich, "Public Aid to Railroads," pp. 410–13; Wallenstein, *From Slave South to New South*, p. 177; General Assembly, *Acts*, 1874, pp. 25, 26–9.

115. James S. Boynton to Governor James Milton Smith, 5 February 1872, Box 60, Governor's Correspondence, GDAH; William J. Northen, *Men of Mark in Georgia*, Vol. 3 (Atlanta: A.B. Caldwell, 1911), pp. 366–72.

116. James S. Boynton to Governor James Milton Smith, 5 February 1872, and F.D. Dimanke to Governor James Milton Smith, 5 February 1872, Box 60, Governor's Correspondence, GDAH; see also A.D. Nunn to Governor James Milton Smith, 5 February 1872, Box 60, Governor's Correspondence, GDAH; Coleman and Gurr, eds., *Dictionary of Georgia Biography*, Vol. 1, pp. 108–9; Northen, *Men of Mark*, Vol. 3, pp. 366–72.

117. For Memphis Branch bids see Wade Coltman, Alfred Shorter, Dunlap Scott, and F.L. Stone to James Milton Smith, 26 February 1872 and 28 February 1872, Box 60, Governor's Correspondence, GDAH. See also General Assembly, *Acts*, 1870, p. 338, for aid to the Memphis Branch; and *Acts*, 1871, p. 25 for the lease law stipulating "public works." For other bids submitted to Smith, see William C. Churry to James Milton Smith, 27 January 1872; V.J. Winn to James Milton Smith, 22 February 1872; M.A. Hardin to James Milton Smith, 28 February 1872; all in Box 60, Governor's Correspondence, GDAH.

118. For Etna Iron Co. bids, see Shorter and Coltman to James Milton Smith, 5 February 1872; John T. Burns [Attorney for Etna] to James Milton Smith, 24 February 1872, Box 60, Governor's Correspondence, GDAH. For background on Alfred Shorter see Coleman and Gurr, eds., Dictionary of *Georgia Biography*, Vol. 2, pp. 887–8.

119 Johnson, Lyons & Co. to James Milton Smith, 29 February 1872, Box 60, Governor's Correspondence, GDAH.

120. Taylor, "Origins of Convict Lease," pp. 115–16; Principal Keeper, *Report*, 1876, pp. 6–7; 1872–73, p. 4; Lamar Cobb, Alex Irwin, and Howell Cobb to James Milton Smith, 27 March 1874, Box 68, Governor's Correspondence, GDAH. See also General Assembly, *Acts*, 1870, pp. 344–6, for the Northeastern Railroad's initial aid charter under the Republicans; *Poor's Manual of Railroads*, 1879, p. 528; 1886, p. 132, for endorsement and issuance of the bonds.

121. General Assembly, *Acts*, 1876, p. 41.

122. Report by E.T. Shubrick to Governor McDaniel, 1 July 1886; Report to Governor Gordon, December 1886; Report to Governor Gordon, November 1887; all in E.T. Shubrick File, Box 215, Names File, File II, GDAH.

123. Principal Keeper, *Report*, 1872–73, p. 26.

124. Ibid., pp. 8–9, 26.

125. General Assembly, *Acts*, 1871, pp. 24–6; 1874, pp. 26–8, emphasis added.

126. J.T. Meador to Governor James Milton Smith, 24 March 1874, Box 68, Governor's Correspondence, GDAH; Henry Stevens to Capt. John Jones, 7 March

1874, Henry Stevens File, Box 223, Names File, File II, GDAH; J.P. Bondurant to James Milton Smith, 20 May 1875, "Convicts" Subject File, Box 64, File II, GDAH. D. Hallahan to James Milton Smith, 13 December 1873, Box 67; William Gibson to James Milton Smith, 30 March 1875, Box 72; Patrick Walsh to James Milton Smith, 14 April 1875, Box 73, in regard to Hallahan's attempt to secure some convicts, all in Governor's Correspondence, GDAH. N.S. Eaves and M.B. McGinty to James Milton Smith, 24 March 1874, Box 68, Governor's Correspondence, GDAH, for "*No dangerous work*," emphasis in the original. For background on Henry Stevens, see Coleman and Gurr, *Dictionary of Georgia Biography*, Vol. 2, pp. 931–2.

127. Robert Hester et al. to James Milton Smith, 20 December 1875, Box 75, Governor's Correspondence, GDAH.

128. Christian and Triplett (publishers of the Thomasville *Times*) to Governor Smith's Secretary, 17 March 1874, Box 68; R. Montfort to James Milton Smith, 3 November 1875, Box 75; Robert J. Jones to James Milton Smith, 23 March 1874, Box 68; all in Governor's Correspondence, GDAH.

129. John T. and William D. Grant to James Milton Smith, 24 March 1874, 25 March 1874, Box 68, Governor's Correspondence, GDAH. The Grants claimed to own over $200,000 worth of property as sufficient bond. Much of their railroad profits had been invested in Atlanta real estate. Thomas Alexander to James Milton Smith, 24 March 1874, Thomas Alexander File, Box 2, Names File, File II, GDAH.

130. Principal Keeper, *Report*, 1874, pp. 6–9; 1875, p. 5; Smith, Riddle & Company to James Milton Smith, 20 March 1874, Box 68, Governor's Correspondence, GDAH.

131. Principal Keeper, *Report*, 1874, p. 9; John T. Brown to James Milton Smith, 15 March 1875 and 8 April 1875, John T. Brown File, Box 18, Names File, File II, GDAH; V.H. Taliaferro (Penitentiary Physician) to James Milton Smith, 6 May 1875 and 24 May 1875, Box 73, Governor's Correspondence, GDAH; Taylor, "Origins of Convict Lease," p. 117.

132. Principal Keeper, *Report*, 1874, pp. 4, 7–8.

133. General Assembly, *Acts*, 1876, pp. 40–44; Principal Keeper, *Report*, 1876, pp. 4, 8–9; Principal Keeper, *Report*, 1877–78; Copy of Bond, 21 June 1876, Box 78, Governor's Correspondence, GDAH.

134. For Brown biographies, see Derrell C. Roberts, *Joseph E. Brown and the Politics of Reconstruction* (University, Ala.: University of Alabama Press, 1973), and Joseph H. Parks, *Joseph E. Brown of Georgia* (Baton Rouge: Louisiana State University Press, 1977); for Brown and the "Bourbon Triumvirate," see Woodward, *Origins of the New South*, pp. 14–15; Lewis Nicholas Wynne, *The Continuity of Cotton: Planter Politics in Georgia 1865–1892* (Macon, Ga.: Mercer University Press, 1986), ch. 8. For details on Dade lease, see Principal Keeper, *Report*, 1877–78; Folder 4, Box 3, Joseph E. Brown Papers, UGA, for bids. See also Derrell Roberts, "Joseph E. Brown and His Georgia Mines," *Georgia Historical Quarterly* 52 (September 1968), pp. 285–92. For a sketch of the so-called "Bourbon System," see Bartley, *Creation of Georgia*, pp. 81–7.

135. On the 1877 Georgia Constitution, see Bartley, *Creation of Georgia*, p. 79; Wynne, *Continuity of Cotton*, ch. 6. Wynne offers the most uncompromising insistence that the planters triumphed in the "New South," making it less than new, at least in Georgia.

136. For a discussion of Redemption that emphasizes the coalition of planters and industrialists, see Foner, *Reconstruction*, ch. 12, esp. pp. 588, 596.

137. US Bureau of Labor, *Convict Labor*, Second Annual Report of the Commissioner of Labor (Washington, DC: GPO, 1887), pp. 98–100, 218. Lawrence N. Powell, "The Prussians are Coming," *Georgia Historical Quarterly* 71 (Winter 1987), p. 649, for observation on textiles; Wiener, *Social Origins of the New South*, on planter antipathy to

industrialization. Neither takes convict labor much into account, though in a foot-note Powell does remark that "convict labor has a 'Prussian Road' flavor about it" (p. 661n). On law, Redemption, and labor control, see Foner, *Reconstruction*, p. 594; Foner, *Nothing But Freedom*, pp. 59–61; Perman, *The Road to Redemption*, pp. 243–5.

138. Foner, *Reconstruction*, p. 594; Foner, *Nothing But Freedom*, pp. 59–61; Perman, *The Road to Redemption*, pp. 243–5. On rural property crime in Georgia as social protest, see Smith, "Down Freedom's Road," esp. ch. 5; on the high proportion of convicts from cities, see Principal Keeper, *Report*, 1886–88, p. 8; on urban crime in the postbellum South, see Ayers, *Vengeance and Justice*, pp. 173–4; Joel Williamson, *A Rage for Order: Black-White Relations in the American South since Emancipation* (New York: Oxford University Press, 1986), p. 146; and Howard Rabinowitz, *Race Relations in the Urban South, 1865–1890* (Urbana: University of Illinois Press, 1980), pp. 49–50. Figures on convicts are from Principal Keeper, *Report*, 1877–78, pp. 71–2; see also Principal Keeper, *Report*, 1872–73, pp. 28–36, for race, crime and county of conviction.

139. Lee Chapman file, Box 22; Charley Hill file, Box 54; Bony Waters file, Box 126; Alfred Flynn file, Box 41; Ed Porter file, Box 97; Applications for Clemency, Executive Department Papers, GDAH.

140. Bill Slaughter file, Box 108; Doc Wilson file, Box 133; Henry Armstrong file, Box 3; Applications for Clemency, Executive Department Papers, GDAH. For black-on-black crime, see also Alfred Smith file, Box 109; Isaac Watson file, Box 127; Mary Battle file, Box 7; and William Wilson file, Box 133.

141. Principal Keeper, *Report*, 1877–78, pp. 71–2; Principal Keeper, *Report*, 1886–88, p. 8; Principal Keeper, *Report*, 1882.

Chapter 4

1. William D. Kelley, *The Old South and the New: A Series of Letters* (New York: G.P. Putnam's Sons, 1888), p. 3.

2. In 1890 there were 733 coal miners in Georgia, and 628 of them were convicts; US Department of the Interior, Census Office, *Compendium of the 11th Census: 1890*, part 2 (Washington, DC: GPO, 1894), p. 486; US Department of the Interior, Census Office, *Report on Crime, Pauperism and Benevolence at the Eleventh Census*, Vol. 3, 1890 (Washington, DC: GPO, 1895), p. 15. On coalfields, see US Department of the Interior, Census Office, *Mineral Industries in the United States*, 1890, Vol. 7 (Washington, DC: GPO, 1892), p. 346; US Department of the Interior, United States Geological Survey, *Mineral Resources of the United States, 1883–1884* (Washington, DC: GPO, 1884), pp. 14, 39, 88 (hereafter cited as USGS, *Mineral Resources*). The three key productive basins in Alabama – the Warrior, Coosa, and Cahaba – consisted of 1,030 square miles, however; USGS, *Mineral Resources*, 1883–84, pp. 14–15. For comparative levels of coke and pig-iron production, see Tennessee Division of Mines, *Second Annual Report of the Commissioner of Labor and Inspector of Mines* (Nashville, Tenn.: State Printer, 1893), pp. 300–303; *Fourth Annual Report of the Bureau of Labor, Statistics and Mines* (Nashville, Tenn.: State Printer, 1895), pp. 233–6.

3. Only Stanley Greenberg, *Race and State in Capitalist Development: Comparative Perspectives* (New Haven, Conn.: Yale University Press, 1980), esp. pp. 209–26, at-tributes adequate significance to the role of convict labor in the industrialization of this region; Gerald Jaynes, *Branches Without Roots: Genesis of the Black Working Class in the American South, 1862–1882* (New York: Oxford University Press, 1986), p. 271, is suggestive, however. Ronald L. Lewis, *Black Coal Miners in America: Race, Class and Community Conflict, 1780–1980* (Lexington: The University Press of Kentucky, 1987), ch. 2, is a good survey of convict mine labor in all three states.

4. T.J. Hill, "Experience in Mining Coal With Convicts," in National Prison Association, *Proceedings of the Annual Congress, 1897* (Pittsburgh: Shaw Bros, 1898), p. 389.

5. Ibid., p. 390.

6. Ibid., pp. 390, 394-5.

7. Ibid., pp. 396-7.

8. US Geological Survey, *Mineral Resources of the United States*, 1883-84, 1889-90, 1891, 1900; Emory Q. Hawk, *Economic History of the South* (New York: Prentice Hall, 1934), p. 482, for the 1896 figure. On industrial growth in this region, and its dependence on northern capital, see Jaynes, *Branches Without Roots*, pp. 268-72; Gavin Wright, *Old South, New South: An Economic History Since the Civil War* (New York: Basic Books, 1986), ch. 6; Victor S. Clark, *History of Manufactures in the United States*, Volume 2 (1929; reprint, New York: Peter Smith, 1949), pp. 211-20; and C. Vann Woodward, *Origins of the New South, 1877-1913* (Baton Rouge: Louisiana State University Press, 1951), chs 5 and 11, for the classic account of the "colonial economy." For an excellent discussion of the various explanations for the relative weakness of southern industry, see Robert J. Norrell, *James Bowron: The Autobiography of a New South Industrialist* (Chapel Hill: University of North Carolina Press, 1991), introduction.

9. Kelley, *The Old South and the New*, p. 3; William G. Atkinson to Governor James M. Smith, 26 September 1872, Box 82, Governor's Incoming Correspondence, Georgia Executive Department Records, GDAH, pp. 3-4; Abram S. Hewitt, quoted in John T. Milner, *Alabama: As It Was, As It Is, and As It Will Be* (Montgomery, Ala.: Barret & Brown, 1876), p. 192; Tennessee Bureau of Agriculture, Statistics and Mines, *Tennessee: Its Agricultural and Mineral Wealth* (Nashville, Tenn.: State Printer, 1876), pp. 129-30; J.W. Burke, "The Coal Fields of Alabama," pamphlet (n.p.: n.pub., c. 1885), p. 5; American Iron and Steel Institute, *Bulletin* 20 (29 December 1886), pp. 346-7.

10. On the antebellum coal and iron industries, see Herman H. Chapman, *The Iron and Steel Industries of the South* (University, Ala: University of Alabama Press, 1953), pp. 98-101; Ethel Armes, *The Story of Coal and Iron in Alabama* (Birmingham, Ala.: Chamber of Commerce, 1910), pp. 58-194; Kenneth Warren, *The American Steel Industry, 1850-1970: A Geographical Interpretation* (Oxford: Clarendon Press, 1973), pp. 25, 65-6; William T. Hogan, *Economic History of the Iron and Steel Industry in the United States*, 4 vols (Lexington, Mass.: D.C. Heath, 1971), Vol. 1, pp. 72-4; James M. Swank, "The American Iron Industry From Its Beginnings in 1619 to 1886," in USGS, *Mineral Resources*, 1886, p. 32; J. Allen Tower, "The Industrial Development of the Birmingham Region," *Bulletin of Birmingham–Southern College* 46 (December 1953), pp. 11-12; Woodward Iron Co., *Alabama Blast Furnaces* (Woodward, Ala.: Woodward Iron Co., 1940), pp. 18-20.

11. On the contiguity of key resources for iron production in the South, see American Institute of Mining Engineers, *Transactions* 14 (1885), pp. 3-11; Tennessee Bureau of Agriculture, Statistics and Mines, *Report for 1876*, pp. 226-7; Chapman, *Iron and Steel Industries*, p. 27.

12. William B. Phillips, *Iron-Making in Alabama*, 2nd edn (Montgomery, Ala.: State Printer, 1898), p. 366; USGS, *Mineral Resources*, 1889-1890, p. 172; US Census Office, *Report on the Mineral Industries of the United States at the Eleventh Census*, Vol. 7, 1890, p. 355; USGS, *Mineral Resources*, 1890, p. 149; Phillips, *Iron-Making*, 1896, p. 25; Mable Mills, *The Coke Industry in Alabama* (University, Ala.: Bureau of Business Research, University of Alabama, 1947), p. 2; Tennessee Division of Mines, *Fourth Annual Report of the Bureau of Labor, Statistics and Mines* (Nashville, Tenn.: State Printer, 1895), p. 234; Woodward Iron Company, *Alabama Blast Furnaces* (1940), p. 19.

13. USGS, *Mineral Resources*, 1882, p. 7; 1889-90, p. 271; Tennessee Division of Mines, *Second Annual Report of the Commissioner of Labor and Inspector of Mines, Jan. 2, 1893* (Nashville, Tenn.: State Printer, 1893), p. 314; Tennessee Division of Mines,

Fourth Annual Report of the Bureau of Labor, Statistics and Mines, January 1895 (Nashville, Tenn.: State Printer, 1895), pp. 223, 283; American Institute of Mining Engineers, *Transactions* 14 (1885), pp. 3–11.

14. American Iron and Steel Association, *Bulletin* 18 (21 May 1884), p. 133; on depressions, see, e.g., Justin Fuller, "History of the Tennessee Coal, Iron and Railroad Company, 1852–1907" (Ph.D. dissertation, University of North Carolina, 1966), p. 54; Clark, *History of Manufactures*, Vol. 2, pp. 286–303.

15. American Iron and Steel Association, *Bulletin* 18 (20 August 1884), p. 210.

16. James M. Swank, "The American Iron Industry From Its Beginnings in 1619 to 1886," in USGS, *Mineral Resources*, 1886, pp. 33–8.

17. Phillips, *Iron-Making*, p. 4; American Institute of Mining Engineers, *Transactions* 14 (1885), pp. 7–11; Chapman, *Iron and Steel Industries*, pp. 47, 51, 155, and Peter Temin, *Iron and Steel in Nineteenth-Century America, An Economic Inquiry* (Cambridge, Mass.: MIT Press, 1964), p. 200 on the low quality of southern ores. See also Chapman, *Iron and Steel Industries*, ch. 6, on the inconsistency of southern coal seams, esp. pp. 51–2, 60, 155, 176. See W.H. Ruffner to J.W. Johnston, 1 January 1884; A.B. Johnston to J.W. Johnston, 17 June 1884; Correspondence, Folder 2, Coalburg Coal Company Records, SRC, for one company's struggle with these constraints.

18. US Congress, Senate Committee on Education and Labor, *Report of the Committee of the Senate Upon the Relations Between Labor and Capital*, 4 vols, 1885, Vol. 4, p. 132; H.H. Campbell, *The Manufacture of Iron and Steel* (New York: The Engineering and Mining Journal, 1903), pp. 674–5.

19. E.W. Tutwiler to J.W. Johnston, 7 February 1884, Correspondence, Folder 2, Coalburg Coal and Coke Company Records, SRC, p. 18; *Relations Between Labor and Capital*, Vol. 4, pp. 286–90. There were similar complaints about white workers in the "mountainous sections of [Alabama]" (p. 23); see also pp. 25–6.

20. *Relations Between Labor and Capital*, Vol. 4, pp. 286–90, 385–6.

21. US Bureau of Labor, *Convict Labor*, p. 301; US Senate, Reports of the Immigration Commission, *Immigrants in Industries*, 61st Congress, 2nd session, Doc. No. 633, part 1, vol. 2, *Bituminous Coal Mining* (Washington, DC: GPO, 1911), p. 218; E.W. Tutwiler to J.W. Johnston, 7 February 1884, Correspondence, Folder 2, Coalburg Coal and Coke Company Records, SRC, pp. 1, 2, 18; *Joint Scale Convention of the Alabama Coal Operators Association and the United Mine Workers of America and the Proceedings of the Board of Arbitration* (Birmingham, Ala.: Roberts and Sons, 1903), p. 7; US Congress, House of Representatives, *Hearings Before the Committee on Investigation of United States Steel Corporation* (Washington, DC: GPO, 1912), p. 2982; see also John A. Fitch, "Birmingham District: Labor Conservation," *The Survey* 27 (6 January 1912), pp. 1527–40.

22. Tennessee Bureau of Agriculture, Statistics and Labor, *Coal: Report of Henry E. Colton, Geologist and Inspector of Mines* (Nashville, Tenn.: State Printer, 1883), pp. 38–9; Tennessee Division of Mines, *Second Annual Report*, p. 152.

23. *Relations Between Labor and Capital*, Vol. 4, p. 249; A.B. Johnston to J.W. Johnston, 17 June 1884, Correspondence, Folder 2, Coalburg Coal and Coke Company Records, SRC, p. 4.

24. *Relations Between Labor and Capital*, Vol. 4, pp. 438, 442; "Operations of Mines at Coalburg, from Feb. 1 to May 31, 1884," Correspondence, Folder 2, Coalburg Coal and Coke Company Records, SRC; *Report of Henry E. Colton*, pp. 42–4, 81. Other sources give the cost of convict labor as $18.50 per month in 1888; free labor in the mines as $2.15 a day, in 1889. Alabama, *Second Biennial Report of the Inspector of Convicts, From Oct. 1, 1886 to Sept. 30, 1888* (Montgomery, Ala.: State Printer, 1888), p. 251; USGS, *Mineral Resources*, 1889–90, pp. 170–71.

25. US Bureau of Labor, *Convict Labor*, 1886, p. 301; *United Mine Workers Journal*

(*UMWJ*), 15 September 1892, p. 4; 26 January 1899, p. 4.

26. J.A. Bartamm to J.W. Johnston, 9 April 1883, Correspondence, Folder 1, Coalburg Coal and Coke Company Records, SRC.

27. E.A. Tutwiler to J.W. Johnston, 7 February 1884, Correspondence, Folder 2, Coalburg Coal and Coke Company Records, SRC.

28. See Kenneth R. Bailey, "A Judicious Mixture: Negroes and Immigrants in the West Virginia Mines, 1880–1917," and the other essays in William H. Turner and Edward J. Cabbell, eds., *Blacks in Appalachia* (Lexington: The University Press of Kentucky, 1985), parts 3, 4 and 5; Lewis, *Black Coal Miners in America*, chs 7 and 8.

29. R.H. Dawson to North Carolina Bureau of Labor Statistics, in North Carolina Bureau of Labor Statistics, *First Annual Report* (Raleigh, N.C.: State Printer, 1887), p. 206.

30. Nashville *Republican Banner*, 20 December 1872; Hill, "Experience in Mining Coal With Convicts," p. 390; *Relations Between Labor and Capital*, Vol. 4, pp. 434, 437, 442; Alabama General Assembly, *Journal of the House of Representatives, 1896–1897* (Montgomery, Ala.: State Printer, 1897), p. 638. For similar trends in Georgia, see Georgia, Principal Keeper of the Penitentiary, *Report*, 1877–78, p. 10; *Investigation of Charges Against Penitentiary Companies One, Two and Three*, 2 vols, *Evidence for the State*, Vol. 1, *Evidence for Julius Brown, Receiver*, Vol. 2: 10–21 February 1896, Box 4, Julius L. Brown Papers, AHC, vol. 1, pp. 120–25, vol. 2, p. 479.

31. *Relations Between Labor and Capital*, Vol. 4, pp. 442, 446; Alabama, *First Biennial Report of the Inspector of Convicts, 1884–1886* (Montgomery, Ala.: State Printer, 1886), p. 21.

32. Letter to *National Labor Tribune*, 4 January 1879, reprinted in Herbert G. Gutman, "Black Coal Miners and the Greenback-Labor Party in Alabama," *Labor History* 10 (Summer 1969), pp. 506–35, 516; *UMWJ*, 4 April 1895, p. 3; Alabama *Sentinel*, 13 June 1891; Thomas Parke Diary, 15 March 1895, 31 July 1895, BPL; Alabama, *First Biennial Report of the Inspectors of Convicts, 1884–1886*, pp. 187–8; Alabama, *Second Biennial Report of the Inspectors of Convicts, 1886–1888*, lists of county convicts; *UMWJ*, 10 February 1898, p. 1. For a later critique of the "fee system," see Shelby Harrison, "A Cash-Nexus for Crime," *The Survey* 27 (6 January 1912).

33. Alabama, *Third Biennial Report of the Inspectors of Convicts* (Montgomery, Ala.: State Printer, 1890), pp. 204, 206. See also Alabama General Assembly, *Testimony Before the Joint Committee of the General Assembly, Appointed to Examine into the Convict System of Alabama* (Montgomery, Ala.: Brown Printing Co., 1889), pp. 11, 119; W.D. Lee to Governor Seay, 26 August 1887, Administrative Files, Governor's Papers, G24, ADAH; S.G. Carradine to Reginald Dawson, 21 November 1890, Reports from Inspectors, Incoming Correspondence, Vol. 2, Corrections Department, ADAH.

34. R.H. Dawson (President of Alabama Board of Inspectors of Convicts), in National Prison Association, *Proceedings*, 1888, p. 84; on percentage of black workers by the turn of the century, see Paul B. Worthman, "Black Workers and Labor Unions in Birmingham, Alabama, 1897–1904," *Labor History* 10 (Summer 1969), pp. 375–407. By 1920, 70 per cent of Alabama miners were black according to one estimate; see Alabama Coal Strike of 1920, File 170–1182, Federal Mediation and Conciliation Service Records, RG280, NA-WNRC; *UMWJ*, 10 February 1898, p. 1; see also Lewis, *Black Coal Miners in America*, pp. 39, 191. On percentage of black convicts, see Alabama, *Second Biennial Report of the Inspectors of Convicts, 1886–1888*, pp. 62–82; Alabama, *Second Biennial Report of the Board of Inspectors of Convicts, 1896–1898* (Montgomery, Ala.: State Printer, 1898), p. 19.

35. Reports of the Immigration Commission, *Immigrants in Industries, Bituminous Coal Mining*, p. 218.

36. *UMWJ*, 2 February 1898, p. 1; 4 January 1894, p. 4; 31 December 1891, p. 6; 22 September 1904, p. 2; 30 April 1891, p. 3.

37. *UMWJ*, 10 February 1898, p. 1; 4 April 1895, p. 3; *U.S. Steel Hearings*, p. 2984. On race relations in the UMW, see Herbert G. Gutman, "The Negro and the United Mine Workers of America," in Julius Jacobson, ed., *The Negro and the American Labor Movement* (Garden City, N.J.: Doubleday, 1968), pp. 49–127; Herbert Hill, "Myth-Making as Labor History: Herbert Gutman and the United Mine Workers of America," *International Journal of Politics, Culture, and Society* 2 (Winter 1988), pp. 132–200; Rick Halpern, "Organized Labor, Black Workers, and the Twentieth Century South: The Emerging Revision," in Melvyn Stokes and Rick Halpern, eds., *Race and Class in the American South Since 1890* (Oxford: Berg, 1994), pp. 47–55; Alex Lichtenstein, "Racial Conflict and Racial Solidarity in the Alabama Coal Strike of 1894: New Evidence for the Gutman–Hill Debate," *Labor History* 36 (Winter 1995), pp. 63–76.

38. On integrated production, see Hogan, *Economic History of the Iron and Steel Industry*, Vol. 1, p. 74; Armes, *The Story of Coal and Iron*, p. 275; Robert Gregg, *Origin and Development of the Tennessee Coal, Iron and Railroad Company* (New York: Newcomen Society, 1948), pp. 13–14; Woodward Iron Co., *Alabama Blast Furnaces*; United States Steel Corporation, Tennessee Coal and Iron Division, *Biography of a Business* (n.p.: US Steel Corporation, 1960), p. 32.

39. Judge Milliken of Tennessee, quoted in American Iron and Steel Association, *Bulletin* 20 (29 December 1886), p. 347; Atkinson quoted in *Proceedings of the Annual Meeting of the Stockholders of the Western Railroad Company*, 1880, p. 17.

40. Tennessee Bureau of Labor, *Report of Henry E. Colton*, p. 51.

41. By 1882 the Pratt mines were the most productive in Alabama; Alabama, *Biennial Report of the Inspectors of the Alabama Penitentiary, 1880–1882* (Montgomery, Ala.: State Printer, 1882), pp. 82–4; Tennessee Bureau of Agriculture, Statistics and Mines, *Hand-Book of Tennessee* (Knoxville, Tenn.: Whig & Chronicle, 1883), p. 24; Tennessee Division of Mines, *Second Annual Report*, p. 303; US Census Office, *Mineral Industries of the United States*, 1880, Vol. 15, p. 926; Tennessee Bureau of Labor, *Report of Henry E. Colton*, pp. 42, 80; USGS, *Mineral Resources*, 1882, p. 7; Tennessee Division of Mines, *Fourth Annual Report of the Bureau of Labor, Statistics and Mines* (Nashville, Tenn.: State Printer, 1895), p. 222. Virtually all of Georgia's 150,000 to 300,000 tons were mined by convicts; on Joseph Brown's mines, see Chapters 5 and 6 below. See Fuller, "History of TCI"; and Gregg, *Origin and Development of TCI*, pp. 8–14 for history of Tracy City; Armes, *Story of Coal and Iron*, pp. 273ff., for history of Pratt mines.

42. Tennessee Bureau of Labor, *Report of Henry E. Colton*, p. 81; Tennessee Bureau of Agriculture, *Hand-Book of Tennessee*, p. 24.

43. TCI, *Annual Report*, 1893, pp. 3–4; TCI, *Annual Report*, 1898.

44. Alabama, *Second Biennial Report of the Inspectors of Mines, 1898* (Birmingham, Ala.: Dispatch Printing Co., 1898), pp. 16, 18.

45. J.B. Killebrew, *Special Report on the Coal-Field of Little Sequatchee* (Nashville, Tenn.: Tavel, Eastman and Howell, 1876), map; Tennessee Department of Education, Division of Geology, *The Southern Tennessee Coal Field*, Bulletin 33-A (Nashville, Tenn.: State Printer, 1925), pp. 4–5; Tennessee Bureau of Labor, *Report of Henry E. Colton*, p. 80; Fuller, "History of TCI," p. 280; Armes, *Story of Coal and Iron*, pp. 362–8. On the antebellum and Civil War history of TCI, see US Steel, TCI Division, *Biography of a Business*, pp. 3–8; *Report of Henry E. Colton*, p. 80.

46. Fuller, "History of TCI," pp. 176, 289; *Report of Henry E. Colton*, p. 80; Nashville *Republican Banner*, 18 December 1872, p. 4; Tennessee Bureau of Agriculture, *Introduction to the Resources of Tennessee* (Nashville, Tenn.: State Printer, 1874), p. 746; Tennessee Bureau of Agriculture, Statistics, and Mines, *Tennessee: Its Agricultural and Mineral Wealth* (Nashville, Tenn.: State Printer, 1876), pp. 90–117.

47. Sewanee Mining and Tennessee Coal, Iron and Railroad Company Records, microfilm, BPL, p. 6.

48. USGS, *Mineral Resources*, 1886, p. 252; Tennessee Division of Mines, *Fifth Annual Report of the Commissioner of Labor and Inspector of Mines* (Nashville, Tenn.: State Printer, 1896), pp. 210–11; Tennessee Division of Mines, *Third Annual Report of the Commissioner of Labor and Inspector of Mines* (Nashville, Tenn.: State Printer, 1894), p. 93; Report by L.E. Bryant, Chief Engineer of Tennessee State Mines, in USGS, *Mineral Resources*, 1894, p. 189; "Report on Tracy City Division of TCI, April 1, 1895," pp. 5–6, Erskine Ramsey Papers, BPL.

49. USGS, *Mineral Resources*, 1883–84, p. 160; Georgia Penitentiary, Principal Physician, *Report*, 1884–86, p. 109; USGS, *Mineral Resources*, 1900, p. 372; 1901, pp. 358, 430, 443; Charles W. Hayes, *The Southern Appalachian Coal Field*, in USGS, *Twenty-Second Annual Report*, part 3, p. 260.

50. Sewanee Mining and Tennessee Coal, Iron and Railroad Company Records, microfilm, BPL, pp. 7, 10–11.

51. *Report of Henry E. Colton*, pp. 79–80; Morrow Chamberlain, *A Brief History of the Pig-iron Industry of East Tennessee* (Chattanooga, Tenn.: privately printed, 1942), p. iii; American Iron and Steel Association, *Bulletin* 10 (5 January 1876), p. 2.

52. Killebrew, *Special Report*, pp. 9, 17–20. See also Gregg, *Origins and Development of TCI*, pp. 13–14.

53. Nashville *Republican Banner*, 10 June, 11 June 1870. For the long-running battle against convict labor by Tennessee's free miners, see Karin Shapiro, "The Tennessee Convict Miner's Revolts of 1891–1892: Industrialization, Politics, and Convict Labor in the Late Nineteenth-Century South" (Ph.D. dissertation, Yale University, 1991).

54. Nashville *Republican Banner*, 14 August 1870.

55. Nashville *Republican Banner*, 12 December 1872, p. 4; 13 December 1872, p. 4.

56. Tennessee Division of Mines, *Second Annual Report*, pp. 314, 341; Armes, *Story of Coal and Iron*, pp. 390–91; Fuller, "History of TCI," p. 49.

57. Tennessee Division of Mines, *Second Annual Report*, pp. 52, 48, 62–3, 303, 50, 342; Tennessee Division of Mines, *Fourth Annual Report of the Bureau of Labor, Statistics and Mines, January 1895*, p. 283; USGS, *Mineral Resources*, 1891, p. 320; "Report on Tracy City Division of TCI, April 1, 1895," Erskine Ramsey Papers, BPL, pp. 4,7; TCI, *Annual Report for the Fiscal Year ending January 31, 1892*, p. 3; Tennessee Division of Mines, *Second Annual Report*, p. 314.

58. Tennessee Division of Mines, *Second Annual Report*, p. 50.

59. For TCI's move to Alabama, see Fuller, "History of TCI," p. 177; Gregg, *Origins and Development*, pp. 15–16; US Steel, TCI Division, *Biography of a Business*, pp. 22–4; for production figures for the company's divisions, see TCI, *Annual Report*, 1892, pp. 3–4. On the transfer of convicts to state-owned mines, see Tennessee, *Report of the Board of Prison Commissioners, December 15, 1896* (n.p.: n.pub., n.d.), pp. 12, 33; "Report on Tracy City Division," 1 April 1895, pp. 2–3; Tennessee Division of Mines, *Sixth Annual Report* (Nashville, Tenn.: State Printer, 1896), pp. 158–9.

60. Alabama Bureau of Industrial Resources, *Report of the Commissioner of Industrial Relations of Alabama* (Montgomery, Ala.: State Printer, 1875), p. 9; Geological Survey of Alabama, *On the Warrior Coal Field* (Montgomery, Ala.: State Printer, 1886), p. 13; Alabama, *First Biennial Report of the Inspector of Convicts, 1884–1886* (Montgomery, Ala.: State Printer, 1886), p. 21; USGS, *Mineral Resources*, 1886, p. 237.

61. USGS, *Mineral Resources*, 1886, p. 237; USGS, *Mineral Resources*, 1882, p. 36. For figures on convicts, see Alabama, *Biennial Report of the Inspectors of the Alabama Penitentiary, 1882–1884* (Montgomery, Ala.: State Printer, 1885), pp. 104–10; *First Biennial Report of the Inspectors of Convicts, 1884–1886* (Montgomery, Ala.; State Printer, 1886), pp. 113, 119, 187–8.

62. John W. DuBose, ed., *The Mineral Wealth of Alabama and Birmingham Illustrated* (Birmingham, Ala.: N.T. Green and Co., 1886), p. 145; American Iron and Steel Asso-

ciation, *Bulletin* 17 (4 July 1883), p. 179; *UMWJ*, 26 April 1894, p. 4. The best secondary sources on DeBardeleben are Armes, *Story of Coal and Iron*; Fuller, "History of TCI"; Justin Fuller, "Henry F. DeBardeleben, Industrialist of the New South," *Alabama Review* 39 (January 1986), pp. 3–18; and Marjorie L. White, *The Birmingham District: An Industrial History and Guide* (Birmingham, Ala.: Birmingham Historical Society, 1981). See also Worthman, "Black Workers and Labor Unions in Birmingham," pp. 376–9.

63. Alabama, *Second Biennial Report of the Inspectors of Mines, 1898*, pp. 16, 19, 21; Armes, *Story of Coal and Iron*, pp. 273, 275; Clark, *History of Manufactures*, Vol. 2, p. 215.

64. Alabama, *Annual Report of the Alabama Penitentiary, From October 1, 1873 to September 30, 1874*, p. 5; US Census Office, *Minerals*, 1880, Vol. 15, p. 866; USGS, *Mineral Resources*, 1886, p. 237; *Biennial Report of the Inspectors of the Alabama Penitentiary, 1880–1882*, p. 4; *First Biennial Report of the Inspectors of Convicts, 1884–1886*, pp. 187–8.

65. American Iron and Steel Association, *Bulletin* 17 (4 July 1883), p. 179.

66. DuBose, *Mineral Wealth of Alabama*, p. 145; White, *The Birmingham District: An Industrial History*, p. 44; Armes, *Story of Coal and Iron*, p. 261; Fuller, "History of TCI," p. 236; *Annual Report of the Inspectors of the Alabama Penitentiary*, 1875–1876, 1876–1877; for the importance of the shift to coke-fueled furnaces, see J. Allen Tower, "The Industrial Development of the Birmingham Region," *Bulletin of Birmingham-Southern College* 46 (December 1953), pp. 11–12.

67. Armes, *Story of Coal and Iron*, p. 273; Fuller, "History of TCI," pp. 183–4. For a good history of Birmingham, see Carl V. Harris, *Political Power in Birmingham, 1871–1921* (Knoxville: University of Tennessee Press, 1977).

68. Alabama, *Second Biennial Report of the Inspectors of Mines, 1898*, pp. 23, 28; *Biennial Report of the Inspectors of the Alabama Penitentiary, 1880–1882* (Montgomery, Ala.: State Printer, 1882), p. 4.

69. DuBose, *Mineral Wealth of Alabama*, p. 67; White, *The Birmingham District: An Industrial History*, p. 46; A.B. Johnston to J.W. Johnston, 17 June 1884, Correspondence, Folder 2, Coalburg Coal and Coke Company Records, SRC, p. 2.

70. White, *The Birmingham District: An Industrial History*, p. 46.

71. Armes, *Story of Coal and Iron*, pp. 283–4, 290–93; DuBose, *Mineral Wealth of Alabama*, pp. 173–4; Clark, *History of Manufactures*, Vol. 2, p. 215.

72. Fuller, "History of TCI," p. 69; DuBose, *Mineral Wealth of Alabama*, pp. 169, 173; Alabama, *First Biennial Report of the Inspectors of Convicts, 1884–1886*, pp. 113, 119, 187–8; Gregg, *Origins and Development*, pp. 15–16; US Steel, TCI Division, *Biography of a Business*, pp. 22–4.

73. Alabama, *Second Biennial Report of the Inspectors of Convicts, 1886–1888*, pp. 2–3, 251; USGS, *Mineral Resources*, 1889–1890, pp. 170–71, for free wages; R.M. Cunningham, "The Convict System of Alabama in Its Relation to Health and Disease," in National Prison Association, *Proceedings*, 1889, pp. 108–41, 132.

74. W. David Lewis, *Sloss Furnaces and the Rise of the Birmingham District: An Industrial Epic* (Tuscaloosa: University of Alabama Press, 1994), pp. 55–8; White, *The Birmingham District: An Industrial History*, pp. 46, 145–6; Alabama, *Second Biennial Report of the Inspectors of Mines, 1898*, pp. 11, 13; DuBose, *Mineral Wealth of Alabama*, pp. 172–3; Armes, *Story of Coal and Iron*, pp. 288–9, 347–53; Woodward Iron Co., *Alabama Blast Furnaces*, pp. 128–9.

75. Armes, *Story of Coal and Iron*, pp. 438–9; "Accounts Receivable," Correspondence, Folder 2, Coalburg Coal and Coke Company Records, SRC; Alabama, *First Biennial Report of the Inspectors of Convicts, 1884–1886*, pp. 187–8; USGS, *Mineral Resources*, 1886, p. 237; Alabama, *Third Biennial Report of the Inspectors of Convicts, 1888–1890*, pp. 51, 97; *Fourth Biennial Report of the Inspectors of Convicts, 1890–1892*; Alabama, Mine Inspector, *First Biennial Report of the State Inspector of Mines, 1892–1894* (n.p.: n.pub., n.d.) p. 56.

76. *Testimony Before the Joint Committee of the General Assembly, Appointed to Examine*

into the Convict System of Alabama (Montgomery, Ala.: Brown Printing Co., 1889), p. 11; W.D. Lee to Governor Seay, 26 August 1887, Administrative Files, Governor's Papers, G24, ADAH; E.W. Tutwiler to J.W. Johnston, 9 November 1885, Correspondence, Folder 3, Coalburg Coal and Coke Company Records, SRC; see also A.B. Johnston to J.W. Johnston, 17 June 1884, and A.B. Johnston to J.W. Johnston, 2 March 1884, both in Folder 2, Coalburg Coal and Coke Company Records, SRC.

77. White, *The Birmingham District: An Industrial History*, pp. 145–6.

78. Alabama General Assembly, *Journal of the House of Representatives*, 1896–97, p. 651. For mergers and acquisitions in Alabama's iron industry, see Chapman, *Iron and Steel Industries*, p. 141; Tower, "Industrial Development of Birmingham Region," pp. 13–16; Gregg, *Origins and Development of TCI*, pp. 16–19; Woodward Iron Co., *Alabama Blast Furnaces*, p. 31.

79. Alabama, *Second Biennial Report of the Board of Inspectors of Convicts, 1896–1898*, p. 19; Barbara J. Mitchell, "Steel Workers in a Boom Town: Birmingham 1900," *Southern Exposure* 12 (November/December 1984), pp. 56–60; White, *The Birmingham District: An Industrial History*, pp. 145–6; Wayne Flynt, *Mine, Mill and Microchip: A Chronicle of Alabama Enterprise* (Northridge, Calif.: Windsor Publications, 1987), p. 115.

80. "The 'Prison-Made' Pig Iron in Canada," *Ironmonger*, n.d., James Bowron Scrapbooks, 1895–1902, BPL.

81. Department of the Interior, US Census Office, *Compendium of the 11th Census: 1890*, part 2, p. 486; US Census Office, *Report on Crime, Pauperism and Benevolence in the U.S. at the 11th census: 1890*, part 2, pp. 15–16, 121. For data on *underground* workers, of which convicts made up a higher percentage, see US Census Office, *Report on Mineral Industries*, 1890, Vol. 7, pp. 350–51; the figures are 5,674 for Alabama and 3,234 for Tennessee. However, between 1889 and 1890 the number of mine workers in Alabama jumped from 6,975 to 10,642; but by 1894 the number had dropped to 8,936, while the number of convicts had increased to 1,727. Alabama, *First Biennial Report of the Board of Inspectors of Convicts, 1894–1896*, pp. ii–xiii, "Report of State Health Officer to the Governor on Coalburg." Alabama, *Second Biennial Report of the Inspector of Mines, 1898*, p. 60; Alabama General Assembly, *Journal of the House*, 1896–97, p. 639.

82. *Southern Miner and Manufacturer*, 29 July 1884, James Bowron Scrapbooks, BPL.

83. Alabama, *Second Biennial Report of the Inspectors of Mines*, pp. 21–34.

84. Ibid.

85. Alabama Mine Inspector, *First Biennial Report of the State Inspector of Mines For the Years Beginning Dec. 31, 1892 and Ending Dec. 31, 1894*, pp. 71–4, 46–51.

86. USGS, *Mineral Resources*, 1893, p. 240.

87. Alabama Mine Inspector, *First Biennial Report of the State Inspector of Mines For the Years Beginning Dec. 31, 1892 and Ending Dec. 31, 1894*, pp. 3, 46–8, 71. For Alabama's total coke output in 1893, see Tennessee Division of Mines, *Fourth Annual Report of the Bureau of Labor, Statistics and Mines* (Nashville, Tenn.: State Printer, 1895), p. 222.

88. Clark, *History of Manufactures* Volume 2, pp. 239–42, 280–85.

89. USGS, *Mineral Resources*, 1889–90, p. 169; Anna Rochester, *Labor and Coal* (New York: International Publishers, 1931), p. 179; *Engineering and Mining Journal* 86 (15 August 1908), pp. 335–6; Richard A. Straw, "The Collapse of Biracial Unionism: The Alabama Coal Strike of 1908," in Turner and Cabbell, eds., *Blacks in Appalachia*, pp. 183–98; Lewis, *Black Coal Miners in America*, pp. 45–58; Robert David Ward and William Warren Rogers, *Convicts, Coal and the Banner Mine Tragedy* (Tuscaloosa: University of Alabama Press, 1987), pp. 49–50.

90. T.J. Hill, "Experience in Mining Coal With Convicts," p. 396; Hilda J. Zimmerman, "Penal Systems and Penal Reforms in the South since the Civil War," (Ph.D. dissertation, University of North Carolina, 1947), p. 220; TCI, *Annual Report*, 1890, p. 7; *UMWJ*, 30 April 1891, p. 3; 28 March 1895, p. 1.

222 NOTES TO PAGES 97–100

91. *UMWJ*, 26 April 1894, p. 4; *U.S. Steel Hearings*, testimony of John A. Fitch,
p. 2940; Norrell, *James Bowron*, p. 241.

92. Arthur Colyar, letter to the Nashville *Republican Banner*, 27 December 1872.

93. Nashville *Republican Banner*, 17 December 1872, 19 December 1872, 27 December 1872.

94. Reprint of letter by A.K. McClure, *Philadelphia Times*, 28 January 1885, in J.W. Burke, "The Coal Fields of Alabama," pamphlet, c. 1885, p. 39.

95. Norrell, *James Bowron*, introduction; Robert David Ward and William Warren Rogers, *Labor Revolt in Alabama: The Great Strike of 1894* (Tuscaloosa: University of Alabama Press, 1965); Clark, *History of Manufactures* Volume 2, pp. 302–3; Alfred M. Shook to Arthur S. Colyar, 30 September 1892; G.B. McCormack to Nat Baxter, 1 April 1892; Alfred M. Shook to Benjamin Talbot, c. 1894, all in Alfred M. Shook Papers, BPL.

96. Fuller, "History of TCI," pp. 293–4; see also letters to the *National Labor Tribune*, 4 January 1879 and 2 August 1879, reprinted in Gutman, "Black Coal Miners and the Greenback-Labor Party," pp. 516, 526; and USGS, *Mineral Resources*, 1896, p. 607; *UMWJ*, 25 August 1892, p. 4.

97. Tennessee Division of Mines, *Second Annual Report*, pp. 141–2; TCI, *Annual Report*, 1890, p. 13; TCI, *Annual Report*, 1891, p. 9; TCI, *Annual Report*, 1892, p. 9.

98. E.g. Tennessee Division of Mines, *Second Annual Report*, pp. 141–2, 193; Erskine Ramsey to G.B. McCormack, 13 February 1896, Erskine Ramsey Papers, BPL.

99. A.M. Shook to G.B. McCormack, 24 November 1890, 4 December 1890, 9 December 1890, and 16 December 1890, Alfred M. Shook Papers, BPL; P. J. Rogers to R.H. Dawson, 8 December 1890, Reports from Inspectors and Other Officers, Incoming Correspondence, Vol. 2, Corrections Department, ADAH; A. T. Henley to R.H. Dawson, 19 December 1890, Reports from Inspectors and Other Officers, Incoming Correspondence, Vol. 4, Corrections Department, ADAH; Ward and Rogers, *Labor Revolt in Alabama*, pp. 32–3.

100. *UMWJ*, 25 August 1892, p. 4.

101. For contemporary descriptions of East Tennessee's "convict war" of 1891–92, see Tennessee Division of Mines, *Second Annual Report*, pp. 63, 142–3, 228–9, 341; USGS, *Mineral Resources*, 1893, pp. 377–83; and Friedrich A. Sorge, *The Labor Movement in the United States: A History of the American Working Class from 1890 to 1896*, translated by Kai Schoenhals (Westport, Conn.: Greenwood Press, 1987), pp. 13–24. Zimmerman, "Penal Systems," pp. 220–30; Pete Daniel, "The Tennessee Convict War," *Tennessee Historical Quarterly* 34 (Fall 1975), pp. 273–92; Archie Green, *Only a Miner: Studies in Recorded Coal-Mining Songs* (Urbana: University of Illinois Press, 1972), pp. 155–91; and especially Shapiro, "Tennessee Convict Mine Revolts," provide good secondary treatments.

102. Fuller, "History of TCI," pp. 126–7; USGS, *Mineral Resources*, 1896, p. 607; P. D. Sims, "The Lease System in Tennessee and Other Southern States," in National Prison Association, *Proceedings of the Annual Meeting, 1893* (Chicago: Knight and Leonard, 1893), pp. 123–4, 126–7.

103. *UMWJ*, 23 July 1891, p. 4.

104. *UMWJ*, 16 July 1891, p. 5; 23 July 1891, pp. 1, 4.

105. *UMWJ*, 24 September 1891, p. 4; 5 November 1891, pp. 1, 8; 18 August 1892, p. 5; "Report of Assistant General Manager, Tennessee Divisions, TCI, Jan. 31st 1893," Shook Papers, BPL, pp. 3, 8; *UMWJ*, 5 November 1891, p. 1.

106. Tennessee, Division of Mines, *Fourth Annual Report of the Bureau of Labor, Statistics and Mines*, p. 282; USGS, *Mineral Resources*, 1892, pp. 491–2; *UMWJ*, 25 August 1892, p. 1; "Report of Assistant General Manager, Tennessee Divisions, TCI, Jan. 31st 1893," pp. 1, 3, 5.

107. "Report of Assistant General Manager, Tennessee Divisions, TCI, Jan. 31st 1893," p. 8; Tennessee Division of Mines, *Second Annual Report*, pp. 141–2, 77; Tennessee Division of Mines, *Third Annual Report*, pp. 90–92; *UMWJ*, 21 September 1899, p. 3.

108. USGS, *Mineral Resources*, 1894, pp. 9–10, 22; 1893, pp. 203–4. See also *The Tradesman* 31 (1 May 1894), p. 50 on the strike in Alabama.

109. Tennessee Division of Mines, *Fourth Annual Report*, pp. 49–52, 66–7.

110. *UMWJ*, 19 April 1894, p. 5.

111. On the 1894 strike in Alabama, see Ward and Rogers, *Labor Revolt in Alabama*; USGS, *Mineral Resources*, 1894, pp. 9–10, 22–3. Mine operators feared an attack by free miners on the convict mines; see Convict Department to G.B. McCormack, 27 June 1893, Letterbooks, 1893–95, Corrections Department, ADAH, p. 297.

112. R.H. Dawson to G.B. McCormack, 12 April 1894, Letterbooks, 1893–95, Corrections Department, ADAH, p. 470; T.H. Aldrich to Governor Jones, 19 April 1894, Minutes, 1893–95, Board of Managers of Convicts, Corrections Department, ADAH, pp. 49–50.

113. Alabama, *First Biennial Report of the Board of Inspectors of Convicts, 1894–1896*, pp. ii–xiii; Alabama, *First Biennial Report of the State Inspector of Mines, 1892–1894*, pp. 65–6.

114. These calculations are made from figures in Alabama's *First Biennial Report of the State Inspector of Mines*, pp. 56–7, 65–6.

115. USGS, *Mineral Resources*, 1894, p. 67; Alabama, *First Biennial Report of the State Inspector of Mines*, p. 66. On the effects of the strike on production, see also J.J. Ormsbee, "The Coal Interests of the South," *The Tradesman* 34 (1 January 1896), p. 111; see Ward and Rogers, *Labor Revolt in Alabama*, pp. 89, 116, for the importance of convict labor in eventually breaking the strike.

116. *The Tradesman* 30 (15 May 1894), pp. 61–2; 30 (1 May 1894), p. 50; Alabama General Assembly, *Journal of the House*, 1896–97, p. 639.

117. A. M. Shook to G.B. McCormack, 10 March 1894, Shook Papers, BPL, pp. 2–3; *UMWJ*, 7 June 1894, p. 2.

118. Alabama, *Second Biennial Report of the Inspectors of Mines, 1898* (Birmingham, Ala.: Dispatch Printing Co., 1898), pp. 16, 19–20, chart; "Report on Tracy City Division," 1 April 1895, Erskine Ramsey Papers, BPL; Alabama, *Second Biennial Report of the Board of Inspectors of Convicts, 1896–1898*, pp. 9–10, 19; TCI, *Annual Report*, 1897, p. 6; Phillips, *Iron-Making*, 2nd edn, 1898, pp. 21, 4.

119. See, e.g., TCI, *Annual Report*, 1898, p. 5; US Steel, TCI Division, *Biography of a Business*, pp. 26–8; Alfred M. Shook to Benjamin Talbot, c. 1894, Shook Papers, BPL; Sewanee Mining and Tennessee Coal, Iron and Railroad Company Records, microfilm, 30 November 1899, BPL, p. 39.

120. Alfred M. Shook to Arthur S. Colyar, 30 September 1892, Shook Papers, BPL; on the late conversion to steel, see Norrell, *James Bowron*, pp. xxvi–xxxii; Wright, *Old South, New South*, pp. 164–70.

121. Minutes, Stockholders and Board of Directors, 1899–1919, Sloss–Sheffield Steel & Iron Company Records, BPL, p. 87; *Second Annual Report of the Sloss–Sheffield Steel and Iron Co.*, 30 November 1901, pp. 10, 13; George Stocking, *Basing Point Pricing and Regional Development* (Chapel Hill: University of North Carolina Press, 1954), pp. 99, 103. On the ability of the Sloss Company to succesfully negotiate a distinctly southern path to industrialization, see W. David Lewis, *Sloss Furnaces and the Rise of the Birmingham District*, pp. 474–504.

122. *Third Annual Report of the Sloss–Sheffield Steel and Iron Co., 1902*, p. 7; Alabama, *Report of the Inspector of Alabama Coal Mines for the Year 1909* (Birmingham, Ala.: Freret and Grant, 1910), pp. 16, 25; White, *The Birmingham District*, p. 274.

123. "Prospectus," c. 1901, Bowron Scrapbooks, 1895–1902, BPL; Sewanee Mining

and Tennessee Coal, Iron and Railroad Company Records, microfilm, BPL, p. 57; Alabama Governor, *Convict Department and Its Management* (Montgomery, Ala.: Brown Printing Co., 1913), pp. 50–51.

124. Marlene Hunt Rikard, "George Gordon Crawford: Man of the New South," *Alabama Review* 31 (July 1978), pp. 163–81, 165; US Steel, TCI Division, *Biography of a Business*, pp. 37–47. On persistent weaknesses in the Birmingham coal and iron industry, see Wright, *Old South, New South*, pp. 167–9; on abolition of the lease in Alabama, see Ward and Rogers, *Convicts, Coal and the Banner Mine Tragedy*, p. 120.

125. John A. Fitch, "Birmingham District: Labor Conservation," *The Survey* 27 (6 January 1912), p. 1527.

126. Richard A. Straw, "'This is Not a Strike, it is Simply a Revolution': Birmingham Miners' Struggle for Power, 1894–1908" (Ph.D. dissertation, University of Missouri, 1980); and Straw, "The Collapse of Biracial Unionism: The Alabama Coal Strike of 1908," pp. 183–98; Lewis, *Black Coal Miners in America*, ch. 3.

127. George Crawford to J.G. Oakley, 24 November 1911, reproduced in *U.S. Steel Hearings*, p. 3112; see also Ward and Rogers, *Convicts, Coal and the Banner Mine Tragedy*, p. 50.

128. Alabama, *Coal Mine Statistics for 1911* (Birmingham: Alabama Mineral Map Co., n.d.), p. 532; *Quadrennial Report of the Board of Inspectors of Convicts, From Sept. 1, 1906 to Aug. 31, 1910* (Montgomery, Ala.: State Printer, 1910), pp. 64, 70. In some of the mines owned by these companies the convicts were worked by the state, not leased to the company. Under this arrangement, the company then purchased the convict-mined coal from the state mines at an agreed-upon below-market rate. The result was the same as convict leasing: a guaranteed supply of cheap coal mined by forced labor. See Ward and Rogers, *Convicts, Coal and the Banner Mine Tragedy*, pp. 44–5.

129. US Steel, TCI Division, *Biography of a Business*, frontispiece.

Chapter 5

1. "Joe Brown," recording on *Cap'n Your So Mean: Negro Songs of Protest*, Volume 2 (Rounder Records 4013).

2. In 1890 these mines produced 70,399 tons of coal; in 1891, 67,000 tons; in 1892, 43,419 tons. Tennessee Division of Mines, *Second Annual Report of the Commissioner of Labor and Inspector of Mines* (Nashville, Tenn.: State Printer, 1893), pp. 191, 146–7 for other complaints about convict workers, and pp. 229–30 for complaints from a customer about the poor quality of convict-mined coal.

3. Alabama General Assembly, *Journal of the House of Representatives*, 1896–97, pp. 627–8, 652–4; "Statement of Classification, Slope No. 2, Pratt Mines, Aug. 1890," Reports from Inspectors and Other Officers, Incoming Correspondence, Vol. 2, Corrections Department, ADAH.

4. A.T. Henley to R.H. Dawson, 11 April 1889, Reports from Inspectors and Other Officers, Incoming Correspondence, Vol. 3, Corrections Department, ADAH; Henley to Dawson, 14 May 1891, Vol. 4; W.D. Lee to Governor Seay, 26 August 1887, Administrative Files, G24, Governors' Papers, ADAH; A.T. Henley to R.H. Dawson, 5 July 1889; Richard Gills to "dr. henley," no date, enclosed with Henley to Dawson, 6 December 1889, both in Reports from Inspectors and Other Officers, Incoming Correspondence, Vol. 3, Corrections Department, ADAH.

5. For slack and lump distinction, see, e.g., Tennessee Division of Mines, *Third Annual Report*, 1893, p. 93; and Tennessee Division of Mines, *Fifth Annual Report*, 1895, pp. 210–11. A.B. Johnston to J.W. Johnston, 17 June 1884, Correspondence, Folder 2, Coalburg Coal Company Records, SRC, p. 10; W.D. Lee to Governor Seay, 26

August 1887, Administrative Files, G24, Governors' Papers, ADAH; USGS, *Mineral Resources*, 1894, p. 189, Report by L.E. Bryant; A.T. Henley to R.H. Dawson, 2 June 1885, Reports from Inspectors and Other Officers, Incoming Correspondence, Vol. 4, Corrections Department, ADAH; Reginald Heber Dawson Diaries, Vol. 2, 20 July 1890, ADAH; Savannah *Tribune*, 21 November 1908.

6. Gary Kulik, "Black Workers and Technological Change in the Birmingham Iron Industry, 1881–1931," in Gary M. Fink and Merl E. Reed, eds., *Southern Workers and their Unions: Selected Papers, the Second Southern Labor History Conference, 1977* (Westport, Conn.: Greenwood Press, 1981), pp. 23–40; Gary Kulik, "Birmingham Furnaces Still Central Element of Industrial City's Skyline," *American Preservation* 1 (February–March 1978), pp. 20–23.

7. In 1896, neither Georgia, Tennessee nor Alabama reported having any coal mining machines, which were coming into widespread use in other coalfields; see figures in USGS, *Mineral Resources*, 1896, p. 462. Mines in Georgia did not adopt machines until 1905; in that year 3.32% of Georgia coal was mined with machinery; 8.04% in Tennessee; 13.36% in Alabama (but only 6.58% in 1904). The US average in 1905 was 35.37%; USGS, *Mineral Resources*, 1905, pp. 496–7, 561. On coal mining and mechanization, see Keith Dix, *What's a Coal Miner to Do?: The Mechanization of Coal Mining* (Pittsburgh, Pa.: University of Pittsburgh Press, 1988).

8. Justin Fuller, "History of the Tennessee Coal, Iron and Railroad Company, 1852–1907" (Ph.D. dissertation, University of North Carolina, 1966), pp. 35–6; "First Annual Report of the Manager of the Coal Mines at Brushy Mountain, Tennessee," in Tennessee, *Report of the Board of Prison Commissioners, December 15, 1896* (n.p.: n.pub., n.d.), p. 25; Alabama, *Journal of the House*, 1896–97, p. 640. One of the contractors who squeezed Colyar in the 1870s was William M. Morrow, who shortly thereafter became a major investor in Joseph Brown's Dade mines.

9. Principal Keeper, *Report*, 1875, pp. 4, 9, 14; 1876, p. 4; 1877–78, p. 9; Joseph E. Brown to James Milton Smith, bid for lease, 15 June 1876, 17 June 1876, Folder 4, Box 3, Joseph E. Brown Papers, UGA; Savannah *Tribune*, 3 December 1892, for "Southern Siberia."

10. USGS, *Mineral Resources*, 1900, pp. 276–9 for output 1887–1900; *Mineral Resources*, 1910, part 2, p. 115, for output 1860–1910.

11. See Principal Keeper, *Annual Reports*.

12. James M. Russell, *Atlanta 1847–1890: City Building in the Old South and the New* (Baton Rouge: Louisiana State University Press, 1988), p. 249; George Little, *Report of Progress of the Mineralogical, Geological and Physical Survey of the State of Georgia ... Sept. 1st to Dec. 31st, 1874* (Atlanta: n.pub., 1875), p. 17; Jonathan McLeod, "Black and White Workers: Atlanta During Reconstruction" (Ph.D. dissertation, University of California, Los Angeles, 1987), pp. 52–3, 101–2, on the Atlanta Rolling Mill, "the largest manufacturing establishment in postbellum Atlanta" (p. 101); US Department of the Interior, Census Office, *Report on the Mineral Industries of the United States at the Tenth Census, 1880*, Vol. 15 (Washington, DC: GPO, 1886), pp. 614, 868; Tennessee Bureau of Agriculture, Statistics and Mining, *Report of the Bureau for 1876* (Nashville, Tenn.: State Printer, 1877), pp. 226–7; Morrow Chamberlain, *A Brief History of the Pig-iron Industry of East Tennessee* (Chattanooga, Tenn.: privately printed, 1942), p. iii; Georgia Geological Survey, *A Preliminary Report on the Coal Deposits of Georgia*, Bulletin no. 12 (Atlanta, Ga.: State Printer, 1904), p. 35, on the Walker County mines. By 1900 48% of Georgia's coal was used for manufacturing fuel and 46% was converted into coke for use in pig-iron production in Georgia and Tennessee; Charles Willard Hayes, *The Southern Appalachian Coal Field*, in United States Geological Survey, *22nd Annual Report*, part 3 (Washington, DC: GPO, 1902), pp. 227–63, esp. p. 260. See also US Geological Survey, *Mineral Resources of the United States*, entry for Georgia, various years between 1884 and 1900,

but esp. 1885, p. 89, and 1888, p. 240 for uses of coke.

13. On the isolation, geography and topography of northwest Georgia, see Dade County Subject File, File II, Central Research Section, GDAH; Thomas W. Hodler and Howard A. Schretter, *The Atlas of Georgia* (Athens, Ga.: Institute of Community and Area Development, 1986), p. 16; Robert Sparks Walker, *Lookout: The Story of a Mountain* (Kingsport, Tenn.: Southern Publishers, 1941). This description is also based on a visit by the author to the region.

14. 1860 Manuscript Census, Georgia, Dade County, Free and Slave Schedules; Augusta *Daily Constitutionalist*, 2 November 1859, p. 2; Allen P. Tankersley, "Zachariah Herndon Gordon: His Life and His Letters on the Battle of King's Mountain," *Georgia Historical Quarterly* 36 (September 1952), pp. 231–49, 237; 1870 Manuscript Census, Dade County, p. 59, refers to the "Gordon Cole [*sic*] Bank" and notes that it was "not in operation at this time."

15. Column by Mark A. Cooper, in Augusta *Daily Constitutionalist*, 29 October 1859, p. 1; Georgia Geological Survey, *A Preliminary Report on a Part of the Iron Ores of Georgia*, Bulletin no. 10A (Atlanta, Ga.: State Printer, 1900), pp. 126, 139, 143, for Cooper's pioneering efforts; Clarence Mohr, *On the Threshold of Freedom: Masters and Slaves in Civil War Georgia* (Athens: University of Georgia Press, 1986), pp. 151–4; Georgia Geological Survey, *A Preliminary Report on the Mineral Resources of Georgia*, Bulletin no. 23 (Atlanta, Ga.: State Printer, 1910), pp. 115–18; Georgia Geological Survey, *Report on the Fossil Iron Ores of Georgia*, Bulletin no. 17 (Atlanta, Ga.: State Printer, 1908); Charles F. Stone, *The Story of Dixisteel: The First Fifty Years, 1901 to 1951* (Atlanta, Ga.: Atlantic Steel Co., 1951), pp. 7–10; USGS, *Mineral Resources*, 1886, pp. 32–3, on weaknesses in industry; Kenneth Warren, *The American Steel Industry, 1850–1970: A Geographical Interpretation* (Oxford: Clarendon Press, 1973), pp. 65–7, quote on reconstruction on p. 67.

16. William G. Atkinson to Governor James M. Smith, 26 September 1872, Box 82, Governor's Incoming Correspondence, Georgia Executive Department Records, GDAH, pp. 3–4.

17. Little, *Report of Progress*, pp. 4, 22, 28–9.

18. Ibid., p. 17.

19. Georgia General Assembly, *Acts*, 1873, pp. 185–8.

20. "Statement of the Properties, Betterments and Earnings of the Georgia Mining, Manufacturing and Investment Company – Historical Sketch," Typescript, Folder 1, Box 1, Julius L. Brown Papers, AHC; Michael Perman, *The Road to Redemption: Southern Politics, 1869–1879* (Chapel Hill: University of North Carolina Press, 1984), pp. 206–7 on the 1877 Georgia Constitution.

21. See "Historical Sketch" and "Charter and Bylaws of Georgia Mining, Manufacturing and Investment Company," both in Folder 1, Box 1, Julius L. Brown Papers, AHC. For the use of coke in the furnaces, see USGS, *Mineral Resources*, 1886, p. 393. For observations on the benefits of the area's coal and iron deposits, see also E. Hulbert, *Georgia, Empire State of the South: Characteristics, Climate, Soil, Agricultural Products...* (Atlanta, Ga.: American Manufacturing Association, 1887), pp. 2–3; USGS, *Mineral Resources*, 1886, p. 382.

22. On the Durham mines, see USGS, *Mineral Resources*, 1892, p. 366; 1893, p. 261; *Investigation of Charges Against Penitentiary Companies One, Two and Three*, 2 vols, *Evidence for the State*, Vol. 1; *Evidence for Julius Brown, Receiver*, Vol. 2: 10–21 February 1896, Box 4, Julius L. Brown Papers, AHC (hereafter cited as *Investigation*, 1896, JLB Papers, AHC), vol. 1, p. 273; vol. 2, p. 814; Hayes, *Southern Appalachian Coal Field*, p. 242; Georgia Geological Survey, *A Preliminary Report on the Coal Deposits of Georgia*, Bulletin No. 12 (Atlanta, Ga.: State Printer, 1904), pp. 35–7; James Alfred Sartain, *History of Walker County, Georgia*, Vol. 1 (Dalton, Ga.: A.J. Showalter, 1932), pp. 185– 6; "Lookout Mountain Communities: Durham," clipping from the Walker County

Historical Society, LaFayette, Georgia, in author's possession. On Captain James Warren English, see clippings in Personality File, AHC; David Berry, "Free Labor He Found Unsatisfactory: James W. English and Convict Labor at the Chattahoochee Brick Company," *Proceedings and Papers of the Georgia Association of Historians* 11 (1990), pp. 117–25.

23. On Atlanta, see Russell, *Atlanta 1847–1890*, p. 249; McLeod, "Black and White Workers," pp. 52–3. On capitalist development in Appalachia more generally, see Ronald D. Eller, *Miners, Millhands and Mountaineers: Industrialization of the Appalachian South, 1880–1930* (Knoxville: University of Tennessee Press, 1982), e.g. p. 44. Pig iron from the Chattanooga Iron Company, for example, was used in the city's Baldwin locomotive works; see "Historical Sketch," Folder 1, Box 1, Julius Brown Papers, AHC, p. 5.

24. Georgia Penitentiary, Principal Physician, *Report*, 1892–93, pp. 13–20.

25. The most direct presentation of this interpretation is found in Christopher Adamson, "Punishment After Slavery: Southern State Penal Systems, 1865–1890," *Social Problems* 30 (June 1983), pp. 555–69; see also J. Thorsten Sellin, *Slavery and the Penal System* (New York: Elsevier, 1976), ch. 11; Blake McKelvey, "A Half Century of Southern Penal Exploitation," *Social Forces* 13 (October 1934), pp. 112–24.

26. *Dixie* 12 (March 1896), p. 37; *Ex Parte Bartow Iron and Manganese Co.*, Bartow Superior Court, Spring Term, 1889, Folder 11, Box 1, Joseph E. Brown Papers, AHC.

27. 1870 Manuscript Census, Georgia, Dade County; US Department of the Interior, Census Office, *Ninth Census of the United States, 1870*, Vol. 1, *Population* (Washington, DC: GPO, 1872), pp. 506, 625, 680, 761. Women were certainly potential recruits to the textile industry, but appear to be absent from the coal and iron industry; hence the number of men in the county seems an appropriate figure in this instance.

28. On the spread of cotton and tenancy in the Georgia Piedmont, see Steven Hahn, *The Roots of Southern Populism: Yeoman Farmers and the Transformation of the Georgia Upcountry, 1850–1890* (New York: Oxford University Press, 1983); US Department of the Interior, Census Office, *Report on the Productions of Agriculture at the Tenth Census of the United States: 1880* (Washington, DC: GPO, 1883), pp. 110, 218; *Report of the Statistics of Agriculture in the United States at the Eleventh Census: 1890* (Washington, DC: GPO, 1895), pp. 129–30.

29. 1880 Manuscript Census, Georgia, Dade County, Militia Districts 1222 (Cole City) and 1038 (Rising Fawn). On the antebellum and Civil War iron industry at the Tredegar Iron Works, Richmond, see Charles B. Dew, *Ironmaker to the Confederacy: Joseph R. Anderson and the Tredegar Iron Works* (New Haven: Yale University Press, 1966).

30. Little, *Report of Progress*, p. 22; Georgia Geological Survey, *Preliminary Report on Coal Deposits*, p. 70; *Report on the Fossil Iron Ores of Georgia*, p. 64,; John T. Milner, *Alabama As It Was, As It Is, And As It Will Be* (Montgomery, Ala.: Barrett & Brown, 1876), p. 205; US Forest Service, Chattahoochee National Forest, Armuchee Ranger District, *Iron Ore Mining in Northwest Georgia* (1985), pp. 6–8.

31. "Statement of facts and opinion of E.D. Graham, Attorney at Law, as to the conditions of the Rising Fawn Iron Company," "Class A," Legal Documents, Iron and Coal Companies, 1879–81, Folder 10, Series II-G-2, James C. Warner Papers, Tennessee State Library and Archives, Nashville.

32. 1880 Manuscript Census, Georgia, Dade County, Militia District 1038; US Department of the Interior, Census Office, *Report on the Mineral Industries of the United States at the Tenth Census*, 1880, Vol. 15 (Washington, DC: GPO, 1886), p. 868; Atlanta *Constitution*, 17 May 1884, p. 7; the Huntsville (Alabama) *Gazette*, 24 May 1884, a black-owned paper, noted that the displaced workers were white.

33. Georgia General Assembly, *Journal of the House*, p. 432; Principal Keeper,

Report, 1884–86, p. 6; 1886–88, p. 105; *Investigation,* 1896, Box 4, JLB Papers, AHC, vol. 2, p. 621.

34. Georgia General Assembly, *Proceedings of the Joint Committee of the Senate and House to Investigate the Convict Lease System of Georgia,* 1908, 5 ms vols (on microfilm), GDAH, Vol. 4, pp. 1220–21 (hereafter cited as *Proceedings,* 1908); Prison Commission, *Report,* 1901–02, pp. 18–20.

35. W.E.B. Du Bois, ed., *Some Notes on Negro Crime, Particularly in Georgia,* Ninth Conference for the Study of Negro Problems (Atlanta, Ga.: Atlanta University Press, 1904), p. 8; Savannah *Tribune,* 26 November 1892. On convicts and white women, see Exhibit A, *Hamby and Toomer v. Georgia Coal and Iron,* Case File A-29478, Box 510, Supreme Court Case Files, Office of the Clerk of the Court, Records of the Supreme Court of Georgia, GDAH; General Assembly, *Acts,* 1897, p. 72; Holland Thompson, "Effects of Industrialisation Upon Political and Social Ideas," *Annals of the American Academy of Political and Social Science* 35 (January 1910), p. 141. See also US Industrial Commission, *Report of the Industrial Commission on Relations and Conditions of Capital and Labor,* Vol. 7 of the Commission's Reports (Washington, DC: GPO, 1901), pp. 483–4, for opposition to black labor in the southern textile industry. Alabama did begin to work convicts in a state-owned textile mill in the 1890s, but the goal was "to divide the competition of convict labor with the different kinds of labor in the state." Report of J.W. Grayton to Governor, December 1896, Governors' Papers, Box 43, ADAH.

36. *Tradesman* 31 (1 July 1894), p. 65; Principal Keeper, *Report,* 1877–78, p. 8; Prison Commission, *Report,* 1901–02, pp. 17–18, 20. For objections to convict labor by free workers, see, e.g., the testimony of J.W. Bridwell, Secretary of the Atlanta Federation of Trades, before the US Industrial Commission in 1900, reprinted in Philip Foner and Ronald L. Lewis, eds., *The Black Worker During the Era of the American Federation of Labor and the Railroad Brotherhoods,* Vol. 4 of *The Black Worker: A Documentary History from the Colonial Times to the Present* (Philadelphia: Temple University Press, 1979), p. 308; US Congress, Senate Committee on Education and Labor, *Report of the Committee of the Senate Upon the Relations Between Labor and Capital,* 1885, 4 vols, testimony by a rolling-mill worker, Vol. 4, p. 367. See Gerald D. Jaynes, *Branches Without Roots: Genesis of the Black Working Class in the American South, 1862–1882* (New York: Oxford University Press, 1986), pp. 267–72, on the racial division of labor in southern industries. For a good statement of the problem of a "labor shortage" in the South, see Enoch M. Banks, "Labor Supply and Labor Problems," *Annals of the American Academy of Political and Social Science,* issue on "The New South" 35 (January 1910), pp. 143–9.

37. "Lookout Mountain Communities," clipping, Walker County Historical Society; Principal Keeper, *Report,* 1888–90, pp. 7–9; 1890–92, pp. 4–5; Report to Governor William J. Northen by Assistant Principal Keeper, 1 February 1891, Box 102, Governor's Correspondence, GDAH.

38. Joseph E. Brown to Governor James M. Smith, 24 March 1874, 25 March 1874, Box 68, Governor's Correspondence, GDAH.

39. Prison Commission, *Report,* 1906–07, p. 6; Georg Rusche and Otto Kirchheimer, *Punishment and Social Structure* (New York: Columbia University Press, 1939), p. 65. Rusche and Kirchheimer offer the theoretical proposition that historically when "the predominant aim [of penal institutions] was ... to obtain the greatest possible benefit from the labor ... the period of detention was determined solely by reference to the needs of the institution or its lessees" (pp. 55–6). On lengthy sentences in Georgia and the South, see Blake McKelvey, *American Prisons: A History of Good Intentions* (1936; reprint, Montclair, N.J.: Patterson Smith, 1977), pp. 210–11; George Washington Cable, *The Silent South, together with the Freedman's Case in Equity*

and the Convict Lease System (1883; reprint, New York: Charles Scribner's Sons, 1907), pp. 177–8; Principal Keeper, *Report*, 1896–97, p. 9; William Jallack [Secretary of the Howard Association, an international prison reform organization] to Governor Alfred H. Colquitt, 12 February 1880, Box 86, Governor's Correspondence, GDAH.

40. General Assembly, *Acts*, 1876, p. 42; Bill of Exceptions, Application for Injunction, *Georgia Penitentiary Co. No. 2 and Georgia Penitentiary Co. No. 3 vs. Marietta and North Georgia Railroad and John W. Nelms, Principal Keeper of the Penitentiary*, Fulton County Superior Court, 15 October 1881, Georgia Room Collection, University of Georgia Library, pp. 52–3.

41. *Investigation*, 1896, JLB Papers, AHC, vol. 1, p. 281; see, e.g., *Penitentiary Co. No. 2 v. Gordon*, 85 Ga. 159 (1890); Principal Keeper, *Report*, 1874, p. 7. See also Prison Commission, *Report*, 1900–01, p. 7: "[Mine] employment is preferable to all others, as the men are more easily guarded and controlled, at less expense to the state".

42. Report to Governor John B. Gordon, December 1886, E.T. Shubrick File, Box 215, Names File, File II, Central Research Section, GDAH.

43. All figures are tabulated from a list of convicts assigned to Penitentiary Company No. 1, which in 1882 was identical to the Dade Coal Company; Principal Keeper, *Report*, 1880–82, pp. 12–22; 1880 Manuscript Census, Georgia, Dade County, for racial breakdown that year. The ever-increasing proportion of life-term convicts was a penitentiary-wide process: from 18% in 1897 to 29% by the time the lease came to an end in 1908, for example; Principal Keeper, *Report*, 1896–97, p. 30; Prison Commission, *Report*, 1907–08, p. 22.

44. Jacob W. Seaver to Joseph E. Brown, 11 August 1874, Folder 1, Box 3, Joseph E. Brown Papers, UGA.

45. General Assembly, *Acts*, 1876, pp. 40–43; Principal Keeper, *Report*, 1895–96, pp. 9, 104.

46. See, e.g., Georgia Geological Survey, *Report on the Coal Deposits*, pp. 35, 38; USGS, *Mineral Resources*, 1886, pp. 252, 394; 1907, part 2, pp. 106–7.

47. USGS, *Mineral Resources*, 1886, p. 252 on the high proportion of slack coal produced in the Dade mines; Tennessee Division of Mines, *Fifth Annual Report*, pp. 210–11; Tennessee Division of Mines, *Third Annual Report*, p. 93; USGS, *Mineral Resources*, 1894, p. 189.

48. USGS, *Mineral Resources*, 1883–84, p. 160; Principal Physician, *Report*, 1884–86, p. 109; USGS, *Mineral Resources*, 1900, p. 372; 1901, pp. 358, 430, 443; Hayes, *Southern Appalachian Coal Field*, p. 260.

49. *Investigation*, 1896, JLB Papers, AHC, vol. 1, pp. 106–7; "Report of Receiver," 4 February 1895, *Sibley Manufacturing Co. v. Georgia Mining & Manufacturing Co*, Fulton Superior Court, Joseph Mackey Brown Papers II (restricted collection), Special Collections, UGA; "Hearing on Receivership," 24 January 1895, Fulton Superior Court, Joseph Mackey Brown Papers II, p. 5.

50. "Original Petition of Georgia Iron and Coal Co.," *Hamby and Toomer v. Georgia Iron and Coal*, Case File A-29478, Box 510, Supreme Court Case Files, GDAH, p. 5; *Hamby and Toomer v. Georgia Iron and Coal Company*, 127 Ga. 792 (1907), pp. 794–5; "Affidavit of Joel Hurt," and "Affidavit of George Hurt," *Georgia Iron and Coal v. Hamby and Toomer*, Case File A-29479, Box 510, Supreme Court Case Files, GDAH.

51. Principal Physician, *Report*, 1888–90, p. 3; Report to Stockholders, 3 May 1893, Folder 1, Box 1, Julius L. Brown Papers, AHC; Minutes of Stockholders Meeting, 8 June 1892, Joseph E. Brown Papers, AHC; Julius L. Brown to Governor William J. Northen, 21 June 1892, Box 103, Governor's Correspondence, GDAH; J.W. Hoffman to Julius Brown, 25 February 1890, 1 March 1890, Folder 2, Box 1, Julius L. Brown Papers, AHC; see also Weekly Register of Convicts in Prison Camp Hospitals, Vol. 1891–92, Cole City, 30 May 1891, 5 March 1892, Prison Commission

Records, Records of the Board of Corrections, GDAH, for other examples of shifting labor from place to place.

52. Julius L. Brown to Jacob W. Seaver, 10 January 1895; Julius L. Brown to O.P. Heath, 31 January 1895, Julius L. Brown Letterbook, 1894–95, Joseph Mackey Brown Papers II, Special Collections, UGA. On receivership, see *Asheville Cigar Co.* v. *Brown,* 100 Ga. 171 (1896); *Brown* v. *Barnes,* 99 Ga. 1 (1896); *Dade Coal Company* v. *Penitentiary Co. No. 2,* 119 Ga. 824 (1904); "Petition for Receiver," 31 January 1895 and "Report of Receiver," 4 February 1895, *Sibley Manufacturing Co.* v. *Georgia Mining, Manufacturing and Investment Co.,* Fulton County Superior Court, Spring Term 1895, Joseph M. Brown Papers II, UGA; Julius L. Brown to A. Pluemer, 16 February 1895, Julius L. Brown Letterbook, 1894–95, Joseph Mackey Brown Papers II, UGA. Julius L. Brown was the appointed receiver for the Georgia Mining, Manufacturing and Investment Company. On reorganization of the company, see "Copy of Deed," 24 July 1897, Fulton County Superior Court, Box 1, Folder 1, Julius L. Brown Papers, AHC; Clifford L. Anderson to Julius L. Brown, 12 February 1896, Box 1, Folder 2, Julius L. Brown Papers, AHC; T.D. Meador to Governor A.D. Candler, 19 December 1898, Box 121, Governor's Correspondence, GDAH; *Southern Mining Co.* v. *Lowe,* 105 Ga. 352 (1898). On Joel Hurt, see *Hamby and Toomer* v. *Georgia Iron and Coal Co.,* Case File A-29478, Box 510, Supreme Court Case Files, GDAH; Julius L. Brown to Joel Hurt, 11 July 1895, 17 January 1895, Julius L. Brown Letterbook, 1894–95, Joseph Mackey Brown Papers II, UGA; Personality Files, Joel Hurt, AHC; Sarah Simms Edge, *Joel Hurt and the Development of Atlanta* (Atlanta, Ga.: Atlanta Historical Society, 1955), esp. pp. 270–71. For a good summary of the effects of the depression of the 1890s on the South, see C. Vann Woodward, *Origins of the New South, 1877–1913* (Baton Rouge: Louisiana State University Press, 1951), pp. 264–72.

53. "Hearing on receivership," 24 January 1895, Fulton County Superior Court; Julius L. Brown to A. Pluemer, 15 February 1895, Julius L. Brown Letterbook, 1894–95; "Report of Receiver," 4 February 1895, Fulton Superior Court; Julius L. Brown to A. Pluemer, 16 February 1895; Julius L. Brown to F.H. Conner, 25 February 1895, Julius L. Brown Letterbook, 1894–95; all in Joseph Mackey Brown Papers II, UGA.

54. Copy of minutes of Georgia Mining & Manufacturing Company meeting, 23 January 1895, Fulton Superior Court, 24 January 1895, p. 10; also "Petition for Receiver," 31 January 1895; Julius L. Brown to Jacob W. Seaver, 8 May 1895, Julius L. Brown Letterbook, 1894–95, all in Joseph Mackey Brown Papers II, UGA.

55. "Report of Receiver," 4 February 1895, Fulton Superior Court, Joseph Mackey Brown Papers II, UGA; "Earnings and Expenses of the Georgia Mining, Manufacturing and Investment Company," 30 September 1896, Folder 1, Box 1, Julius L. Brown Papers, AHC.

56. J.J. Ormsbee, "The Coal Interests of the South," *Tradesman* 36 (1 January 1897), pp. 120–23; *Investigation,* 1896, JLB Papers, AHC, vol. 1, pp. 917, 979.

57. *Investigation,* 1896, JLB Papers, AHC, vol. 1, pp. 917, 925; *Asheville Cigar Co.* v. *Brown,* 100 Ga. 171 (1896), p. 174. See also *Investigation,* 1896, JLB Papers, AHC, vol. 1, p. 747.

58. Julius L. Brown to Joseph T. Orme, 14 October 1895, Julius L. Brown Letterbook, 1894–95, Joseph M. Brown Papers II, UGA.

59. Georgia, *Journal of the House,* 1895, pp. 829–30; *Investigation,* 1896, JLB Papers, AHC, vol. 1, p. 276, for a comparison with conditions at the Durham mines, which remained solvent (perhaps because their owner, James English of the Chattahoochee Brick Company, had more diverse holdings). On the "water treatment," see *Investigation,* 1896, JLB Papers, AHC, vol. 1, pp. 17, 275; vol. 2, p. 460.

60. Prison Commission, *Report,* 1901–02, p. 8; "Executive Order *In Re* Proceedings Against Georgia Penitentiary Co. No. 2," 21 July 1896, Box 112, Governor's

Correspondence, GDAH; *Dade Coal Co.* v. *Penitentiary Co. No. 2*, 119 Ga. 824 (1904), p. 825; Principal Keeper, *Report*, 1895–96, p. 7; Principal Physician, *Report*, 1895–96, p. 135; "Original Petition," *Dade Coal Co.* v. *Penitentiary Co. No. 3*, Fulton Superior Court, Spring Term 1899 (no. 7013), Case File A-26381, Box 446, Supreme Court Case Files, GDAH, p. 8.

61. General Assembly, *Acts*, 1897, pp. 71–8, especially pp. 75–6; see Prison Commission, *Report*, 1897–98, pp. 44–6 for the bids received for this lease.

62. Prison Commission, *Report*, 1897–98, pp. 12–14; 1898–99, pp. 8–9; 1901–02, pp. 17–18; 1903–04, pp. 8–10; 1906–07, p. 6; Matthew J. Mancini, "Race, Economics and the Abandonment of Convict Leasing," *Journal of Negro History* 63 (Fall 1978), pp. 339–52, 348–9; *Proceedings*, 1908, Vol. 2, pp. 428–9, for subleasing when coal price declined. On problems recruiting free labor, especially in the lumber and turpentine industries, see, e.g., Letter to Editor, *Savannah Naval Stores Review* 14 (6 August 1904), p. 8; *Southern Lumberman* 39 (1 April 1901), p. 6; 39 (15 March 1901), p. 5 (for quotation). These industries were major sublessees of convicts after 1900.

63. Tom Brass, "Review Essay: Slavery Now: Unfree Labour and Modern Capitalism," *Slavery and Abolition* 9 (September 1988), pp. 183–97, 187.

64. *State of Dade News*, 19 June 1891, p. 3; Prison Commission, *Report*, 1906–07, p. 6; *Proceedings*, 1908, Vol. 5, pp. 1562–3. On difficulty in recruiting mine labor see Eller, *Miners, Millhands and Mountaineers*, pp. 165–8, 193.

65. Prison Commission, *Report*, 1901–02, pp. 17–18; *Proceedings*, 1908, Vol. 3, p. 965.

Chapter 6

1. Harold Courlander, *Negro Folk Music, U.S.A.* (New York: Columbia University Press, 1963), pp. 106–7.

2. Telegrams from John Towers to Governor Henry McDaniel, 13 July 1886, 9:40 a.m., 11:43 a.m., 1:30 p.m.; 14 July 1886, 9:17 a.m., 4:50 p.m.; in "Convicts" Subject File, Box 64, File II, Central Research Section, GDAH; Atlanta *Constitution*, 13 July 1886, p. 1; 14 July 1886, p. 5; 15 July 1886, p. 1; Atlanta *Journal*, 13 July 1886, p. 1.

3. Principal Keeper, *Report*, 1884–86, p. 10; Georgia, *Journal of the House*, pp. 429, 432.

4. Report to Governor Gordon, December 1886 and "Special Report," E. T. Shubrick to Governor, 18 January 1887, E.T. Shubrick File, Box 215, Names File, File II, Central Research Section, GDAH; *State of Dade News*, 26 June 1891, p. 2; *Investigation of Charges Against Penitentiary Companies One, Two and Three*, 2 vols, *Evidence for the State*, Vol. 1, *Evidence for Julius Brown, Receiver*, Vol. 2: 10–21 February 1896, Box 4, Julius L. Brown Papers, AHC, vol. 1, pp. 474–5, 567, 570–71, 668 (hereafter cited as *Investigation*, 1896); Minutes of Stockholders Meeting, Dade Coal Company, 2 February 1892, Joseph E. Brown Papers, AHC; Principal Keeper, *Report*, 1890–92, p. 7; Atlanta *Constitution*, 23 June 1891, 25 June 1891; Report to Governor William J. Northen from R.F. Wright (Assistant Keeper), 6 July 1891, Box 102, Governor's Correspondence, Executive Department Papers, GDAH, p. 2; Julius L. Brown to Governor William J. Northen, 26 October 1891, Box 102, Governor's Correspondence, GDAH.

5. Keith Dix, *Work Relations in the Coal Industry: The Hand-Loading Era, 1880–1930* (Morgantown: Institute for Labor Studies, West Virginia University, 1977), introduction and pp. 12–16, 105–6; Curtis Seltzer, *Fire in the Hole: Miners and Managers in the American Coal Industry* (Lexington: The University Press of Kentucky, 1985), pp. 10–

12; Carter Goodrich, *The Miner's Freedom: A Study of the Working Life in a Changing Industry* (Boston: Marshall Jones Co., 1925) is the classic tale of the persistence of the independent labor process into the twentieth century, written in the twilight of the "hand-loading era." See Priscilla Long, *Where the Sun Never Shines: A History of America's Bloody Coal Industry* (New York: Paragon House, 1989), part 1, for a wide-ranging discussion of nineteenth-century coal mining.

    6. Dix, *Work Relations in the Coal Industry*, pp. 50–51.

    7. Seltzer, *Fire in the Hole*, pp. 10–12; Dix, *Work Relations in the Coal Industry*, pp. 39, 52–5; Ronald D. Eller, *Miners, Millhands and Mountaineers: Industrialization of the Appalachian South, 1880–1930* (Knoxville: University of Tennessee Press, 1982), pp. 161–98, esp. 178, 188, 192–4. See Chapter 4, above, for the use of convicts to break strikes.

    8. See, for example, US Bureau of Labor, *Convict Labor*, 20th Annual Report of the Commissioner of Labor (Washington, DC: GPO, 1905), pp. 30–31.

    9. Philip D. Morgan, "Task and Gang Systems: The Organization of Labor on New World Plantations," in Stephen Innes, ed., *Work and Labor in Early America* (Chapel Hill: University of North Carolina Press, 1988), pp. 189–220, offers the most complete summary of research on antebellum task work, with some allusions to piece work; see also his "Work and Culture: The Task System and the World of Lowcountry Blacks," *William and Mary Quarterly*, 3rd series, 39 (October 1982), pp. 563–99; Thomas Armstrong, "From Task Labor to Free Labor: The Transition Along Georgia's Rice Coast," *Georgia Historical Quarterly* 64 (Winter 1980), pp. 432–47; John Scott Strickland, "Traditional Culture and Moral Economy: Social and Economic Change in the South Carolina Low Country, 1865–1910," in Steven Hahn and Jonathan Prude, eds., *The Countryside in the Age of Capitalist Transformation* (Chapel Hill: University of North Carolina Press, 1985), pp. 145–7; and the essays in Ira Berlin and Philip D. Morgan, eds., *Cultivation and Culture: Labor and the Shaping of Slave Life in the Americas* (Charlottesville: University of Virginia Press, 1993). Leslie Rowland has offered a critique of this approach in a paper presented at the "Culture and Cultivation in Slave Societies" conference at the University of Maryland, College Park, April 1989, and emphasizes instead exploitation over autonomy.

    10. For industrial task work under slavery, see Clarence Mohr, *On the Threshold of Freedom: Masters and Slaves in Civil War Georgia* (Athens: University of Georgia Press, 1986), pp. 179–81; Charles B. Dew, "Disciplining Slave Ironworkers in the Antebellum South: Coercion, Conciliation, and Accommodation," *American Historical Review* 79 (April 1974), pp. 405–6; Charles B. Dew, *Bond of Iron: Master and Slave at Buffalo Forge* (New York: Norton, 1994), pp. 108–21, for positive accounts; Robert S. Starobin, *Industrial Slavery in the Old South* (New York: Oxford University Press, 1970), pp. 99–104 offers the dimmer view.

    11. William H. Worger, "Industrialization and Incarceration: Punishment and Society in South Africa," paper presented at the Stanford-Emory Conference on Law in Colonial Africa, 7–9 April 1988, p. 52, in author's possession.

    12. Georgia General Assembly, *Proceedings of the Joint Committee of the Senate and House to Investigate the Convict Lease System of Georgia*, 1908, 5 ms vols (on microfilm), GDAH, Vol. 1, p. 170 (hereafter cited as *Proceedings*, 1908).

    13. E.g., *Proceedings*, 1908, Vol. 1, pp. 146–7, 150, 177.

    14. Hearing before the Prison Commission, Prison Commission Folder, Box 19 (Pratt, J.L.–Ransom, Richard), Hoke Smith Collection, Richard B. Russell Memorial Library, University of Georgia, Athens.

    15. *Dixie* 12 (March 1896), p. 12; see also "Senator Brown's Argument Before the Governor: In Defense of Dade Coal Company, on Convict Question," pamphlet, 1887, Folder 11, Box 1, Joseph E. Brown Papers, AHC.

16. W.E.B. Du Bois, ed., *Some Notes on Negro Crime, Particularly in Georgia*, Ninth Conference for the Study of Negro Problems (Atlanta, Ga.: Atlanta University Press, 1904), p. 6.

17. Principal Keeper, *Report*, 1874, pp. 7–8.

18. US Congress, Senate Committee on Education and Labor, *Report of the Committee of the Senate Upon the Relations Between Labor and Capital*, 4 vols, 1885, Vol. 4, pp. 435–7, testimony of Zeke Archey.

19. Starobin, *Industrial Slavery*, pp. 99–100; *Investigation*, 1896, Vol. 1, pp. 100, 115, 315. Scrip was also used at the Coalburg mines in Alabama, but cash was paid at Pratt mines; A.T. Henley to R.H. Dawson, 5 May 1891, Reports from Inspectors and Other Officers, Incoming Correspondence, vol. 4, Corrections Department, ADAH.

20. *Proceedings*, 1908, Vol. 1, p. 171.

21. President's Report to Stockholders of the Georgia Mining and Manufacturing Co., 3 May 1893, Folder 1, Box 1, Julius L. Brown Papers, AHC.

22. *Investigation*, 1896, Vol. 1, pp. 95, 102; Vol. 2, pp. 619–20; Monthly Reports of Convicts Punished ("Whipping Reports"), Vol. 1, Cole [*sic*] City Camp, 1901–04, Records of the Prison Commission, Records of the Board of Corrections, GDAH; A.T. Henley to R.H. Dawson, 5 May 1891, Reports from Inspectors and Other Officers, Incoming Correspondence, vol. 4, Corrections Department, ADAH; Georgia, *Journal of the House*, 1890, p. 722.

23. *Investigation*, 1896, Vol. 2, p. 461.

24. After 1879, by law county grand juries had to inspect the condition of the convict camps in their county, and report on them along with their evaluations of other county matters; General Assembly, *Acts*, 1878–79, pp. 140–41.

25. "The Georgia Convict Lease System," letter from Joseph E. Brown to *The Christian Union*, 24 December 1879, p. 549; Georgia, *Journal of the House*, 1881, p. 74; Dade County Grand Jury Presentments, March Term 1897, Dade County Superior Court Minutes, Book F (1896–1906), on microfilm, GDAH, p. 66.

26. Dade County Grand Jury Presentments, March Term 1898, Dade County Superior Court Minutes, Book F, GDAH, p. 165; Dade County Grand Jury Presentments, September Term 1901, Sup. Ct. Mins., Book F, GDAH, p. 35.

27. Georgia, *Journal of the House*, 1890, pp. 722–3.

28. Georgia, *Journal of the House*, 1908, Extraordinary Session, p. 53; "Report of the Investigating Committee," General Assembly, *Acts*, 1908, Extraordinary Session, p. 1084 (hereafter cited as General Assembly, "Report," 1908). Task work for convicts also prevailed in the turpentine and brick industries; see, e.g., *Proceedings*, 1908, Vol. 1, pp. 90–92, 105; Vol. 2, pp. 471, 529–31, 655.

29. Georgia, *Journal of the House*, 1908, Ext. Sess., p. 54; *Proceedings*, 1908, Vol. 1, p. 179.

30. *Proceedings*, 1908, Vol. 3, p. 800.

31. General Assembly, "Report," 1908, p. 1082; *Proceedings*, 1908, Vol. 3, pp. 873–4.

32. See, e.g., *Proceedings*, 1908, Vol. 3, pp. 877, 895; Vol. 4, p. 1304.

33. *Investigation*, 1896, Vol. 2, pp. 462, 470–71.

34. *Investigation*, 1896, Vol. 1, pp. 220–26; Vol. 2, pp. 462, 967; "Declaration," 14 July 1888, *Dade Coal Company* v. *Haslett*, 83 Ga. 549 (1889), Case File A-15904, Box 252, Supreme Court Case Files, Office of the Clerk of the Court, Records of the Supreme Court of Georgia, GDAH; Georgia, *Journal of the House*, 1886, pp. 433–4.

35. *Proceedings*, 1908, Vol. 4, p. 1556.

36. On free miners, see, e.g., US Industrial Commission, *Report on Trusts and Industrial Combinations*, Vol. 13 of the Commission's Reports (Washington, DC: GPO,

1901), p. 508; USGS, *Mineral Resources*, 1889–90, pp. 170–71; Alfred M. Shook to James T. Woodward, 22 June 1897, A.M. Shook Papers, BPL. On convicts, see "Declaration," 14 July 1888, *Dade Coal Co.* v. *Haslett*, Box 252, Supreme Court Case Files, GDAH; *Proceedings*, 1908, Vol. 1, pp. 28, 147; Vol. 4, p. 1244.

37. *Proceedings*, 1908, Vol. 1, p. 171.

38. *Investigation*, 1896, Vol. 1, pp. 278, 405.

39. *Proceedings*, 1908, Vol. 1, pp. 28, 147, 386; Vol. 3, 789–90.

40. Ibid., Vol. 1, p. 195.

41. Ibid., Vol. 1, pp. 156, 63.

42. Georgia Penitentiary, Principal Physician, *Report*, 1895–96, p. 111; see Weekly Register of Convicts in Prison Camp Hospitals, Cole City, vol. 1891–92 and vol. 1892–1895, Records of the Georgia Prison Commission, GDAH; Principal Physician, *Report*, 1888–90, pp. 13–14; 1890–92, pp. 12–13; USGS, *Mineral Resources*, 1900, pp. 276–79, 451; 1909, part 2, pp. 47, 52. The national fatality rate in bituminous mining in 1896 was approximately 230,000 tons per fatality.

43. Dade County Grand Jury Presentments, March Term 1897, Sup. Ct. Mins., Book F, GDAH, p. 66; *Proceedings*, 1908, Vol. 3, p. 779; Georgia, *Journal of the House*, 1908, Ext. Sess., p. 53; *Proceedings*, 1908, Vol. 4, pp. 1501, 1509. On the racial division of labor, see e.g. *Proceedings*, 1908, Vol. 1, pp. 148, 170; *Investigation*, 1896, Vol. 2, pp. 450, 675.

44. *Proceedings*, 1908, Vol. 1, pp. 157, 180–81.

45. Georgia, *Journal of the House*, 1908, Ext. Sess., p. 52.

46. *Proceedings*, 1908, Vol. 4, p. 1556; Warden E.D. Brock to George Hurt, 22 January 1902, included in *Proceedings*, 1908, Vol. 3, p. 863.

47. *Investigation*, 1896, Vol. 2, pp. 693, 788. There is evidence of this practice in the Tennessee convict mines as well; see US Department of the Interior, United States Geological Survey, *Mineral Resources of the United States*, 1894 (Washington, DC: GPO, 1894), p. 189.

48. *Proceedings*, 1908, Vol. 3, p. 783; *Investigation*, 1896, Vol. 2, p. 643.

49. *Investigation*, 1896, Vol. 2, pp. 617–18.

50. Monthly Reports of Convicts Punished ("Whipping Reports"), Vol. 1, Cole [*sic*] City Camp, 1901–04, Records of the Prison Commission, Records of the Board of Corrections, GDAH.

51. *Investigation*, 1896, Vol. 2, pp. 462, 469–70, 474; on difficulty of task due to work place in mine, see *Investigation*, 1896, Vol. 1, pp. 314, 951; for further evidence of homosexuality in the mines, see, e.g., *Investigation*, 1896, Vol. 1, pp. 281–2; Georgia, *Journal of the House*, 1892, p. 655.

52. Dade County Grand Jury Presentments, September Term 1901, Sup. Ct. Mins., Book F, GDAH, p. 351; *Proceedings*, 1908, Vol. 1, pp. 386–7; *Investigation*, 1896, Vol. 1, pp. 679–80; *Proceedings*, 1908, Vol. 1, p. 155; R.H. Dawson to Governor Seay, Corrections Department Letterbook, September 1888–May 1889, p. 119; W.D. Lee to R.H. Dawson, 31 March 1889, Reports from Inspectors and Other Officers, Incoming Correspondence, Vol. 3, Corrections Department, ADAH.

53. Pamphlet, Folder 11, Box 1, Joseph E. Brown Papers, AHC, pp. 11–12; *Hamby and Toomer* v. *Georgia Iron and Coal Company*, 127 Ga. 792 (1906), p. 801; Georgia, *Journal of the House*, 1895, p. 830

54. William D. Grant, "Georgia Penitentiary Co. No. 3 and the Convicts," pamphlet, *c.* 1881, Georgia Room, University of Georgia Library. The grand-jury reports, legislative investigations, and "special investigations" commissioned by the governor cited throughout this chapter are fine examples of scrutiny of convict food, clothing, quarters, sanitation, labor conditions, and overall treatment. See also Georgia, *Journal of the House*, 1897, pp. 1264–72; 1903, pp. 885–91; Grant, "Georgia

Penitentiary Co. No. 3," contains several excerpts from investigations, as do the "Exhibits" in Benjamin G. Lockett, "Memorial to the Senate and House of Representatives … of the State of Georgia," *c.* 1881, Georgia Room, University of Georgia Library, pp. 7–12. For rules guaranteeing oversight and inspection, see *The Code of the State of Georgia, Adopted December 15th, 1895,* Vol. 3 (Atlanta, Ga.: Foote & Davies, 1896), pp. 334 (inspectors), 335 (grand juries), 336 (physician), 338 (principal keeper and assistant principal keeper[s]).

55. Principal Physician, *Report,* 1886–88, pp. 97–101.

56. "General Notice to Lessees of the Georgia Penitentiary," 1 June 1875, Box 73, Governor's Correspondence, GDAH; *The Code of the State of Georgia,* 4th edn (Atlanta, Ga.: James P. Harrison, 1882), p. 1245.

57. *Proceedings,* 1908, Vol. 2, pp. 461, 465, 529.

58. See, e.g., Georgia, *Journal of the House,* 1886, p. 433.

59. *Investigation,* 1896, Vol. 2, pp. 555–6; see also US Senate Committee on Education and Labor, *Relations Between Labor and Capital,* Vol. 4, pp. 291–2, for the same rationale in Alabama; *Investigation,* 1896, Vol. 1, pp. 103, 115 on coal mines.

60. *Investigation,* Vol. 2, p. 621; see also pamphlet, Folder 11, Box 1, Joseph E. Brown Papers, AHC, p. 9, for Joseph Brown's justification of this practice.

61. Report on Conditions of Convict Camps, August 1887, Grand Jury Presentments, Polk County Grand Jury, Miscellaneous Records, Records of the Georgia Prison Commission, GDAH; Georgia, *Journal of the House,* 1886, p. 433.

62. Pamphlet, Folder 11, Box 1, Joseph E. Brown Papers, AHC, p. 9; *Investigation,* 1896, Vol. 1, pp. 105, 115, 315.

63. *Investigation,* 1896, Vol. 1, pp. 115, 316; Georgia, *Journal of the House,* 1886, p. 433; General Assembly, "Report," 1908, p. 1084.

64. President's Report to Stockholders of the Georgia Mining and Manufacturing Co., 3 May 1893, Folder 1, Box 1, Julius L. Brown Papers, AHC.

65. Anonymous to Governor John B. Gordon, 22 January 1887, Box 93, Governor's Correspondence, GDAH.

66. For details of the investigation, see E.T. Shubrick to John B. Gordon, 26 August 1887; John Towers to John Brown Gordon, 26 August 1887, both in Box 94, Governor's Correspondence, GDAH.

67. Georgia Executive Minutes, 23 September 1887, 8 November 1887, pp. 489–90, GDAH; James W. English to John B. Gordon, 26 November 1887, J.W. English File, Box 42, Names File, File II, Central Research Section, GDAH; Ralph Lowell Eckert, *John Brown Gordon: Soldier, Southerner, American* (Baton Rouge: Louisiana State University Press, 1989), p. 280; Woodward, *Origins of the New South,* pp. 15–17.

68. Reports of September 1885, December 1885, January 1887, February 1887, E.T. Shubrick File, Box 215, Names File, File II, Central Research Section, GDAH; Principal Keeper, *Report,* 1877–78, p. 7; 1895–96, pp. 4–5; Georgia, *Journal of the House,* 1890, p. 721; Selena S. Butler, "The Chain-Gang System," speech before the National Association of Colored Women, 16 September 1897, Nashville, Tennessee (Tuskegee, Ala.: Normal School Steam Press, 1897), Georgia Room, University of Georgia Library, p. 6; Anonymous to Governor John B. Gordon, 22 January 1887, Box 93, Governor's Correspondence, GDAH.

69. Lockett, "Memorial to the Senate and House of Representatives," p. 3; Report of Legislative Committee on the Penitentiary to Governor Colquitt, 20 February 1877, Box 82, Governor's Correspondence, GDAH, p. 2; Principal Physician, *Report,* 1888–90, p. 8; see also Principal Physician, *Report,* 1893–94, p. 5.

70. For example, Principal Physician, *Report,* 1884–86, pp. 108–13.

71. Charles Van Onselen, *Chibaro: African Mine Labour in Southern Rhodesia, 1900–1933* (London: Pluto Press, 1976), p. 73.

72. *Investigation*, 1896, Vol. 1, p. 397; Vol. 2, pp. 542; H.H. Tucker, "Prison Labor," in American Prison Association, *Proceedings*, 1886 (Chicago: Donnelly and Sons, 1887), p. 257; Prison Commission, *Report*, 1899–1900, p. 6; *Investigation*, 1896, Vol. 2, p. 881. See also *Investigation*, 1896, Vol. 1, pp. 20, 32 (for a comparison with "beds in the Confederate Army"!), 33, 35. Further examples are found in the 1908 investigation of the convict lease, *Proceedings*, 1908, Vol. 4, p. 1514, for comparison with "slavery times," and Vol. 5, p. 1640 for "average negro."

73. *Investigation*, 1896, Vol. 2, p. 606; Joseph E. Brown, "The Georgia Convict System," *The Christian Century*, 24 December 1879, p. 549. These sorts of views still have not disappeared in the 1990s. When confronted with the abysmal conditions endured by West Indian workers in Florida's migrant camps in the sugarcane industry, a state legislator insisted that "U.S. Sugar has very nice villages for their people to live in. However, many of these people don't know how to take care of property"; Miami *Herald*, 31 May 1990, p. 2G.

74. *Bulletin of Atlanta University* 42 (January 1893), pp. 3–4; Savannah *Tribune*, 10 December 1892; Georgia, *Journal of the House*, 1892, pp. 652–3.

75. Georgia, *Journal of the House*, 1881, pp. 66–76, quotations from p. 76; see Georgia, *Journal of the House*, 1892, p. 657, for a similar recommendation by Joseph S. Turner, chairman of the Committee on the Penitentiary. Turner was appointed chairman of the Prison Commission in 1897, when this form of direct supervision was passed into law.

76. Julius L. Brown to Governor William J. Northen, 30 May 1894, Box 105, Governor's Correspondence, GDAH.

77. General Assembly, *Acts*, 1880–81, p. 107.

78. *Investigation*, 1896, Vol. 1, p. 824. For a whipping boss who doubled as "superintendent" at the Dade mines, see Georgia, *Journal of the House*, 1895, p. 829; for Governor Gordon, see Georgia Executive Minutes, 8 November 1887, p. 488, GDAH.

79. W.O. Reese to Joseph E. Brown, 24 October 1889, and Joseph E. Brown to Governor John B. Gordon, 30 October 1889, Box 98; Julius L. Brown to Governor William J. Northen, 26 October 1891, Box 102; Julius L. Brown to Governor W. Y. Atkinson, 28 March 1896, Box 112; all in Governor's Correspondence, GDAH.

80. For additional examples, see Georgia Executive Minutes, 16 February 1897, 21 January 1893, GDAH; J.C. Moore to Governor W.Y. Atkinson, 22 October 1895, Box 111, Governor's Correspondence, GDAH.

81. Julius L. Brown to Governor William J. Northen, 17 October 1893, Box 104; 5 June 1894, Box 105, Governor's Correspondence, GDAH.

82. General Assembly, *Acts*, 1897, pp. 71–8, esp. p. 72.

83. General Assembly, *Acts*, 1897, pp. 75–6; Prison Commission, *Report*, 1899–1900, p. 4; 1901–02, p. 17; see also Prison Commission, *Report*, 1907–08, for repetition of this myth on the eve of abolition of leasing – "no convicts are in the custody or control of any company" (pp. 5–6). For "good and faithful labor," see Prison Commission, *Report*, 1898–99, pp. 46–7; see also *Proceedings*, 1908, Vol. 2, p. 660; US Bureau of Labor, *Convict Labor*, 20th Annual Report of the Commissioner of Labor (Washington, DC: GPO, 1905), p. 236.

84. See General Assembly, "Report," 1908, pp. 1068–9, for a good statement of this relationship; *Proceedings*, 1908, Vol. 4, p. 1382.

85. General Assembly, "Report," 1908, pp. 1082–3; *Proceedings*, 1908, Vol. 3, p. 800.

86. *Proceedings*, 1908, Vol. 2, pp. 614–15, 660–61, 719, 726; Vol. 3, pp. 1114, 1156.

87. The evidence of this practice, which was apparently endemic, is widespread and conclusive. See General Assembly, "Report," 1908, pp. 1063–70; *Proceedings*, 1908,

Vol. 1, pp. 38 (quotation), 117, 152, 163, 168; Vol. 2, pp. 459 (quotation), 522, 549, 581, 589, 623, 651, 674, 678; Vol. 3, pp. 776, 931, 1099. *Proceedings*, 1908, Vol. 1, p. 678; Vol. 2, pp. 804, 878, on its "customary" nature.

88. *Proceedings*, 1908, Vol. 2, pp. 547–8; General Assembly, "Report," 1908, p. 1069; Petitioners Amendment, Transcript of Record, 28 April 1909, *Chattahoochee Brick Company* v. *Goings*, Case File A-31445, Box 558, Supreme Court Case Files, GDAH; Hurt in *Proceedings*, 1908, Vol. 2, p. 438, also p. 457.

89. General Assembly, "Report," 1908, p. 1079; Georgia, *Journal of the House*, 1908, Ext. Sess., pp. 53–4.

90. General Assembly, "Report," 1908, p. 1079; *Proceedings*, 1908, Vol. 1, pp. 159, 180; Vol. 3, 782, 788–90.

91. *Proceedings*, 1908, Vol. 1, p. 170.

92. *Proceedings*, 1908, Vol. 2, pp. 531, 719; see also Vol. 4, p. 1213 for similar hairsplitting.

93. *Proceedings*, 1908, Vol. 2, p. 589; Vol. 3, p. 772; Vol. 4, pp. 1231–2.

94. *Proceedings*, 1908, Vol. 3, pp. 739–40, 1158–9; Vol. 4, pp. 1298–301, 1306.

95. *Proceedings*, 1908, Vol. 1, pp. 91–2, 129–31; US Bureau of Labor, *Convict Labor*, p. 30.

96. US Bureau of Labor, *Convict Labor*, pp. 30–31; Gerald D. Jaynes, *Branches Without Roots: Genesis of the Black Working Class in the American South, 1862–1882* (New York: Oxford University Press, 1986), pp. 270–71; *Proceedings*, 1908, Vol. 4, p. 1228; George Washington Cable, *The Silent South, together with the Freedmen's Case in Equity and the Convict Lease System* (1883; reprint, New York: Charles Scribner's Sons, 1907), pp. 177–8.

97. USGS, *Mineral Resources*, 1883–1910.

98. On days worked, see, e.g., USGS, *Mineral Resources*, 1900, pp. 301–2; J.J. Ormsbee, "The Coal Interests of the South," *Tradesman* 36 (1 January 1897), pp. 120–23.

99. Report to Stockholders, 3 May 1893, Folder 1, Box 1, Julius L. Brown Papers, AHC; *Investigation*, 1896, Vol. 1, p. 750; USGS, *Mineral Resources*, 1896, p. 482; USGS, *Mineral Resources*, 1906, p. 659; USGS, *Mineral Resources*, 1886, p. 252; Charles Willard Hayes, *The Southern Appalachian Coal Field*, in USGS, *22nd Annual Report*, part 3 (Washington, DC: GPO, 1902), p. 243.

100. USGS, *Mineral Resources*, 1905, p. 561; 1900, pp. 309, 372; 1910, part 2, pp. 9–10, 113; 1907, part 2, pp. 50–52, 106. On the impact of mechanization on the coal industry, see Keith Dix, *What's a Coal Miner to Do?: The Mechanization of Coal Mining* (Pittsburgh, Pa.: University of Pittsburgh Press, 1988).

101. See USGS, *Mineral Resources*, 1888, p. 207, for a good summary of factors bearing on productivity in the bituminous coal industry.

102. USGS, *Mineral Resources*, 1918, part 2, pp. 701, 727, 744; 1907, part 2, p. 107; *Appalachian Trade Journal* 6 (January 1911), pp. 20–21; W.F. Blevins to Otto E. Sherman, 18 December 1911, Wiley Redding file, Box 100, Applications for Clemency, Georgia Executive Department Papers, GDAH.

103. USGS, *Mineral Resources*, 1908, part 2, pp. 105–6; 1909, part 2, pp. 108–9.

104. USGS, *Mineral Resources*, 1909, part 2, pp. 108–9; 1910, part 2, p. 113; on pig-iron decline, see James H. Dodd, *A History of Production in the Iron and Steel Industry in the Southern Appalachian States, 1901–1926* (Nashville, Tenn.: George Peabody College, 1928), pp. 67–8, 84, 129.

105. Prison Commission, *Report*, 1901–2, p. 18; 1897–98, pp. 12–14, 44–5; 1900–01, p. 7; 1901–02, pp. 19–20; 1903–04, pp. 7–9; 1907–08, p. 4.

106. On the abolition of leasing in Georgia, see A. Elizabeth Taylor, "The Abolition of the Convict Lease System in Georgia," *Georgia Historical Quarterly* 26 (June

1942), pp. 273–87; Matthew J. Mancini, "Race, Economics, and the Abandonment of Convict Leasing," *Journal of Negro History* 63 (Fall 1978), pp. 339–52; Dewey Grantham, *Hoke Smith and the Politics of the New South* (Baton Rouge: Louisiana State University Press, 1958), pp. 172–5.

107. Principal Physician, *Report*, 1896–97, pp. v–vi. The following year, as part of the "reforms" instituted in the convict system, the office of the Principal Physician was abolished; Prison Commission, *Report*, 1897–98, p. 5.

Chapter 7

1. Sterling Brown, *The Collected Poems of Sterling Brown*, edited by Michael Harper (Chicago: TriQuarterly Books, 1989), p. 56.

2. United States Geological Survey, *Mineral Resources of the United States*, 1900, (Washington, DC: GPO, 1901), p. 372; 1907, part 2, p. 106.

3. On peonage, see Pete Daniel, *The Shadow of Slavery: Peonage in the South, 1901–1969* (Urbana: University of Illinois Press, 1972); Charles W. Russell, *Report on Peonage*, US Department of Justice (Washington, DC: GPO, 1908), p. 19 on mining. On the *Padrone* system, see Luciano J. Iorizzo, *Italian Immigration and the Impact of the Padrone System* (New York: Arno Press, 1980).

4. Louis B. Magid to Editor, 25 November 1911, Box 200, Governor's Incoming Correspondence, GDAH; see also Magid to Governor Hoke Smith, 3 November 1911, Box 200, Governor's Correspondence, GDAH, in which he urged Smith to participate in a conference on southern immigration.

5. Copy of Contract, 10 March 1910; James W. English, Jr. to Governor Joseph M. Brown, 7 June 1910, p. 1, both in "Durham Riot" (DR) File, Box 200, Governor's Correspondence, GDAH.

6. James English, Jr. to Joseph M. Brown, 7 June 1910, pp. 2–3; Affidavit of J.C. Cheatham, 9 June 1910, p. 2; Affidavit of John Mitchell, 10 June 1910; Affidavit of E.A. Turner, 10 June 1910, pp. 1–2; Captain H.P. Meikleham to General A.J. Scott, 27 May 1910; all in DR File, Box 200, Governor's Correspondence, GDAH.

7. H.P. Meikleham to A.J. Scott, 21 June 1910, Box 163, Governor's Correspondence, GDAH; James English, Jr. to Joseph M. Brown, 7 June 1910, pp. 4–5; H.P. Meikleham to A.J. Scott, 27 May 1910, pp. 3–4; Affidavit of R.S. Garmany, n.d., p. 3; all in DR File, Box 200, Gov. Corr., GDAH. On the relationship between English and Brown, see James W. English to Joseph M. Brown, 25 May 1910, Folder 9, Box 1; on the same day as the strike, English introduced Brown to a Chattanooga realtor with some property Brown was interested in. This letter, of course, is in the Joseph Mackey Brown Papers, AHC, rather than the official Governor's Correspondence.

8. Montagliari to [US] Secretary of State, 9 June 1910; Huntington Wilson to Joseph M. Brown, 7 June 1910; both in DR File, Box 200, Governor's Correspondence, GDAH; *Journal of Labor*, 29 July 1910; Wesley Shropshire to Joseph M. Brown, 11 June 1910, DR File, Box 200, Governor's Correspondence, GDAH.

9. Copy of Speech to Georgia House of Representatives, n.d., DR File, Box 200, Governor's Correspondence, GDAH, p. 6.

10. E.A. Turner to Joseph M. Brown, 23 July 1910, Folder 11, Box 1, Joseph M. Brown Papers, AHC. Included with this communication was a "letter" from a "Georgia working man" questioning the governor's actions, to which Brown was ostensibly going to respond publicly; from all appearances this "letter" was a fabrication.

11. *Appalachian Trade Journal* 6 (January 1911), pp. 20–21.

12. On the Chattahoochee Brick Company and convicts, see Principal Physician to the Penitentiary, *Report*, 1884–86, pp. 129–30; 1886–88, p. 115; 1895–96, pp. 133–

4; Principal Keeper, *Report*, 1884–86, p. 96 (which shows 270 convicts at the brick-yard); 1888–90, pp. 7–9; Georgia General Assembly, *Proceedings of the Joint Committee of the Senate and House to Investigate the Convict Lease System of Georgia*, 1908, 5 ms vols (on microfilm), GDAH (hereafter cited as *Proceedings*, 1908), Vol. 1, pp. 81–143; Vol. 2, pp. 695–722; Vol. 4, pp. 1209–32; Minute Books, 1903–18 (2 vols), 14 November 1903, Box 6, Chattahoochee Brick Company (CBC) Papers, AHC, Vol. 1, p. 11 for the final lease of 175 convicts at $223.25 per annum; Atlanta *Constitution*, 27 September 1887, p. 5 for economic significance of brick to Atlanta. On productive capacity, see letterhead of the company, e.g., W.B. Lowe to Joseph S. Turner, 28 April 1896, Box 112, Governor's Correspondence, GDAH; Production & Shipments and Annual Statements, 1902–16, Folder 2, Box 1, Financial Records, CBC Papers, AHC, which shows at its peak in May 1906, 3,486,226 brick produced, or about 145,000 daily. The warden at the brickyard estimated daily production to be 140,000 brick; see *Proceedings*, 1908, Vol. 2, p. 696. The company appears to have produced around 30 million bricks annually while it used convicts. For its history, see David Charles Berry, "Free Labor He Found Unsatisfactory: James W. English and Convict Lease Labor at the Chattahoochee Brick Company," (M.A. thesis, Georgia State University, 1991), pp. 29–40.

13. US Bureau of Labor, *Convict Labor*, Second Annual Report of the Commissioner of Labor (Washington, DC: GPO, 1887), pp. 194–5, 300–301; *Proceedings*, 1908, Vol. 2, pp. 656, 661; testimony of J.W. Bridwell, Secretary, Atlanta Federation of Trades, in US Industrial Commission, *Report on the Relations and Conditions of Capital and Labor*, Vol. 7 of the Commissioner's Reports (Washington, DC: GPO, 1901), p. 242. By 1909 only four brickyards existed in Fulton County, and three of them had previously worked convicts; Georgia Geological Survey, *Second Report on the Clay Deposits of Georgia*, Bulletin No. 18 (Atlanta, Ga.: State Printer, 1909), p. 329.

14. Harry English, Report to Stockholders, Minute Books, 25 June 1908, Box 6, CBC Papers, AHC, vol. 1, p. 94.

15. Georgia General Assembly, *Acts and Resolutions*, Extraordinary Session, 1908, pp. 1119–30 for the legislation ending convict leasing; Directors' Meeting and Report by Harry English, Minute Books, 4 January 1909, Box 6, CBC Papers, AHC, vol. 1, pp. 99–100.

16. *Journal of Labor*, 29 November 1907, p. 4; Directors' Meeting and Report by Harry English, Minute Books, 4 January 1909, Box 6, CBC Papers, AHC, vol. 1, pp. 99–100; for production figures, see Production & Shipment, Folder 2, Box 1, Financial Records, CBC Records, AHC.

17. Harry English to Stockholders, Minute Books, 25 June 1908, vol. 1, p. 94; Harry English, Report to Directors, Minute Books, 4 January 1909, vol. 1, p. 99; Report by General Manager to Board of Directors, Minute Books, 3 May 1909, vol. 1, p. 107; all in Box 6, CBC Papers, AHC.

18. Minute Books, 5 April 1909, vol. 1, p. 104, and 3 May 1909, vol. 1, p. 107; both in Box 6, CBC Papers, AHC; production statistics are from Folder 2, Box 1, Financial Records, CBC Papers, AHC.

19. Minute Books, 11 June 1909, vol. 1, p. 109; Stockholders Meeting, Minute Books, 22 July 1912, vol. 2, p. 4; Board of Directors Meeting, Minute Books, 8 March 1911, vol. 2; all in Box 6, CBC Papers, AHC.

20. Folder 2, Box 1, Financial Records, CBC Papers, AHC, for production and labor costs, esp. Annual Statement, 1 June 1908 to 1 April 1909, and Annual Statement, 1 June 1909 to 1 June 1910; Harry English, Report, Minute Books, 25 June 1908, Box 6, CBC Papers, AHC, vol. 1, p. 94.

21. Stockholders Meeting, Minute Books, 23 October 1912, Box 6, CBC Records, AHC, vol. 2.

22. Board of Directors Meeting, Minute Books, 3 May 1909, p. 106; General Manager's Report to Directors, Minute Books, 16 May 1910, vol. 1, p. 137, both in Box 6, CBC Papers, AHC; Inventory: Buildings and Machinery, 24 October 1916, Folder 5, Box 1, Financial Records, CBC Papers, AHC, p. 1; Stockholders Meeting, Minute Books, 22 July 1912, Box 6, CBC Records, AHC, vol. 2, p. 4.

23. Minute Books, Box 6, CBC Papers, AHC, vol. 2, *passim*, esp. Rebie Rosenkrantz to Board of Directors, Minute Books, 21 June 1912; on mechanization, see Board of Directors Meeting, Minute Books, 18 May 1910, vol. 1, p. 138; General Manager's Report, Minute Books, 16 May 1910, vol. 1, p. 137; Stockholders Meeting, Minute Books, 22 July 1912, vol. 2, p. 5.

24. Stockholders Meeting, Minute Books, 23 October 1912, Box 6, CBC Papers, AHC, vol. 2; Harry W. English to James W. English, Minute Books, 22 September 1914, Box 6, CBC Papers, AHC, vol. 2.

25. *Journal of Labor*, 7 August 1908, p. 4; also 2 April 1909, p. 4. For evidence of early labor opposition to convict leasing in Atlanta, see Atlanta City Council, Minute Books, vol. 10, 6 April 1885 and vol. 13, 18 January 1892, Records of the City of Atlanta, AHC.

26. H.L. Garrett, F.W. McCabe and J.L. Jones [Officers of the International Association of Machinists, Local No. 1, Atlanta] to Senator Dobbs and Representatives Slaton, Blackburn and Bell, 31 July 1908, "Convicts" Subject File, Box 64, File II, Central Research Section, GDAH; *Journal of Labor*, 2 April 1909, p. 4.

27. *Journal of Labor*, 17 July 1908, p. 4; 31 July 1908, p. 6; for farmer–worker alliance on this question, and quotation on "unfair competition," see the petition to the legislature of the Georgia Federation of Labor, Georgia, *Journal of the House*, Extraordinary Session, 1908, p. 550; also Editorial, *Southern Good Roads* 2 (August 1910), p. 17 for the contention that "if there is any possible work that convicts may do and not conflict with free labor it is road work"; Martin Dodge, "Government Cooperation in Object-Lesson Road Work," in US Department of Agriculture, *Yearbook*, 1901 (Washington, DC: GPO, 1901), p. 412, and Joseph Hyde Pratt, "Convict Labor in Good Roads Construction," *Southern Good Roads* 2 (November 1910), p. 29 for reiteration of this point. Labor's opposition to leasing and support for placing convicts on the roads is also found in *Journal of Labor*, 3 July 1908, p. 4; 21 August 1908, p. 6; 15 January 1909, p. 2; 29 November 1907, p. 4 (which stresses the question of competition with free labor); and the petitions and memorials to the legislative session considering abolishing the lease, Georgia, *Journal of the House*, Ext. Sess., 1908, pp. 11, 277, 300–302, 315–16. For the black press, see, e.g., Savannah *Tribune*, 19 December 1908, p. 7.

28. *Journal of Labor*, 17 July 1908, p. 4; Resolutions of Mass Meeting, Rising Fawn, Georgia, 2 August 1908, "Convicts" Subject File, Box 64, File II, GDAH.

29. Savannah *Tribune*, 12 September 1908, 18 August 1908.

30. Hicks File, Box 57; Horace Hammond File, Box 51, Applications for Clemency, Executive Department Papers, GDAH.

31. Frank Tannenbaum, *Darker Phases of the South* (London: G.P. Putnam's Sons, 1924), pp. 74–115; George Washington Cable, *The Silent South, together with the Freedman's Case in Equity and the Convict Lease System* (1883; reprint, New York: Charles Scribner's Sons, 1907); *The Nation* 136 (4 January 1933), p. 2; Robert Elliot Burns, *I am a Fugitive from the Georgia Chain Gang!* (New York: Vanguard Press, 1932). For a description of the creation of the image of the "benighted" South, see George B. Tindall, "The Benighted South: Origins of a Modern Image," *Virginia Quarterly Review* 40 (Spring 1964), pp. 281–94.

32. Joseph Brown in *Southern Good Roads* 1 (March 1910), p. 17; Logan Waller Page, "The Necessity for Road Improvement in the South," *South Atlantic Quarterly* 9

(April 1910), pp. 156–60; see also *Southern Good Roads* 3 (January 1911), p. 26.

33. On the good roads movement, which still awaits its historian, see George B. Tindall, *The Emergence of the New South, 1913–1945* (Baton Rouge: Louisiana State University Press, 1967), pp. 254–7; Harry McKown, "Roads and Reform: The Good Roads Movement in North Carolina, 1885–1921" (M.A. thesis, University of North Carolina, 1972); Bruce Seely, *Building the American Highway System: Engineers as Policy Makers* (Philadelphia: Temple University Press, 1987), part 1; Howard L. Preston, *Dirt Roads to Dixie: Accessibility and Modernization in the South, 1885–1935* (Knoxville: University of Tennessee Press, 1990); Cecil K. Brown, *The State Highway System of North Carolina: Its Evolution and Present Status* (Chapel Hill: University of North Carolina Press, 1931); Dewey Grantham, *Southern Progressivism: The Reconciliation of Progress and Tradition* (Knoxville: University of Tennessee Press, 1983), pp. 134–5, 307–10; Alton DuMar Jones, "Progressivism in Georgia, 1898–1918," (Ph.D. dissertation, Emory University, 1963), p. 3, notes that opposition to convict leasing and support for good roads were both continuities between Populism and Progressivism.

The best expression of the good roads philosophy is found in the numerous publications of the US Office of Public Roads (OPR); US Department of Agriculture annual reports and yearbooks; North Carolina Geological Survey (NCGS) reports, economic papers, bulletins, and good roads circulars; and articles in *Southern Good Roads* magazine. See, for example, USDA, Office of Road Inquiry, *Addresses on Road Improvement*, Circular No. 14 (Washington, DC: GPO, 1894); USDA, Office of Public Road Information, *Road Conventions in the Southern States*, Bulletin No. 23 (Washington, DC: GPO, 1902); North Carolina Geological Survey, *Highway Work in North Carolina*, Economic Paper No. 27 (Raleigh, N.C.: State Printer, 1912); J.H. Pratt, "Public Roads – Their Beneficial Results and How to Obtain Them," *Southern Good Roads* 3 (May 1911), pp. 7–14; Logan Waller Page, "Progress and Present Status of the Good Roads Movement in the United States," in USDA, *Yearbook, 1910* (Washington, DC: GPO, 1911), pp. 265–74; G. Grosvenor Dawes, "The Good Roads Movement Throughout the Southern States," *Southern Good Roads* 1 (January 1910), pp. 3–9; Maurice Eldridge, "Construction of Good County Roads," in USDA, *Yearbook, 1898*, pp. 317–24.

34. Brown, *State Highway System*, p. 30. The papers of the NCGS, in the Southern Historical Collection, University of North Carolina, show the importance of good roads in the Survey's day-to-day work. For Holmes's advocacy of road improvement, see, e.g., J.A. Holmes, "Road Building in North Carolina," in USDA, Office of Public Roads, *Proceedings of the North Carolina Good Roads Convention*, Bulletin No. 24 (Washington, DC: GPO, 1902), pp. 65–72. On Pratt, see Robert Ireland, "Prison Reform, Road Building, and Southern Progressivism: Joseph Hyde Pratt and the Campaign for Good Roads and Good Men," *North Carolina Historical Review* 68 (April 1991), pp. 125–57.

35. Good roads publications provide numerous examples of the emphasis on the importance of convict labor. See, for representative examples, J.A. Holmes, "Road Building With Convict Labor in the Southern States," USDA, *Yearbook, 1901*, pp. 319–32 (Washington, DC: GPO, 1902); J.E. Pennybacker, H.S. Fairbank, and W.F. Draper, *Convict Labor For Road Work*, USDA Bulletin No. 414 (Washington, DC: GPO, 1916); Maurice O. Eldridge, "The Evolution of Convict Labor," *Good Roads* N.S. 6 (February 1905), pp. 59–64; J.H. Pratt, "Economics of Convict Labor in Road Construction," NCGS, Good Roads Circular No. 97, 18 February 1914; William L. Spoon, "Road Work and the Convict," *Southern Good Roads* 2 (November 1910), pp. 13–15; J.H. Pratt, "Convict Labor in Good Roads Construction," *Southern Good Roads* 2 (November 1910), pp. 29–32; Editorial, *Southern Good Roads* 2 (October 1910), p. 18; J.E. Pennybacker, "The Road Situation in the South," *Southern Good Roads* 1 (January 1910), pp. 9–14; USDA, *Yearbook, 1895*, p. 491.

36. USDA, Office of Public Roads, *Proceedings of the North Carolina Good Roads Convention*, p. 36; USDA, Office of Public Roads, *Public Roads of North Carolina: Mileage and Expenditures in 1904*, Circular No. 45 (Washington, DC: GPO, 1907); USDA, Office of Public Roads, *Public Roads of Georgia: Mileage and Expenditures in 1904*, Circular No. 76 (Washington, DC: GPO, 1907); Speech by Governor Carr to the North Carolina Good Roads Convention, *c.* 1894, Box 31, Folder 348, NCGS Papers, SHC. Critiques of statute labor can also be found in Martin Dodge, "Government Cooperation in Object-Lesson Road Work," in USDA, *Yearbook, 1901*, pp. 411–12; Editorial, *Southern Good Roads* 1 (February 1910), p. 15; Joseph Hyde Pratt, "The Construction of Good Roads in the South," *South Atlantic Quarterly* 9 (January 1910), p. 57. On Georgia's experience with statute labor, and its replacement with convicts, see Peter Wallenstein, *From Slave South to New South: Public Policy in Nineteenth-Century Georgia* (Chapel Hill: University of North Carolina Press, 1987), pp. 196–207.

37. J.A. Holmes to Martin Dodge, 21 August 1901, Folder 8, Box 9, NCGS Papers, SHC; *Proceedings of the North Carolina Good Roads Convention*, p. 67.

38. Undated draft speech, Folder 355, Box 31, NCGS Papers, SHC.

39. North Carolina Bureau of Labor Statistics, *Third Annual Report ... for the Year 1889* (Raleigh, N.C.: State Printer, 1890), p. 175.

40. W.E. Spencer to North Carolina Good Roads Association (NCGRA), 29 April 1902, Folder 91, Box 10, NCGS Papers, SHC.

41. See the William Luther Spoon Papers, SHC, e.g., W.H. Kinsey to William L. Spoon, 21 September 1897, Folder 35; 16 May 1898, Folder 42; 22 November 1897, Folder 37; W.S. Clark to William L. Spoon, 16 December 1899, Folder 54; Report by Road Supervisor A.L. McPherson, 28 August 1899, Folder 653; Report by J.F. Garrison, August 1899, Folder 653; V.S. Freeland to William L. Spoon, 14 September 1900, Folder 58.

42. D.L. McLean to Joseph A. Holmes, 20 July 1900, Folder 70, Box 8, NCGS Papers, SHC.

43. For origins of this tension, see Michael Hyman, "Taxation, Public Policy, and Political Dissent: Yeoman Disaffection in the Post-Reconstruction Lower South," *Journal of Southern History* 55 (February 1989), pp. 49–76, 72–3.

44. Gilmore Welch to Joseph A. Holmes, 7 July 1900; H.H. Farthing to Joseph A. Holmes, 13 July 1900, Folder 69, Box 8, NCGS Papers, SHC.

45. W.L. Spoon to Road Supervisors, Chapel Hill, 13 September 1902, Folder 95, Box 10, NCGS Papers, SHC.

46. J.W. Putnam to Joseph A. Holmes, 10 July 1900, Folder 69, Box 8, NCGS Papers, SHC.

47. USDA, Office of Public Road Information, *Road Conventions in the Southern States*, Bulletin No. 23 (Washington, DC: GPO, 1902), p. 13, speech by S.L. Patterson, North Carolina Commissioner of Agriculture.

48. J.M. Paterson to Joseph A. Holmes, 10 July 1900, Folder 69, Box 8, NCGS Papers, SHC.

49. J.H. German to Joseph A. Holmes, 9 July 1900, Folder 69, Box 8, NCGS Papers, SHC.

50. Road Reports, 3 January 1908, Folder 625; see also William L. Spoon to W.H. Carrell, 7 January 1899, Folder 47; W.J. Gibson to William L. Spoon, 24 February 1898, Folder 39; Spoon Papers, SHC.

51. J.T. Bradshaw to William L. Spoon, 18 April 1898, Folder 41, Spoon Papers, SHC; O.H. Rowland to Joseph A. Holmes, 11 July 1900, Folder 69, Box 8, NCGS Papers, SHC; Road Reports, 1907, Folder 624, Spoon Papers, SHC; North Carolina Good Roads Association convention, n.d., Folder 348, Box 31, NCGS Papers, SHC.

52. Paul Garrett to R.H. Sykes, 11 September 1902, Folder 95, Box 10, NCGS Papers, SHC.

53. North Carolina Highway Commission, *First Biennial Report, 1902*, p. 9.

54. USDA, *Report of the Secretary of Agriculture*, 1904 (Washington, DC: GPO, 1904), pp. 421–2; *Proceedings of the North Carolina Good Roads Convention*, p. 70.

55. E. Stagg Whitin, "Convicts and Road Building," *Southern Good Roads* 5 (June 1912), p. 16; Harlan H. Stone, "Good Roads," *Methodist Review* 78 (July–August 1896), p. 421; see also W.G. Whidby to Joseph A. Holmes, 10 September 1894, Box 2, NCGS Papers, SHC, on the Georgia Road Congress's discussion of convict labor.

56. See, e.g., H.B. Varner, "Why Convicts Should be Worked on Public Roads," *Southern Good Roads* 8 (September 1913), pp. 22–3.

57. USDA, Office of Public Road Information, *Road Conventions in the Southern States*, p. 45; Fred L. White to Logan Waller Page, 17 May 1909, Box 49, File 135, "Georgia Roads," General Correspondence Files, 1893–1912, OPR Records, RG 30, NA-WNRC.

58. O.H. Sheffield, *Improvement of the Road System in Georgia*, USDA, Office of Road Inquiry, Bulletin No. 3 (Washington, DC: GPO, 1894), p. 26.

59. Principal Keeper, *Report*, 1894; for changes in sentencing law, see S. W. McCallie, "Convicts on the Public Roads of Georgia," *Southern Good Roads*, 2 (December 1910), p. 3; Prison Commission, *Report*, 1907–08, pp. 7–9; and Georgia, *Journal of the Senate*, 1903, pp. 466–8.

60. A. Elizabeth Taylor, "The Abolition of the Convict Lease System in Georgia," *Georgia Historical Quarterly* 26 (June 1942), pp. 273–87; Matthew J. Mancini, "Race, Economics, and the Abandonment of Convict Leasing," *Journal of Negro History* 63 (Fall 1978), pp. 339–52; Dewey Grantham, *Hoke Smith and the Politics of the New South* (Baton Rouge: Louisiana State University Press, 1958), pp. 172–5.

61. E.C. Branson to Unnamed Correspondent, 13 June 1908, Correspondence, Folder 3, E.C. Branson Papers, SHC; *Journal of Labor*, 17 July 1908, p. 4; 31 July 1908, p. 6; Hilda Jane Zimmerman, "Penal Systems and Penal Reform in the South Since the Civil War" (Ph.D. dissertation, University of North Carolina, 1947), pp. 322–33; Dewey Grantham, *Southern Progressivism: The Reconciliation of Progress and Tradition* (Knoxville: University of Tennessee Press, 1983), pp. 127–42; Blake McKelvey, *American Prisons: A History of Good Intentions* (1936; reprint, Montclair, N.J.: Patterson Smith, 1977), pp. 214–15; David Oshinsky, "Prison Plantation: Parchman Prison and Forced Labor," paper presented at the Annual Meeting of the Southern Historical Association, 8–11 November 1989, copy in author's possession; Mark T. Carleton, *Politics and Punishment: The History of the Louisiana State Penal System* (Baton Rouge: Louisiana State University Press, 1971); Donald Walker, *Penology for Profit: A History of the Texas Prison System, 1867–1912* (College Station: Texas A & M Press, 1988); Jesse F. Steiner and Roy M. Brown, *The North Carolina Chain Gang: A Study of County Convict Road Work* (Chapel Hill: University of North Carolina Press, 1927). In Tennessee the chain-gang movement was spearheaded by capital; the Southern Appalachian Coal Operators Association objected to the state working convicts in coal mines after the abolition of leasing in 1895, and vigorously advocated convict road work. For examples, see *Appalachian Trade Journal* 2 (May 1909), p. 1; 2 (June 1909), p. 1; 3 (July 1909), pp. 5–7; 3 (September 1909), pp. 5–6; 9 (August 1912), p. 26, among others.

62. On the racial ideology of southern Progressivism, see John Dittmer, *Black Georgia in the Progressive Era, 1900–1920* (Urbana: University of Illinois Press, 1977), pp. 110–15; George Fredrickson, *The Black Image in the White Mind* (New York: Harper and Row, 1971), pp. 286–319; Grantham, *Southern Progressivism*, pp. 230–45; Jack Temple Kirby, *Darkness at the Dawning: Race and Reform in the Progressive South* (Philadelphia: J.B. Lippincott, 1972).

63. Alexander McKelway, "The Convict Lease System of Georgia," *The Outlook* 90 (12 September 1908), p. 67; Prison Commission, *Report*, 1908–09, pp. 7–8; H.H. Tucker, "Prison Labor," in National Prison Association, *Proceedings*, 1886 (Chicago: Donnelly and Sons, 1887), p. 262; J.E. Pennybacker to H.G. Buchanan, 20 January 1912, Box 35, File 97, "Convict Labor," General Correspondence, 1893–1912, OPR Records, RG30, NA-WNRC, pp. 2–3. For evidence of segregated sentencing in North Carolina, see North Carolina Prison Department, *Report*, 1897, p. 32; 1898, p. 128; 1903–04, p. 106; 1905–06, p. 22.

64. Alexander McKelway, "The Atlanta Riots: A Southern White Point of View," *The Outlook* 84 (3 November 1906), pp. 559, 562; McKelway, "The Convict Lease System of Georgia"; McKelway, "Abolition of the Convict Lease System of Georgia," in American Prison Association, *Proceedings, 1908* (Indianapolis, Ind.: William H. Buford, 1909), pp. 219–27.

65. Edgar G. Murphy, *Problems of the Present South* (New York: MacMillan, 1905), pp. 151–201; Dittmer, *Black Georgia*, pp. 110–15; Fredrickson, *Black Image*, pp. 286–96; Kirby, *Darkness at the Dawning*, pp. 62–78.

66. Murphy, *Problems of the Present South*, p. 164.

67. Grantham, *Hoke Smith*, pp. 172–5; J. Morgan Kousser, *The Shaping of Southern Politics: Suffrage Restriction and the Establishment of the One-Party South, 1880–1910* (New Haven, Conn.: Yale University Press, 1974), pp. 221–3; Savannah *Tribune*, 26 September 1908, 10 October 1908.

68. E. Stagg Whitin, "The Spirit of Convict Road-Building," *Southern Good Roads* 6 (December 1912), pp. 12–13.

69. Hooper Alexander, "The Convict Lease and the System of Contract Labor – Their Place in History," in James E. McCulloch, ed., *The South Mobilizing for Social Service* (Nashville, Tenn.: Southern Sociological Congress, 1913), pp. 161–74.

70. For criticism of the deplorable conditions in Georgia's misdemeanor camps, and the impossible task of regulating them, see Selena S. Butler, "The Chain-Gang System," speech before the National Association of Colored Women, Nashville, Tennessee, 16 September 1897, Georgia Room, University of Georgia (Tuskeegee, Ala.: Normal School Steam Press, 1897); Georgia, *Journal of the House*, 1894, pp. 33–5; 1895, pp. 245–51; Prison Commission, *Report*, 1898–99, pp. 17–18; 1899–1900, pp. 16–23; 1901–02, p. 14.

71. Savannah *Tribune*, 9 October 1897. For five weeks the *Tribune* serialized a special report made to the governor about these camps. For a description of a Georgia county road camp in 1906 that easily could have been written thirty years later, see George Herbert Clarke, "Georgia and the Chain-Gang," *Outlook* 82 (13 January 1906), pp. 73–9. On George V. Gress, Georgia's "Lumber King," see Mary Lou L. McDonald and Samuel Jordan Lawson III, *The Passing of the Pines: A History of Wilcox County, Georgia* (Roswell, Ga.: W.H. Wolfe, 1984), pp. 42–3, 69; Principal Keeper, *Report*, 1896, Table 7.

72. Chain Gang Sentences Imposed by Recorder (Macon, Georgia), March 1904, "Exhibit," *Jamison* v. *E. A. Wimbish*, File 53A386, Box 488, Case Files, US District Court, Southern District of Georgia, Western Division (Macon), RG 21, Atlanta Regional Archives, National Archives and Records Service (hereafter cited as RG21, ARA); for the summary procedures of the Macon Recorder's Court, see *Pearson* v. *Wimbish*, 124 Ga. 701 (1905), and "Criminal Docket," *Jamison* v. *Wimbish*, Case File A-28901, Box 499, Case Files, Records of the Supreme Court of Georgia, GDAH, pp. 2–3; Petition for Habeas Corpus, 20 June 1904, pp. 40–54, 61, Petition for Writ of Habeas Corpus, n.d. (for Jamison's sentence), and habeas corpus proceedings, Savannah, 23 March 1904, p. 3H, all in *Jamison* v. *E. A. Wimbish*, File 53A386, Box 488, Case Files, US District Court, Southern District of Georgia,

Western Division (Macon), RG21, ARA. See also *Voice of the Negro* 1 (August 1904), pp. 300–301, and Clarke, "Georgia and the Chain-Gang," on the importance of the *Jamison* case.

73. The racial breakdown is found in Petition for Habeas Corpus, 20 June 1904, *Jamison v. E. A. Wimbish*, File 53A386, Box 488, Case Files, US District Court, Southern District of Georgia, Western Division (Macon), RG21, ARA, p. 81; *Macon City Directory*, 1904; *Savannah Tribune*, 18 September 1897.

74. Report, Donalson Lumber Company, October 1899; Report, E.J. Smith Camp, May 1900; both in Monthly Reports of Misdemeanor Chain Gangs, Georgia Prison Commission Records, Records of the Georgia Board of Corrections, GDAH.

75. Colquitt County Superior Court, County Court, Minutes, 1894–1901, Book A, GDAH, pp. 1, 4, 7, 10, 14, 42; *Moultrie Weekly Observer*, 13 November 1903, p. 3; Wilcox County Superior Court Minutes, September Term 1893, vols 3–4, 1892–1902, GDAH, p. 8. For the deals made between lessees and county officials, including judges, to obtain this labor, see for example *Proceedings*, 1908, Vol. 2, pp. 684–9; Transcript of Record, 14 October 1897, *Russell v. Tatum*, Case File A-21517, Box 352, Records of the Supreme Court of Georgia, GDAH; on fees, fines and costs see, e.g., *Black v. Fite*, 88 Ga. 238 (1891); *Rountree v. Durden*, 95 Ga. 221 (1894); *Pulaski County v. DeLacy*, 114 Ga. 583 (1901); *Barron v. Terrell*, 124 Ga. 1077 (1905); and *Sapp v. DeLacy*, 127 Ga. 659 (1906).

76. H. Bruce Franklin, *Prison Literature in America: The Victim as Criminal and Artist*, 1st revised edn (Westport, Conn.: Lawrence Hill, 1982), p. 117.

77. L.F. Hawley, "Turpentine and Rosin," unpublished study, 1919, Box 13, US Forest Service Records, RG95, National Archives, Washington, DC, pp. 13–14; Charles H. Herty, *A New Method of Turpentine Orcharding*, USDA, Bureau of Forestry, Bulletin No. 40 (Washington, DC: GPO, 1903), pp. 10, 43; A.W. Schrager and H.S. Betts, *The Naval Stores Industry*, USDA Bulletin No. 229 (Washington, DC: GPO, 1915), pp. 1–2, 12–18; USDA, *Report of the Secretary*, 1892, pp. 332–58; *Northwest Lumberman*, 22 May 1897, p. 12; Mark V. Wetherington, *The New South Comes to Wiregrass Georgia, 1860–1910* (Knoxville: University of Tennessee Press, 1994), pp. 116–22; Jeffrey A. Drobney, "Where Palm and Pine are Blowing: Convict Labor in the North Florida Turpentine Industry, 1877–1923," *Florida Historical Quarterly* 72 (April 1994), pp. 411–34. On task labor, see, e.g., *Proceedings*, 1908, Vol. 2, pp. 529–31.

78. *Investigation of Charges Against Penitentiary Companies One, Two and Three*, 2 vols, *Evidence for the State*, Vol. 1; *Evidence for Julius Brown, Receiver*, Vol. 2: 10–21 February 1896, Box 4, Julius L. Brown Papers, AHC, Vol. 1, pp. 128, 134, 145–51, 157–8, 331–2; Hearing, Investigation of Connaly & Pinson Camp in Turner County, 9 September 1908, Prison Commission 1908 Folder, Box 19, Prison Commission Correspondence, 1908–09, Hoke Smith Collection, Richard B. Russell Library, University of Georgia, p. 26; J.B. Crabb to W.B. Lowe, 9 September 1895, Box 111, Governor's Correspondence, GDAH; *Savannah Tribune*, 9 October 1897, 13 November 1897. On wildcat camps, and their legal ambiguity, see Prison Commission, *Report*, 1899–1900, pp. 17–18; 1901–02, pp. 9, 16; 1904–05, p. 7; Georgia, *Journal of the House*, 1894, pp. 33–5; 1895, pp. 245–51; *Russell v. Tatum*, 104 Ga. 332 (1898); *Daniel v. State*, 59 Ga. 533 (1901); *Proceedings*, 1908, Vol. 4, pp. 1266–8; Hearing, Investigation of Connaly & Pinson Camp in Turner County, 9 September 1908, Prison Commission 1908 Folder, pp. 3–13; Joseph Turner to Hoke Smith, 16 September 1908, Prison Commission Correspondence, 1908–09, both in Box 19, Hoke Smith Collection, Richard B. Russell Library, University of Georgia. This area of the penal system frequently overlapped – and was confused with – peonage; Daniel, *Shadow of Slavery*, pp. 24–5; Daniel Novak, *The Wheel of Servitude: Black Forced Labor After Slavery* (Lexington: The University Press of Kentucky, 1978), p. 24; Russell, *Report on Peonage*.

79. On competition between the public and private sectors for misdemeanor convicts, see, e.g., Minutes of County Commissioners (MCC), Worth County, Georgia, vol. A, 1904–26, pp. 54–5, 64–7, 168–70, 173, 180; Minutes of Court of Ordinary, Worth County, vol. C, 1897–1903, pp. 430, 451, both in Box 71, Georgia County Records, Works Progress Administration (WPA) Historical Records Survey, UGA; MCC, Colquitt County, Georgia, Minute Book D, 1898–1902, pp. 198, 235, 240, 244; Grand Jury Presentments, Minutes of the Superior Court, Colquitt County, Minute Book E, 1902–07, pp. 140–41, 197, 261–2, 308, 366, both in Box 19, Georgia County Records, WPA Records UGA. For the effects of the free labor market on the supply of and demand for misdemeanor convicts, especially in the turpentine and lumber industries, see Letter to the Editor, *Savannah Naval Stores Review* 14 (6 August 1904), p. 8 ("the loafing negro"); *Southern Lumberman* 39 (1 April 1901), p. 6; 1 May 1901, p. 7; W.E.B. Du Bois, *Some Notes on Negro Crime, Particularly in Georgia*, (Atlanta, Ga.: Atlanta University Press, 1904), p. 47; Prison Commission, *Report*, 1898–99, pp. 8–9; 1900–01, pp. 7–10; 1901–02, pp. 19–20; 1903–04, pp. 9–10; 1906–07, p. 6; and *Proceedings*, 1908, Vol. 3, p. 967.

80. Grand Jury Presentments (GJP), Colquitt County, Minute Book E, pp. 197 (first quotation), 308, 366, 500 (second quotation); MCC, Colquitt County, Book No. 1, 1902–19, p. 22; GJP, Colquitt County, Minute Book F, 1907–12, p. 364 (third quotation), all in Box 20, WPA Records, UGA.

81. DuBois, *Some Notes on Negro Crime*, pp. 46, 48.

82. On the racial composition of misdemeanants, see for example, Prison Commission, *Report*, 1901–02, pp. 9, 31, which shows that 2,113 of 2,221 misdemeanor convicts were black; Monthly Reports of Misdemeanor Chain Gangs, Georgia Prison Commission Records, GDAH; Savannah *Tribune*, 9 October 1897. On Populism and the convict lease, see Barton C. Shaw, *The Wool-Hat Boys: Georgia's Populist Party* (Baton Rouge: Louisiana State University Press, 1984), pp. 79, 133, 189; Zimmerman, "Penal Systems and Penal Reform," pp. 239–44; Alton Jones, "Progressivism in Georgia, 1898–1918," p. 3; *People's Party Paper*, 1 November 1895, p. 4. On the chain gang as a form of social control for urban blacks, see Joel Williamson, *A Rage for Order: Black-White Relations in the American South since Emancipation* (New York: Oxford University Press, 1986), p. 146; Howard Rabinowitz, *Race Relations in the Urban South, 1865–1890* (Urbana: University of Illinois Press, 1980), pp. 49–50. Figures on road improvement and use of convicts are from Georgia Geological Survey, *A Preliminary Report of the Roads and Road-Building Materials of Georgia*, Bulletin No. 8 (Atlanta, Ga.: State Printer, 1901).

83. Georgia Geological Survey, *A Preliminary Report on the Roads and Road-Building Materials of Georgia*, pp. 235 (Irwin County Commissioner), 207 (Richmond County), 173 (Greene County), 191 (Upson County), 225 (Stewart County), 150–51 (Fulton County). On roads and the growth of Atlanta, see Howard L. Preston, *Automobile Age Atlanta: The Making of a Southern Metropolis* (Athens: University of Georgia Press, 1979). Automobile License Register, 1904–10, 3 vols, Records of the City of Atlanta, AHC, shows that 86 auto licenses were granted in six months of 1904; by 1908, 738 had been issued; two years later, 2,397.

84. General Assembly, *Acts*, 1903, pp. 65–71 (quotation on p. 70); Prison Commission, *Report*, 1907–08, pp. 23–4.

85. Prison Commission, *Report*, 1907–08, 1908–09, Table 2; General Assembly, *Acts*, Extraordinary Session, 1908, pp. 1119–30; S.W. McCallie, "Convicts on the Public Roads of Georgia," *Southern Good Roads* 2 (December 1910), pp. 3–4; Goodloe Yancey to Logan Waller Page, 25 November 1908, Box 35, File 97, "Convict Labor," General Correspondence, 1893–1912, OPR Records, RG30, NA-WNRC; Atlanta *Journal*, 19 August 1908, p. 1.

86. Hoke Smith to Logan Waller Page, 29 September 1908, Box 49, File 135, "Georgia Roads," General Correspondence, 1893–1912, OPR Records, RG30, NA-WNRC; Georgia, *Journal of the House*, 1909, pp. 33–4; see also Prison Commission, *Report*, 1908–09, p. 5; Speech by C.B. Goodyear to Good Roads Meeting, Brunswick, Georgia, 22 February 1909, Folder 4, Box 2, Joseph Mackey Brown Papers, UGA, p. 5; Hoke Smith, Inaugural Address, 1911, Folder 15, Box 15, E. Merton Coulter Pamphlet Collection, UGA, p. 8.

87. *Southern Good Roads* 3 (January 1911), p. 26.

88. Georgia, *Journal of the Senate*, 1912, p. 883.

89. Prison Commission, *Report*, 1910–11, p. 7; see also Prison Commission, *Report*, 1909–10, p. 11; S.W. McCallie [Georgia State Geologist], "Road Improvement in Georgia," in Southern Appalachian Good Roads Association, *Bulletin No. 3* (Durham, N.C.: Seeman Printery, 1910), pp. 6–7; for delegates to the National Good Roads Convention, see List of Delegates to the National Good Roads Convention, April 1912, Box 183, Governor's Correspondence, GDAH. In 1916 the Prison Commission was merged with the newly created Highway Department; General Assembly, *Acts*, 1916, p. 125.

90. *Southern Good Roads* 5 (February 1912), pp. 20–21; 5 (May 1912), p. 18. Georgia did serve as a southwide example for successful convict road work; G. Grosvenor Dawes, "The Good Roads Movement Throughout the South," in Southern Appalachian Good Roads Association, *Bulletin No. 2* (Durham, N.C.: Seeman Printery, 1909), p. 19; also Logan W. Page, "Progress and Present Status of the Good Roads Movement in the United States," in USDA, *Yearbook, 1910*, p. 273, for the federal view; *Appalachian Trade Journal* 4 (March 1910), pp. 10–12; 6 (March 1911), pp. 15–16; 8 (June 1912), p. 14; and Cyrus Kehr to Director, Office of Public Roads, 25 July 1914, Folder 3, Box 112, File 712, "Convict Labor," General Correspondence, 1893–1916, OPR Records, RG30, on Tennessee; H.B. Varner, "Why Convicts Should Be Worked on the Public Roads," *Southern Good Roads* 8 (September 1913), pp. 22–3 (speech to the North Carolina Good Roads Association, 31 July 1913); Press Release, Asheville Board of Trade, 27 March 1916, and N. Buckner to J.C. Forester, 27 March 1916, Folder 52, Box 2, Eugene C. Branson Papers, SHC, for North Carolina. For the economic benefits of road improvement, see *Southern Good Roads* 1 (June 1910), p. 21; 2 (August 1910), pp. 20–21; 2 (October 1910), p. 22.

91. USDA, Office of Public Roads, *Mileage and Cost of Public Roads in the United States in 1904*, Bulletin No. 32 (Washington, DC: GPO, 1907), p. 8; Georgia Geological Survey, *Second Report on the Public Roads of Georgia*, Bulletin No. 24 (Atlanta, Ga.: State Printer, 1910), tables; USDA, Office of Public Roads, *Mileage and Cost of Public Roads in the United States in 1909*, Bulletin No. 41 (Washington, DC: GPO, 1912), pp. 16–17, 40; USDA, Office of Public Roads and Rural Engineering, *Public Road Mileage and Revenues in the Southern States*, Bulletin No. 387 (Washington, DC: GPO, 1917), p. 20; American Highway Association, *Good Roads Yearbook, 1917* (Washington, DC: AHA, 1917), p. 473. Discrepancies in mileage counts were due to inaccurate or incomplete reports from counties, different measurements of total roads, different definitions of "surfaced" and "improved" roads, and the decision to omit or include rural and urban roads. The American Highway Association, *Good Roads Yearbook, 1913* (Washington, DC: AHA, 1913), p. 390, gives the figure 26.2% of Georgia's roads being "improved," perhaps because that year they added "partially improved" roads to the usual figure of "surfaced" roads. Fifteen per cent by 1914 appears to be an accurate minimum figure.

92. Walter B. Hill, "Rural Survey of Clarke County, Georgia, with Special Reference to the Negroes," Phelps-Stokes Fellowship Study, No. 2, *Bulletin of the University of Georgia* 15 (March 1915), pp. 5–63, 24; Georgia Geological Survey,

Preliminary Report on the Roads and Road-Building Materials of Georgia, 1901, p. 167. The number of convicts in each county can be correlated with the miles of paved road in 1914 by matching the Prison Commission, *Report*, 1914, pp. 15–17, with Table 41 (Georgia) in the appendix of USDA, Office of Public Roads and Rural Engineering, *Public Road Mileage and Revenues in the Southern States*, Bulletin No. 387, pp. li–liii; and, for 1909 and 1911, by matching the Prison Commission *Report* of those years with the tables in Georgia Geological Survey, *Second Report on the Public Roads of Georgia* (1910), and *A Third Report on the Public Roads of Georgia*, Bulletin No. 28 (Atlanta, Ga.: State Printer, 1912) respectively. On the University of Georgia and the good roads movement, see C.M. Strahan, "Good Roads for Georgia," *Journal of Labor*, 15 January 1909, p. 2; *Southern Good Roads* 5 (February 1912), pp. 23–4; Harry Hodson to Governor Joseph M. Brown, n.d.; Conference Proceedings, 9–10 January 1912; C. M. Strahan to A. H. Ulm, 2 December 1912, 31 December 1912, all in "Roads" File, Box 200, Governor's Correspondence, GDAH.

93. Georgia, *Journal of the Senate*, 1912, p. 884; J.E. Pennybacker, H.S. Fairbank, and W.F. Draper, *Convict Labor for Road Work*, USDA, Office of Public Roads and Rural Engineering, Bulletin No. 414 (Washington, DC: GPO, 1916), pp. 20–21; P. St. Julien Wilson, "Convict Labor on the Roads of Virginia," *Southern Good Roads* 2 (November 1910), p. 11.

94. Joseph A. Holmes, "Convicts on the Public Roads," *Manufacturers Record* 26 (16 November 1894), p. 238; William L. Spoon, "Road Work and the Convict," *Southern Good Roads* 2 (November 1910), p. 15. See also Charles Dew, "Convicts as Builders of Public Roads," *Southern Good Roads* 6 (December 1912), pp. 18–19; Joseph Hyde Pratt, "Convict Labor in Good Roads Construction," *Southern Good Roads* 2 (November 1910), p. 29; Joseph Hyde Pratt to Walter R. Markley, 21 January 1911, Folder 170, Box 19, NCGS Papers, SHC; and J.E. Pennybacker to H.G. Buchanan, 20 January 1910, Box 35, File 97, "Convict Labor," General Correspondence 1893–1912, OPR Records, RG30, NA-WNRC, for further examples of the elimination of labor uncertainty and the labor control afforded by reliance on a convict force; see Wade H. Harris, "Processes of Good Roads Building and the Value of Improved Highways," *Southern Good Roads* 1 (February 1910), p. 5 for the view that convict labor was the "cheapest" way to improve roads. Other material in the NCGS Papers, SHC, suggests the cost savings of convict labor. On "object lesson" roads, see USDA, *Report of the Secretary of Agriculture*, 1909, p. 724; 1910, p. 775; 1911, pp. 726–8.

95. E. Stagg Whitin, "Convicts and Road Building," *Southern Good Roads* 5 (June 1912), p. 16. According to oral historian Cliff Kuhn, "bad boys make good roads" was a popular folk saying in early-twentieth-century Georgia; Cliff Kuhn, personal communication, 11 July 1988, based on his interview with Forrest Turner, tape recording in Living Atlanta Collection, AHC. For the ameliorative aspect of road work, see, e.g., editorial, *Southern Good Roads* 2 (November 1910), p. 19.

96. A.J. McKelway, "Abolition of the Convict Lease System in Georgia," p. 226.

97. Editorial, *Southern Good Roads* 2 (November 1910), p. 19; Logan Waller Page to Judson M. Bemis, 7 September 1911, Box 35, File 97, "Convict Labor," General Correspondence, 1893–1912, OPR Records, RG30, NA-WNRC, for the song.

98. Joseph Hyde Pratt, "Convict Labor in Good Roads Construction," *Southern Good Roads* 2 (November 1910), p. 30; P. St. Julien Wilson [assistant director, US Office of Public Roads], "Convict Camps in the South," in *Proceedings of the National Conference of Charities and Corrections, 1915* (Chicago: Hildman Printing Co., 1915), p. 382; J.E. Pennybacker et al., *Convict Labor for Road Work*, p. 13; Joseph Hyde Pratt, "Convict Labor in Highway Construction," *Annals of the American Academy of Political and Social Science* 46 (March 1913), pp. 78–87, 86. See also *Southern Good Roads* 2 (August 1910), p. 14; 2 (October 1910), p. 18. The most fully developed view of the moral/

physical benefits of road labor, which manages to make republican manhood compatible with forced labor, is E. Stagg Whitin, "The Spirit of Convict Road Building," *Southern Good Roads* 6 (December 1912), pp. 12–13; and Whitin, "Convicts and Road Building," *Southern Good Roads* 5 (June 1912), pp. 16–18. See Jackson Lears, *No Place of Grace: Antimodernism and the Transformation of American Culture, 1880–1920* (New York: Pantheon, 1981), on the moral and physical elements of the "strenuous life."

99. Zimmerman, "Penal Systems and Penal Reform," pp. 332–3; J.E. Pennybacker to H.G. Buchanan, 20 January 1912, Box 35, File 97, "Convict Labor," General Correspondence, 1893–1912, OPR Records, RG30, NA-WNRC, pp. 2–3; P. St. Julien Wilson, "Convict Camps in the South," p. 379.

100. J. E. Pennybacker et al., *Convict Labor for Roads*, pp. 18–19, 26; see also Logan Waller Page to William D. Scheir, 21 June 1916, Box 4119, File 712, General Correspondence 1912–50, OPR Records, RG30, NA-WNRC. On convict road work in other regions, see *Annals of the American Academy of Political and Social Science* 46 (March 1913), an issue devoted to "Prison Labor."

101. Editorial, *Southern Good Roads* 2 (August 1910), p. 17.

102. E. Stagg Whitin, "Convicts and Road Building," p. 16; Letters to *Southern Good Roads* 2 (July 1910), p. 23. See also North Carolina Geological Survey, Good Roads Circular No. 53, 15 January 1910, p. 3; Joseph Hyde Pratt to H.W. Horton, 4 September 1913, Folder 301, Box 28, NCGS Papers, SHC, for some specific examples of this line of argument. On similar trends in states other than Georgia, see note 90, above. North Carolina offers a good example; see NCGS, *Proceedings of the Annual Convention of the North Carolina Good Roads Association, 1913*, Economic Paper No. 36 (Raleigh, N.C.: State Printer, 1913), pp. 89–94, for a full-blown debate between advocates of convict road work and defenders of leasing convicts to railroads. The issue of the *Annals of the American Academy of Political and Social Science* 25 (January 1910) devoted to "The New South" exemplifies the belief that the South needed to shift from extractive industries to manufacturing and value-added sectors based on its own raw materials.

103. Zimmerman, "Penal Systems and Penal Reform," p. 327; D.C. Hamilton to Governor Joseph M. Brown, 4 April 1912, Box 183; Charlie Bailey to Governor Joseph M. Brown, 7 March 1912, Box 182, both in Governor's Correspondence, GDAH; L.R. Livingston to Governor Joseph M. Brown, 10 February 1912, "Pardons" File, Box 201, Governor's Correspondence, GDAH, for description of the overseer in an automobile, emphasis in original. For other complaints about the brutal conditions on Georgia's chain gangs from convicts and citizens, see Monroe Watson to Governor J.M. Slaton, 28 February 1914, Box 210; Jess C. Page to Governor Slaton, 17 March 1914, Box 210, both in Governor's Correspondnce, GDAH. Steiner and Brown, *The North Carolina Chain Gang*, pp. 173–84, claimed that decentralized administration was the crucial defect in the organization of southern chain gangs.

104. Convicts to Governor, 7 March 1920; Convicts to Governor Bickett, 17 March 1919; Joe Bisset to T.T. Thorne, 22 January 1918; Mrs. Dr. D.D. Bennet to Gov. Bickett, 8 July 1918; T.T. Thorne to R.F. Beasley, 16 July 1918, Box 8, "Prisons 1917–1925, General and Miscellaneous"; Wiley Woodard [a black convict] to Kate Burr Johnson [Commissioner of Public Welfare], 10 August 1925, Box 9, "Prison Complaints, 1915–1929"; Urban A. Woodbury to Governor Bickett, 8 February 1920, Box 8, "Prisons 1917–1925, General and Miscellaneous," all in Subject Files, Department of Social Services Records, State Board of Public Welfare (State Board of Public Charities) Records, North Carolina State Archives, Raleigh. These subject files contain numerous pleas for help addressed to Kate Johnson, most of which emphasize poor food, hard work, and brutal punishment.

105. This composite picture is drawn from Tannenbaum, *Darker Phases of the South*,

pp. 73–113; John Spivak, "On the Chain Gang," *International Pamphlets* No. 32 (New York: International Publishers, 1932); Arthur Raper, *Preface to Peasantry: A Tale of Two Black Belt Counties* (Chapel Hill: University of North Carolina Press, 1936), pp. 294–6; Bayard Rustin, "Twenty-Two Days on a Chain Gang," in *Down the Line: The Collected Writings of Bayard Rustin* (Chicago: Quadrangle, 1971), pp. 26–49, written in 1949.

106. Georgia, *Journal of the Senate*, p. 880–82; Prison Commission, *Report*, 1911–12, p. 8; Philip Weltner to Governor Emmet O'Neal, 14 July 1913, Administrative Files (Convict Department), Box 97, Governors' Papers, ADAH.

107. Cross examination by Minton Wimberly, p. 36; Testimony of E.A. Wimbish, p. 80; Testimony of Henry Jamison, p. 9; Testimony of Richard Ruff, p. 17; all in Transcript, Petition for Habeas Corpus, 20 June 1904, *Jamison* v. *E.A. Wimbish*, File 53A386, Box 488, Case Files, US District Court, Southern District of Georgia, Western Division (Macon), RG21, ARA.

108. D.H. Winslow, "Defects in Southern Road Laws," *Southern Good Roads* 6 (July 1912), p. 11; see Benno C. Schmidt, Jr., "Principle and Prejudice: The Supreme Court and Race in the Progressive Era. Part 2: The *Peonage Cases*," *Columbia Law Review* 82 (April 1982), pp. 646–718, 649, 653, on the functions of legal terror in the South.

109. J.H. Dodge to A.N. Johnson, 18 June 1905, Box 35, File 97, "Convict Labor," General Correspondence, 1893–1912, OPR Records, RG30, NA-WNRC.

110. James W. Abbott to "My dear Senator," 24 June 1904 and 27 June 1904, Box 35, File 97, "Convict Labor," OPR Records, RG30, NA-WNRC. In North Carolina the original legislation placing convicts on the roads was referred to as the "Mecklenburg Road Law"; Joseph A. Holmes, "Some Recent Road Legislation in North Carolina," North Carolina Geological Survey, Economic Paper No. 2 (Raleigh, N.C.: State Printer, 1899); Steiner and Brown, *The North Carolina Chain Gang*, pp. 29, 34; see State Geologist to John B. Cunningham, 5 February 1905, Folder 107, Box 11, NCGS Papers, SHC, for Mecklenburg as the "best illustration" of what could be done with convict labor on the roads.

111. Dewey Grantham uses the phrase "reconciliation of progress and tradition" without irony to describe southern Progressivism in *Southern Progressivism*; see p. 419 for an example of this argument. For more critical assessments of southern Progressivism, with reference to Georgia, see Numan V. Bartley, *The Creation of Modern Georgia* (Athens: University of Georgia Press, 1983), pp. 147–78; Dittmer, *Black Georgia in the Progressive Era*; and Kousser, *The Shaping of Southern Politics*.

Chapter 8

1. Walter Benjamin, *Illuminations*, edited by Hannah Arendt (New York: Schocken Books, 1969), p. 256.

2. Willemina Kloosterboer, *Involuntary Labour Since the Abolition of Slavery: A Survey of Compulsory Labour Throughout the World* (Leiden: E.J. Brill, 1960), pp. 190–200; J. Thorsten Sellin, *Slavery and the Penal System* (New York: Elsevier, 1976); Georg Rusche and Otto Kirchheimer, *Punishment and Social Structure* (New York: Columbia University Press, 1939), p. 42; and Sidney Mintz, "The Dignity of Honest Toil: A Review Article," *Comparative Studies in Society and History* 21 (October 1979), pp. 558–66, on some of the common elements in forced labor.

Much of this analysis is based on a distillation of many works that have influenced my thinking on the subject of forced labor, progress, and modernity. For a complete list, see Alex Lichtenstein, "The Political Economy of Convict Labor in the New South" (Ph.D. dissertation, University of Pennsylvania, 1990), pp. 419–20.

3. Georgia General Assembly, *Journal of the House of Representatives*, 1909, p. 33.

4. Interesting critiques of southern "modernization" are found in Pete Daniel, *Breaking the Land: The Transformation of Cotton, Tobacco, and Rice Cultures since 1880* (Urbana: University of Illinois Press, 1985) and Jack Temple Kirby, *Rural Worlds Lost: The American South 1920–1960* (Baton Rouge: Louisiana State University Press, 1987). Daniel in particular is highly critical of the federal role, a view I find reinforced by the USDA's enthusiastic promotion of convict labor on the roads. See *Southern Good Roads* 5 (February 1912) for several articles on federal aid – in money and expertise – to southern road programs which relied on convict labor.

The civil engineers who worked for the USDA Office of Public Roads were not just bureaucrats; they got their hands dirty. One of the most popular methods of Federal aid to counties was actually to send an OPR engineer "to assist ... in organizing and working [the] convict road gang for the improvement of roads" (Office of Public Roads to J.D. Coleman [Chairman, County Commissioners, Tatnall County, Ga.], 10 May 1911); also R.H. Sheffield to Logan W. Page, 25 November 1909; and E.L. Bardwell to Page, 24 October 1911, all in Box 49, File 135, General Correspondence, 1893–1916, "Georgia Roads," OPR Records, RG30, NA-WNRC. This was the Progressive application of expertise with a vengeance.

5. For a good articulation of this point, see James Oakes, *Slavery and Freedom: An Interpretation of the Old South* (New York: Knopf, 1990), pp. 40–79, esp. p. 52.

6. Tom Brass, "Review Essay: Slavery Now: Unfree Labour and Modern Capitalism," *Slavery and Abolition* 9 (September 1988), pp. 183–97.

7. The concept of "underdevelopment" here does not contradict the notion of economic progress; regions and nations can sustain rapid economic growth and remain underdeveloped, particularly in their social and labor relations – indeed this is often one of the reasons for the persistence of unfree labor relations. In other words, an *under*developed society is quite distinct from an *un*developed one; see Barbara J. Fields, "The Nineteenth-Century American South: History and Theory," *Plantation Society in the Americas* 2 (April 1983), pp. 7–27.

8. George Washington Cable, *The Silent South, together with the Freedman's Case in Equity and the Convict Lease System* (1883; reprint, New York: Charles Scribner's Sons, 1907); Rebecca Latimer Felton, *My Memoirs of Georgia Politics* (Atlanta, Ga.: n.pub., 1911), pp. 438–9, 463–6; Rebecca Felton, "The Convict System of Georgia," *The Forum* 2 (January 1887), pp. 484–90; Frank Tannenbaum, *Darker Phases of the South* (London: G.P. Putnam's Sons, 1924), pp. 74–115.

9. John Spivak, *Georgia Nigger* (New York: Brewer, Warren and Putnam, 1932); Walter Wilson, *Forced Labor in the United States* (New York: International Publishers, 1933).

10. W.E.B. Du Bois, ed., *Some Notes on Negro Crime, Particularly in Georgia*, Ninth Conference for the Study of Negro Problems (Atlanta, Ga.: Atlanta University Press, 1904), pp. 5–6.

11. Prison Commission, *Report*, 1929–30, p. 22; US Department of Justice, *Historical Corrections Statistics in the United States, 1850–1984* (Washington, DC: GPO, 1986), p. 30; US Department of Commerce and Labor, Bureau of the Census, *Thirteenth Census of the United States*, Vol. 2, *Population* (Washington, DC: GPO, 1910), p. 372.

12. Jesse Crawford, "Cheating the Georgia Chain Gang," *The Crisis* 45 (June 1938), pp. 168–9, 178.

13. USDA, *Yearbook, 1918* (Washington, DC: GPO, 1918), pp. 67–8; H.M. Berry to Earle Godbey, 11 January 1921, Folder 17, Box 1, Harriet Morehead Berry Papers, SHC; W.R. Neel to A.E. Loder, 24 January 1922, Box 2187, File 481, General Correspondence, Georgia, 1912–50, OPR Records, RG30, NA-WNRC.

14. Report by Chairman of the North Carolina State Highway Commission,

n.d. [c. 1932], Folder 56, Box 2, Berry Papers, SHC; M.C. Tarver to Thomas McDonald [director, US Bureau of Public Roads], 21 August 1931, and McDonald to Tarver, 25 August 1931, Box 2183, File 481, General Correspondence, Georgia, 1933–31, OPR Records, NA-WNRC.

15. For the evolution of this decision in Georgia (cemented in 1916, with the Federal Road Aid Act), see C.M. Strahan to A.H. Ulm, 2 December 1912, 31 December 1912, Subject Files, "Roads," Box 200; A.S. Burleson [postmaster general] to Gov. Joseph M. Brown, 18 March 1913, and Brown to Burleson, 31 March 1913, "Roads" File, Box 200; Gov. J. M. Slaton to Congressman Frank Park (GA), 11 February 1914, and Park to Slaton, 13 February 1914, Box 209, all in Governor's Correspondence, GDAH; R.M. Jones to T.E. Patterson, 21 November 1916, Box 2188, File 481, General Correspondence, Georgia, 1912–50, OPR Records, RG30, NA-WNRC; Atlanta *Constitution*, 24 September, 3 October, 23 October 1916.

16. Thomas McDonald to Senator Walter F. George, 25 November 1930, Box 2184, File 481, General Correspondence, Georgia, 1912–50, OPR Records, RG30, NA-WNRC; E.L. Rainey [Chairman, Georgia Prison Commission] to Sen. Walter F. George, 6 November 1930, enclosed with above letter; Georgia State Highway Department, Minutes, Box 2, 25 April 1933, 2 May 1933; Minutes, Box 4, 28 September 1938, 30 November 1938, Department of Transportation Records, GDAH.

17. Blake McKelvey, "A Half Century of Southern Penal Exploitation," *Social Forces* 13 (October 1934), pp. 121–2. McKelvey contended that, despite its obvious cruelties, at least the southern penal system kept convicts at work; "in the long run southern convicts have enjoyed a measurable advantage over the thousands of idle prisoners in the North," he claimed with considerable exaggeration. At the same time, he noted that the National Penal Information Society "rank[ed] the penal system of Georgia at the bottom of the list, even in the South" (p. 118).

18. Elliot Currie, *Confronting Crime: An American Challenge* (New York: Pantheon Books, 1985), pp. 28–9; George M. Camp and Camille G. Camp, *The Corrections Yearbook* (South Salem, N.Y.: Criminal Justice Institute, 1987), p. 4; Marc Miller, "The Numbers Game: A *Southern Exposure* Special Report," *Southern Exposure* 6 (Winter 1978), pp. 25–9; US Department of Justice, Bureau of Justice Statistics, *Sourcebook of Criminal Justice Statistics, 1986* (Washington, DC: GPO, 1987), pp. 405–6; Scott Christianson, *Black Incarceration Rate in the United States – A Nationwide Problem*, National Institute of Justice (Washington, DC: National Criminal Justice Reference Service, 1980), esp. pp. 19, 23; Michael Tonry, *Malign Neglect: Race, Crime, and Punishment in America* (New York: Oxford University Press, 1995), pp. 49–80.

19. H. Bruce Franklin, *Prison Literature in America: The Victim as Criminal and Artist*, 2nd edn (Westport, Conn.: Lawrence Hill & Co., 1982), pp. xiv–xv, xxiii–xxx, 3–30, 73–123, 233–76; Lawrence Levine, *Black Culture and Black Consciousness: Afro-American Folk Thought from Slavery to Freedom* (New York: Oxford University Press, 1977), pp. 246–70; see for examples, George Jackson, *Soledad Brother: The Prison Letters of George Jackson* (New York: Bantam Books, 1970), p. 9; Alex Haley and Malcolm X, *The Autobiography of Malcolm X* (New York: Grove Press, 1964), the classic of the genre. Prison work songs also offer powerful testament to this, e.g. Bruce Jackson, comp., *Wake Up Dead Man: Afro-American Work Songs From Texas Prisons* (Cambridge, Mass.: Harvard University Press, 1972).

20. On Parchman, and its enduring significance, see David Oshinsky, "Prison Plantation: Parchman Prison and Forced Labor," paper presented at the Annual Meeting of the Southern Historical Association, 8–11 November 1989, copy in author's possession; on Angola, John Vodicka, "Prison Plantation: The Story of Angola," *Southern Exposure* 6 (Winter 1978), pp. 32–8; Wilbert Rideau and Ron Wikberg, *Life Sentences: Rage and Survival Behind Bars* (New York: Times Books, 1992).

21. Samuel L. Myers, "Employment Opportunities and Crime," Technical Report for the National Institute of Justice (Washington, DC: National Criminal Justice Reference Service, 1980), p. 16; Gerald D. Jaynes, *Branches Without Roots: Genesis of the Black Working Class in the American South, 1862–1882* (New York: Oxford University Press, 1986), pp. 261–79.

22. Franklin, *Prison Literature in America*, pp. 122–3, for a succinct presentation of this periodization; Neil McMillen, *Dark Journey: Black Mississippians in the Age of Jim Crow* (Urbana: University of Illinois Press, 1989), ch. 6, offers a striking discussion of southern "criminal justice," which was definitely not an oxymoron. For a good summary of approaches to the question of joblessness, race, and the "underclass," see Michael B. Katz, *The Undeserving Poor: From the War on Poverty to the War on Welfare* (New York: Pantheon Books, 1989), pp. 195–215.

Obviously, here I treat the question of punishment as distinct from, and relatively unconnected with, crime. This approach falls within a particular tradition of Marxist criminological thought, pioneered by Georg Rusche and Otto Kirchheimer in *Punishment and Social Structure* (New York: Columbia University Press, 1939), which regards penal developments as more responsive to changes in political economy than to criminal behavior per se. See Dario Melossi, "Georg Rusche and Otto Kirchheimer: *Punishment and Social Structure*," *Crime and Social Justice* 9 (Spring–Summer 1978), pp. 73–85 for the background and influence of this work on modern criminology; Christopher Adamson, "Toward a Marxian Penology," *Social Problems* 31 (April 1984), pp. 435–58, for a theoretical application to the nineteenth-century United States; Ivan Jankovich, "Labor Market and Imprisonment," *Crime and Social Justice* 8 (Fall–Winter), pp. 17–31, for an analysis of twentieth-century developments; and Ivan Jankovich, "Prison and Postindustrial Society" (Ph.D. dissertation, University of California, Santa Barbara, 1976), for a suggestive consideration of the role of incarceration in the postindustrial political economy. When crime itself is considered in these models it is understood primarily as the threat posed to stability and capital accumulation by the reserve army of labor, with, in the United States, obvious implications for race relations.

23. Mike Davis, "A Prison-Industrial Complex: Hell Factories in the Field," *The Nation*, 20 February 1995, pp. 229–34.

24. Criminal Justice Associates, *Private Sector Involvement in Prison-Based Business: A National Assessment*, National Institute of Justice Research Report (Washington, DC: GPO, 1985), pp. 6–7.

25. Joan Mullen, Kent J. Chabotar, and Deborah M. Carrow, *The Privatization of Corrections*, National Institute of Justice, *Issues and Practices* (Washington, DC: GPO, 1985), p. 24; on privatization, see also George E. Sexton, Franklin C. Farrow, and Barbara J. Auerbach, "The Private Sector and Prison Industries," National Institute of Justice, *Research in Brief*, August 1985, and articles in "Corrections and Privatization: An Overview," *The Prison Journal* 65 (Autumn–Winter 1985); Scott Christianson, "Prison Labor and Unionization – Legal Developments," *Criminal Law Bulletin* 14 (May–June 1978), pp. 243–7, notes the absence of legal rights and benefits in the prison workplace; on the current constitutional legal ramifications of privatized prisons and prison labor, see Ira P. Robbins, *The Legal Dimensions of Private Incarceration* (Washington, DC: American Bar Association, 1988), pp. 120–33; for an unapologetic advocacy of private prisons, see Charles Logan, *Private Prisons: Cons and Pros* (New York: Oxford University Press, 1990).

26. On industrial forced labor in Nazi Germany, see Raul Hilberg, *The Destruction of European Jewery*, 3 vols (New York: Holmes and Meier, 1985), Vol. 1, pp. 249–59; Vol. 3, pp. 917–36; Benjamin B. Ferencz, *Less Than Slaves: Jewish Forced Labor and the Quest for Compensation* (Cambridge, Mass.: Harvard University Press, 1979), esp.

pp. 17–30; Peter Hayes, *Industry and Ideology: IG Farben in the Nazi Era* (Cambridge: Cambridge University Press, 1987), pp. 332–76; on Stalinist forced labor, see Tony Cliff, *State Capitalism in Russia* (London: Pluto Press, 1974), p. 33; and S. Swianiewicz, *Forced Labour and Economic Development: An Enquiry into the Experience of Soviet Industrialization* (London: Oxford University Press, 1965), a provocative and fascinating examination of the Soviet Gulag which attributes forced labor in the Soviet Union to changes in the Soviet political economy and problems with labor recruitment during the attempt (in the 1930s) to industrialize rapidly an overwhelmingly agrarian country (see pp. 2–4, 18–19).

27. Wilson, *Forced Labor in the United States*, compares southern chain gangs unfavorably to Soviet labor camps; Fletcher Green, "Some Aspects of the Convict Lease System in the Southern States," in Fletcher Green, ed., *Essays in Southern History* (Chapel Hill: University of North Carolina Press, 1949), p. 122, for a direct comparison with Nazism.

28. This is the view associated with the work of Eugene D. Genovese; see his *Roll, Jordan, Roll: The World the Slaves Made* (New York: Random House, 1974), and "Marxian Interpretations of the Slave South," in *In Red and Black: Marxian Explorations in Southern and Afro-American History* (Knoxville: University of Tennessee Press, 1984).

29. Fields, "The Nineteenth-Century American South," pp. 24–5. Fields confines this analysis to the agricultural sector, however, thus missing the significance of convict labor, which perfectly illustrates her point.

30. Milovan Djilas, *Of Prisons and Ideas* (San Diego, Calif.: Harcourt Brace Jovanovich, 1986), p. 139.

Index

Abbott, James, 184
absenteeism, of free labor, 128
African-Americans: alleged capacity for convict work, 148; alleged need for corporal punishment, 184, 185; among prison population, 59; and legacy of slavery, 130; as agricultural workers, 113; as majority in coal mining labor force, 86, 117; as majority of chain gang prisoners, 173, 183, 184; as majority of misdemeanor convicts, 175; as majority of prison population, xiv, 3, 15, 27, 70, 159, 180, 189, 191, 193; as miners, 86; as strikebreakers, 87, 115; assumed inferiority of, 142; barred from mechanical trades, 75; estimated capabilities of, 26; harsh treatment by judicial system, 18; in iron industry, 114; in modern prison system, 191; on road gangs, 159; penal oppression of, 59; perceived requirement of compulsion, 195; prescribed place in Southern society, 195; Progressive agenda for, 167; seen as suited to road work, 180; shunted out of labor market, 192; taboo on proximity to white women, 115
agriculture, 40, 66, 67, 77, 83, 114, 124, 160, 173; labor force in, 19, 62, 75, 80, 81, 117, 184 (black, 4; control of, 39; convicts, 20; repression of, 9, 13); labor relations in, 83; monocrop, 4, 7; slavery in, 129
Alabama, xv, 7, 9, 12, 39, 44, 73, 75, 78, 79, 81, 83, 84, 85, 86, 87, 89, 90, 93,
94, 96, 97, 99, 100, 101, 102, 104, 105, 107, 118, 123, 131; coal mining in, 91; growth of industry, 77
Alexander, Hooper, 168
Alexander, Thomas, 47, 52, 58, 67, 68
Allen and Holmes turpentine camp, 173
anti-enticement statutes, 7, 72
Appalachian coalfield, 73
Armstrong, Henry, 71
arson: in mines, 107; sentencing for, 71, 117
Atkinson, Edward, 87
Atkinson, William G., 110, 111, 122
Atlanta, xvii–xix, 16, 50, 126, 175; development of, 44, 46, 51, 62
Atlanta and Charlotte Air-Line, 45, 50
Atlanta and Hawkinsville Railroad, 64
Atlanta Federation of Trades, 153
Atlanta Rolling Mill, 109

"backwardness" of South, 12
bad weather, working in, 52
Bailey, Nathan, 61
bankruptcy of railroads, 65
Bartamm, J.A., 83
Bartow Iron and Manganese Company, 111, 113; abolition of convict camp, 122
Bateman, W.S., 66
Beall, Rack, 37
beatings of convict labor, 52, 134, 182 *see also* whipping
Benjamin, Walter, 186
Bibb County chain gang, 183
Billings, Dwight, 9